EMPLOYEE'S RECEIPT

I acknowledge receipt of the 2000 Emergency Response Guidebook (14-ORS-0), detailing emergency response procedures as developed under the supervision of the Office of Hazardous Materials Initiatives and Training, Research and Special Programs Administration, U.S. Department of Transpo

D0558625

EMPLOYEE'S SIGNATURE   DATE

COMPANY

COMPANY SUPERVISOR'S SIGNATURE

NOTE: This receipt shall be read and signed by the employee. A responsible company supervisor shall countersign the receipt and place it in the employee's personnel file.

HOW TO USE THIS GUIDEBOOK DURING AN INCIDENT INVOLVING DANGEROUS GOODS

ONE IDENTIFY THE MATERIAL BY FINDING ANY **ONE** OF THE FOLLOWING:

> THE 4-DIGIT ID NUMBER ON A PLACARD OR ORANGE PANEL
>
> THE 4-DIGIT ID NUMBER (after UN/NA) ON A SHIPPING DOCUMENT OR PACKAGE
>
> THE NAME OF THE MATERIAL ON A SHIPPING DOCUMENT, PLACARD OR PACKAGE

> IF AN **ID NUMBER** OR THE **NAME OF THE MATERIAL** CANNOT BE FOUND, SKIP TO THE NOTES BELOW.

TWO LOOK UP THE MATERIAL'S 3-DIGIT GUIDE NUMBER IN EITHER:

> THE ID NUMBER INDEX..(the yellow-bordered pages of the guidebook)
>
> THE NAME OF MATERIAL INDEX..(the blue-bordered pages of the guidebook)

> If the guide number is supplemented with the letter "P", it indicates that the material may undergo violent polymerization if subjected to heat or contamination.
>
> If the index entry is highlighted (in either yellow or blue), it is a TIH (Toxic Inhalation Hazard) material or a Dangerous Water Reactive Material (produces toxic gas upon contact with water). **LOOK FOR THE ID NUMBER AND NAME OF THE MATERIAL** IN THE TABLE OF INITIAL ISOLATION AND PROTECTIVE ACTION DISTANCES (the green-bordered pages). Then, if necessary, **BEGIN PROTECTIVE ACTIONS IMMEDIATELY** (see Protective Actions on page 314). If protective action is not required, use the information jointly with the 3-digit guide.

> **USE GUIDE 112 FOR ALL EXPLOSIVES EXCEPT FOR EXPLOSIVES 1.4 (EXPLOSIVES C) WHERE GUIDE 114 IS TO BE CONSULTED.**

THREE TURN TO THE NUMBERED GUIDE (the orange-bordered pages) AND READ CAREFULLY.

NOTES IF A NUMBERED GUIDE CANNOT BE OBTAINED BY FOLLOWING THE ABOVE STEPS, AND A PLACARD CAN BE SEEN, LOCATE THE PLACARD IN THE TABLE OF PLACARDS (pages 16-17), THEN GO TO THE 3-DIGIT GUIDE SHOWN NEXT TO THE SAMPLE PLACARD.

IF A REFERENCE TO A GUIDE CANNOT BE FOUND AND THIS INCIDENT IS BELIEVED TO INVOLVE DANGEROUS GOODS, TURN TO GUIDE 111 NOW, AND USE IT UNTIL ADDITIONAL INFORMATION BECOMES AVAILABLE. If the shipping document lists an emergency response telephone number, call that number. If the shipping document is not available, or no emergency response telephone number is listed, IMMEDIATELY CALL the appropriate **emergency response agency listed on the inside back cover of this guidebook**. Provide as much information as possible, such as the name of the carrier (trucking company or railroad) and vehicle number. AS A LAST RESORT, CONSULT THE TABLE OF RAIL CAR AND ROAD TRAILER IDENTIFICATION CHART (pages 18-19). IF THE CONTAINER CAN BE IDENTIFIED, REMEMBER THAT THE INFORMATION ASSOCIATED WITH THESE CONTAINERS IS FOR THE WORST CASE POSSIBLE.

ERG2000 USER'S GUIDE

The 2000 Emergency Response Guidebook (ERG2000) was developed jointly by Transport Canada (TC), the U.S. Department of Transportation (DOT) and the Secretariat of Transport and Communications of Mexico (SCT) for use by fire fighters, police, and other emergency services personnel who may be the first to arrive at the scene of a transportation incident involving dangerous goods. **It is primarily a guide to aid first responders in quickly identifying the specific or generic hazards of the material(s) involved in the incident, and protecting themselves and the general public during the initial response phase of the incident.** For the purposes of this guidebook, the "initial response phase" is that period following arrival at the scene of an incident during which the presence and/or identification of dangerous goods is confirmed, protective actions and area securement are initiated, and assistance of qualified personnel is requested. It is not intended to provide information on the physical or chemical properties of dangerous goods.

This guidebook will assist responders in making initial decisions upon arriving at the scene of a dangerous goods incident. It should not be considered as a substitute for emergency response training, knowledge or sound judgment. ERG2000 does not address all possible circumstances that may be associated with a dangerous goods incident. It is primarily designed for use at a dangerous goods incident occurring on a highway or railroad. Be mindful that there may be limited value in its application at fixed facility locations.

ERG2000 incorporates dangerous goods lists from the most recent United Nations Recommendations as well as from other international and national regulations. Explosives are not listed individually by either proper shipping name or ID Number. They do, however, appear under the general heading "Explosives" on the first page of the ID Number index (yellow-bordered pages) and alphabetically in the Name of Material index (blue-bordered pages). Also, the letter **"P"** following the guide number in the yellow-bordered and blue-bordered pages identifies those materials which present a polymerization hazard under certain conditions; for example, Acrolein, inhibited, Guide **131P**.

First responders at the scene of a dangerous goods incident should seek additional specific information about any material in question as soon as possible. The information received by contacting the appropriate emergency response agency, the emergency response number on the shipping document, or by consulting the information on or accompanying the shipping document, may be more specific and accurate than this guidebook in providing guidance for the materials involved.

BECOME FAMILIAR WITH THIS GUIDEBOOK BEFORE USING IT DURING AN EMERGENCY! In the U.S., according to the requirements of the U.S. Department of Labor's Occupational Safety and Health Administration (OSHA, 29 CFR 1910.120), and regulations issued by the U.S. Environmental Protection Agency (EPA, 40 CFR Part 311), first responders must be trained regarding the use of this guidebook.

GUIDEBOOK CONTENTS

1-Yellow-bordered pages: Index list of dangerous goods in numerical order of ID number. This section quickly identifies the guide to be consulted from the ID Number of the material involved. This list displays the 4-digit ID number of the material followed by its assigned emergency response guide and the material name.

For example:	ID No.	Guide No.	Name of Material
	1090	127	Acetone

2-Blue-bordered pages: Index list of dangerous goods in alphabetical order of material name. This section quickly identifies the guide to be consulted from the name of the material involved. This list displays the name of the material followed by its assigned emergency response guide and 4-digit ID number.

For example:	Name of Material	Guide No.	ID No.
	Sulfuric acid	137	1830

3-Orange-bordered pages: This section is the most important section of the guidebook because it is where all safety recommendations are provided. It comprises a total of 62 individual guides, presented in a two-page format. Each guide provides safety recommendations and emergency response information to protect yourself and the public. The left hand page provides safety related information whereas the right hand page provides emergency response guidance and activities for fire situations, spill or leak incidents and first aid. Each guide is designed to cover a group of materials which possess similar chemical and toxicological characteristics.

The guide title identifies the general hazards of the dangerous goods covered.

For example: Guide 124 - Gases-Toxic and/or Corrosive-Oxidizing.

Each guide is divided into three main sections: the first section describes **potential hazards** that the material may display in terms of fire/explosion and health effects upon exposure. The highest potential is listed first. The emergency responder should consult this section first. This allows the responder to make decisions regarding the protection of the emergency response team as well as the surrounding population.

The second section outlines suggested **public safety** measures based on the situation at hand. It provides general information regarding immediate isolation of the incident site, recommended type of protective clothing and respiratory protection. Suggested evacuation distances are listed for small and large spills and for fire situations (fragmentation hazard). It also directs the reader to consult the tables listing Toxic Inhalation Hazard materials (TIH) and water-reactive materials (green-bordered pages) when the material name is highlighted in the yellow-bordered and blue-bordered pages.

The third section covers **emergency response** actions, including first aid. It outlines special precautions for incidents which involve fire, spill or chemical exposure. Several recommendations are listed under each part which will further assist in the decision making process. The information on first aid is general guidance prior to seeking medical care.

4-Green-bordered pages: This section contains a table which lists, by ID number, TIH materials, including certain chemical warfare agents, and water-reactive materials which produce toxic gases upon contact with water. The table provides two different types of recommended safe distances which are "Initial isolation distances" and "Protective action distances." The materials are highlighted for easy identification in both numeric (yellow-bordered pages) and alphabetic (blue-bordered pages) lists of the guidebook. The table provides distances for both small (approximately 200 liters or less) and large spills (more than 200 liters) for all highlighted materials. The list is further subdivided into daytime and nighttime situations. This is necessary due to varying atmospheric conditions which greatly affect the size of the hazardous area. The distances change from daytime to nighttime due to different mixing and dispersion conditions in the air. During the night, the air is generally calmer and this causes the chemical to disperse less and therefore create a toxicity zone which is greater than would usually occur during the day. During the day, the chemical is generally dispersed by a more active atmosphere. The chemical will be present in a larger area; however, the actual area where toxic levels are reached will be smaller (due to increased dispersion). It is the quantity of the chemical that poses problems not its mere presence.

The "Initial Isolation Distance" is a distance within which all persons should be considered for evacuation in all directions from the actual spill/leak source. It is a distance (radius) which defines a circle (Initial Isolation Zone) within which persons may be exposed to dangerous concentrations upwind of the source and may be exposed to life threatening concentrations downwind of the source. For example, in the case of Compressed gas, toxic, n.o.s., ID No. 1955, Inhalation Hazard Zone A, the isolation distance for small spills is 430 meters, therefore, representing an evacuation circle of 860 meters in diameter.

For the same material, the "Protective Action Distance" is 4.2 kilometers for a daytime incident and 8.4 kilometers for a nighttime incident, these distances represent a downwind distance from the spill/leak source within which Protective Actions could be implemented. Protective Actions are those steps taken to preserve the health and safety of emergency responders and the public. People in this area could be evacuated and/or sheltered in-place. For more information, consult the INTRODUCTION TO THE TABLE OF INITIAL ISOLATION AND PROTECTIVE ACTION DISTANCES (pages 311-312).

What is a TIH?

It is a liquid or a gas which is known to be so toxic to humans as to pose a hazard to health during transportation, or in the absence of adequate data on human toxicity, is presumed to be toxic to humans because when tested on laboratory animals it has an LC50 value of not more than 5000 ppm.

It is important to note that even though the term zone is used, the hazard zones do not represent any actual area or distance. The assignment of the zones is strictly a function of their Lethal Concentration 50 (LC50); for example, TIH Zone A is more toxic than Zone D. All distances which are listed in the green-bordered pages are calculated by the use of mathematical models for each TIH material.

Assignment of hazard zones:

HAZARD ZONE A: LC50 of less than or equal to 200 ppm,
HAZARD ZONE B: LC50 greater than 200 ppm and less than or equal to 1000 ppm,
HAZARD ZONE C: LC50 greater than 1000 ppm and less than or equal to 3000 ppm,
HAZARD ZONE D: LC50 greater than 3000 ppm and less than or equal to 5000 ppm.

ISOLATION AND EVACUATION DISTANCES

Isolation or evacuation distances are shown in the guides (orange-bordered pages) and in the Table of Initial Isolation and Protective Action Distances (green-bordered pages). This may confuse users not thoroughly familiar with ERG2000.

It is important to note that some guides refer to non-TIH materials only (40 guides) and some refer to both TIH and non-TIH materials (22 guides). A guide refers to both TIH and non-TIH materials only when the following sentence appears under the title EVACUATION-SPILLS: "See the Table of Initial Isolation and Protective Action Distances for highlighted substances. For non-highlighted substances, increase, in the downwind direction, as necessary, the isolation distance shown under 'PUBLIC SAFETY.'" If this sentence does not appear in the guide, then this particular guide refers to non-TIH materials only.

If you are dealing with a TIH material (highlighted entries in the index lists), the isolation and evacuation distances are found directly in the green-bordered pages. The guides (orange-bordered pages) also remind the user to refer to the green-bordered pages for evacuation specific information involving highlighted materials.

If you are dealing with a non-TIH material but the guide refers to both TIH and non-TIH materials, an immediate isolation distance is provided under the heading PUBLIC SAFETY. It applies to the non-TIH materials only. In addition, for evacuation purposes, the guide informs the user under the title EVACUATION-SPILLS to increase, for non-highlighted substances, in the downwind direction, if necessary, the immediate isolation distance listed under "Public Safety." For example, Guide 124 - Gases-Toxic and/or Corrosive-Oxidizing, instructs the user to: Isolate the spill or leak area immediately for at least 100 to 200 meters (330 to 660 feet) in all directions. In case of a large spill, the isolation area could be expanded from 100 meters to a distance deemed as safe by the On-scene-commander and emergency responders.

If you are dealing with a non-TIH material and the guide refers only to non-TIH materials, the immediate isolation and evacuation distances are specified as actual distances in the guide (orange-bordered pages) and are not referenced in the green-bordered pages.

SAFETY PRECAUTIONS

APPROACH CAUTIOUSLY FROM UPWIND. Resist the urge to rush in; others cannot be helped until the situation has been fully assessed.

SECURE THE SCENE. Without entering the immediate hazard area, isolate the area and assure the safety of people and the environment, keep people away from the scene and outside the safety perimeter. Allow enough room to move and remove your own equipment.

IDENTIFY THE HAZARDS. Placards, container labels, shipping documents, material safety data sheets, Rail Car and Road Trailer Identification Charts, and/or knowledgeable persons on the scene are valuable information sources. Evaluate all available information and consult the recommended guide to reduce immediate risks. **Additional information, provided by the shipper or obtained from another authoritative source, may change some of the emphasis or details found in the guide.** Remember, the guide provides only the most important and worst case scenario information for the initial response in relation to a family or class of dangerous goods. As more material-specific information becomes available, the response should be tailored to the situation.

ASSESS THE SITUATION. Consider the following:
- Is there a fire, a spill or a leak?
- What are the weather conditions?
- What is the terrain like?
- Who/what is at risk: people, property or the environment?
- What actions should be taken: Is an evacuation necessary? Is diking necessary? What resources (human and equipment) are required and are readily available?
- What can be done immediately?

OBTAIN HELP. Advise your headquarters to notify responsible agencies and call for assistance from qualified personnel.

DECIDE ON SITE ENTRY. Any efforts made to rescue persons, protect property or the environment must be weighed against the possibility that you could become part of the problem. Enter the area only when wearing appropriate protective gear (see PROTECTIVE CLOTHING, page 364).

RESPOND. Respond in an appropriate manner. Establish a command post and lines of communication. Rescue casualties where possible and evacuate if necessary. Maintain control of the site. Continually reassess the situation and modify the response accordingly. The first duty is to consider the safety of people in the immediate area, including your own.

ABOVE ALL — Do not walk into or touch spilled material. Avoid inhalation of fumes, smoke and vapors, even if no dangerous goods are known to be involved. Do not assume that gases or vapors are harmless because of lack of a smell—odorless gases or vapors may be harmful.

WHO TO CALL FOR ASSISTANCE

Upon arrival at the scene, a first responder is expected to recognize the presence of dangerous goods, protect oneself and the public, secure the area, and call for the assistance of trained personnel as soon as conditions permit. Follow the steps outlined in your organization's standard operating procedures and/or local emergency response plan for obtaining qualified assistance. Generally, the notification sequence and requests for technical information beyond what is available in this guidebook should occur in the following order:

1. ORGANIZATION/AGENCY

Notify your organization/agency. This will set in motion a series of events based upon the information provided. Actions may range from dispatching additional trained personnel to the scene to activating the local emergency response plan. Ensure that local fire and police departments have been notified.

2. EMERGENCY RESPONSE TELEPHONE NUMBER

Locate and call the telephone number listed on the shipping document. The person answering the phone at the listed emergency response number must be knowledgeable of the materials and mitigation actions to be taken, or must have immediate access to a person who has the required knowledge.

3. NATIONAL ASSISTANCE

Contact the appropriate emergency response agency listed on the inside back cover of this guidebook when the emergency response telephone number is not available. Upon receipt of a call describing the nature of the incident, the agency will provide immediate advice on handling the early stages of the incident. The agency will also contact the shipper or manufacturer of the material for more detailed information and request on-scene assistance when necessary.

Collect and provide as much of the following information as can safely be obtained to your chain-of-command and specialists contacted for technical guidance:

Your name, call back telephone number, FAX number
Location and nature of problem (spill, fire, etc.)
Name and identification number of material(s) involved
Shipper/consignee/point of origin
Carrier name, rail car or truck number
Container type and size
Quantity of material transported/released
Local conditions (weather, terrain, proximity to schools, hospitals, waterways, etc.)
Injuries and exposures
Local emergency services that have been notified

CANADA

1. CANUTEC

CANUTEC is the **Canadian Transport Emergency Centre** operated by the Transport Dangerous Goods Directorate of Transport Canada.
CANUTEC provides a national bilingual (French and English) advisory service and is staffed by professional chemists experienced and trained in interpreting technical information and providing emergency response advice.

> **In an emergency, CANUTEC may be called collect at**
> **613-996-6666 (24 hours)**
> ***666 cellular (Press Star 666, Canada only)**

In a non-emergency situation, please call the information line at 613-992-4624 (24 hours).

2. PROVINCIAL AGENCIES

Although technical information and emergency response assistance can be obtained from **CANUTEC**, there are federal and provincial regulations requiring the reporting of dangerous goods incidents to certain authorities.

The following list of provincial agencies is supplied for your convenience.

Province	Emergency Authority and/or Telephone Number
Alberta	Local Police and Provincial Authorities 1-800-272-9600*
British Columbia	Local Police or 1-800-663-3456
Manitoba	Local Police or fire brigade, as appropriate, or 204-945-4888
New Brunswick	Local Police or 1-800-565-1633** or 902-426-6030
Newfoundland	Local Police or 709-772-2083
Northwest Territories	867-920-8130
Nova Scotia	Local Police or 1-800-565-1633** or 902-426-6030
Nunavut	867-920-8130
Ontario	Local Police
Prince Edward Island	Local Police or 1-800-565-1633** or 902-426-6030
Quebec	Local Police
Saskatchewan	Local Police or 1-800-667-7525
Yukon Territory	867-667-7244

* This number is not accessible from outside Alberta.

** This number is not accessible from outside of New Brunswick, Nova Scotia or Prince Edward Island.

NOTE:

1. The appropriate federal agency must be notified in the case of rail, air or marine incidents.

2. The nearest police department must be notified in the case of lost, stolen or misplaced explosives, radioactive materials or infectious substances.

3. **CANUTEC must** be notified in the case of:

   a. lost, stolen or misplaced infectious substances;
   b. an incident involving infectious substances;
   c. an incident where the shipping documents display **CANUTEC's** telephone number 613-996-6666 as the emergency telephone number; or
   d. a dangerous goods incident in which a railway vehicle is involved.

UNITED STATES

1. **CHEMTREC®**, a 24-hour emergency response communication service, can be reached as follows:

    CALL **CHEMTREC®** (24 hours)
    1-800-424-9300
    (Toll-free in the U.S., Canada, and the U.S. Virgin Islands)
    For calls originating elsewhere:
    703-527-3887 (Collect calls are accepted)

    or

2. **CHEM-TEL, INC.**, a 24-hour emergency response communication service, can be reached as follows:

    CALL **CHEM-TEL, INC.** (24 hours)
    1-800-255-3924
    (Toll-free in the U.S., Canada, and the U.S. Virgin Islands)
    For calls originating elsewhere:
    813-248-0585 (Collect calls are accepted)

    or

3. **INFOTRAC**, a 24-hour emergency response communication service, can be reached as follows:

    CALL **INFOTRAC** (24 hours)
    1-800-535-5053
    (Toll-free in the U.S., Canada, and the U.S. Virgin Islands)
    For calls originating elsewhere:
    352-323-3500 (Collect calls are accepted)

    or

4. **3E COMPANY**, a 24-hour emergency response communication service, can be reached as follows:

    CALL **3E COMPANY** (24 hours)
    1-800-451-8346
    (Toll-free in the U.S., Canada, and the U.S. Virgin Islands)
    For calls originating elsewhere:
    760-602-8703 (Collect calls are accepted)

The emergency response information services shown above have requested to be listed as providers of emergency response information and have agreed to provide emergency response information to all callers. They maintain periodically updated lists of state and Federal radiation authorities who provide information and technical assistance on handling incidents involving radioactive materials.

5. NATIONAL RESPONSE CENTER (NRC)

The NRC, which is operated by the U.S. Coast Guard, receives reports required when dangerous goods and hazardous substances are spilled. After receiving notification of an incident, the NRC will immediately notify the appropriate Federal On-Scene Coordinator and concerned Federal agencies. Federal law requires that anyone who releases into the environment a reportable quantity of a hazardous substance (including oil when water is, or may be affected) or a material identified as a marine pollutant, must **immediately** notify the NRC. When in doubt as to whether the amount released equals the required reporting levels for these materials, the NRC should be notified.

CALL NRC (24 hours)
1-800-424-8802
(Toll-free in the U.S., Canada, and the U.S. Virgin Islands)
202-267-2675 in the District of Columbia

Calling the emergency response telephone number, CHEMTREC®, CHEM-TEL, INC., INFOTRAC or 3E COMPANY, does not constitute compliance with regulatory requirements to call the NRC.

6. MILITARY SHIPMENTS

For assistance at incidents involving materials being shipped by, for, or to the Department of Defense (DOD), call one of the following numbers (24 hours):

703-697-0218 (call collect) (U.S. Army Operations Center) for incidents involving explosives and ammunition.

1-800-851-8061 (toll free in the U.S.) (Defense Logistics Agency) for incidents involving dangerous goods other than explosives and ammunition.

The above numbers are for **emergencies** only.

MEXICO

1. **SETIQ** (Emergency Transportation System for the Chemical Industry), a service of the National Association of Chemical Industries (ANIQ), can be reached as follows:

    Call **SETIQ** (24 hours)
    01-800-00-214-00 in the Mexican Republic
    For calls originating in Mexico City and the Metropolitan Area
    5559-1588
    For calls originating elsewhere, call
    0-11-52-5-559-1588

2. **CECOM**, the National Center for Communications of the Civil Protection Agency, can be reached as follows:

    CALL **CECOM** (24 hours)
    01-800-00-413-00 in the Mexican Republic
    For calls originating in Mexico City and the Metropolitan Area
    5550-1496, 5550-1552, 5550-1485, or 5550-4885
    For calls originating elsewhere, call
    0-11-52-5-550-1496, or 0-11-52-5-550-1552
    0-11-52-5-550-1485, or 0-11-52-5-550-4885

HAZARD CLASSIFICATION SYSTEM

The hazard class of dangerous goods is indicated either by its class (or division) number or name. For a placard corresponding to the primary hazard class of a material, the hazard class or division number must be displayed in the lower corner of the placard. However, no hazard class or division number may be displayed on a placard representing the subsidiary hazard of a material. For other than Class 7 or the OXYGEN placard, text indicating a hazard (for example, "CORROSIVE") is not required. Text is shown only in the U.S. The hazard class or division number must appear on the shipping document after each shipping name.

Class 1 - Explosives

Division 1.1	Explosives with a mass explosion hazard
Division 1.2	Explosives with a projection hazard
Division 1.3	Explosives with predominantly a fire hazard
Division 1.4	Explosives with no significant blast hazard
Division 1.5	Very insensitive explosives; blasting agents
Division 1.6	Extremely insensitive detonating articles

Class 2 - Gases

Division 2.1	Flammable gases
Division 2.2	Non-flammable, non-toxic* compressed gases
Division 2.3	Gases toxic* by inhalation
Division 2.4	Corrosive gases (Canada)

Class 3 - Flammable liquids (and Combustible liquids [U.S.])

Class 4 - Flammable solids; Spontaneously combustible materials; and Dangerous when wet materials

Division 4.1	Flammable solids
Division 4.2	Spontaneously combustible materials
Division 4.3	Dangerous when wet materials

Class 5 - Oxidizers and Organic peroxides

Division 5.1	Oxidizers
Division 5.2	Organic peroxides

Class 6 - Toxic* materials and Infectious substances

Division 6.1	Toxic* materials
Division 6.2	Infectious substances

Class 7 - Radioactive materials

Class 8 - Corrosive materials

Class 9 - Miscellaneous dangerous goods

Division 9.1	Miscellaneous dangerous goods (Canada)
Division 9.2	Environmentally hazardous substances (Canada)
Division 9.3	Dangerous wastes (Canada)

* The words "poison" or "poisonous" are synonymous with the word "toxic".

INTRODUCTION TO THE TABLE OF PLACARDS

USE THIS TABLE ONLY IF YOU HAVE NOT BEEN ABLE TO IDENTIFY THE MATERIAL(S) IN TRANSPORT BY ID NUMBER OR NAME

The next two pages display the placards used on transport vehicles carrying dangerous goods. As you approach a reported or suspected dangerous goods incident involving a placarded vehicle:

1. **Approach the incident cautiously from upwind to a point from which you can safely identify and/or read the placard or orange panel information.** If wind direction allows, consider approaching the incident from uphill. Use binoculars, if available.

2. **Match the vehicle placard(s) with one of the placards displayed on the following pages.**

3. **Consult the numbered guide associated with the sample placard. Use that information for now.** For example, a FLAMMABLE (Class 3) placard leads to Guide **127**. A CORROSIVE (Class 8) placard leads to Guide **153**. If multiple placards point to more than one guide, initially use the most conservative guide (i.e., the guide requiring the greatest degree of protective actions).

4. **Remember that the guides associated with the placards provide the most significant risk and/or hazard information.**

5. **When specific information,** such as ID number or shipping name, **becomes available, the more specific guide recommended for that material must be consulted.**

6. **If Guide 111 is being used because only the DANGER/DANGEROUS placard is displayed or the nature of the spilled, leaking, or burning material is not known, as soon as possible, get more specific information concerning the material(s) involved.**

7. Asterisks (*) on orange placards represent explosives "Compatibility Group" letters; refer to the Glossary (page 372).

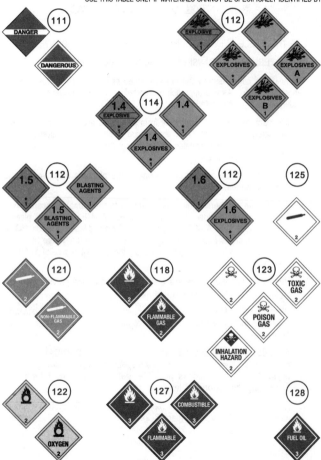

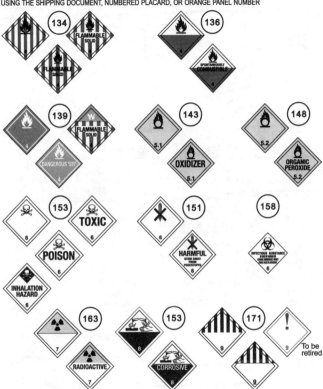

RAIL CAR IDENTIFICATION CHART*

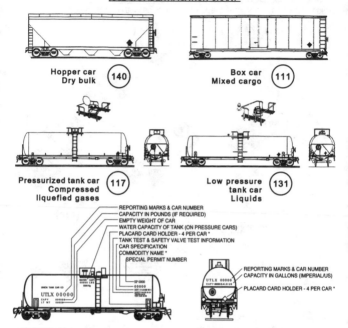

Hopper car (140)
Dry bulk

Box car (111)
Mixed cargo

Pressurized tank car (117)
Compressed
liquefied gases

Low pressure (131)
tank car
Liquids

REPORTING MARKS & CAR NUMBER
CAPACITY IN POUNDS (IF REQUIRED)
EMPTY WEIGHT OF CAR
WATER CAPACITY OF TANK (ON PRESSURE CARS)
PLACARD CARD HOLDER - 4 PER CAR *
TANK TEST & SAFETY VALVE TEST INFORMATION
CAR SPECIFICATION
COMMODITY NAME *
SPECIAL PERMIT NUMBER

REPORTING MARKS & CAR NUMBER
CAPACITY IN GALLONS (IMPERIAL/US)
PLACARD CARD HOLDER - 4 PER CAR *

CAUTION: Emergency response personnel must be aware that rail tank cars vary widely in construction, fittings and purpose. Tank cars could transport products that may be solids, liquids or gases. The products may be under pressure. It is essential that products be identified by consulting shipping documents or train consist or contacting dispatch centers before emergency response is initiated.

The information stenciled on the sides or ends of tank cars, as illustrated above, may be used to identify the product utilizing:

a.   the commodity name shown; or

b.   the other information shown, especially reporting marks and car number which, when supplied to a dispatch center, will facilitate the identification of the product.

*   **The recommended guides should be considered as last resort if product cannot be identified by any other means.**

ROAD TRAILER IDENTIFICATION CHART*

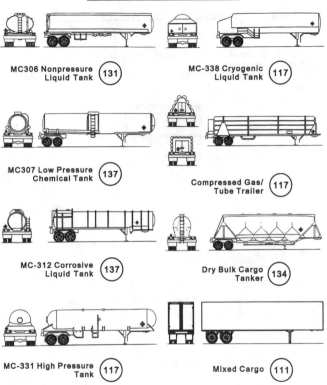

MC306 Nonpressure Liquid Tank (131)

MC-338 Cryogenic Liquid Tank (117)

MC307 Low Pressure Chemical Tank (137)

Compressed Gas/ Tube Trailer (117)

MC-312 Corrosive Liquid Tank (137)

Dry Bulk Cargo Tanker (134)

MC-331 High Pressure Tank (117)

Mixed Cargo (111)

CAUTION: This chart depicts only the most general shapes of road trailers. Emergency response personnel must be aware that there are many variations of road trailers, not illustrated above, that are used for shipping chemical products. The suggested guides are for the most hazardous products that may be transported in these trailer types.

* The recommended guides should be considered as last resort if product cannot be identified by any other means.

HAZARD IDENTIFICATION CODES
DISPLAYED ON SOME INTERMODAL CONTAINERS

Hazard identification codes, referred to as "hazard identification numbers" under European and some South American regulations, may be found in the top half of an orange panel on some intermodal bulk containers. The 4-digit identification number is in the bottom half of the orange panel.

The hazard identification code in the top half of the orange panel consists of two or three figures. In general, the figures indicate the following hazards:

2 - EMISSION OF GAS DUE TO PRESSURE OR CHEMICAL REACTION

3 - FLAMMABILITY OF LIQUIDS (VAPORS) AND GASES OR SELF-HEATING LIQUID

4 - FLAMMABILITY OF SOLIDS OR SELF-HEATING SOLID

5 - OXIDIZING (FIRE-INTENSIFYING) EFFECT

6 - TOXICITY OR RISK OF INFECTION

7 - RADIOACTIVITY

8 - CORROSIVITY

9 - RISK OF SPONTANEOUS VIOLENT REACTION

- Doubling of a figure indicates an intensification of that particular hazard (i.e. 33, 66, 88).

- Where the hazard associated with a material can be adequately indicated by a single figure, the figure is followed by a zero (i.e. 30, 40, 50).

- A hazard identification code prefixed by the letter "X" indicates that the material will react dangerously with water (i.e. X88).

HAZARD IDENTIFICATION CODES
DISPLAYED ON SOME INTERMODAL CONTAINERS

The hazard identification codes listed below have the following meanings:

20	Inert gas
22	Refrigerated gas
223	Refrigerated gas, flammable
225	Refrigerated gas, oxidizing (fire-intensifying)
23	Flammable gas
236	Flammable gas, toxic
239	Flammable gas which can spontaneously lead to violent reaction
25	Oxidizing (fire-intensifying) gas
26	Toxic gas
263	Toxic gas, flammable
265	Toxic gas, oxidizing (fire-intensifying)
266	Highly toxic gas
268	Toxic gas, corrosive

30	Flammable liquid
323	Flammable liquid which reacts with water, emitting flammable gas
X323	Flammable liquid which reacts dangerously with water, emitting flammable gas
33	Highly flammable liquid
333	Pyrophoric liquid
X333	Pyrophoric liquid which reacts dangerously with water
336	Highly flammable liquid, toxic
338	Highly flammable liquid, corrosive
X338	Highly flammable liquid, corrosive, which reacts dangerously with water
339	Highly flammable liquid which can spontaneously lead to violent reaction
36	Flammable liquid, toxic, or self-heating liquid, toxic
362	Flammable liquid, toxic, which reacts with water, emitting flammable gas
X362	Flammable liquid, toxic, which reacts dangerously with water, emitting flammable gas
368	Flammable liquid, toxic, corrosive
38	Flammable liquid, corrosive
382	Flammable liquid, corrosive, which reacts with water, emitting flammable gas
X382	Flammable liquid, corrosive, which reacts dangerously with water, emitting flammable gas
39	Flammable liquid which can spontaneously lead to violent reaction

40	Flammable solid, or self-reactive material, or self-heating material
423	Solid which reacts with water, emitting flammable gas

HAZARD IDENTIFICATION CODES
DISPLAYED ON SOME INTERMODAL CONTAINERS

X423	Flammable solid which reacts dangerously with water, emitting flammable gas
43	Spontaneously flammable (pyrophoric) solid
44	Flammable solid, in the molten state at an elevated temperature
446	Flammable solid, toxic, in the molten state at an elevated temperature
46	Flammable solid, toxic, or self-heating solid, toxic
462	Toxic solid which reacts with water, emitting flammable gas
X462	Solid which reacts with water, emitting toxic gas
48	Flammable or self-heating solid, corrosive
482	Corrosive solid which reacts with water, emitting flammable gas
X482	Solid which reacts dangerously with water, emitting corrosive gas

50	Oxidizing (fire-intensifying) substance
539	Flammable organic peroxide
55	Strongly oxidizing (fire-intensifying) substance
556	Strongly oxidizing (fire-intensifying) substance, toxic
558	Strongly oxidizing (fire-intensifying) substance, corrosive
559	Strongly oxidizing (fire-intensifying) substance which can spontaneously lead to violent reaction
56	Oxidizing (fire-intensifying) substance, toxic
568	Oxidizing (fire-intensifying) substance, toxic, corrosive
58	Oxidizing (fire-intensifying) substance, corrosive
59	Oxidizing (fire intensifying) substance which can spontaneously lead to violent reaction

60	Toxic material
606	Infectious substance
623	Toxic liquid which reacts with water, emitting flammable gas
63	Toxic liquid, flammable
638	Toxic liquid, flammable, corrosive
639	Toxic liquid, flammable, which can spontaneously lead to violent reaction
64	Toxic solid, flammable or self-heating
642	Toxic solid which reacts with water, emitting flammable gas
65	Toxic material, oxidizing (fire-intensifying)
66	Highly toxic material
663	Highly toxic liquid, flammable
664	Highly toxic solid, flammable or self-heating
665	Highly toxic material, oxidizing (fire-intensifying)
668	Highly toxic material, corrosive

HAZARD IDENTIFICATION CODES
DISPLAYED ON SOME INTERMODAL CONTAINERS

669	Highly toxic material which can spontaneously lead to violent reaction
68	Toxic material, corrosive
69	Toxic material which can spontaneously lead to violent reaction

70	Radioactive material
72	Radioactive gas
723	Radioactive gas, flammable
73	Radioactive liquid, flammable
74	Radioactive solid, flammable
75	Radioactive material, oxidizing (fire-intensifying)
76	Radioactive material, toxic
78	Radioactive material, corrosive

80	Corrosive material
X80	Corrosive material which reacts dangerously with water
823	Corrosive liquid which reacts with water, emitting flammable gas
83	Corrosive liquid, flammable
X83	Corrosive liquid, flammable, which reacts dangerously with water
839	Corrosive liquid, flammable, which can spontaneously lead to violent reaction
X839	Corrosive liquid, flammable, which can spontaneously lead to violent reaction and which reacts dangerously with water
84	Corrosive solid, flammable or self-heating
842	Corrosive solid which reacts with water, emitting flammable gas
85	Corrosive material, oxidizing (fire-intensifying)
856	Corrosive material, oxidizing and toxic
86	Corrosive material, toxic
88	Highly corrosive material
X88	Highly corrosive material which reacts dangerously with water
883	Highly corrosive liquid, flammable
884	Highly corrosive solid, flammable or self-heating
885	Highly corrosive material, oxidizing (fire-intensifying)
886	Highly corrosive material, toxic
X886	Highly corrosive material, toxic, which reacts dangerously with water
89	Corrosive material which can spontaneously lead to violent reaction

90	Miscellaneous dangerous substance; environmentally hazardous substance
99	Miscellaneous dangerous substance transported at elevated temperature

Note: If an entry is highlighted in either the yellow-bordered or blue-bordered pages AND THERE IS NO FIRE, go directly to the Table of Initial Isolation and Protective Action Distances (green-bordered pages) and look up the ID number and name of material to obtain initial isolation and protective action distances. IF THERE IS A FIRE, or IF A FIRE IS INVOLVED, go directly to the appropriate guide (orange-bordered pages) and use the evacuation information shown under PUBLIC SAFETY.

ID No.	Guide No.	Name of Material	ID No.	Guide No.	Name of Material
—	112	Ammonium nitrate-fuel oil mixtures	—	159	Methylbromoacetone
—	158	Biological agents	—	135	p-Nitrosodiethylaniline
—	112	Blasting agent, n.o.s.	—	171	Plastic molding material
—	171	Cargo transport unit under fumigation	—	171P	Polymerizable material, stabilized with dry ice
—	154	Chemical kits (containing corrosive substances)	—	153	Toxins
—	128	Chemical kits (containing flammable liquids)	—	133	Wool waste, wet
—	133	Chemical kits (containing flammable solids)	1001	116	Acetylene
—	140	Chemical kits (containing oxidizing substances)	1001	116	Acetylene, dissolved
—	153	Chemical kits (containing poisonous liquids)	1002	122	Air, compressed
—	154	Chemical kits (containing poisonous solids)	1003	122	Air, refrigerated liquid (cryogenic liquid)
—	153	Chemical kits (containing toxic liquids)	1003	122	Air, refrigerated liquid (cryogenic liquid), non-pressurized
—	154	Chemical kits (containing toxic solids)	1005	125	Ammonia, anhydrous
—	129	1-Chloroheptane	1005	125	Ammonia, anhydrous, liquefied
—	129	1-Chlorohexane	1005	125	Ammonia solution, with more than 50% Ammonia
—	152	m-Dichlorobenzene	1005	125	Anhydrous ammonia
—	136	p-Diethylnitrosoaniline	1005	125	Anhydrous ammonia, liquefied
—	153	2-Ethyl-3-propylacrolein	1006	121	Argon
—	112	Explosive A	1006	121	Argon, compressed
—	112	Explosive B	1008	125	Boron trifluoride
—	114	Explosive C	1008	125	Boron trifluoride, compressed
—	112	Explosives, division 1.1, 1.2, 1.3, 1.5 or 1.6	1009	126	Bromotrifluoromethane
—	114	Explosives, division 1.4	1009	126	Refrigerant gas R-13B1
—	133	Fibres, animal or vegetable, burnt, wet or damp	1010	116P	Butadienes, inhibited
—	133	Fibres, vegetable, dry	1011	115	Butane
			1011	115	Butane mixture
			1012	115	Butylene
			1013	120	Carbon dioxide
			1013	120	Carbon dioxide, compressed
			1014	122	Carbon dioxide and Oxygen mixture

ID No.	Guide No.	Name of Material
1014	122	Carbon dioxide and Oxygen mixture, compressed
1014	122	Oxygen and Carbon dioxide mixture
1014	122	Oxygen and Carbon dioxide mixture, compressed
1015	126	Carbon dioxide and Nitrous oxide mixture
1015	126	Nitrous oxide and Carbon dioxide mixture
1016	119	Carbon monoxide
1016	119	Carbon monoxide, compressed
1017	124	Chlorine
1018	126	Chlorodifluoromethane
1018	126	Refrigerant gas R-22
1020	126	Chloropentafluoroethane
1020	126	Refrigerant gas R-115
1021	126	1-Chloro-1,2,2,2-tetrafluoroethane
1021	126	Chlorotetrafluoroethane
1021	126	Refrigerant gas R-124
1022	126	Chlorotrifluoromethane
1022	126	Refrigerant gas R-13
1023	119	Coal gas
1023	119	Coal gas, compressed
1026	119	Cyanogen
1026	119	Cyanogen, liquefied
1026	119	Cyanogen gas
1027	115	Cyclopropane
1027	115	Cyclopropane, liquefied
1028	126	Dichlorodifluoromethane
1028	126	Refrigerant gas R-12
1029	126	Dichlorofluoromethane
1029	126	Refrigerant gas R-21
1030	115	1,1-Difluoroethane
1030	115	Difluoroethane
1030	115	Refrigerant gas R-152a
1032	118	Dimethylamine, anhydrous
1033	115	Dimethyl ether
1035	115	Ethane
1035	115	Ethane, compressed
1036	118	Ethylamine
1037	115	Ethyl chloride
1038	115	Ethylene, refrigerated liquid (cryogenic liquid)
1039	115	Ethyl methyl ether
1039	115	Methyl ethyl ether
1040	119P	Ethylene oxide
1040	119P	Ethylene oxide with Nitrogen
1041	115	Carbon dioxide and Ethylene oxide mixture, with more than 9% but not more than 87% Ethylene oxide
1041	115	Carbon dioxide and Ethylene oxide mixtures, with more than 6% Ethylene oxide
1041	115	Ethylene oxide and Carbon dioxide mixture, with more than 9% but not more than 87% Ethylene oxide
1041	115	Ethylene oxide and Carbon dioxide mixtures, with more than 6 % Ethylene oxide
1043	125	Fertilizer, ammoniating solution, with free Ammonia
1044	126	Fire extinguishers with compressed gas
1044	126	Fire extinguishers with liquefied gas
1045	124	Fluorine

ID No.	Guide No.	Name of Material
1045	124	Fluorine, compressed
1046	121	Helium
1046	121	Helium, compressed
1048	125	Hydrogen bromide, anhydrous
1049	115	Hydrogen
1049	115	Hydrogen, compressed
1050	125	Hydrogen chloride, anhydrous
1051	117	AC
1051	117	Hydrocyanic acid, aqueous solutions, with more than 20% Hydrogen cyanide
1051	117	Hydrocyanic acid, liquefied
1051	117	Hydrogen cyanide, anhydrous, stabilized
1051	117	Hydrogen cyanide, stabilized
1052	125	Hydrogen fluoride, anhydrous
1053	117	Hydrogen sulfide
1053	117	Hydrogen sulfide, liquefied
1053	117	Hydrogen sulphide
1053	117	Hydrogen sulphide, liquefied
1055	115	Isobutylene
1056	121	Krypton
1056	121	Krypton, compressed
1057	115	Cigarette lighter, with flammable gas
1057	115	Flammable gas in lighter for cigars, cigarettes, etc.
1057	115	Lighter refills (cigarettes) (flammable gas)
1057	115	Lighters (cigarettes) (flammable gas)
1058	121	Liquefied gas (nonflammable)
1058	121	Liquefied gases, non-flammable, charged with Nitrogen, Carbon dioxide or Air
1060	116P	Methylacetylene and Propadiene mixture, stabilized
1060	116P	Propadiene and Methylacetylene mixture, stabilized
1061	118	Methylamine, anhydrous
1062	123	Methyl bromide
1063	115	Methyl chloride
1063	115	Refrigerant gas R-40
1064	117	Methyl mercaptan
1065	121	Neon
1065	121	Neon, compressed
1066	121	Nitrogen
1066	121	Nitrogen, compressed
1067	124	Dinitrogen tetroxide
1067	124	Dinitrogen tetroxide, liquefied
1067	124	Nitrogen dioxide
1067	124	Nitrogen dioxide, liquefied
1067	124	Nitrogen peroxide, liquid
1067	124	Nitrogen tetroxide, liquid
1069	125	Nitrosyl chloride
1070	122	Nitrous oxide
1070	122	Nitrous oxide, compressed
1071	119	Oil gas
1071	119	Oil gas, compressed
1072	122	Oxygen
1072	122	Oxygen, compressed
1073	122	Oxygen, refrigerated liquid (cryogenic liquid)
1075	115	Butane
1075	115	Butane mixture
1075	115	Butylene
1075	115	Isobutane

ID No.	Guide No.	Name of Material	ID No.	Guide No.	Name of Material
1075	115	Isobutane mixture	1089	129	Acetaldehyde
1075	115	Isobutylene	1090	127	Acetone
1075	115	Liquefied petroleum gas	1091	127	Acetone oils
1075	115	LPG	1092	131P	Acrolein, inhibited
1075	115	Petroleum gases, liquefied	1093	131P	Acrylonitrile, inhibited
1075	115	Propane	1098	131	Allyl alcohol
1075	115	Propane mixture	1099	131	Allyl bromide
1075	115	Propylene	1100	131	Allyl chloride
1076	125	CG	1104	129	Amyl acetates
1076	125	Diphosgene	1105	129	Amyl alcohols
1076	125	DP	1105	129	Pentanols
1076	125	Phosgene	1106	132	Amylamines
1077	115	Propylene	1107	129	Amyl chloride
1078	126	Dispersant gas, n.o.s.	1108	127	n-Amylene
1078	126	Refrigerant gas, n.o.s.	1108	127	1-Pentene
1079	125	Sulfur dioxide	1109	129	Amyl formates
1079	125	Sulfur dioxide, liquefied	1110	127	n-Amyl methyl ketone
1079	125	Sulphur dioxide	1110	127	Amyl methyl ketone
1079	125	Sulphur dioxide, liquefied	1110	127	Methyl amyl ketone
1080	126	Sulfur hexafluoride	1111	130	Amyl mercaptan
1080	126	Sulphur hexafluoride	1112	140	Amyl nitrate
1081	116P	Tetrafluoroethylene, inhibited	1113	129	Amyl nitrite
1082	119P	Trifluorochloroethylene	1114	130	Benzene
1082	119P	Trifluorochloroethylene, inhibited	1118	130	Brake fluid, hydraulic
1083	118	Trimethylamine, anhydrous	1120	129	Butanols
1085	116P	Vinyl bromide, inhibited	1120	129	Butyl alcohol
1086	116P	Vinyl chloride	1123	129	Butyl acetates
1086	116P	Vinyl chloride, inhibited	1125	132	n-Butylamine
1086	116P	Vinyl chloride, stabilized	1126	129	1-Bromobutane
1087	116P	Vinyl methyl ether	1126	129	n-Butyl bromide
1087	116P	Vinyl methyl ether, inhibited	1127	130	Butyl chloride
1088	127	Acetal	1127	130	Chlorobutanes
			1128	129	n-Butyl formate

ID No.	Guide No.	Name of Material
1129	129	Butyraldehyde
1130	128	Camphor oil
1131	131	Carbon bisulfide
1131	131	Carbon bisulphide
1131	131	Carbon disulfide
1131	131	Carbon disulphide
1133	128	Adhesives (flammable)
1133	128	Cement (flammable)
1133	128	Cement, container, linoleum, tile or wallboard, liquid
1133	128	Cement, leather
1133	128	Cement, liquid, n.o.s.
1133	128	Cement, pyroxlin
1133	128	Cement, roofing, liquid
1133	128	Cement, rubber
1134	130	Chlorobenzene
1135	131	Ethylene chlorohydrin
1136	128	Coal tar distillates, flammable
1137	128	Coal tar distillate
1139	127	Coating solution
1142	127	Compound, vulcanizing, liquid (flammable)
1142	127	Compounds, polishing, liquid, etc. (flammable)
1142	127	Flammable liquid preparations, n.o.s.
1143	131P	Crotonaldehyde, inhibited
1143	131P	Crotonaldehyde, stabilized
1144	128	Crotonylene
1145	128	Cyclohexane
1146	128	Cyclopentane
1147	130	Decahydronaphthalene
1148	129	Diacetone alcohol
1149	127	Butyl ethers
1149	127	Dibutyl ethers
1150	130P	1,2-Dichloroethylene
1150	130P	Dichloroethylene
1152	130	Dichloropentanes
1153	127	Ethylene glycol diethyl ether
1154	132	Diethylamine
1155	127	Diethyl ether
1155	127	Ethyl ether
1156	127	Diethyl ketone
1157	127	Diisobutyl ketone
1158	132	Diisopropylamine
1159	127	Diisopropyl ether
1160	129	Dimethylamine, aqueous solution
1160	129	Dimethylamine, solution
1161	129	Dimethyl carbonate
1162	155	Dimethyldichlorosilane
1163	131	1,1-Dimethylhydrazine
1163	131	Dimethylhydrazine, unsymmetrical
1164	130	Dimethyl sulfide
1164	130	Dimethyl sulphide
1165	127	Dioxane
1166	127	Dioxolane
1167	131P	Divinyl ether, inhibited
1168	127	Driers, paint or varnish, liquid, n.o.s.
1169	127	Extracts, aromatic, liquid
1170	127	Ethanol
1170	127	Ethanol, solution
1170	127	Ethyl alcohol
1170	127	Ethyl alcohol, solution
1171	127	Ethylene glycol monoethyl ether

ID No.	Guide No.	Name of Material	ID No.	Guide No.	Name of Material
1172	129	Ethylene glycol monoethyl ether acetate	1199	132P	Furaldehydes
1173	129	Ethyl acetate	1199	132P	Furfural
1175	129	Ethylbenzene	1199	132P	Furfuraldehydes
1176	129	Ethyl borate	1201	127	Fusel oil
1177	129	2-Ethylbutyl acetate	1202	128	Diesel fuel
1177	129	Ethylbutyl acetate	1202	128	Fuel oil
1178	129	2-Ethylbutyraldehyde	1202	128	Fuel oil, no. 1,2,4,5,6
1179	127	Ethyl butyl ether	1202	128	Gas oil
1180	129	Ethyl butyrate	1202	128	Heating oil, light
1181	155	Ethyl chloroacetate	1203	128	Gasohol
1182	155	Ethyl chloroformate	1203	128	Gasoline
1183	139	Ethyldichlorosilane	1203	128	Motor spirit
1184	129	Ethylene dichloride	1203	128	Petrol
1185	131P	Ethyleneimine, inhibited	1204	127	Nitroglycerin, solution in alcohol, with not more than 1% Nitroglycerin
1188	127	Ethylene glycol monomethyl ether	1204	127	Spirits of Nitroglycerin, not exceeding 1 % Nitroglycerin
1189	129	Ethylene glycol monomethyl ether acetate	1206	128	Heptanes
1190	129	Ethyl formate	1207	129	Hexaldehyde
1191	129	Ethylhexaldehydes	1208	128	Hexanes
1191	129	Octyl aldehydes	1208	128	Neohexane
1192	129	Ethyl lactate	1210	129	Ink, printer's, flammable
1193	127	Ethyl methyl ketone	1210	129	Printing ink, flammable
1193	127	Methyl ethyl ketone	1210	129	Printing ink related material
1194	131	Ethyl nitrite, solution	1212	129	Isobutanol
1195	129	Ethyl propionate	1212	129	Isobutyl alcohol
1196	155	Ethyltrichlorosilane	1213	129	Isobutyl acetate
1197	127	Extracts, flavoring, liquid	1214	132	Isobutylamine
1197	127	Extracts, flavouring, liquid	1216	128	Isooctene
1198	132	Formaldehyde, solution, flammable	1218	130P	Isoprene, inhibited
1198	132	Formaldehyde, solutions (Formalin)	1219	129	Isopropanol
			1219	129	Isopropyl alcohol

ID No.	Guide No.	Name of Material
1220	129	Isopropyl acetate
1221	132	Isopropylamine
1222	130	Isopropyl nitrate
1223	128	Kerosene
1224	127	Ketones, liquid, n.o.s.
1226	127	Cigarette lighter, with flammable liquid
1226	127	Lighters for cigars, cigarettes etc. with lighter fluid
1226	127	Lighters for cigars, cigarettes (flammable liquid)
1228	131	Mercaptan mixture, aliphatic
1228	131	Mercaptan mixture, liquid, flammable, poisonous, n.o.s.
1228	131	Mercaptan mixture, liquid, flammable, toxic, n.o.s.
1228	131	Mercaptan mixtures, liquid, n.o.s.
1228	131	Mercaptans, liquid, flammable, poisonous, n.o.s.
1228	131	Mercaptans, liquid, flammable, toxic, n.o.s.
1229	129	Mesityl oxide
1230	131	Methanol
1230	131	Methyl alcohol
1231	129	Methyl acetate
1232	127	Methyl acetone
1233	129	Methylamyl acetate
1234	127	Methylal
1235	132	Methylamine, aqueous solution
1237	129	Methyl butyrate
1238	155	Methyl chloroformate
1239	131	Methyl chloromethyl ether
1242	139	Methyldichlorosilane
1243	129	Methyl formate

ID No.	Guide No.	Name of Material
1244	131	Methylhydrazine
1245	127	Methyl isobutyl ketone
1246	127P	Methyl isopropenyl ketone, inhibited
1247	129P	Methyl methacrylate monomer, inhibited
1247	129P	Methyl methacrylate monomer, uninhibited
1248	129	Methyl propionate
1249	127	Methyl propyl ketone
1250	155	Methyltrichlorosilane
1251	131P	Methyl vinyl ketone
1251	131P	Methyl vinyl ketone, stabilized
1255	128	Naphtha, petroleum
1255	128	Petroleum naphtha
1256	128	Naphtha, solvent
1257	128	Natural gasoline
1259	131	Nickel carbonyl
1261	129	Nitromethane
1262	128	Isooctane
1262	128	Octanes
1263	128	Paint (flammable)
1263	128	Paint related material (flammable)
1264	129	Paraldehyde
1265	128	Isopentane
1265	128	n-Pentane
1265	128	Pentanes
1266	127	Perfumery products, with flammable solvents
1267	128	Petroleum crude oil
1268	128	Petroleum distillates, n.o.s.
1268	128	Petroleum products, n.o.s.
1270	128	Oil, petroleum, n.o.s.

ID No.	Guide No.	Name of Material	ID No.	Guide No.	Name of Material
1270	128	Petroleum oil	1298	155	Trimethylchlorosilane
1271	128	Petroleum ether	1299	128	Turpentine
1271	128	Petroleum spirit	1300	128	Turpentine substitute
1272	129	Pine oil	1301	129P	Vinyl acetate
1274	129	n-Propanol	1301	129P	Vinyl acetate, inhibited
1274	129	normal Propyl alcohol	1302	127P	Vinyl ethyl ether
1274	129	Propyl alcohol, normal	1302	127P	Vinyl ethyl ether, inhibited
1275	129	Propionaldehyde	1303	129P	Vinylidene chloride, inhibited
1276	129	n-Propyl acetate	1304	127P	Vinyl isobutyl ether
1277	132	Monopropylamine	1304	127P	Vinyl isobutyl ether, inhibited
1277	132	Propylamine	1305	155	Vinyltrichlorosilane
1278	129	1-Chloropropane	1305	155	Vinyltrichlorosilane, inhibited
1278	129	Propyl chloride	1306	129	Wood preservatives, liquid
1279	130	1,2-Dichloropropane	1307	130	Xylenes
1279	130	Dichloropropane	1308	170	Zirconium metal, liquid, suspension
1279	130	Propylene dichloride	1308	170	Zirconium suspended in a flammable liquid
1280	127P	Propylene oxide			
1281	129	Propyl formates	1308	170	Zirconium suspended in a liquid (flammable)
1282	129	Pyridine			
1286	127	Rosin oil	1309	170	Aluminum powder, coated
1287	127	Rubber solution	1310	113	Ammonium picrate, wetted with not less than 10% water
1288	128	Shale oil			
1289	132	Sodium methylate, alcohol mixture	1312	133	Borneol
			1313	133	Calcium resinate
1289	132	Sodium methylate, solution in alcohol	1314	133	Calcium resinate, fused
			1318	133	Cobalt resinate, precipitated
1292	132	Ethyl silicate	1320	113	Dinitrophenol, wetted with not less than 15% water
1292	132	Tetraethyl silicate			
1293	127	Tinctures, medicinal	1321	113	Dinitrophenolates, wetted with not less than 15% water
1294	130	Toluene			
1295	139	Trichlorosilane	1322	113	Dinitroresorcinol, wetted with not less than 15% water
1296	132	Triethylamine			
1297	132	Trimethylamine, aqueous solution	1323	170	Ferrocerium
			1324	133	Film

ID No.	Guide No.	Name of Material
1324	133	Films, nitrocellulose base
1325	133	Air bag inflators
1325	133	Air bag modules
1325	133	Antimony sulfide, solid
1325	133	Antimony sulphide, solid
1325	133	Burnt cotton, not picked
1325	133	Cosmetics, n.o.s.
1325	133	Drugs, n.o.s.
1325	133	Flammable solid, n.o.s.
1325	133	Flammable solid, organic, n.o.s.
1325	133	Fusee (rail or highway)
1325	133	Medicines, flammable, solid, n.o.s.
1325	133	N-Methyl-N'-Nitro-N-Nitrosoguanidine
1325	133	Pyroxylin plastic, rod, sheet, roll, tube or scrap
1325	133	Smokeless powder for small arms
1326	170	Hafnium powder, wetted with not less than 25% water
1327	133	Bhusa, wet, damp or contaminated with oil
1327	133	Hay, wet, damp or contaminated with oil
1327	133	Straw, wet, damp or contaminated with oil
1328	133	Hexamethylenetetramine
1328	133	Hexamine
1330	133	Manganese resinate
1331	133	Matches, "strike anywhere"
1332	133	Metaldehyde
1333	170	Cerium, slabs, ingots or rods
1334	133	Naphthalene, crude
1334	133	Naphthalene, refined
1336	113	Nitroguanidine (Picrite), wetted with not less than 20% water
1336	113	Nitroguanidine, wetted with not less than 20% water
1336	113	Picrite, wetted
1337	113	Nitrostarch, wet, with not less than 30% alcohol or solvent
1337	113	Nitrostarch, wetted with not less than 20% water
1337	113	Nitrostarch, wetted with not less than 30% solvent
1338	133	Phosphorus, amorphous
1338	133	Phosphorus, amorphous, red
1338	133	Red phosphorus
1338	133	Red phosphorus, amorphous
1339	139	Phosphorus heptasulfide, free from yellow and white Phosphorus
1339	139	Phosphorus heptasulphide, free from yellow and white Phosphorus
1340	139	Phosphorus pentasulfide, free from yellow and white Phosphorus
1340	139	Phosphorus pentasulphide, free from yellow and white Phosphorus
1341	139	Phosphorus sesquisulfide, free from yellow and white Phosphorus
1341	139	Phosphorus sesquisulphide, free from yellow and white Phosphorus
1343	139	Phosphorus trisulfide, free from yellow and white Phosphorus
1343	139	Phosphorus trisulphide, free from yellow and white Phosphorus

ID No.	Guide No.	Name of Material
1344	113	Picric acid, wet, with not less than 10% water
1344	113	Trinitrophenol, wetted with not less than 30% water
1345	133	Rubber scrap, powdered or granulated
1345	133	Rubber shoddy, powdered or granulated
1346	170	Silicon powder, amorphous
1347	113	Silver picrate, wetted with not less than 30% water
1348	113	Sodium dinitro-o-cresolate, wetted with not less than 15% water
1348	113	Sodium dinitro-ortho-cresolate, wetted
1349	113	Sodium picramate, wetted with not less than 20% water
1350	133	Sulfur
1350	133	Sulphur
1352	170	Titanium powder, wetted with not less than 25% water
1353	133	Fabrics impregnated with weakly nitrated Nitrocellulose, n.o.s.
1353	133	Fibers impregnated with weakly nitrated Nitrocellulose, n.o.s.
1353	133	Fibres impregnated with weakly nitrated Nitrocellulose, n.o.s.
1353	133	Toe puffs, nitrocellulose base
1354	113	Trinitrobenzene, wetted with not less than 30% water
1355	113	Trinitrobenzoic acid, wetted with not less than 30% water
1356	113	TNT, wetted with not less than 30% water
1356	113	Trinitrotoluene, wetted with not less than 30% water
1357	113	Urea nitrate, wetted with not less than 20% water
1358	170	Zirconium metal, powder, wet
1358	170	Zirconium powder, wetted with not less than 25% water
1360	139	Calcium phosphide
1361	133	Carbon, animal or vegetable origin
1361	133	Charcoal
1361	133	Charcoal, briquettes
1361	133	Charcoal, shell
1361	133	Charcoal, wood, ground, crushed, granulated or pulverized
1361	133	Charcoal screenings, made from "Pinon" wood
1361	133	Charcoal screenings, other than "Pinon" wood screenings
1362	133	Carbon, activated
1363	135	Copra
1364	133	Cotton waste, oily
1365	133	Cotton
1365	133	Cotton, wet
1366	135	Diethylzinc
1369	135	p-Nitrosodimethylaniline
1370	135	Dimethylzinc
1372	133	Fiber, animal or vegetable, n.o.s., burnt, wet or damp
1372	133	Fibers
1373	133	Fabrics, animal, synthetic or vegetable, n.o.s., with oil
1373	133	Fiber, animal, synthetic or vegetable, n.o.s., with oil
1373	133	Fibres, animal, synthetic or vegetable, n.o.s., with oil
1374	133	Fish meal, unstabilized

ID No.	Guide No.	Name of Material
1374	133	Fish meal containing less than 6% or more than 12% water
1374	133	Fish scrap, unstabilized
1374	133	Fish scrap containing less than 6% or more than 12% water
1376	135	Iron oxide, spent
1376	135	Iron sponge, spent
1378	170	Metal catalyst, wetted
1379	133	Paper, unsaturated oil treated
1380	135	Pentaborane
1381	136	Phosphorus, white, dry or under water or in solution
1381	136	Phosphorus, yellow, dry or under water or in solution
1381	136	White phosphorus, dry
1381	136	White phosphorus, in solution
1381	136	White phosphorus, under water
1381	136	Yellow phosphorus, dry
1381	136	Yellow phosphorus, in solution
1381	136	Yellow phosphorus, under water
1382	135	Potassium sulfide, anhydrous
1382	135	Potassium sulfide, with less than 30% water of crystallization
1382	135	Potassium sulfide, with less than 30% water of hydration
1382	135	Potassium sulphide, anhydrous
1382	135	Potassium sulphide, with less than 30% water of crystallization
1382	135	Potassium sulphide, with less than 30% water of hydration
1383	135	Aluminum powder, pyrophoric
1383	135	Pyrophoric alloy, n.o.s.
1383	135	Pyrophoric metal, n.o.s.
1384	135	Sodium dithionite
1384	135	Sodium hydrosulfite
1384	135	Sodium hydrosulphite
1385	135	Sodium sulfide, anhydrous
1385	135	Sodium sulfide, with less than 30% water of crystallization
1385	135	Sodium sulphide, anhydrous
1385	135	Sodium sulphide, with less than 30% water of crystallization
1386	135	Seed cake, with more than 1.5% oil and not more than 11% moisture
1389	138	Alkali metal amalgam
1389	138	Alkali metal amalgam, liquid
1389	138	Alkali metal amalgam, solid
1390	139	Alkali metal amides
1391	138	Alkali metal dispersion
1391	138	Alkaline earth metal dispersion
1392	138	Alkaline earth metal amalgam
1393	138	Alkaline earth metal alloy, n.o.s.
1394	138	Aluminum carbide
1395	139	Aluminum ferrosilicon powder
1396	138	Aluminum powder, uncoated
1397	139	Aluminum phosphide
1398	138	Aluminum silicon powder, uncoated
1400	138	Barium
1401	138	Calcium
1401	138	Calcium metal, crystalline
1402	138	Calcium carbide
1403	138	Calcium cyanamide, with more than 0.1% Calcium carbide
1404	138	Calcium hydride
1405	138	Calcium silicide
1406	138	Calcium silicon

ID No.	Guide No.	Name of Material	ID No.	Guide No.	Name of Material
1407	138	Caesium	1435	138	Zinc residue
1407	138	Cesium	1435	138	Zinc skimmings
1408	139	Ferrosilicon	1436	138	Zinc dust
1409	138	Hydrides, metal, n.o.s.	1436	138	Zinc powder
1409	138	Metal hydrides, water-reactive, n.o.s.	1437	138	Zirconium hydride
1410	138	Lithium aluminum hydride	1438	140	Aluminum nitrate
1411	138	Lithium aluminum hydride, ethereal	1439	141	Ammonium dichromate
1412	139	Lithium amide	1442	143	Ammonium perchlorate
1413	138	Lithium borohydride	1444	140	Ammonium persulfate
1414	138	Lithium hydride	1444	140	Ammonium persulphate
1415	138	Lithium	1445	141	Barium chlorate
1417	138	Lithium silicon	1445	141	Barium chlorate, wet
1418	138	Magnesium alloys powder	1446	141	Barium nitrate
1418	138	Magnesium powder	1447	141	Barium perchlorate
1419	139	Magnesium aluminum phosphide	1448	141	Barium permanganate
1420	138	Potassium, metal alloys	1449	141	Barium peroxide
1420	138	Potassium, metal liquid alloy	1450	141	Bromates, inorganic, n.o.s.
1421	138	Alkali metal alloy, liquid, n.o.s.	1451	140	Caesium nitrate
1422	138	Potassium sodium alloys	1451	140	Cesium nitrate
1422	138	Sodium potassium alloys	1452	140	Calcium chlorate
1423	138	Rubidium	1453	140	Calcium chlorite
1423	138	Rubidium metal	1454	140	Calcium nitrate
1426	138	Sodium borohydride	1455	140	Calcium perchlorate
1427	138	Sodium hydride	1456	140	Calcium permanganate
1428	138	Sodium	1457	140	Calcium peroxide
1431	138	Sodium methylate	1458	140	Borate and Chlorate mixtures
1431	138	Sodium methylate, dry	1458	140	Chlorate and Borate mixtures
1432	139	Sodium phosphide	1459	140	Chlorate and Magnesium chloride mixture
1433	139	Stannic phosphides	1459	140	Magnesium chloride and Chlorate mixture
1435	138	Zinc ashes	1461	140	Chlorate, n.o.s., wet
1435	138	Zinc dross	1461	140	Chlorates, inorganic, n.o.s.

ID No.	Guide No.	Name of Material	ID No.	Guide No.	Name of Material
1462	143	Chlorites, inorganic, n.o.s.	1481	140	Perchlorates, inorganic, n.o.s.
1463	141	Chromic acid, solid	1482	140	Permanganate, n.o.s.
1463	141	Chromic acid mixture, dry	1482	140	Permanganates, inorganic, n.o.s.
1463	141	Chromium trioxide, anhydrous	1483	140	Peroxides, inorganic, n.o.s.
1465	140	Didymium nitrate	1484	140	Potassium bromate
1466	140	Ferric nitrate	1485	140	Potassium chlorate
1467	143	Guanidine nitrate	1486	140	Potassium nitrate
1469	141	Lead nitrate	1487	140	Potassium nitrate and Sodium nitrite mixture
1470	141	Lead perchlorate	1487	140	Sodium nitrite and Potassium nitrate mixtures
1470	141	Lead perchlorate, solid			
1470	141	Lead perchlorate, solution	1487	140	Sodium nitrite mixture
1471	140	Lithium hypochlorite, dry	1488	140	Potassium nitrite
1471	140	Lithium hypochlorite mixture	1489	140	Potassium perchlorate
1471	140	Lithium hypochlorite mixtures, dry	1490	140	Potassium permanganate
1472	143	Lithium peroxide	1491	144	Potassium peroxide
1473	140	Magnesium bromate	1492	140	Potassium persulfate
1474	140	Magnesium nitrate	1492	140	Potassium persulphate
1475	140	Magnesium perchlorate	1493	140	Silver nitrate
1476	140	Magnesium peroxide	1494	141	Sodium bromate
1477	140	Ammonium sulfate nitrate	1495	140	Sodium chlorate
1477	140	Ammonium sulphate nitrate	1496	143	Sodium chlorite
1477	140	Nitrate, n.o.s.	1498	140	Sodium nitrate
1477	140	Nitrates, inorganic, n.o.s.	1499	140	Potassium nitrate and Sodium nitrate mixture
1479	140	Compound, tree or weed killing, solid (oxidizer)	1499	140	Sodium nitrate and Potassium nitrate mixture
1479	140	Cosmetics, n.o.s.			
1479	140	Drugs, n.o.s.	1500	140	Sodium nitrite
1479	140	Medicines, oxidizing substances, solid, n.o.s.	1502	140	Sodium perchlorate
1479	140	Oxidizing solid, n.o.s.	1503	140	Sodium permanganate
1479	140	Oxidizing substances, solid, n.o.s.	1504	144	Sodium peroxide
			1505	140	Sodium persulfate
1481	140	Perchlorate, n.o.s.	1505	140	Sodium persulphate

ID No.	Guide No.	Name of Material
1506	143	Strontium chlorate
1506	143	Strontium chlorate, solid
1506	143	Strontium chlorate, solution
1507	140	Strontium nitrate
1508	140	Strontium perchlorate
1509	143	Strontium peroxide
1510	143	Tetranitromethane
1511	140	Urea hydrogen peroxide
1511	140	Urea peroxide
1512	140	Zinc ammonium nitrite
1513	140	Zinc chlorate
1514	140	Zinc nitrate
1515	140	Zinc permanganate
1516	143	Zinc peroxide
1517	113	Zirconium picramate, wetted with not less than 20% water
1541	155	Acetone cyanohydrin, stabilized
1544	151	Alkaloids, solid, n.o.s. (poisonous)
1544	151	Alkaloid salts, solid, n.o.s. (poisonous)
1545	155	Allyl isothiocyanate, inhibited
1545	155	Allyl isothiocyanate, stabilized
1546	151	Ammonium arsenate
1547	153	Aniline
1548	153	Aniline hydrochloride
1549	157	Antimony compound, inorganic, n.o.s.
1549	157	Antimony compound, inorganic, solid, n.o.s.
1549	157	Antimony tribromide, solid
1549	157	Antimony tribromide, solution
1549	157	Antimony trifluoride, solid
1549	157	Antimony trifluoride, solution
1550	151	Antimony lactate
1551	151	Antimony potassium tartrate
1553	154	Arsenic acid, liquid
1554	154	Arsenic acid, solid
1555	151	Arsenic bromide
1556	152	Arsenic compound, liquid, n.o.s.
1556	152	Arsenic compound, liquid, n.o.s., inorganic
1556	152	MD
1556	152	Methyldichloroarsine
1556	152	PD
1556	152	Phenyldichloroarsine
1557	152	Arsenic compound, solid, n.o.s.
1557	152	Arsenic compound, solid, n.o.s., inorganic
1557	152	Arsenic iodide, solid
1557	152	Arsenic sulfide
1557	152	Arsenic sulphide
1557	152	Arsenic trisulfide
1557	152	Arsenic trisulphide
1558	152	Arsenic
1559	151	Arsenic pentoxide
1560	157	Arsenic chloride
1560	157	Arsenic trichloride
1561	151	Arsenic trioxide
1562	152	Arsenical dust
1564	154	Barium compound, n.o.s.
1565	157	Barium cyanide
1566	154	Beryllium chloride
1566	154	Beryllium compound, n.o.s.
1566	154	Beryllium fluoride
1567	134	Beryllium powder
1569	131	Bromoacetone

ID No.	Guide No.	Name of Material
1570	152	Brucine
1571	113	Barium azide, wetted with not less than 50% water
1572	151	Cacodylic acid
1573	151	Calcium arsenate
1574	151	Calcium arsenate and Calcium arsenite mixture, solid
1574	151	Calcium arsenate, solid
1574	151	Calcium arsenite and Calcium arsenate mixture, solid
1575	157	Calcium cyanide
1577	153	Chlorodinitrobenzenes
1577	153	Dinitrochlorobenzene
1578	152	Chloronitrobenzenes
1578	152	Chloronitrobenzenes, liquid
1578	152	Chloronitrobenzenes, solid
1578	152	Nitrochlorobenzenes, liquid
1578	152	Nitrochlorobenzenes, solid
1579	153	4-Chloro-o-toluidine hydrochloride
1580	154	Chloropicrin
1581	123	Chloropicrin and Methyl bromide mixture
1581	123	Methyl bromide and Chloropicrin mixtures
1581	123	Methyl bromide and more than 2% Chloropicrin mixture, liquid
1582	119	Chloropicrin and Methyl chloride mixture
1582	119	Methyl chloride and Chloropicrin mixtures
1583	154	Chloropicrin, absorbed
1583	154	Chloropicrin mixture, n.o.s.
1584	151	Cocculus
1585	151	Copper acetoarsenite
1586	151	Copper arsenite
1587	151	Copper cyanide
1588	157	Cyanides, inorganic, n.o.s.
1588	157	Cyanides, inorganic, solid, n.o.s.
1589	125	CK
1589	125	Cyanogen chloride, inhibited
1590	153	Dichloroanilines
1590	153	Dichloroanilines, liquid
1590	153	Dichloroanilines, solid
1591	152	o-Dichlorobenzene
1592	152	p-Dichlorobenzene
1593	160	Dichloromethane
1593	160	Methylene chloride
1594	152	Diethyl sulfate
1594	152	Diethyl sulphate
1595	156	Dimethyl sulfate
1595	156	Dimethyl sulphate
1596	153	Dinitroanilines
1597	152	Dinitrobenzenes
1598	153	Dinitro-o-cresol
1599	153	Dinitrophenol, solution
1600	152	Dinitrotoluenes, molten
1601	151	Disinfectant, solid, poisonous, n.o.s.
1601	151	Disinfectant, solid, toxic, n.o.s.
1601	151	Disinfectants, solid, n.o.s. (poisonous)
1602	151	Dye, liquid, poisonous, n.o.s.
1602	151	Dye, liquid, toxic, n.o.s.
1602	151	Dye intermediate, liquid, poisonous, n.o.s.
1602	151	Dye intermediate, liquid, toxic, n.o.s.

ID No.	Guide No.	Name of Material	ID No.	Guide No.	Name of Material
1603	155	Ethyl bromoacetate	1627	141	Mercurous nitrate
1604	132	Ethylenediamine	1628	151	Mercurous sulfate
1605	154	Ethylene dibromide	1628	151	Mercurous sulphate
1606	151	Ferric arsenate	1629	151	Mercury acetate
1607	151	Ferric arsenite	1630	151	Mercury ammonium chloride
1608	151	Ferrous arsenate	1631	154	Mercury benzoate
1610	159	Halogenated irritating liquid, n.o.s.	1633	151	Mercury bisulfate
1611	151	Hexaethyl tetraphosphate	1633	151	Mercury bisulphate
1611	151	Hexaethyl tetraphosphate, liquid	1634	154	Mercuric bromide
1611	151	Hexaethyl tetraphosphate, solid	1634	154	Mercurous bromide
1612	123	Hexaethyl tetraphosphate and compressed gas mixture	1634	154	Mercury bromides
			1636	154	Mercuric cyanide
1613	154	Hydrocyanic acid, aqueous solution, with less than 5% Hydrogen cyanide	1636	154	Mercury cyanide
			1637	151	Mercury gluconate
1613	154	Hydrocyanic acid, aqueous solution, with not more than 20% Hydrogen cyanide	1638	151	Mercury iodide
			1639	151	Mercury nucleate
			1640	151	Mercury oleate
1613	154	Hydrogen cyanide, aqueous solution, with not more than 20% Hydrogen cyanide	1641	151	Mercury oxide
			1642	151	Mercuric oxycyanide
1614	131	Hydrogen cyanide, anhydrous, stabilized (absorbed)	1642	151	Mercury oxycyanide, desensitized
			1643	151	Mercury potassium iodide
1614	131	Hydrogen cyanide, stabilized (absorbed)	1644	151	Mercury salicylate
			1645	151	Mercuric sulfate
1616	151	Lead acetate	1645	151	Mercuric sulphate
1617	151	Lead arsenates	1645	151	Mercury sulfate
1618	151	Lead arsenites	1645	151	Mercury sulphate
1620	151	Lead cyanide	1646	151	Mercury thiocyanate
1621	151	London purple	1647	151	Ethylene dibromide and Methyl bromide mixture, liquid
1622	151	Magnesium arsenate			
1623	151	Mercuric arsenate	1647	151	Methyl bromide and Ethylene dibromide mixture, liquid
1624	154	Mercuric chloride			
1625	141	Mercuric nitrate	1648	131	Acetonitrile
1626	157	Mercuric potassium cyanide	1648	131	Methyl cyanide

ID No.	Guide No.	Name of Material
1649	131	Motor fuel anti-knock compound
1649	131	Motor fuel anti-knock mixture
1649	131	Tetraethyl lead, liquid
1650	153	beta-Naphthylamine
1650	153	Naphthylamine (beta)
1651	153	Naphthylthiourea
1652	153	Naphthylurea
1653	151	Nickel cyanide
1654	151	Nicotine
1655	151	Nicotine compound, solid, n.o.s.
1655	151	Nicotine preparation, solid, n.o.s.
1656	151	Nicotine hydrochloride
1656	151	Nicotine hydrochloride, solution
1657	151	Nicotine salicylate
1658	151	Nicotine sulfate, solid
1658	151	Nicotine sulfate, solution
1658	151	Nicotine sulphate, solid
1658	151	Nicotine sulphate, solution
1659	151	Nicotine tartrate
1660	124	Nitric oxide
1660	124	Nitric oxide, compressed
1661	153	Nitroanilines
1662	152	Nitrobenzene
1663	153	Nitrophenols
1664	152	Nitrotoluenes
1664	152	Nitrotoluenes, liquid
1664	152	Nitrotoluenes, solid
1665	152	Nitroxylenes
1665	152	Nitroxylol
1669	151	Pentachloroethane
1670	157	Perchloromethyl mercaptan
1671	153	Phenol, solid
1672	151	Phenylcarbylamine chloride
1673	153	Phenylenediamines
1674	151	Phenylmercuric acetate
1677	151	Potassium arsenate
1678	154	Potassium arsenite
1679	157	Potassium cuprocyanide
1680	157	Potassium cyanide
1683	151	Silver arsenite
1684	151	Silver cyanide
1685	151	Sodium arsenate
1686	154	Sodium arsenite, aqueous solution
1687	153	Sodium azide
1688	152	Sodium cacodylate
1689	157	Sodium cyanide
1690	154	Sodium fluoride
1690	154	Sodium fluoride, solid
1690	154	Sodium fluoride, solution
1691	151	Strontium arsenite
1692	151	Strychnine
1692	151	Strychnine salts
1693	159	Irritating agent, n.o.s.
1693	159	ORM-A, n.o.s.
1693	159	Tear gas devices
1693	159	Tear gas substance, liquid, n.o.s.
1693	159	Tear gas substance, solid, n.o.s.
1694	159	Bromobenzyl cyanides
1694	159	CA
1695	131	Chloroacetone, stabilized
1697	153	Chloroacetophenone
1697	153	Chloroacetophenone, liquid
1697	153	Chloroacetophenone, solid
1697	153	CN
1698	154	Adamsite

ID No.	Guide No.	Name of Material
1698	154	Diphenylamine chloroarsine
1698	154	DM
1699	151	DA
1699	151	Diphenylchloroarsine
1699	151	Diphenylchloroarsine, liquid
1699	151	Diphenylchloroarsine, solid
1700	159	Tear gas candles
1700	159	Tear gas grenades
1701	152	Xylyl bromide
1702	151	1,1,2,2-Tetrachloroethane
1702	151	Tetrachloroethane
1703	123	Tetraethyl dithiopyrophosphate and gases, in solution
1703	123	Tetraethyl dithiopyrophosphate and gases, mixtures
1703	123	Tetraethyl dithiopyrophosphate and gases, mixtures, or in solution (LC50 more than 200 ppm but not more than 5000 ppm)
1703	123	Tetraethyl dithiopyrophosphate and gases, mixtures, or in solution (LC50 not more than 200 ppm)
1704	153	Tetraethyl dithiopyrophosphate
1704	153	Tetraethyl dithiopyrophosphate, mixture, dry or liquid
1705	123	Tetraethyl pyrophosphate and compressed gas mixtures
1705	123	Tetraethyl pyrophosphate and compressed gas mixtures (LC50 more than 200 ppm but not more than 5000 ppm)
1705	123	Tetraethyl pyrophosphate and compressed gas mixtures (LC50 not more than 200 ppm)
1707	151	Thallium compound, n.o.s.
1707	151	Thallium sulfate, solid
1707	151	Thallium sulphate, solid
1708	153	Toluidines
1708	153	Toluidines, liquid
1708	153	Toluidines, solid
1709	151	2,4-Toluenediamine
1709	151	Toluenediamine
1709	151	2,4-Toluylenediamine
1710	160	Trichloroethylene
1711	153	Xylidines
1712	151	Zinc arsenate
1712	151	Zinc arsenate and Zinc arsenite mixture
1712	151	Zinc arsenite
1712	151	Zinc arsenite and Zinc arsenate mixture
1713	151	Zinc cyanide
1714	139	Zinc phosphide
1715	137	Acetic anhydride
1716	156	Acetyl bromide
1717	132	Acetyl chloride
1718	153	Acid butyl phosphate
1718	153	Butyl acid phosphate
1719	154	Alkaline liquid, n.o.s.
1719	154	Caustic alkali liquid, n.o.s.
1722	155	Allyl chlorocarbonate
1722	155	Allyl chloroformate
1723	132	Allyl iodide
1724	155	Allyltrichlorosilane, stabilized
1725	137	Aluminum bromide, anhydrous
1726	137	Aluminum chloride, anhydrous
1727	154	Ammonium bifluoride, solid
1727	154	Ammonium hydrogendifluoride, solid

ID No.	Guide No.	Name of Material
1727	154	Ammonium hydrogen fluoride, solid
1728	155	Amyltrichlorosilane
1729	156	Anisoyl chloride
1730	157	Antimony pentachloride, liquid
1731	157	Antimony pentachloride, solution
1732	157	Antimony pentafluoride
1733	157	Antimony trichloride
1733	157	Antimony trichloride, liquid
1733	157	Antimony trichloride, solid
1733	157	Antimony trichloride, solution
1736	137	Benzoyl chloride
1737	156	Benzyl bromide
1738	156	Benzyl chloride
1739	137	Benzyl chloroformate
1740	154	Bifluorides, n.o.s.
1740	154	Hydrogendifluorides, n.o.s.
1741	125	Boron trichloride
1742	157	Boron trifluoride acetic acid complex
1743	157	Boron trifluoride propionic acid complex
1744	154	Bromine
1744	154	Bromine, solution
1745	144	Bromine pentafluoride
1746	144	Bromine trifluoride
1747	155	Butyltrichlorosilane
1748	140	Calcium hypochlorite, dry
1748	140	Calcium hypochlorite mixture, dry, with more than 39% available Chlorine (8.8% available Oxygen)
1749	124	Chlorine trifluoride
1750	153	Chloroacetic acid, liquid
1750	153	Chloroacetic acid, solution
1751	153	Chloroacetic acid, solid
1752	156	Chloroacetyl chloride
1753	156	Chlorophenyltrichlorosilane
1754	137	Chlorosulfonic acid
1754	137	Chlorosulfonic acid and Sulfur trioxide mixture
1754	137	Chlorosulphonic acid
1754	137	Chlorosulphonic acid and Sulphur trioxide mixture
1754	137	Sulfur trioxide and Chlorosulfonic acid mixture
1754	137	Sulphur trioxide and Chlorosulphonic acid mixture
1755	154	Chromic acid, solution
1756	154	Chromic fluoride, solid
1757	154	Chromic fluoride, solution
1758	137	Chromium oxychloride
1759	154	Corrosive solid, n.o.s.
1759	154	Cosmetics, solid, n.o.s.
1759	154	Drugs, solid, n.o.s.
1759	154	Ferrous chloride, solid
1759	154	Medicines, corrosive, solid, n.o.s.
1759	154	Stannous chloride, solid
1760	154	Acid, liquid, n.o.s.
1760	154	Aluminum phosphate, solution
1760	154	Aluminum sulfate, solution
1760	154	Aluminum sulphate, solution
1760	154	2-(2-Aminoethoxy)ethanol
1760	154	Aminopropyldiethanolamine
1760	154	N-Aminopropylmorpholine
1760	154	Chemical kit
1760	154	Compound, rust preventing (corrosive)

ID No.	Guide No.	Name of Material
1760	154	Compound, rust removing (corrosive)
1760	154	Compound, tree or weed killing, liquid (corrosive)
1760	154	Compound, vulcanizing, liquid (corrosive)
1760	154	Compounds, cleaning, liquid (corrosive)
1760	154	Corrosive liquid, n.o.s.
1760	154	Cosmetics, liquid, n.o.s.
1760	154	2,2-Dichloropropionic acid
1760	154	Drugs, liquid, n.o.s.
1760	154	Ferrous chloride, solution
1760	154	Flame retardant compound, liquid (corrosive)
1760	154	Hexanoic acid
1760	154	Isopentanoic acid
1760	154	Medicines, corrosive, liquid, n.o.s.
1760	154	Morpholine, aqueous mixture
1760	154	Nitric acid, 40% or less
1760	154	ORM-B, n.o.s.
1760	154	Paint (corrosive)
1760	154	Paint related material (corrosive)
1760	154	Textile treating compound or mixture, liquid (corrosive)
1760	154	Titanium sulfate, solution
1760	154	Titanium sulphate, solution
1761	154	Cupriethylenediamine, solution
1762	156	Cyclohexenyltrichlorosilane
1763	156	Cyclohexyltrichlorosilane
1764	153	Dichloroacetic acid
1765	156	Dichloroacetyl chloride
1766	156	Dichlorophenyltrichlorosilane
1767	155	Diethyldichlorosilane
1768	154	Difluorophosphoric acid, anhydrous
1769	156	Diphenyldichlorosilane
1770	153	Diphenylmethyl bromide
1771	156	Dodecyltrichlorosilane
1773	157	Ferric chloride
1773	157	Ferric chloride, anhydrous
1774	154	Fire extinguisher charges, corrosive liquid
1775	154	Fluoboric acid
1775	154	Fluoroboric acid
1776	154	Fluorophosphoric acid, anhydrous
1777	137	Fluorosulfonic acid
1777	137	Fluorosulphonic acid
1778	154	Fluorosilicic acid
1778	154	Fluosilicic acid
1778	154	Hydrofluorosilicic acid
1778	154	Hydrofluosilicic acid
1779	153	Formic acid
1780	156	Fumaryl chloride
1781	156	Hexadecyltrichlorosilane
1782	154	Hexafluorophosphoric acid
1783	153	Hexamethylenediamine, solution
1784	156	Hexyltrichlorosilane
1786	157	Hydrofluoric acid and Sulfuric acid mixture
1786	157	Hydrofluoric acid and Sulphuric acid mixture
1786	157	Sulfuric acid and Hydrofluoric acid mixtures
1786	157	Sulphuric acid and Hydrofluoric acid mixtures
1787	154	Hydriodic acid

ID No.	Guide No.	Name of Material
1787	154	Hydriodic acid, solution
1788	154	Hydrobromic acid
1788	154	Hydrobromic acid, solution
1789	157	Compound, cleaning liquid (containing Hydrochloric (muriatic) acid)
1789	157	Hydrochloric acid
1789	157	Hydrochloric acid, mixture
1789	157	Hydrochloric acid, solution
1789	157	Muriatic acid
1790	157	Compound, cleaning liquid (containing Hydrofluoric acid)
1790	157	Etching acid, liquid, n.o.s.
1790	157	Hydrofluoric acid
1790	157	Hydrofluoric acid, solution
1791	154	Hypochlorite solution
1791	154	Hypochlorite solution, with more than 5% available Chlorine
1792	157	Iodine monochloride
1793	153	Isopropyl acid phosphate
1794	154	Lead sulfate, with more than 3% free acid
1794	154	Lead sulphate, with more than 3% free acid
1796	157	Nitrating acid mixture
1798	157	Aqua regia
1798	157	Nitrohydrochloric acid
1799	156	Nonyltrichlorosilane
1800	156	Octadecyltrichlorosilane
1801	156	Octyltrichlorosilane
1802	140	Perchloric acid, with not more than 50% acid
1803	153	Phenolsulfonic acid, liquid
1803	153	Phenolsulphonic acid, liquid
1804	156	Phenyltrichlorosilane
1805	154	Phosphoric acid
1806	137	Phosphorus pentachloride
1807	137	Phosphoric anhydride
1807	137	Phosphorus pentoxide
1808	137	Phosphorus tribromide
1809	137	Phosphorus trichloride
1810	137	Phosphorus oxychloride
1811	154	Potassium bifluoride
1811	154	Potassium hydrogendifluoride
1811	154	Potassium hydrogen fluoride, solution
1812	154	Potassium fluoride
1813	154	Battery
1813	154	Caustic potash, dry, solid
1813	154	Potassium hydroxide, dry, solid
1813	154	Potassium hydroxide, flake
1813	154	Potassium hydroxide, solid
1814	154	Caustic potash, liquid
1814	154	Caustic potash, solution
1814	154	Potassium hydroxide, solution
1815	132	Propionyl chloride
1816	155	Propyltrichlorosilane
1817	137	Pyrosulfuryl chloride
1817	137	Pyrosulphuryl chloride
1818	157	Silicon tetrachloride
1819	154	Sodium aluminate, solution
1821	154	Sodium bisulfate, solid
1821	154	Sodium bisulphate, solid
1821	154	Sodium hydrogen sulfate, solid
1821	154	Sodium hydrogen sulphate, solid
1823	154	Caustic soda, bead
1823	154	Caustic soda, flake
1823	154	Caustic soda, granular

ID No.	Guide No.	Name of Material
1823	154	Caustic soda, solid
1823	154	Sodium hydroxide, dry
1823	154	Sodium hydroxide, bead
1823	154	Sodium hydroxide, flake
1823	154	Sodium hydroxide, granular
1823	154	Sodium hydroxide, solid
1824	154	Caustic soda, solution
1824	154	Sodium hydroxide, solution
1825	157	Sodium monoxide
1826	157	Nitrating acid, spent
1826	157	Nitrating acid mixture, spent
1827	137	Stannic chloride, anhydrous
1827	137	Tin tetrachloride
1828	137	Sulfur chlorides
1828	137	Sulphur chlorides
1829	137	Sulfur trioxide
1829	137	Sulfur trioxide, inhibited
1829	137	Sulfur trioxide, stabilized
1829	137	Sulfur trioxide, uninhibited
1829	137	Sulphur trioxide
1829	137	Sulphur trioxide, inhibited
1829	137	Sulphur trioxide, stabilized
1829	137	Sulphur trioxide, uninhibited
1830	137	Sulfuric acid
1830	137	Sulfuric acid, with more than 51% acid
1830	137	Sulphuric acid
1830	137	Sulphuric acid, with more than 51% acid
1831	137	Oleum
1831	137	Oleum, with less than 30% free Sulfur trioxide
1831	137	Oleum, with less than 30% free Sulphur trioxide
1831	137	Oleum, with not less than 30% free Sulfur trioxide
1831	137	Oleum, with not less than 30% free Sulphur trioxide
1831	137	Sulfuric acid, fuming
1831	137	Sulfuric acid, fuming, with less than 30% free Sulfur trioxide
1831	137	Sulfuric acid, fuming, with not less than 30% free Sulfur trioxide
1831	137	Sulphuric acid, fuming
1831	137	Sulphuric acid, fuming, with less than 30% free Sulphur trioxide
1831	137	Sulphuric acid, fuming, with not less than 30% free Sulphur trioxide
1832	137	Sulfuric acid, spent
1832	137	Sulphuric acid, spent
1833	154	Sulfurous acid
1833	154	Sulphurous acid
1834	137	Sulfuryl chloride
1834	137	Sulphuryl chloride
1835	153	Tetramethylammonium hydroxide
1836	137	Thionyl chloride
1837	157	Thiophosphoryl chloride
1838	137	Titanium tetrachloride
1839	153	Trichloroacetic acid
1840	154	Zinc chloride, solution
1841	171	Acetaldehyde ammonia
1843	141	Ammonium dinitro-o-cresolate
1845	120	Carbon dioxide, solid
1845	120	Dry ice
1846	151	Carbon tetrachloride

ID No.	Guide No.	Name of Material
1847	153	Potassium sulfide, hydrated, with not less than 30% water of crystallization
1847	153	Potassium sulfide, hydrated, with not less than 30% water of hydration
1847	153	Potassium sulphide, hydrated, with not less than 30% water of crystallization
1847	153	Potassium sulphide, hydrated, with not less than 30% water of hydration
1848	132	Propionic acid
1849	153	Sodium sulfide, hydrated, with not less than 30% water
1849	153	Sodium sulphide, hydrated, with not less than 30% water
1851	151	Medicine, liquid, poisonous, n.o.s.
1851	151	Medicine, liquid, toxic, n.o.s.
1854	135	Barium alloys, pyrophoric
1855	135	Calcium, metal and alloys, pyrophoric
1855	135	Calcium, pyrophoric
1855	135	Calcium alloys, pyrophoric
1856	133	Rags, oily
1858	126	Hexafluoropropylene
1858	126	Refrigerant gas R-1216
1859	125	Silicon tetrafluoride
1859	125	Silicon tetrafluoride, compressed
1860	116P	Vinyl fluoride, inhibited
1862	129	Ethyl crotonate
1863	128	Fuel, aviation, turbine engine
1864	128	Gas drips, hydrocarbon
1865	131	n-Propyl nitrate
1866	127	Resin solution
1867	133	Cigarettes, self-lighting
1868	134	Decaborane
1869	138	Magnesium
1869	138	Magnesium, in pellets, turnings or ribbons
1869	138	Magnesium alloys, with more than 50% Magnesium, in pellets, turnings or ribbons
1869	138	Magnesium scrap
1870	138	Potassium borohydride
1871	170	Titanium hydride
1872	141	Lead dioxide
1872	141	Lead peroxide
1873	143	Perchloric acid, with more than 50% but not more than 72% acid
1884	157	Barium oxide
1885	153	Benzidine
1886	156	Benzylidene chloride
1887	160	Bromochloromethane
1888	151	Chloroform
1889	157	Cyanogen bromide
1891	131	Ethyl bromide
1892	151	ED
1892	151	Ethyldichloroarsine
1894	151	Phenylmercuric hydroxide
1895	151	Phenylmercuric nitrate
1897	160	Perchloroethylene
1897	160	Tetrachloroethylene
1898	156	Acetyl iodide
1902	153	Di-(2-ethylhexyl)phosphoric acid
1902	153	Diisooctyl acid phosphate
1903	153	Disinfectant, liquid, corrosive, n.o.s.

ID No.	Guide No.	Name of Material
1903	153	Disinfectants, corrosive, liquid, n.o.s.
1905	154	Selenic acid
1906	153	Acid, sludge
1906	153	Sludge acid
1907	154	Soda lime, with more than 4% Sodium hydroxide
1908	154	Chlorite solution
1908	154	Chlorite solution, with more than 5% available Chlorine
1908	154	Sodium chlorite, solution, with more than 5% available Chlorine
1910	157	Calcium oxide
1911	119	Diborane
1911	119	Diborane, compressed
1911	119	Diborane mixtures
1912	115	Methyl chloride and Methylene chloride mixture
1912	115	Methylene chloride and Methyl chloride mixture
1913	120	Neon, refrigerated liquid (cryogenic liquid)
1914	130	Butyl propionates
1915	127	Cyclohexanone
1916	152	2,2'-Dichlorodiethyl ether
1916	152	Dichloroethyl ether
1917	129P	Ethyl acrylate, inhibited
1918	130	Cumene
1918	130	Isopropylbenzene
1919	129P	Methyl acrylate, inhibited
1920	128	Nonanes
1921	131P	Propyleneimine, inhibited
1922	132	Pyrrolidine
1923	135	Calcium dithionite
1923	135	Calcium hydrosulfite
1923	135	Calcium hydrosulphite
1928	135	Methyl magnesium bromide in Ethyl ether
1929	135	Potassium dithionite
1929	135	Potassium hydrosulfite
1929	135	Potassium hydrosulphite
1931	171	Zinc dithionite
1931	171	Zinc hydrosulfite
1931	171	Zinc hydrosulphite
1932	135	Zirconium scrap
1935	157	Cyanide solution, n.o.s.
1938	156	Bromoacetic acid
1938	156	Bromoacetic acid, solid
1938	156	Bromoacetic acid, solution
1939	137	Phosphorus oxybromide
1939	137	Phosphorus oxybromide, solid
1940	153	Thioglycolic acid
1941	171	Dibromodifluoromethane
1942	140	Ammonium nitrate, with not more than 0.2% combustible substances
1942	140	Ammonium nitrate, with organic coating
1944	133	Matches, safety
1945	133	Matches, wax "vesta"
1950	126	Aerosol dispensers
1950	126	Aerosols
1951	120	Argon, refrigerated liquid (cryogenic liquid)
1952	126	Carbon dioxide and Ethylene oxide mixtures, with not more than 6% Ethylene oxide
1952	126	Carbon dioxide and Ethylene oxide mixtures, with not more than 9% Ethylene oxide

ID No.	Guide No.	Name of Material
1952	126	Ethylene oxide and Carbon dioxide mixtures, with not more than 6% Ethylene oxide
1952	126	Ethylene oxide and Carbon dioxide mixtures, with not more than 9% Ethylene oxide
1953	119	Compressed gas, flammable, poisonous, n.o.s. (Inhalation Hazard Zone A)
1953	119	Compressed gas, flammable, poisonous, n.o.s. (Inhalation Hazard Zone B)
1953	119	Compressed gas, flammable, poisonous, n.o.s. (Inhalation Hazard Zone C)
1953	119	Compressed gas, flammable, poisonous, n.o.s. (Inhalation Hazard Zone D)
1953	119	Compressed gas, flammable, toxic, n.o.s. (Inhalation Hazard Zone A)
1953	119	Compressed gas, flammable, toxic, n.o.s. (Inhalation Hazard Zone B)
1953	119	Compressed gas, flammable, toxic, n.o.s. (Inhalation Hazard Zone C)
1953	119	Compressed gas, flammable, toxic, n.o.s. (Inhalation Hazard Zone D)
1953	119	Compressed gas, poisonous, flammable, n.o.s.
1953	119	Compressed gas, poisonous, flammable, n.o.s. (Inhalation Hazard Zone A)
1953	119	Compressed gas, poisonous, flammable, n.o.s. (Inhalation Hazard Zone B)
1953	119	Compressed gas, poisonous, flammable, n.o.s. (Inhalation Hazard Zone C)
1953	119	Compressed gas, poisonous, flammable, n.o.s. (Inhalation Hazard Zone D)
1953	119	Compressed gas, toxic, flammable, n.o.s.
1953	119	Compressed gas, toxic, flammable, n.o.s. (Inhalation Hazard Zone A)
1953	119	Compressed gas, toxic, flammable, n.o.s. (Inhalation Hazard Zone B)
1953	119	Compressed gas, toxic, flammable, n.o.s. (Inhalation Hazard Zone C)
1953	119	Compressed gas, toxic, flammable, n.o.s. (Inhalation Hazard Zone D)
1953	119	Liquefied gas, flammable, poisonous, n.o.s.
1953	119	Liquefied gas, flammable, poisonous, n.o.s. (Inhalation Hazard Zone A)
1953	119	Liquefied gas, flammable, poisonous, n.o.s. (Inhalation Hazard Zone B)
1953	119	Liquefied gas, flammable, poisonous, n.o.s. (Inhalation Hazard Zone C)
1953	119	Liquefied gas, flammable, poisonous, n.o.s. (Inhalation Hazard Zone D)
1953	119	Liquefied gas, flammable, toxic, n.o.s.
1953	119	Liquefied gas, flammable, toxic, n.o.s. (Inhalation Hazard Zone A)

ID No.	Guide No.	Name of Material
1953	119	Liquefied gas, flammable, toxic, n.o.s. (Inhalation Hazard Zone B)
1953	119	Liquefied gas, flammable, toxic, n.o.s. (Inhalation Hazard Zone C)
1953	119	Liquefied gas, flammable, toxic, n.o.s. (Inhalation Hazard Zone D)
1953	119	Poisonous gas, flammable, n.o.s.
1953	119	Poisonous liquid, flammable, n.o.s.
1954	115	Compressed gas, flammable, n.o.s.
1954	115	Dispersant gas, n.o.s. (flammable)
1954	115	Insecticide gas, flammable, n.o.s.
1954	115	Liquefied gas, flammable, n.o.s.
1954	115	Refrigerant gas, n.o.s. (flammable)
1954	115	Refrigerating machines, containing flammable, liquefied gas
1954	115	Refrigerating machines, containing flammable, non-poisonous, non-corrosive, liquefied gas
1955	123	Chloropicrin and non-flammable, non-liquefied compressed gas mixture
1955	123	Compressed gas, poisonous, n.o.s.
1955	123	Compressed gas, poisonous, n.o.s. (Inhalation Hazard Zone A)
1955	123	Compressed gas, poisonous, n.o.s. (Inhalation Hazard Zone B)
1955	123	Compressed gas, poisonous, n.o.s. (Inhalation Hazard Zone C)
1955	123	Compressed gas, poisonous, n.o.s. (Inhalation Hazard Zone D)
1955	123	Compressed gas, toxic, n.o.s.
1955	123	Compressed gas, toxic, n.o.s. (Inhalation Hazard Zone A)
1955	123	Compressed gas, toxic, n.o.s. (Inhalation Hazard Zone B)
1955	123	Compressed gas, toxic, n.o.s. (Inhalation Hazard Zone C)
1955	123	Compressed gas, toxic, n.o.s. (Inhalation Hazard Zone D)
1955	123	Liquefied gas, poisonous, n.o.s.
1955	123	Liquefied gas, poisonous, n.o.s. (Inhalation Hazard Zone A)
1955	123	Liquefied gas, poisonous, n.o.s. (Inhalation Hazard Zone B)
1955	123	Liquefied gas, poisonous, n.o.s. (Inhalation Hazard Zone C)
1955	123	Liquefied gas, poisonous, n.o.s. (Inhalation Hazard Zone D)
1955	123	Liquefied gas, toxic, n.o.s.
1955	123	Liquefied gas, toxic, n.o.s. (Inhalation Hazard Zone A)
1955	123	Liquefied gas, toxic, n.o.s. (Inhalation Hazard Zone B)
1955	123	Liquefied gas, toxic, n.o.s. (Inhalation Hazard Zone C)
1955	123	Liquefied gas, toxic, n.o.s. (Inhalation Hazard Zone D)
1955	123	Methyl bromide and nonflammable, nonliquefied compressed gas mixture
1955	123	Organic phosphate compound mixed with compressed gas
1955	123	Organic phosphate mixed with compressed gas

ID No.	Guide No.	Name of Material
1955	123	Organic phosphorus compound mixed with compressed gas
1955	123	Poisonous gas, n.o.s.
1955	123	Poisonous liquid, n.o.s.
1956	126	Accumulators, pressurized, pneumatic or hydraulic
1956	126	Compressed gas, n.o.s.
1956	126	Hexafluoropropylene oxide
1956	126	Liquefied gas, n.o.s.
1956	126	Water pump system
1957	115	Deuterium
1957	115	Deuterium, compressed
1958	126	1,2-Dichloro-1,1,2,2-tetrafluoroethane
1958	126	Dichlorotetrafluoroethane
1958	126	Refrigerant gas R-114
1959	116P	1,1-Difluoroethylene
1959	116P	Refrigerant gas R-1132a
1960	115	Engine starting fluid
1961	115	Ethane, refrigerated liquid
1961	115	Ethane-Propane mixture, refrigerated liquid
1961	115	Propane-Ethane mixture, refrigerated liquid
1962	116P	Ethylene
1962	116P	Ethylene, compressed
1963	120	Helium, refrigerated liquid (cryogenic liquid)
1964	115	Hydrocarbon gas, compressed, n.o.s.
1964	115	Hydrocarbon gas mixture, compressed, n.o.s.
1965	115	Hydrocarbon gas, liquefied, n.o.s.
1965	115	Hydrocarbon gas mixture, liquefied, n.o.s.
1966	115	Hydrogen, refrigerated liquid (cryogenic liquid)
1967	123	Insecticide, liquefied gas, containing Poison A or Poison B material
1967	123	Insecticide gas, poisonous, n.o.s.
1967	123	Insecticide gas, toxic, n.o.s.
1967	123	Parathion and compressed gas mixture
1968	126	Insecticide, liquefied gas
1968	126	Insecticide gas, n.o.s.
1969	115	Isobutane
1969	115	Isobutane mixture
1970	120	Krypton, refrigerated liquid (cryogenic liquid)
1971	115	Methane
1971	115	Methane, compressed
1971	115	Natural gas, compressed
1972	115	Liquefied natural gas (cryogenic liquid)
1972	115	LNG (cryogenic liquid)
1972	115	Methane, refrigerated liquid (cryogenic liquid)
1972	115	Natural gas, refrigerated liquid (cryogenic liquid)
1973	126	Chlorodifluoromethane and Chloropentafluoroethane mixture
1973	126	Chloropentafluoroethane and Chlorodifluoromethane mixture
1973	126	Refrigerant gas R-502
1974	126	Bromochlorodifluoromethane
1974	126	Chlorodifluorobromomethane
1974	126	Refrigerant gas R-12B1

ID No.	Guide No.	Name of Material
1975	124	Dinitrogen tetroxide and Nitric oxide mixture
1975	124	Nitric oxide and Dinitrogen tetroxide mixture
1975	124	Nitric oxide and Nitrogen dioxide mixture
1975	124	Nitric oxide and Nitrogen tetroxide mixture
1975	124	Nitrogen dioxide and Nitric oxide mixture
1975	124	Nitrogen tetroxide and Nitric oxide mixture
1976	126	Octafluorocyclobutane
1976	126	Refrigerant gas RC-318
1977	120	Nitrogen, refrigerated liquid (cryogenic liquid)
1978	115	Propane
1978	115	Propane mixture
1979	121	Rare gases mixture
1979	121	Rare gases mixture, compressed
1980	122	Helium-Oxygen mixture
1980	122	Oxygen and Rare gases mixture
1980	122	Oxygen and Rare gases mixture, compressed
1980	122	Rare gases and Oxygen mixture
1980	122	Rare gases and Oxygen mixture, compressed
1981	121	Nitrogen and Rare gases mixture
1981	121	Nitrogen and Rare gases mixture, compressed
1981	121	Rare gases and Nitrogen mixture
1981	121	Rare gases and Nitrogen mixture, compressed
1982	126	Refrigerant gas R-14, compressed
1982	126	Tetrafluoromethane
1982	126	Tetrafluoromethane, compressed
1983	126	1-Chloro-2,2,2-trifluoroethane
1983	126	Chlorotrifluoroethane
1983	126	Refrigerant gas R-133a
1984	126	Refrigerant gas R-23
1984	126	Trifluoromethane
1986	131	Alcohols, flammable, poisonous, n.o.s.
1986	131	Alcohols, flammable, toxic, n.o.s.
1986	131	Alcohols, poisonous, n.o.s.
1986	131	Alcohols, toxic, n.o.s.
1986	131	Denatured alcohol (toxic)
1986	131	Propargyl alcohol
1987	127	Alcohols, n.o.s.
1987	127	Denatured alcohol
1988	131	Aldehydes, flammable, poisonous, n.o.s.
1988	131	Aldehydes, flammable, toxic, n.o.s.
1988	131	Aldehydes, poisonous, n.o.s.
1988	131	Aldehydes, toxic, n.o.s.
1989	129	Aldehydes, n.o.s.
1989	129	Benzaldehyde
1990	129	Benzaldehyde
1991	131P	Chloroprene, inhibited
1992	131	Flammable liquid, poisonous, n.o.s.
1992	131	Flammable liquid, toxic, n.o.s.
1993	128	Combustible liquid, n.o.s.
1993	128	Compound, tree or weed killing, liquid (flammable)
1993	128	Compounds, cleaning, liquid (flammable)
1993	128	Cosmetics, n.o.s.

ID No.	Guide No.	Name of Material
1993	128	Diesel fuel
1993	128	Disinfectant, liquid, n.o.s.
1993	128	Drugs, n.o.s.
1993	128	Ethyl nitrate
1993	128	Flammable liquid, n.o.s.
1993	128	Fuel oil
1993	128	Heater for refrigerator car, liquid fuel type
1993	128	Medicines, flammable, liquid, n.o.s.
1993	128	Refrigerating machine
1994	131	Iron pentacarbonyl
1999	130	Asphalt
1999	130	Asphalt, cutback
1999	130	Tars, liquid
2000	133	Celluloid, in blocks, rods, rolls, sheets, tubes, etc., except scrap
2001	133	Cobalt naphthenates, powder
2002	135	Celluloid, scrap
2003	135	Metal alkyls, n.o.s.
2003	135	Metal alkyls, water-reactive, n.o.s.
2003	135	Metal aryls, n.o.s
2003	135	Metal aryls, water-reactive, n.o.s.
2004	135	Magnesium diamide
2005	135	Magnesium diphenyl
2006	135	Plastic, nitrocellulose-based, spontaneously combustible, n.o.s.
2006	135	Plastics, nitrocellulose-based, self-heating, n.o.s.
2008	135	Zirconium powder, dry
2009	135	Zirconium, dry, finished sheets, strips or coiled wire
2010	138	Magnesium hydride
2011	139	Magnesium phosphide
2012	139	Potassium phosphide
2013	139	Strontium phosphide
2014	140	Hydrogen peroxide, aqueous solution, with not less than 20% but not more than 60% Hydrogen peroxide (stabilized as necessary)
2015	143	Hydrogen peroxide, aqueous solution, stabilized, with more than 60% Hydrogen peroxide
2015	143	Hydrogen peroxide, stabilized
2016	151	Ammunition, poisonous, non-explosive
2016	151	Ammunition, toxic, non-explosive
2017	159	Ammunition, tear-producing, non-explosive
2017	159	Grenade, tear gas
2018	152	Chloroanilines, solid
2019	152	Chloroanilines, liquid
2020	153	Chlorophenols, solid
2020	153	Trichlorophenol
2021	153	Chlorophenols, liquid
2022	153	Cresylic acid
2022	153	Mining reagent, liquid
2023	131P	1-Chloro-2,3-epoxypropane
2023	131P	Epichlorohydrin
2024	151	Mercury compound, liquid, n.o.s.
2025	151	Mercury compound, solid, n.o.s.
2026	151	Phenylmercuric compound, n.o.s.
2027	151	Sodium arsenite, solid
2028	153	Bombs, smoke, non-explosive, with corrosive liquid, without initiating device

ID No.	Guide No.	Name of Material	ID No.	Guide No.	Name of Material
2029	132	Hydrazine, anhydrous	2049	130	Diethylbenzene
2029	132	Hydrazine, aqueous solutions, with more than 64% Hydrazine	2050	127	Diisobutylene, isomeric compounds
2030	153	Hydrazine, aqueous solution, with not less than 37% but not more than 64% Hydrazine	2051	132	2-Dimethylaminoethanol
			2051	132	Dimethylethanolamine
			2052	128	Dipentene
2030	153	Hydrazine, aqueous solutions, with not more than 64% Hydrazine	2053	129	Methylamyl alcohol
			2053	129	Methyl isobutyl carbinol
2030	153	Hydrazine hydrate	2053	129	M.I.B.C.
2031	157	Nitric acid, other than red fuming	2054	132	Morpholine
2032	157	Nitric acid, fuming	2054	132	Morpholine, aqueous mixture
2032	157	Nitric acid, red fuming	2055	128P	Styrene monomer, inhibited
2033	154	Potassium monoxide	2056	127	Tetrahydrofuran
2034	115	Hydrogen and Methane mixture, compressed	2057	128	Tripropylene
			2058	129	Valeraldehyde
2034	115	Methane and Hydrogen mixture, compressed	2059	127	Collodion
			2059	127	Nitrocellulose, block, wet, with not less than 25% alcohol
2035	115	Refrigerant gas R-143a			
2035	115	1,1,1-Trifluoroethane	2059	127	Nitrocellulose, colloided, granular or flake, wet, with not less than 20% alcohol or solvent
2035	115	Trifluoroethane, compressed			
2036	121	Xenon			
2036	121	Xenon, compressed	2059	127	Nitrocellulose, solution, flammable
2037	115	Gas cartridges			
2037	115	Receptacles, small, containing gas	2059	127	Nitrocellulose, solution, in a flammable liquid
2038	152	Dinitrotoluenes	2067	140	Ammonium nitrate fertilizers
2038	152	Dinitrotoluenes, liquid	2068	140	Ammonium nitrate fertilizers, with Calcium carbonate
2038	152	Dinitrotoluenes, solid			
2044	115	2,2-Dimethylpropane	2069	140	Ammonium nitrate fertilizers, with Ammonium sulfate
2045	129	Isobutyl aldehyde			
2045	129	Isobutyraldehyde	2069	140	Ammonium nitrate fertilizers, with Ammonium sulphate
2046	130	Cymenes			
2047	132	Dichloropropenes	2069	140	Ammonium nitrate mixed fertilizers
2048	129	Dicyclopentadiene			

ID No.	Guide No.	Name of Material
2070	143	Ammonium nitrate fertilizers, with Phosphate or Potash
2071	140	Ammonium nitrate fertilizer, with not more than 0.4% combustible material
2071	140	Ammonium nitrate fertilizers
2072	140	Ammonium nitrate fertilizer, n.o.s.
2072	140	Ammonium nitrate fertilizers
2073	125	Ammonia, solution, with more than 35% but not more than 50% Ammonia
2074	153P	Acrylamide
2075	153	Chloral, anhydrous, inhibited
2076	153	Cresols
2077	153	alpha-Naphthylamine
2077	153	Naphthylamine (alpha)
2078	156	Toluene diisocyanate
2079	154	Diethylenetriamine
2080	145	Acetyl acetone peroxide
2081	147	Acetyl benzoyl peroxide
2082	148	Acetyl cyclohexanesulfonyl peroxide
2082	148	Acetyl cyclohexanesulphonyl peroxide
2083	148	Acetyl cyclohexanesulfonyl peroxide
2083	148	Acetyl cyclohexanesulphonyl peroxide
2084	148	Acetyl peroxide
2085	146	Benzoyl peroxide
2087	146	Benzoyl peroxide
2088	146	Benzoyl peroxide
2089	145	Benzoyl peroxide
2090	146	Benzoyl peroxide
2091	145	tert-Butyl cumene peroxide
2091	145	tert-Butyl cumyl peroxide
2091	145	tert-Butyl isopropyl benzene hydroperoxide
2092	147	tert-Butyl hydroperoxide, not more than 80% in Di-tert-butyl peroxide and/or solvent
2093	147	tert-Butyl hydroperoxide
2094	147	tert-Butyl hydroperoxide
2095	146	tert-Butyl peroxyacetate
2096	146	tert-Butyl peroxyacetate
2097	146	tert-Butyl peroxybenzoate
2098	145	tert-Butyl peroxybenzoate
2099	146	tert-Butyl monoperoxymaleate
2102	145	Di-tert-butyl peroxide
2103	146	tert-Butyl peroxyisopropyl carbonate
2104	145	tert-Butyl peroxyisononanoate
2104	145	tert-Butyl peroxy-3,5,5-trimethylhexanoate
2106	146	Di-(tert-butylperoxy)phthalate
2107	145	Di-(tert-butylperoxy)phthalate
2108	145	Di-(tert-butylperoxy)phthalate
2110	148	tert-Butyl peroxypivalate
2111	146	2,2-Di-(tert-butylperoxy)butane
2112	145	1,3-Di-(2-tert-butylperoxy-isopropyl)benzene and 1,4-Di-(2-tert-butylperoxy-isopropyl)benzene mixtures
2112	145	1,4-Di-(2-tert-butylperoxy-isopropyl)benzene and 1,3-Di-(2-tert-butylperoxy-isopropyl)benzene mixtures
2113	146	p-Chlorobenzoyl peroxide
2114	145	p-Chlorobenzoyl peroxide
2115	145	p-Chlorobenzoyl peroxide
2116	147	Cumene hydroperoxide

ID No.	Guide No.	Name of Material
2118	147	Cyclohexanone peroxide, not more than 72% in solution
2119	147	Cyclohexanone peroxide, not more than 90%, with not less than 10% water
2120	148	Decanoyl peroxide
2121	145	Dicumyl peroxide
2122	148	Di-(2-ethylhexyl)-peroxydicarbonate
2123	148	Di-(2-ethylhexyl)-peroxydicarbonate
2124	145	Lauroyl peroxide
2125	147	p-Menthane hydroperoxide
2126	147	Methyl isobutyl ketone peroxide
2128	148	Isononanoyl peroxide
2129	148	Caprylyl peroxide
2129	148	Caprylyl peroxide, solution
2129	148	Octanoyl peroxide
2130	148	Pelargonyl peroxide
2131	147	Peracetic acid, solution
2131	147	Peroxyacetic acid, solution
2132	148	Propionyl peroxide
2133	148	Isopropyl percarbonate, unstabilized
2133	148	Isopropyl peroxydicarbonate
2134	148	Isopropyl peroxydicarbonate
2135	146	Succinic acid peroxide
2136	145	Tetralin hydroperoxide
2137	146	2,4-Dichlorobenzoyl peroxide
2138	145	2,4-Dichlorobenzoyl peroxide
2139	145	2,4-Dichlorobenzoyl peroxide
2140	146	n-Butyl-4,4-di-(tert-butylperoxy)valerate
2141	145	n-Butyl-4,4-di-(tert-butylperoxy)valerate
2142	148	tert-Butyl peroxyisobutyrate
2143	148	tert-Butyl peroxy-2-ethylhexanoate
2144	148	tert-Butyl peroxydiethylacetate
2145	146	1,1-Di-(tert-butylperoxy)-3,3,5-trimethyl cyclohexane
2146	145	1,1-Di-(tert-butylperoxy)-3,3,5-trimethyl cyclohexane
2147	145	1,1-Di-(tert-butylperoxy)-3,3,5-trimethyl cyclohexane
2148	145	Di-(1-hydroxycyclohexyl)-peroxide
2149	148	Dibenzyl peroxydicarbonate
2150	148	Di-(sec-butyl)peroxydicarbonate
2151	148	Di-(sec-butyl)peroxydicarbonate
2152	148	Dicyclohexyl peroxydicarbonate
2153	148	Dicyclohexyl peroxydicarbonate
2154	148	Di-(4-tert-butylcyclohexyl)-peroxydicarbonate
2155	145	2,5-Dimethyl-2,5-di-(tert-butylperoxy)hexane
2156	145	2,5-Dimethyl-2,5-di-(tert-butylperoxy)hexane
2157	148	2,5-Dimethyl-2,5-di-(2-ethyl-hexanoylperoxy)hexane
2158	145	2,5-Dimethyl-2,5-di-(tert-butylperoxy)hexyne-3
2159	145	2,5-Dimethyl-2,5-di-(tert-butylperoxy)hexyne-3, with not more than 52% Peroxide in inert solid
2160	145	1,1,3,3-Tetramethylbutyl hydroperoxide
2161	148	1,1,3,3-Tetramethylbutyl peroxy-2-ethylhexanoate
2162	147	Pinane hydroperoxide
2163	148	Diacetone alcohol peroxides

ID No.	Guide No.	Name of Material
2164	148	Dicetyl peroxydicarbonate
2165	146	3,3,6,6,9,9-Hexamethyl-1,2,4,5-tetraoxacyclononane
2166	145	3,3,6,6,9,9-Hexamethyl-1,2,4,5-tetraoxacyclononane
2167	145	3,3,6,6,9,9-Hexamethyl-1,2,4,5-tetraoxacyclononane
2168	145	2,2-Di-(4,4-tert-butyl-peroxycyclohexyl)propane
2169	148	Butyl peroxydicarbonate
2170	148	Butyl peroxydicarbonate
2171	145	Diisopropylbenzene hydroperoxide
2172	146	2,5-Dimethyl-2,5-di-(benzoylperoxy)hexane
2173	145	2,5-Dimethyl-2,5-di-(benzoylperoxy)hexane
2174	146	2,5-Dimethyl-2,5-dihydroperoxy hexane, not more than 82% with water
2174	146	Dimethylhexane dihydroperoxide, with 18% or more water
2175	148	Diethyl peroxydicarbonate
2176	148	Di-n-propyl peroxydicarbonate
2177	148	tert-Butyl peroxyneodecanoate
2178	146	2,2-Dihydroperoxypropane
2179	146	1,1-Di-(tert-butylperoxy)-cyclohexane
2180	146	1,1-Di-(tert-butylperoxy)-cyclohexane
2182	148	Diisobutyryl peroxide
2183	145	tert-Butyl peroxycrotonate
2184	146	Ethyl-3,3-di-(tert-butyl-peroxy)butyrate
2185	145	Ethyl-3,3-di-(tert-butyl-peroxy)butyrate, not more than 77% in solution
2186	125	Hydrogen chloride, refrigerated liquid
2187	120	Carbon dioxide, refrigerated liquid
2188	119	Arsine
2188	119	SA
2189	119	Dichlorosilane
2190	124	Oxygen difluoride
2190	124	Oxygen difluoride, compressed
2191	123	Sulfuryl fluoride
2191	123	Sulphuryl fluoride
2192	119	Germane
2193	126	Hexafluoroethane
2193	126	Hexafluoroethane, compressed
2193	126	Refrigerant gas R-116, compressed
2194	125	Selenium hexafluoride
2195	125	Tellurium hexafluoride
2196	125	Tungsten hexafluoride
2197	125	Hydrogen iodide, anhydrous
2198	125	Phosphorus pentafluoride
2198	125	Phosphorus pentafluoride, compressed
2199	119	Phosphine
2200	116P	Propadiene, inhibited
2201	122	Nitrous oxide, refrigerated liquid
2202	117	Hydrogen selenide, anhydrous
2203	116	Silane
2203	116	Silane, compressed
2204	119	Carbonyl sulfide
2204	119	Carbonyl sulphide
2205	153	Adiponitrile
2206	155	Isocyanate solution, poisonous, n.o.s.

ID No.	Guide No.	Name of Material
2206	155	Isocyanate solution, toxic, n.o.s.
2206	155	Isocyanate solutions, n.o.s.
2206	155	Isocyanates, n.o.s.
2206	155	Isocyanates, poisonous, n.o.s.
2206	155	Isocyanates, toxic, n.o.s.
2207	155	Isocyanate solutions, n.o.s. (toxic)
2207	155	Isocyanates, n.o.s. (toxic)
2208	140	Bleaching powder
2208	140	Calcium hypochlorite mixture, dry, with more than 10% but not more than 39% available Chlorine
2209	132	Formaldehyde, solutions (Formalin) (corrosive)
2210	135	Maneb
2210	135	Maneb preparation, with not less than 60% Maneb
2210	135	Pesticide, water-reactive
2211	133	Polymeric beads, expandable
2211	133	Polystyrene beads, expandable
2212	171	Asbestos
2212	171	Asbestos, blue
2212	171	Asbestos, brown
2212	171	Blue asbestos
2212	171	Brown asbestos
2213	133	Paraformaldehyde
2214	156	Phthalic anhydride
2215	156	Maleic acid
2215	156	Maleic anhydride
2216	171	Fish meal, stabilized
2216	171	Fish meal containing 6% to 12% water
2216	171	Fish scrap, stabilized
2216	171	Fish scrap containing 6% to 12% water
2217	135	Seed cake, with not more than 1.5% oil and not more than 11% moisture
2218	132P	Acrylic acid, inhibited
2219	129	Allyl glycidyl ether
2222	127	Anisole
2224	152	Benzonitrile
2225	156	Benzenesulfonyl chloride
2225	156	Benzenesulphonyl chloride
2226	156	Benzotrichloride
2227	129P	n-Butyl methacrylate
2227	129P	n-Butyl methacrylate, inhibited
2228	153	Butylphenols, liquid
2229	153	Butylphenols, solid
2232	153	Chloroacetaldehyde
2232	153	2-Chloroethanal
2233	152	Chloroanisidines
2234	130	Chlorobenzotrifluorides
2235	153	Chlorobenzyl chlorides
2236	156	3-Chloro-4-methylphenyl isocyanate
2237	153	Chloronitroanilines
2238	130	Chlorotoluenes
2239	153	Chlorotoluidines
2239	153	Chlorotoluidines, liquid
2239	153	Chlorotoluidines, solid
2240	154	Chromosulfuric acid
2240	154	Chromosulphuric acid
2241	128	Cycloheptane
2242	128	Cycloheptene
2243	130	Cyclohexyl acetate
2244	129	Cyclopentanol

ID No.	Guide No.	Name of Material
2245	127	Cyclopentanone
2246	128	Cyclopentene
2247	128	n-Decane
2248	132	Di-n-butylamine
2249	153	Dichlorodimethyl ether, symmetrical
2250	156	Dichlorophenyl isocyanates
2251	127P	Bicyclo[2.2.1]hepta-2,5-diene
2251	127P	Bicyclo[2.2.1]hepta-2,5-diene, inhibited
2251	127P	Dicycloheptadiene
2251	127P	2,5-Norbornadiene
2251	127P	2,5-Norbornadiene, inhibited
2252	127	1,2-Dimethoxyethane
2253	153	N,N-Dimethylaniline
2254	133	Matches, fusee
2255	146	Organic peroxides, samples, n.o.s
2255	146	Polyester resin kit
2256	130	Cyclohexene
2257	138	Potassium
2257	138	Potassium, metal
2258	132	1,2-Propylenediamine
2258	132	1,3-Propylenediamine
2259	153	Triethylenetetramine
2260	132	Tripropylamine
2261	153	Xylenols
2262	156	Dimethylcarbamoyl chloride
2263	128	Dimethylcyclohexanes
2264	132	Dimethylcyclohexylamine
2265	129	N,N-Dimethylformamide
2266	132	Dimethyl-N-propylamine
2267	156	Dimethyl chlorothiophosphate
2267	156	Dimethyl phosphorochloridothioate
2267	156	Dimethyl thiophosphoryl chloride
2269	153	3,3'-Iminodipropylamine
2270	132	Ethylamine, aqueous solution, with not less than 50% but not more than 70% Ethylamine
2271	127	Ethyl amyl ketone
2272	153	N-Ethylaniline
2273	153	2-Ethylaniline
2274	153	N-Ethyl-N-benzylaniline
2275	129	2-Ethylbutanol
2276	132	2-Ethylhexylamine
2277	129P	Ethyl methacrylate
2277	129P	Ethyl methacrylate, inhibited
2278	128	n-Heptene
2279	151	Hexachlorobutadiene
2280	153	Hexamethylenediamine, solid
2281	156	Hexamethylene diisocyanate
2282	129	Hexanols
2283	130P	Isobutyl methacrylate
2283	130P	Isobutyl methacrylate, inhibited
2284	131	Isobutyronitrile
2285	156	Isocyanatobenzotrifluorides
2286	128	Pentamethylheptane
2287	128	Isoheptene
2288	128	Isohexene
2289	153	Isophoronediamine
2290	156	IPDI
2290	156	Isophorone diisocyanate
2291	151	Lead chloride
2291	151	Lead compound, soluble, n.o.s.
2291	151	Lead fluoborate

ID No.	Guide No.	Name of Material
2293	127	4-Methoxy-4-methyl-pentan-2-one
2294	153	N-Methylaniline
2295	155	Methyl chloroacetate
2296	128	Methylcyclohexane
2297	127	Methylcyclohexanone
2298	128	Methylcyclopentane
2299	155	Methyl dichloroacetate
2300	153	2-Methyl-5-ethylpyridine
2301	127	2-Methylfuran
2302	127	5-Methylhexan-2-one
2303	128	Isopropenylbenzene
2304	133	Naphthalene, molten
2305	153	Nitrobenzenesulfonic acid
2305	153	Nitrobenzenesulphonic acid
2306	152	Nitrobenzotrifluorides
2307	152	3-Nitro-4-chlorobenzotrifluoride
2308	157	Nitrosylsulfuric acid
2308	157	Nitrosylsulphuric acid
2309	128P	Octadiene
2310	131	Pentan-2,4-dione
2310	131	2,4-Pentanedione
2310	131	Pentane-2,4-dione
2311	153	Phenetidines
2312	153	Phenol, molten
2313	130	Picolines
2315	171	Articles containing Polychlorinated biphenyls (PCB)
2315	171	PCB
2315	171	Polychlorinated biphenyls
2315	171	Polychlorinated biphenyls, liquid
2315	171	Polychlorinated biphenyls, solid
2316	157	Sodium cuprocyanide, solid
2317	157	Sodium cuprocyanide, solution
2318	135	Sodium hydrosulfide, solid, with less than 25% water of crystallization
2318	135	Sodium hydrosulfide, with less than 25% water of crystallization
2318	135	Sodium hydrosulphide, solid, with less than 25% water of crystallization
2318	135	Sodium hydrosulphide, with less than 25% water of crystallization
2319	128	Terpene hydrocarbons, n.o.s.
2320	153	Tetraethylenepentamine
2321	153	Trichlorobenzenes, liquid
2322	152	Trichlorobutene
2323	129	Triethyl phosphite
2324	128	Triisobutylene
2325	129	1,3,5-Trimethylbenzene
2326	153	Trimethylcyclohexylamine
2327	153	Trimethylhexamethylenediamines
2328	156	Trimethylhexamethylene diisocyanate
2329	129	Trimethyl phosphite
2330	128	Undecane
2331	154	Zinc chloride, anhydrous
2332	129	Acetaldehyde oxime
2333	131	Allyl acetate
2334	131	Allylamine
2335	131	Allyl ethyl ether
2336	131	Allyl formate
2337	131	Phenyl mercaptan
2338	131	Benzotrifluoride
2339	130	2-Bromobutane
2340	130	2-Bromoethyl ethyl ether

ID No.	Guide No.	Name of Material	ID No.	Guide No.	Name of Material
2341	130	1-Bromo-3-methylbutane	2372	129	1,2-Di-(dimethylamino)ethane
2342	130	Bromomethylpropanes	2373	127	Diethoxymethane
2343	130	2-Bromopentane	2374	127	3,3-Diethoxypropene
2344	130	2-Bromopropane	2375	129	Diethyl sulfide
2344	130	Bromopropanes	2375	129	Diethyl sulphide
2345	129	3-Bromopropyne	2376	127	2,3-Dihydropyran
2346	127	Butanedione	2377	127	1,1-Dimethoxyethane
2346	127	Diacetyl	2378	131	2-Dimethylaminoacetonitrile
2347	130	Butyl mercaptan	2379	132	1,3-Dimethylbutylamine
2348	129P	Butyl acrylate	2380	127	Dimethyldiethoxysilane
2348	129P	Butyl acrylates, inhibited	2381	130	Dimethyl disulfide
2350	127	Butyl methyl ether	2381	130	Dimethyl disulphide
2351	129	Butyl nitrites	2382	131	1,2-Dimethylhydrazine
2352	127P	Butyl vinyl ether, inhibited	2382	131	Dimethylhydrazine, symmetrical
2353	132	Butyryl chloride	2383	132	Dipropylamine
2354	131	Chloromethyl ethyl ether	2384	127	Di-n-propyl ether
2356	129	2-Chloropropane	2384	127	Dipropyl ether
2357	132	Cyclohexylamine	2385	129	Ethyl isobutyrate
2358	128P	Cyclooctatetraene	2386	132	1-Ethylpiperidine
2359	132	Diallylamine	2387	130	Fluorobenzene
2360	131P	Diallyl ether	2388	130	Fluorotoluenes
2361	132	Diisobutylamine	2389	127	Furan
2362	130	1,1-Dichloroethane	2390	129	2-Iodobutane
2363	130	Ethyl mercaptan	2391	129	Iodomethylpropanes
2364	127	n-Propyl benzene	2392	129	Iodopropanes
2366	127	Diethyl carbonate	2393	132	Isobutyl formate
2367	130	alpha-Methylvaleraldehyde	2394	129	Isobutyl propionate
2367	130	Methyl valeraldehyde (alpha)	2395	132	Isobutyryl chloride
2368	127	alpha-Pinene	2396	131P	Methacrylaldehyde
2368	127	Pinene (alpha)	2396	131P	Methacrylaldehyde, inhibited
2369	152	Ethylene glycol monobutyl ether	2397	127	3-Methylbutan-2-one
2370	128	1-Hexene	2398	127	Methyl tert-butyl ether
2371	128	Isopentenes	2399	132	1-Methylpiperidine

ID No.	Guide No.	Name of Material
2400	130	Methyl isovalerate
2401	132	Piperidine
2402	130	Isopropyl mercaptan
2402	130	Propanethiols
2402	130	Propyl mercaptan
2403	129P	Isopropenyl acetate
2404	131	Propionitrile
2405	129	Isopropyl butyrate
2406	131	Isopropyl isobutyrate
2407	155	Isopropyl chloroformate
2409	129	Isopropyl propionate
2410	129	1,2,3,6-Tetrahydropyridine
2410	129	1,2,5,6-Tetrahydropyridine
2411	131	Butyronitrile
2412	129	Tetrahydrothiophene
2413	128	Tetrapropyl orthotitanate
2414	130	Thiophene
2416	129	Trimethyl borate
2417	125	Carbonyl fluoride
2417	125	Carbonyl fluoride, compressed
2418	125	Sulfur tetrafluoride
2418	125	Sulphur tetrafluoride
2419	116	Bromotrifluoroethylene
2420	125	Hexafluoroacetone
2421	124	Nitrogen trioxide
2422	126	Octafluorobut-2-ene
2422	126	Refrigerant gas R-1318
2424	126	Octafluoropropane
2424	126	Refrigerant gas R-218
2426	140	Ammonium nitrate, liquid (hot concentrated solution)
2427	140	Potassium chlorate, aqueous solution
2427	140	Potassium chlorate, solution
2428	140	Sodium chlorate, aqueous solution
2429	140	Calcium chlorate, aqueous solution
2429	140	Calcium chlorate, solution
2430	153	Alkyl phenols, solid, n.o.s. (including C2-C12 homologues)
2431	153	Anisidines
2431	153	Anisidines, liquid
2431	153	Anisidines, solid
2432	153	N,N-Diethylaniline
2433	152	Chloronitrotoluenes
2433	152	Chloronitrotoluenes, liquid
2433	152	Chloronitrotoluenes, solid
2434	156	Dibenzyldichlorosilane
2435	156	Ethylphenyldichlorosilane
2436	129	Thioacetic acid
2437	156	Methylphenyldichlorosilane
2438	132	Trimethylacetyl chloride
2439	154	Sodium bifluoride, solid
2439	154	Sodium bifluoride, solution
2439	154	Sodium hydrogendifluoride
2439	154	Sodium hydrogen fluoride
2440	154	Stannic chloride, pentahydrate
2440	154	Tin tetrachloride, pentahydrate
2441	135	Titanium trichloride, pyrophoric
2441	135	Titanium trichloride mixture, pyrophoric
2442	156	Trichloroacetyl chloride
2443	137	Titanium tetrachloride and Vanadium oxytrichloride, mixture
2443	137	Vanadium oxytrichloride

ID No.	Guide No.	Name of Material
2443	137	Vanadium oxytrichloride and Titanium tetrachloride, mixture
2444	137	Vanadium tetrachloride
2445	135	Lithium alkyls
2446	153	Nitrocresols
2447	136	Phosphorus, white, molten
2447	136	White phosphorus, molten
2447	136	Yellow phosphorus, molten
2448	133	Sulfur, molten
2448	133	Sulphur, molten
2449	154	Ammonium oxalate
2449	154	Oxalates, water soluble
2451	122	Nitrogen trifluoride
2451	122	Nitrogen trifluoride, compressed
2452	116P	Ethylacetylene, inhibited
2453	115	Ethyl fluoride
2453	115	Refrigerant gas R-161
2454	115	Methyl fluoride
2454	115	Refrigerant gas R-41
2455	116	Methyl nitrite
2456	130P	2-Chloropropene
2457	128	2,3-Dimethylbutane
2458	130	Hexadiene
2459	127	2-Methyl-1-butene
2460	127	2-Methyl-2-butene
2461	127	Methylpentadiene
2462	128	Methyl pentane
2463	138	Aluminum hydride
2464	141	Beryllium nitrate
2465	140	Dichloroisocyanuric acid, dry
2465	140	Dichloroisocyanuric acid salts
2465	140	Potassium dichloro-s-triazinetrione, dry
2465	140	Sodium dichloroisocyanurate
2465	140	Sodium dichloro-s-triazinetrione
2466	143	Potassium superoxide
2467	140	Sodium percarbonates
2468	140	Trichloroisocyanuric acid, dry
2468	140	Trichloro-s-triazinetrione, dry
2468	140	(mono)-(Trichloro)-tetra-(monopotassium dichloro)-penta-s-triazinetrione, dry
2469	140	Zinc bromate
2470	152	Phenylacetonitrile, liquid
2471	154	Osmium tetroxide
2473	154	Sodium arsanilate
2474	157	Thiophosgene
2475	157	Vanadium trichloride
2477	131	Methyl isothiocyanate
2478	155	Isocyanate solution, flammable, poisonous, n.o.s.
2478	155	Isocyanate solution, flammable, toxic, n.o.s.
2478	155	Isocyanate solutions, n.o.s.
2478	155	Isocyanates, flammable, poisonous, n.o.s.
2478	155	Isocyanates, flammable, toxic, n.o.s.
2478	155	Isocyanates, n.o.s.
2480	155	Methyl isocyanate
2481	155	Ethyl isocyanate
2482	155	n-Propyl isocyanate
2483	155	Isopropyl isocyanate
2484	155	tert-Butyl isocyanate
2485	155	n-Butyl isocyanate
2486	155	Isobutyl isocyanate
2487	155	Phenyl isocyanate

ID No.	Guide No.	Name of Material	ID No.	Guide No.	Name of Material
2488	155	Cyclohexyl isocyanate	2514	129	Bromobenzene
2489	156	Diphenylmethane-4,4'-diisocyanate	2515	159	Bromoform
			2516	151	Carbon tetrabromide
2490	153	Dichloroisopropyl ether	2517	115	1-Chloro-1,1-difluoroethane
2491	153	Ethanolamine	2517	115	Chlorodifluoroethanes
2491	153	Ethanolamine, solution	2517	115	Difluorochloroethanes
2491	153	Monoethanolamine	2517	115	Refrigerant gas R-142b
2493	132	Hexamethyleneimine	2518	153	1,5,9-Cyclododecatriene
2495	144	Iodine pentafluoride	2520	130P	Cyclooctadienes
2496	156	Propionic anhydride	2521	131P	Diketene, inhibited
2497	153	Sodium phenolate, solid	2522	153P	2-Dimethylaminoethyl methacrylate
2498	132	1,2,3,6-Tetrahydro-benzaldehyde	2522	153P	Dimethylaminoethyl methacrylate
2501	152	1-Aziridinyl phosphine oxide (Tris)	2524	129	Ethyl orthoformate
2501	152	Tri-(1-aziridinyl)phosphine oxide, solution	2525	156	Ethyl oxalate
			2526	132	Furfurylamine
2501	152	Tris-(1-aziridinyl)phosphine oxide, solution	2527	130P	Isobutyl acrylate
			2527	130P	Isobutyl acrylate, inhibited
2502	132	Valeryl chloride	2528	129	Isobutyl isobutyrate
2503	137	Zirconium tetrachloride	2529	132	Isobutyric acid
2504	159	Acetylene tetrabromide	2530	132	Isobutyric anhydride
2504	159	Tetrabromoethane	2531	153P	Methacrylic acid, inhibited
2505	154	Ammonium fluoride	2533	156	Methyl trichloroacetate
2506	154	Ammonium hydrogen sulfate	2534	119	Methylchlorosilane
2506	154	Ammonium hydrogen sulphate	2535	132	4-Methylmorpholine
2507	154	Chloroplatinic acid, solid	2535	132	N-Methylmorpholine
2508	156	Molybdenum pentachloride	2535	132	Methylmorpholine
2509	154	Potassium hydrogen sulfate	2536	127	Methyltetrahydrofuran
2509	154	Potassium hydrogen sulphate	2538	133	Nitronaphthalene
2511	153	2-Chloropropionic acid	2541	128	Terpinolene
2511	153	alpha-Chloropropionic acid	2542	153	Tributylamine
2512	152	Aminophenols	2545	135	Hafnium powder, dry
2513	156	Bromoacetyl bromide			

ID No.	Guide No.	Name of Material	ID No.	Guide No.	Name of Material
2546	135	Titanium powder, dry	2565	153	Dicyclohexylamine
2547	143	Sodium superoxide	2567	154	Sodium pentachlorophenate
2548	124	Chlorine pentafluoride	2570	154	Cadmium compound
2550	147	Methyl ethyl ketone peroxide	2571	156	Alkylsulfuric acids
2551	145	tert-Butyl peroxydiethylacetate, with tert-Butyl peroxybenzoate	2571	156	Alkylsulphuric acids
			2571	156	Ethylsulfuric acid
2552	151	Hexafluoroacetone hydrate	2571	156	Ethylsulphuric acid
2553	128	Naphtha	2572	153	Phenylhydrazine
2554	129P	Methylallyl chloride	2573	141	Thallium chlorate
2555	113	Nitrocellulose, colloided, granular or flake, wet, with not less than 20% water	2574	151	Tricresyl phosphate
			2576	137	Phosphorus oxybromide, molten
			2577	156	Phenylacetyl chloride
2555	113	Nitrocellulose with water, not less than 25% water	2578	157	Phosphorus trioxide
			2579	153	Piperazine
2556	113	Nitrocellulose, wet, with not less than 30% alcohol or solvent	2580	154	Aluminum bromide, solution
			2581	154	Aluminum chloride, solution
2556	113	Nitrocellulose with alcohol	2582	154	Ferric chloride, solution
2556	113	Nitrocellulose with not less than 25% alcohol	2583	153	Alkyl sulfonic acids, solid, with more than 5% free Sulfuric acid
2557	133	Lacquer chips, dry			
2557	133	Nitrocellulose mixture, without plasticizer, without pigment	2583	153	Alkyl sulphonic acids, solid, with more than 5% free Sulphuric acid
2557	133	Nitrocellulose mixture, without plasticizer, with pigment	2583	153	Aryl sulfonic acids, solid, with more than 5% free Sulfuric acid
2557	133	Nitrocellulose mixture, with plasticizer, without pigment	2583	153	Aryl sulphonic acids, solid, with more than 5% free Sulphuric acid
2557	133	Nitrocellulose mixture, with plasticizer, with pigment	2583	153	Toluene sulfonic acid, solid, with more than 5% free Sulfuric acid
2557	133	Nitrocellulose with plasticizing substance			
2558	131	Epibromohydrin	2583	153	Toluene sulphonic acid, solid, with more than 5% free Sulphuric acid
2560	129	2-Methylpentan-2-ol			
2561	127	3-Methyl-1-butene			
2562	148	tert-Butyl peroxyisobutyrate			
2564	153	Trichloroacetic acid, solution			

ID No.	Guide No.	Name of Material
2584	153	Alkyl sulfonic acids, liquid, with more than 5% free Sulfuric acid
2584	153	Alkyl sulphonic acids, liquid, with more than 5% free Sulphuric acid
2584	153	Aryl sulfonic acids, liquid, with more than 5% free Sulfuric acid
2584	153	Aryl sulphonic acids, liquid, with more than 5% free Sulphuric acid
2584	153	Dodecylbenzenesulfonic acid
2584	153	Dodecylbenzenesulphonic acid
2584	153	Toluene sulfonic acid, liquid, with more than 5% free Sulfuric acid
2584	153	Toluene sulphonic acid, liquid, with more than 5% free Sulphuric acid
2585	153	Alkyl sulfonic acids, solid, with not more than 5% free Sulfuric acid
2585	153	Alkyl sulphonic acids, solid, with not more than 5% free Sulphuric acid
2585	153	Aryl sulfonic acids, solid, with not more than 5% free Sulfuric acid
2585	153	Aryl sulphonic acids, solid, with not more than 5% free Sulphuric acid
2585	153	Toluene sulfonic acid, solid, with not more than 5% free Sulfuric acid
2585	153	Toluene sulphonic acid, solid, with not more than 5% free Sulphuric acid
2586	153	Alkyl sulfonic acids, liquid, with not more than 5% free Sulfuric acid
2586	153	Alkyl sulphonic acids, liquid, with not more than 5% free Sulphuric acid
2586	153	Aryl sulfonic acids, liquid, with not more than 5% free Sulfuric acid
2586	153	Aryl sulphonic acids, liquid, with not more than 5% free Sulphuric acid
2586	153	Toluene sulfonic acid, liquid, with not more than 5% free Sulfuric acid
2586	153	Toluene sulphonic acid, liquid, with not more than 5% free Sulphuric acid
2587	153	Benzoquinone
2588	151	Insecticide, dry, n.o.s.
2588	151	Pesticide, solid, poisonous
2588	151	Pesticide, solid, poisonous, n.o.s.
2588	151	Pesticide, solid, toxic, n.o.s.
2589	155	Vinyl chloroacetate
2590	171	Asbestos, white
2590	171	White asbestos
2591	120	Xenon, refrigerated liquid (cryogenic liquid)
2592	145	Distearyl peroxydicarbonate
2593	148	Di-(2-methylbenzoyl)peroxide
2594	148	tert-Butyl peroxyneodecanoate
2595	148	Dimyristyl peroxydicarbonate
2596	145	tert-Butyl peroxy-3-phenylphthalide
2597	148	Di-(3,5,5-trimethyl-1,2-dioxolanyl-3)peroxide
2598	145	Ethyl-3,3-di-(tert-butylperoxy)butyrate

ID No.	Guide No.	Name of Material
2599	126	Chlorotrifluoromethane and Trifluoromethane azeotropic mixture with approximately 60% Chlorotrifluoromethane
2599	126	Refrigerant gas R-13 and Refrigerant gas R-23 azeotropic mixture with 60% Refrigerant gas R-13
2599	126	Refrigerant gas R-23 and Refrigerant gas R-13 azeotropic mixture with 60% Refrigerant gas R-13
2599	126	Refrigerant gas R-503 (azeotropic mixture of Refrigerant gas R-13 and Refrigerant gas R-23 with approximately 60% Refrigerant gas R-13)
2599	126	Trifluoromethane and Chlorotrifluoromethane azeotropic mixture with approximately 60% Chlorotrifluoromethane
2600	119	Carbon monoxide and Hydrogen mixture
2600	119	Carbon monoxide and Hydrogen mixture, compressed
2600	119	Hydrogen and Carbon monoxide mixture
2600	119	Hydrogen and Carbon monoxide mixture, compressed
2601	115	Cyclobutane
2602	126	Dichlorodifluoromethane and Difluoroethane azeotropic mixture with approximately 74% Dichlorodifluoromethane
2602	126	Difluoroethane and Dichlorodifluoromethane azeotropic mixture with approximately 74% dichlorodifluoromethane
2602	126	Refrigerant gas R-12 and Refrigerant gas R-152a azeotropic mixture with 74% Refrigerant gas R-12
2602	126	Refrigerant gas R-152a and Refrigerant gas R-12 azeotropic mixture with 74% Refrigerant gas R-12
2602	126	Refrigerant gas R-500 (azeotropic mixture of Refrigerant gas R-12 and Refrigerant gas R-152a with approximately 74% Refrigerant gas R-12)
2603	131	Cycloheptatriene
2604	132	Boron trifluoride diethyl etherate
2605	155	Methoxymethyl isocyanate
2606	155	Methyl orthosilicate
2607	129P	Acrolein dimer, stabilized
2608	129	Nitropropanes
2609	156	Triallyl borate
2610	132	Triallylamine
2611	131	Propylene chlorohydrin
2612	127	Methyl propyl ether
2614	129	Methallyl alcohol
2615	127	Ethyl propyl ether
2616	129	Triisopropyl borate
2617	129	Methylcyclohexanols
2618	130P	Vinyltoluenes, inhibited
2619	132	Benzyldimethylamine
2620	130	Amyl butyrates
2621	127	Acetyl methyl carbinol
2622	131P	Glycidaldehyde
2623	133	Firelighters, solid, with flammable liquid
2624	138	Magnesium silicide

ID No.	Guide No.	Name of Material
2626	140	Chloric acid
2626	140	Chloric acid, aqueous solution, with not more than 10% Chloric acid
2627	140	Nitrites, inorganic, n.o.s.
2628	151	Potassium fluoroacetate
2629	151	Sodium fluoroacetate
2630	151	Barium selenate
2630	151	Barium selenite
2630	151	Calcium selenate
2630	151	Potassium selenate
2630	151	Potassium selenite
2630	151	Selenates
2630	151	Selenites
2630	151	Sodium selenite
2630	151	Zinc selenate
2630	151	Zinc selenite
2642	154	Fluoroacetic acid
2643	155	Methyl bromoacetate
2644	151	Methyl iodide
2645	153	Phenacyl bromide
2646	151	Hexachlorocyclopentadiene
2647	153	Malononitrile
2648	154	1,2-Dibromobutan-3-one
2649	153	1,3-Dichloroacetone
2650	153	1,1-Dichloro-1-nitroethane
2651	153	4,4'-Diaminodiphenylmethane
2653	156	Benzyl iodide
2655	151	Potassium fluorosilicate
2655	151	Potassium silicofluoride
2656	154	Quinoline
2657	153	Selenium disulfide
2657	153	Selenium disulphide
2658	152	Selenium powder
2659	151	Sodium chloroacetate
2660	153	Mononitrotoluidines
2660	153	Nitrotoluidines (mono)
2661	153	Hexachloroacetone
2662	153	Hydroquinone
2664	160	Dibromomethane
2666	156	Ethyl cyanoacetate
2667	131	Butyltoluenes
2668	131	Chloroacetonitrile
2669	152	Chlorocresols
2669	152	Chlorocresols, liquid
2669	152	Chlorocresols, solid
2670	157	Cyanuric chloride
2671	153	Aminopyridines
2672	154	Ammonia, solution, with more than 10% but not more than 35% Ammonia
2672	154	Ammonium hydroxide
2672	154	Ammonium hydroxide, with more than 10% but not more than 35% Ammonia
2673	151	2-Amino-4-chlorophenol
2674	154	Sodium fluorosilicate
2674	154	Sodium silicofluoride
2676	119	Stibine
2677	154	Rubidium hydroxide, solution
2678	154	Rubidium hydroxide
2678	154	Rubidium hydroxide, solid
2679	154	Lithium hydroxide, solution
2680	154	Lithium hydroxide, monohydrate
2680	154	Lithium hydroxide, solid
2681	154	Caesium hydroxide, solution
2681	154	Cesium hydroxide, solution

ID No.	Guide No.	Name of Material	ID No.	Guide No.	Name of Material
2682	157	Caesium hydroxide	2693	154	Calcium hydrogen sulphite, solution
2682	157	Cesium hydroxide	2693	154	Magnesium bisulfite solution
2683	132	Ammonium hydrosulfide, solution	2693	154	Magnesium bisulphite solution
2683	132	Ammonium hydrosulphide, solution	2693	154	Potassium bisulfite solution
2683	132	Ammonium sulfide, solution	2693	154	Potassium bisulphite solution
2683	132	Ammonium sulphide, solution	2693	154	Zinc bisulfite solution
2684	132	3-Diethylaminopropylamine	2693	154	Zinc bisulphite solution
2684	132	Diethylaminopropylamine	2698	156	Tetrahydrophthalic anhydrides
2685	132	N,N-Diethylethylenediamine	2699	154	Trifluoroacetic acid
2686	132	2-Diethylaminoethanol	2705	153P	1-Pentol
2686	132	Diethylaminoethanol	2707	128	Dimethyldioxanes
2687	133	Dicyclohexylammonium nitrite	2708	127	Butoxyl
2688	159	1-Bromo-3-chloropropane	2709	128	Butylbenzenes
2688	159	1-Chloro-3-bromopropane	2710	127	Dipropyl ketone
2689	153	Glycerol alpha-monochlorohydrin	2711	129	Dibromobenzene
2690	152	N,n-Butylimidazole	2713	153	Acridine
2691	137	Phosphorus pentabromide	2714	133	Zinc resinate
2692	157	Boron tribromide	2715	133	Aluminum resinate
2693	154	Ammonium bisulfite, solid	2716	153	1,4-Butynediol
2693	154	Ammonium bisulfite, solution	2717	133	Camphor
2693	154	Ammonium bisulphite, solid	2717	133	Camphor, synthetic
2693	154	Ammonium bisulphite, solution	2719	141	Barium bromate
2693	154	Bisulfites, aqueous solution, n.o.s.	2720	141	Chromium nitrate
2693	154	Bisulfites, inorganic, aqueous solutions, n.o.s.	2721	141	Copper chlorate
2693	154	Bisulphites, aqueous solution, n.o.s.	2722	140	Lithium nitrate
2693	154	Bisulphites, inorganic, aqueous solutions, n.o.s.	2723	140	Magnesium chlorate
2693	154	Calcium hydrogen sulfite, solution	2724	140	Manganese nitrate
			2725	140	Nickel nitrate
			2726	140	Nickel nitrite
			2727	141	Thallium nitrate
			2728	140	Zirconium nitrate
			2729	152	Hexachlorobenzene

ID No.	Guide No.	Name of Material
2730	152	Nitroanisole
2730	152	Nitroanisole, liquid
2730	152	Nitroanisole, solid
2732	152	Nitrobromobenzene
2732	152	Nitrobromobenzene, liquid
2732	152	Nitrobromobenzene, solid
2733	132	Alkylamines, n.o.s.
2733	132	Amines, flammable, corrosive, n.o.s.
2733	132	Polyalkylamines, n.o.s.
2733	132	Polyamines, flammable, corrosive, n.o.s.
2734	132	Alkylamines, n.o.s.
2734	132	Amines, liquid, corrosive, flammable, n.o.s.
2734	132	Polyalkylamines, n.o.s.
2734	132	Polyamines, liquid, corrosive, flammable, n.o.s.
2735	153	Alkylamines, n.o.s.
2735	153	Amines, liquid, corrosive, n.o.s.
2735	153	Polyalkylamines, n.o.s.
2735	153	Polyamines, liquid, corrosive, n.o.s.
2738	153	N-Butylaniline
2739	156	Butyric anhydride
2740	155	n-Propyl chloroformate
2741	141	Barium hypochlorite, with more than 22% available Chlorine
2742	155	sec-Butyl chloroformate
2742	155	Chloroformates, n.o.s.
2742	155	Chloroformates, poisonous, corrosive, flammable, n.o.s.
2742	155	Chloroformates, toxic, corrosive, flammable, n.o.s.
2742	155	Isobutyl chloroformate
2743	155	n-Butyl chloroformate
2744	155	Cyclobutyl chloroformate
2745	157	Chloromethyl chloroformate
2746	156	Phenyl chloroformate
2747	156	tert-Butylcyclohexyl chloroformate
2748	156	2-Ethylhexyl chloroformate
2749	130	Tetramethylsilane
2750	153	1,3-Dichloropropanol-2
2751	155	Diethylthiophosphoryl chloride
2752	127	1,2-Epoxy-3-ethoxypropane
2753	153	N-Ethylbenzyltoluidines
2754	153	N-Ethyltoluidines
2755	146	3-Chloroperoxybenzoic acid
2756	146	Organic peroxides, mixtures
2757	151	Carbamate pesticide, solid, poisonous
2757	151	Carbamate pesticide, solid, toxic
2757	151	Carbaryl
2757	151	Carbofuran
2757	151	Mexacarbate
2758	131	Carbamate pesticide, liquid, flammable, poisonous
2758	131	Carbamate pesticide, liquid, flammable, toxic
2759	151	Arsenical pesticide, solid, poisonous
2759	151	Arsenical pesticide, solid, toxic
2760	131	Arsenical pesticide, liquid, flammable, poisonous
2760	131	Arsenical pesticide, liquid, flammable, toxic
2761	151	Aldrin, solid
2761	151	Aldrin mixture, dry

ID No.	Guide No.	Name of Material
2761	151	DDT
2761	151	Dichlorodiphenyltrichloroethane (DDT)
2761	151	Dieldrin
2761	151	Endosulfan
2761	151	Lindane
2761	151	Organochlorine pesticide, solid, poisonous
2761	151	Organochlorine pesticide, solid, toxic
2761	151	TDE (1,1-Dichloro-2,2-bis-(p-chlorophenyl)ethane)
2761	151	Toxaphene
2762	131	Aldrin, liquid
2762	131	Aldrin mixture, liquid
2762	131	Organochlorine pesticide, liquid, flammable, poisonous
2762	131	Organochlorine pesticide, liquid, flammable, toxic
2763	151	Triazine pesticide, solid, poisonous
2763	151	Triazine pesticide, solid, toxic
2764	131	Triazine pesticide, liquid, flammable, poisonous
2764	131	Triazine pesticide, liquid, flammable, toxic
2765	152	2,4-Dichlorophenoxyacetic acid
2765	152	Phenoxy pesticide, solid, poisonous
2765	152	Phenoxy pesticide, solid, toxic
2765	152	2,4,5-Trichlorophenoxyacetic acid
2765	152	2,4,5-Trichlorophenoxy-propionic acid
2766	131	Phenoxy pesticide, liquid, flammable, poisonous
2766	131	Phenoxy pesticide, liquid, flammable, toxic
2767	151	Phenyl urea pesticide, solid, poisonous
2767	151	Phenyl urea pesticide, solid, toxic
2768	131	Phenyl urea pesticide, liquid, flammable, poisonous
2768	131	Phenyl urea pesticide, liquid, flammable, toxic
2769	151	Benzoic derivative pesticide, solid, poisonous
2769	151	Benzoic derivative pesticide, solid, toxic
2770	131	Benzoic derivative pesticide, liquid, flammable, poisonous
2770	131	Benzoic derivative pesticide, liquid, flammable, toxic
2771	151	Dithiocarbamate pesticide, solid, poisonous
2771	151	Dithiocarbamate pesticide, solid, toxic
2771	151	Thiocarbamate pesticide, solid, poisonous
2771	151	Thiocarbamate pesticide, solid, toxic
2771	151	Thiram
2772	131	Dithiocarbamate pesticide, liquid, flammable, poisonous
2772	131	Dithiocarbamate pesticide, liquid, flammable, toxic
2772	131	Thiocarbamate pesticide, liquid, flammable, poisonous
2772	131	Thiocarbamate pesticide, liquid, flammable, toxic
2773	151	Phthalimide derivative pesticide, solid, poisonous

ID No.	Guide No.	Name of Material
2773	151	Phthalimide derivative pesticide, solid, toxic
2774	131	Phthalimide derivative pesticide, liquid, flammable, poisonous
2774	131	Phthalimide derivative pesticide, liquid, flammable, toxic
2775	151	Copper based pesticide, solid, poisonous
2775	151	Copper based pesticide, solid, toxic
2776	131	Copper based pesticide, liquid, flammable, poisonous
2776	131	Copper based pesticide, liquid, flammable, toxic
2777	151	Mercury based pesticide, solid, poisonous
2777	151	Mercury based pesticide, solid, toxic
2778	131	Mercury based pesticide, liquid, flammable, poisonous
2778	131	Mercury based pesticide, liquid, flammable, toxic
2779	153	Substituted nitrophenol pesticide, solid, poisonous
2779	153	Substituted nitrophenol pesticide, solid, toxic
2780	131	Substituted nitrophenol pesticide, liquid, flammable, poisonous
2780	131	Substituted nitrophenol pesticide, liquid, flammable, toxic
2781	151	Bipyridilium pesticide, solid, poisonous
2781	151	Bipyridilium pesticide, solid, toxic
2782	131	Bipyridilium pesticide, liquid, flammable, poisonous
2782	131	Bipyridilium pesticide, liquid, flammable, toxic
2783	152	Azinphos methyl
2783	152	Chlorpyrifos
2783	152	Coumaphos
2783	152	Diazinon
2783	152	Dichlorvos
2783	152	Disulfoton
2783	152	Ethion
2783	152	Hexaethyl tetraphosphate mixture, liquid
2783	152	Methyl parathion, liquid
2783	152	Methyl parathion, mixture, dry
2783	152	Methyl parathion, solid
2783	152	Mevinphos
2783	152	Organic phosphate, dry
2783	152	Organic phosphate, solid
2783	152	Organic phosphate compound, dry
2783	152	Organic phosphate compound, solid
2783	152	Organic phosphorus compound, dry
2783	152	Organic phosphorus compound, solid
2783	152	Organophosphorus pesticide, solid, poisonous
2783	152	Organophosphorus pesticide, solid, toxic
2783	152	Parathion
2783	152	Parathion mixture, dry
2783	152	Parathion mixture, liquid
2783	152	Tetraethyl pyrophosphate, liquid

ID No.	Guide No.	Name of Material
2783	152	Tetraethyl pyrophosphate, solid
2783	152	Tetraethyl pyrophosphate mixture, dry
2783	152	Trichlorfon
2784	131	Organophosphorus pesticide, liquid, flammable, poisonous
2784	131	Organophosphorus pesticide, liquid, flammable, toxic
2785	152	4-Thiapentanal
2785	152	Thia-4-pentanal
2786	153	Organotin pesticide, solid, poisonous
2786	153	Organotin pesticide, solid, toxic
2787	131	Organotin pesticide, liquid, flammable, poisonous
2787	131	Organotin pesticide, liquid, flammable, toxic
2788	153	Organotin compound, liquid, n.o.s.
2789	132	Acetic acid, glacial
2789	132	Acetic acid, solution, more than 80% acid
2790	153	Acetic acid, solution, more than 10% but not more than 80% acid
2793	170	Ferrous metal borings, shavings, turnings or cuttings
2793	170	Steel swarf
2794	154	Batteries, wet, filled with acid
2794	154	Battery
2795	154	Batteries, wet, filled with alkali
2795	154	Battery
2796	157	Battery fluid, acid
2796	157	Battery fluid, acid, with battery
2796	157	Battery fluid, acid, with electronic equipment or actuating device
2796	157	Sulfuric acid, with not more than 51% acid
2796	157	Sulphuric acid, with not more than 51% acid
2797	154	Battery fluid, alkali
2797	154	Battery fluid, alkali, with battery
2797	154	Battery fluid, alkali, with electronic equipment or actuating device
2798	137	Benzene phosphorus dichloride
2798	137	Phenylphosphorus dichloride
2799	137	Benzene phosphorus thiodichloride
2799	137	Phenylphosphorus thiodichloride
2800	154	Batteries, wet, non-spillable
2801	154	Coal tar dye, liquid
2801	154	Dye, liquid, corrosive, n.o.s.
2801	154	Dye intermediate, liquid, corrosive, n.o.s.
2802	154	Copper chloride
2803	172	Gallium
2805	138	Lithium hydride, fused solid
2806	138	Lithium nitride
2807	171	Magnetized material
2809	172	Mercury
2809	172	Mercury, metallic
2809	172	Mercury metal
2810	153	Bis-(2-chloroethyl) ethylamine
2810	153	Bis-(2-chloroethyl) methylamine
2810	153	Bis-(2-chloroethyl) sulfide
2810	153	Bis-(2-chloroethyl) sulphide
2810	153	Buzz
2810	153	BZ

ID No.	Guide No.	Name of Material
2810	153	o-Chlorobenzylidene malononitrile
2810	153	Compound, tree or weed killing, liquid (toxic)
2810	153	CS
2810	153	DC
2810	153	Dichloro-(2-chlorovinyl) arsine
2810	153	Diphenylcyanoarsine
2810	153	Drugs, liquid, n.o.s.
2810	153	O-Ethyl S-(2-diisopropylaminoethyl) methylphosphonothiolate
2810	153	Ethyl N,N-dimethylphosphoramidocyanidate
2810	153	GA
2810	153	GB
2810	153	GD
2810	153	GF
2810	153	H
2810	153	HD
2810	153	HL
2810	153	HN-1 (nitrogen mustard)
2810	153	HN-2
2810	153	HN-3
2810	153	Isopropyl methylphosphonofluoridate
2810	153	L (Lewisite)
2810	153	Lewisite
2810	153	Medicines, poisonous, liquid, n.o.s.
2810	153	Medicines, toxic, liquid, n.o.s.
2810	153	Mustard
2810	153	Mustard Lewisite
2810	153	Poison B, liquid, n.o.s.
2810	153	Pinacolyl methylphosphonofluoridate
2810	153	Poisonous liquid, n.o.s.
2810	153	Poisonous liquid, n.o.s. (Inhalation Hazard Zone A)
2810	153	Poisonous liquid, n.o.s. (Inhalation Hazard Zone B)
2810	153	Poisonous liquid, organic, n.o.s.
2810	153	Poisonous liquid, organic, n.o.s. (Inhalation Hazard Zone A)
2810	153	Poisonous liquid, organic, n.o.s. (Inhalation Hazard Zone B)
2810	153	Sarin
2810	153	Soman
2810	153	Tabun
2810	153	Thickened GD
2810	153	Toxic liquid, n.o.s.
2810	153	Toxic liquid, n.o.s. (Inhalation Hazard Zone A)
2810	153	Toxic liquid, n.o.s. (Inhalation Hazard Zone B)
2810	153	Toxic liquid, organic, n.o.s.
2810	153	Toxic liquid, organic, n.o.s. (Inhalation Hazard Zone A)
2810	153	Toxic liquid, organic, n.o.s. (Inhalation Hazard Zone B)
2810	153	Tris-(2-chloroethyl) amine
2810	153	VX
2811	154	CX
2811	154	Drugs, solid, n.o.s.
2811	154	Flue dust, poisonous
2811	154	Lead fluoride
2811	154	Medicines, poisonous, solid, n.o.s.
2811	154	Medicines, toxic, solid, n.o.s.
2811	154	Phosgene oxime

ID No.	Guide No.	Name of Material
2811	154	Poison B, solid, n.o.s.
2811	154	Poisonous solid, n.o.s.
2811	154	Poisonous solid, organic, n.o.s.
2811	154	Selenium oxide
2811	154	Toxic solid, n.o.s.
2811	154	Toxic solid, organic, n.o.s.
2812	154	Sodium aluminate, solid
2813	138	Lithium acetylide-Ethylenediamine complex
2813	138	Substances, which in contact with water emit flammable gases, solid, n.o.s.
2813	138	Water-reactive solid, n.o.s.
2813	138	Water-reactive substances, solid, n.o.s.
2814	158	Etiologic agent, n.o.s.
2814	158	Infectious substance, affecting humans
2815	153	N-Aminoethylpiperazine
2817	154	Ammonium bifluoride, solution
2817	154	Ammonium hydrogendifluoride, solution
2817	154	Ammonium hydrogen fluoride, solution
2818	154	Ammonium polysulfide, solution
2818	154	Ammonium polysulphide, solution
2819	153	Amyl acid phosphate
2820	153	Butyric acid
2821	153	Phenol, liquid
2821	153	Phenol solution
2822	153	2-Chloropyridine
2823	153	Crotonic acid
2823	153	Crotonic acid, liquid
2823	153	Crotonic acid, solid
2826	155	Ethyl chlorothioformate
2829	153	Caproic acid
2829	153	Hexanoic acid
2830	139	Lithium ferrosilicon
2831	160	1,1,1-Trichloroethane
2834	154	Phosphorous acid
2834	154	Phosphorous acid, ortho
2835	138	Sodium aluminum hydride
2837	154	Bisulfates, aqueous solution
2837	154	Bisulphates, aqueous solution
2837	154	Sodium bisulfate, solution
2837	154	Sodium bisulphate, solution
2837	154	Sodium hydrogen sulfate, solution
2837	154	Sodium hydrogen sulphate, solution
2838	129P	Vinyl butyrate, inhibited
2839	153	Aldol
2840	129	Butyraldoxime
2841	131	Di-n-amylamine
2842	129	Nitroethane
2844	138	Calcium manganese silicon
2845	135	Ethyl phosphonous dichloride, anhydrous
2845	135	Methyl phosphonous dichloride
2845	135	Pyrophoric liquid, n.o.s.
2845	135	Pyrophoric liquid, organic, n.o.s.
2846	135	Pyrophoric solid, n.o.s.
2846	135	Pyrophoric solid, organic, n.o.s.
2849	153	3-Chloropropanol-1
2850	128	Propylene tetramer
2851	157	Boron trifluoride, dihydrate
2852	113	Dipicryl sulfide, wetted with not less than 10% water

ID No.	Guide No.	Name of Material
2852	113	Dipicryl sulphide, wetted with not less than 10% water
2853	151	Magnesium fluorosilicate
2853	151	Magnesium silicofluoride
2854	151	Ammonium fluorosilicate
2854	151	Ammonium silicofluoride
2855	151	Zinc fluorosilicate
2855	151	Zinc silicofluoride
2856	151	Fluorosilicates, n.o.s.
2856	151	Silicofluorides, n.o.s.
2857	126	Refrigerating machines, containing Ammonia solutions (UN2073)
2857	126	Refrigerating machines, containing Ammonia solutions (UN2672)
2857	126	Refrigerating machines, containing non-flammable, liquefied gas
2857	126	Refrigerating machines, containing non-flammable, non-poisonous, liquefied gas
2857	126	Refrigerating machines, containing non-flammable, non-poisonous, non-corrosive, liquefied gas
2857	126	Refrigerating machines, containing non-flammable, non-toxic, liquefied gas
2857	126	Refrigerating machines, containing non-flammable, non-toxic, non-corrosive, liquefied gas
2858	170	Zirconium, dry, coiled wire, finished metal sheets or strips
2859	154	Ammonium metavanadate
2860	154	Vanadium trioxide
2861	151	Ammonium polyvanadate
2862	151	Vanadium pentoxide
2863	154	Sodium ammonium vanadate
2864	151	Potassium metavanadate
2865	154	Hydroxylamine sulfate
2865	154	Hydroxylamine sulphate
2869	157	Titanium trichloride mixture
2870	135	Aluminum borohydride
2870	135	Aluminum borohydride in devices
2871	170	Antimony powder
2872	159	Dibromochloropropanes
2873	153	Dibutylaminoethanol
2874	153	Furfuryl alcohol
2875	151	Hexachlorophene
2876	153	Resorcinol
2878	170	Titanium sponge granules
2878	170	Titanium sponge powders
2879	157	Selenium oxychloride
2880	140	Calcium hypochlorite, hydrated, with not less than 5.5% but not more than 10% water
2880	140	Calcium hypochlorite, hydrated mixture, with not less than 5.5% but not more than 10% water
2881	135	Metal catalyst, dry
2881	135	Nickel catalyst, dry
2883	145	2,2-Di-(tert-butylperoxy)-propane
2884	145	2,2-Di-(tert-butylperoxy)-propane
2885	145	1,1-Di-(tert-butylperoxy)-cyclohexane
2886	148	tert-Butyl peroxy-2-ethylhexanoate, with 2,2-Di-(tert-butylperoxy)butane

ID No.	Guide No.	Name of Material	ID No.	Guide No.	Name of Material
2887	145	tert-Butyl peroxy-2-ethylhexanoate, with 2,2-Di-(tert-butylperoxy)butane	2903	131	Pesticide, liquid, toxic, flammable, n.o.s.
2888	148	tert-Butyl peroxy-2-ethylhexanoate, not more than 50%, with phlegmatizer	2904	154	Chlorophenates, liquid
			2904	154	Chlorophenolates, liquid
			2904	154	Phenolates, liquid
2889	148	Diisotridecyl peroxydicarbonate	2905	154	Chlorophenates, solid
2890	145	tert-Butyl peroxybenzoate	2905	154	Chlorophenolates, solid
2891	148	tert-Amyl peroxyneodecanoate	2905	154	Phenolates, solid
2892	148	Dimyristyl peroxydicarbonate, not more than 42%, in water	2906	127	Triisocyanatoisocyanurate of Isophoronediisocyanate, solution (70%)
2893	145	Lauroyl peroxide, not more than 42%, stable dispersion, in water	2907	133	Isosorbide dinitrate mixture
2894	148	Di-(4-tert-butylcyclohexyl)-peroxydicarbonate	2908	161	Radioactive material, empty packages
2895	148	Dicetyl peroxydicarbonate, not more than 42%, in water	2908	161	Radioactive material, excepted package, empty packaging
2896	147	Cyclohexanone peroxide, not more than 72% as a paste	2909	161	Radioactive material, articles manufactured from depleted Uranium
2897	145	1,1-Di-(tert-butylperoxy)-cyclohexane	2909	161	Radioactive material, articles manufactured from natural Thorium
2898	148	tert-Amyl peroxy-2-ethylhexanoate	2909	161	Radioactive material, articles manufactured from natural Uranium
2899	148	Organic peroxides, n.o.s. (including trial quantities)	2909	161	Radioactive material, excepted package, articles manufactured from depleted Uranium
2900	158	Infectious substance, affecting animals only	2909	161	Radioactive material, excepted package, articles manufactured from natural Thorium
2901	124	Bromine chloride			
2902	151	Allethrin	2909	161	Radioactive material, excepted package, articles manufactured from natural Uranium
2902	151	Insecticide, liquid, poisonous, n.o.s.			
2902	151	Pesticide, liquid, poisonous, n.o.s.			
2902	151	Pesticide, liquid, toxic, n.o.s.			
2903	131	Pesticide, liquid, poisonous, flammable, n.o.s.			

ID No.	Guide No.	Name of Material	ID No.	Guide No.	Name of Material
2910	161	Radioactive material, excepted package, articles manufactured from depleted Uranium	2916	163	Radioactive material, Type B(U) package
2910	161	Radioactive material, excepted package, articles manufactured from natural Thorium	2917	163	Radioactive material, Type B(M) package
2910	161	Radioactive material, excepted package, articles manufactured from natural Uranium	2918	165	Radioactive material, fissile, n.o.s.
2910	161	Radioactive material, excepted package, empty packaging	2919	163	Radioactive material, transported under special arrangement
2910	161	Radioactive material, excepted package, instruments or articles	2920	132	Corrosive liquid, flammable, n.o.s.
			2920	132	Dichlorobutene
2910	161	Radioactive material, excepted package, limited quantity of material	2921	134	Corrosive solid, flammable, n.o.s.
			2922	154	Corrosive liquid, poisonous, n.o.s.
2910	161	Radioactive material, limited quantity, n.o.s.	2922	154	Corrosive liquid, toxic, n.o.s.
			2922	154	Sodium hydrosulfide, solution
2911	161	Radioactive material, excepted package, instruments or articles	2922	154	Sodium hydrosulphide, solution
			2923	154	Corrosive solid, poisonous, n.o.s.
			2923	154	Corrosive solid, toxic, n.o.s.
2911	161	Radioactive material, instruments or articles	2923	154	Sodium hydrosulfide, solid
			2923	154	Sodium hydrosulphide, solid
2912	162	Radioactive material, low specific activity (LSA), n.o.s.	2924	132	Dichlorobutene
			2924	132	Flammable liquid, corrosive, n.o.s
2912	162	Radioactive material, low specific activity (LSA-I)	2925	134	Flammable solid, corrosive, n.o.s.
2913	162	Radioactive material, surface contaminated objects (SCO)	2925	134	Flammable solid, corrosive, organic, n.o.s.
2913	162	Radioactive material, surface contaminated objects (SCO-I)	2926	134	Flammable solid, poisonous, n.o.s.
2913	162	Radioactive material, surface contaminated objects (SCO-II)	2926	134	Flammable solid, poisonous, organic, n.o.s.
			2926	134	Flammable solid, toxic, organic, n.o.s.
2915	163	Radioactive material, Type A package	2927	154	Ethyl phosphonothioic dichloride, anhydrous
			2927	154	Ethyl phosphorodichloridate
			2927	154	Poisonous liquid, corrosive, n.o.s.

ID No.	Guide No.	Name of Material
2927	154	Poisonous liquid, corrosive, n.o.s. (Inhalation Hazard Zone A)
2927	154	Poisonous liquid, corrosive, n.o.s. (Inhalation Hazard Zone B)
2927	154	Toxic liquid, corrosive, organic, n.o.s.
2927	154	Toxic liquid, corrosive, organic, n.o.s. (Inhalation Hazard Zone A)
2927	154	Toxic liquid, corrosive, organic, n.o.s. (Inhalation Hazard Zone B)
2928	154	Poisonous solid, corrosive, n.o.s.
2928	154	Toxic solid, corrosive, organic, n.o.s.
2929	131	Chloropicrin mixture, flammable
2929	131	Poisonous liquid, flammable, n.o.s.
2929	131	Poisonous liquid, flammable, n.o.s. (Inhalation Hazard Zone A)
2929	131	Poisonous liquid, flammable, n.o.s. (Inhalation Hazard Zone B)
2929	131	Poisonous liquid, flammable, organic, n.o.s.
2929	131	Poisonous liquid, flammable, organic, n.o.s. (Inhalation Hazard Zone A)
2929	131	Poisonous liquid, flammable, organic, n.o.s. (Inhalation Hazard Zone B)
2929	131	Toxic liquid, flammable, n.o.s.
2929	131	Toxic liquid, flammable, n.o.s. (Inhalation Hazard Zone A)
2929	131	Toxic liquid, flammable, n.o.s. (Inhalation Hazard Zone B)
2929	131	Toxic liquid, flammable, organic, n.o.s.
2929	131	Toxic liquid, flammable, organic, n.o.s. (Inhalation Hazard Zone A)
2929	131	Toxic liquid, flammable, organic, n.o.s. (Inhalation Hazard Zone B)
2930	134	Poisonous solid, flammable, n.o.s.
2930	134	Poisonous solid, flammable, organic, n.o.s.
2930	134	Toxic solid, flammable, n.o.s.
2930	134	Toxic solid, flammable, organic, n.o.s.
2931	151	Vanadyl sulfate
2931	151	Vanadyl sulphate
2933	132	Methyl 2-chloropropionate
2934	132	Isopropyl 2-chloropropionate
2935	132	Ethyl 2-chloropropionate
2936	153	Thiolactic acid
2937	153	alpha-Methylbenzyl alcohol
2937	153	Methylbenzyl alcohol (alpha)
2938	152	Methyl benzoate
2940	135	Cyclooctadiene phosphines
2940	135	9-Phosphabicyclononanes
2941	153	Fluoroanilines
2942	153	2-Trifluoromethylaniline
2943	129	Tetrahydrofurfurylamine
2945	132	N-Methylbutylamine
2946	153	2-Amino-5-diethylaminopentane
2947	155	Isopropyl chloroacetate
2948	153	3-Trifluoromethylaniline
2949	154	Sodium hydrosulfide, with not less than 25% water of crystallization

ID No.	Guide No.	Name of Material
2949	154	Sodium hydrosulphide, with not less than 25% water of crystallization
2950	138	Magnesium granules, coated
2951	149	Diphenyloxide-4,4'-disulfohydrazide
2951	149	Diphenyloxide-4,4'-disulphohydrazide
2952	150	Azodiisobutyronitrile
2953	150	2,2'-Azodi-(2,4-dimethylvaleronitrile)
2954	149	1,1'-Azodi-(hexahydrobenzonitrile)
2955	150	2,2'-Azodi-(2,4-dimethyl-4-methoxyvaleronitrile)
2956	149	5-tert-Butyl-2,4,6-trinitro-m-xylene
2956	149	Musk xylene
2965	139	Boron trifluoride dimethyl etherate
2966	153	Thioglycol
2967	154	Sulfamic acid
2967	154	Sulphamic acid
2968	135	Maneb, stabilized
2968	135	Maneb preparation, stabilized
2969	171	Castor beans, meal, pomace or flake
2970	149	Benzene sulfohydrazide
2970	149	Benzene sulphohydrazide
2971	149	Benzene-1,3-disulfohydrazide
2971	149	Benzene-1,3-disulphohydrazide
2972	149	N,N'-Dinitrosopentamethylene tetramine
2973	149	N,N'-Dinitroso-N,N'-dimethyl terephthalamide
2974	164	Radioactive material, special form, n.o.s.
2975	162	Thorium metal, pyrophoric
2976	162	Thorium nitrate, solid
2977	166	Radioactive material, Uranium hexafluoride, fissile
2977	166	Uranium hexafluoride, fissile containing more than 1% Uranium-235
2978	166	Radioactive material, Uranium hexafluoride, non fissile or fissile-excepted
2978	166	Uranium hexafluoride, fissile-excepted
2978	166	Uranium hexafluoride, low specific activity
2978	166	Uranium hexafluoride, non-fissile
2979	162	Uranium metal, pyrophoric
2980	162	Uranyl nitrate, hexahydrate, solution
2981	162	Uranyl nitrate, solid
2982	163	Radioactive material, n.o.s.
2983	129P	Ethylene oxide and Propylene oxide mixture, with not more than 30% Ethylene oxide
2983	129P	Propylene oxide and Ethylene oxide mixture, with not more than 30% Ethylene oxide
2984	140	Hydrogen peroxide, aqueous solution, with not less than 8% but less than 20% Hydrogen peroxide
2985	155	Chlorosilanes, flammable, corrosive, n.o.s.
2985	155	Chlorosilanes, n.o.s.
2986	155	Chlorosilanes, corrosive, flammable, n.o.s.

ID No.	Guide No.	Name of Material
2986	155	Chlorosilanes, n.o.s.
2987	156	Chlorosilanes, corrosive, n.o.s.
2987	156	Chlorosilanes, n.o.s.
2988	139	Chlorosilanes, n.o.s.
2988	139	Chlorosilanes, water-reactive, flammable, corrosive, n.o.s.
2989	133	Lead phosphite, dibasic
2990	171	Aircraft evacuation slides
2990	171	Life-saving appliances, self-inflating
2991	131	Carbamate pesticide, liquid, poisonous, flammable
2991	131	Carbamate pesticide, liquid, toxic, flammable
2992	151	Carbamate pesticide, liquid, poisonous
2992	151	Carbamate pesticide, liquid, toxic
2993	131	Arsenical pesticide, liquid, poisonous, flammable
2993	131	Arsenical pesticide, liquid, toxic, flammable
2994	151	Arsenical pesticide, liquid, poisonous
2994	151	Arsenical pesticide, liquid, toxic
2995	131	Organochlorine pesticide, liquid, poisonous, flammable
2995	131	Organochlorine pesticide, liquid, toxic, flammable
2996	151	Organochlorine pesticide, liquid, poisonous
2996	151	Organochlorine pesticide, liquid, toxic
2997	131	Triazine pesticide, liquid, poisonous, flammable
2997	131	Triazine pesticide, liquid, toxic, flammable
2998	151	Triazine pesticide, liquid, poisonous
2998	151	Triazine pesticide, liquid, toxic
2999	131	Phenoxy pesticide, liquid, poisonous, flammable
2999	131	Phenoxy pesticide, liquid, toxic, flammable
3000	152	Phenoxy pesticide, liquid, poisonous
3000	152	Phenoxy pesticide, liquid, toxic
3001	131	Phenyl urea pesticide, liquid, poisonous, flammable
3001	131	Phenyl urea pesticide, liquid, toxic, flammable
3002	151	Phenyl urea pesticide, liquid, poisonous
3002	151	Phenyl urea pesticide, liquid, toxic
3003	131	Benzoic derivative pesticide, liquid, poisonous, flammable
3003	131	Benzoic derivative pesticide, liquid, toxic, flammable
3004	151	Benzoic derivative pesticide, liquid, poisonous
3004	151	Benzoic derivative pesticide, liquid, toxic
3005	131	Dithiocarbamate pesticide, liquid, poisonous, flammable
3005	131	Dithiocarbamate pesticide, liquid, toxic, flammable
3005	131	Thiocarbamate pesticide, liquid, poisonous, flammable
3005	131	Thiocarbamate pesticide, liquid, toxic, flammable
3006	151	Dithiocarbamate pesticide, liquid, poisonous
3006	151	Dithiocarbamate pesticide, liquid, toxic

ID No.	Guide No.	Name of Material
3006	151	Thiocarbamate pesticide, liquid, poisonous
3006	151	Thiocarbamate pesticide, liquid, toxic
3007	131	Phthalimide derivative pesticide, liquid, poisonous, flammable
3007	131	Phthalimide derivative pesticide, liquid, toxic, flammable
3008	151	Phthalimide derivative pesticide, liquid, poisonous
3008	151	Phthalimide derivative pesticide, liquid, toxic
3009	131	Copper based pesticide, liquid, poisonous, flammable
3009	131	Copper based pesticide, liquid, toxic, flammable
3010	151	Copper based pesticide, liquid, poisonous
3010	151	Copper based pesticide, liquid, toxic
3011	131	Mercury based pesticide, liquid, poisonous, flammable
3011	131	Mercury based pesticide, liquid, toxic, flammable
3012	151	Mercury based pesticide, liquid, poisonous
3012	151	Mercury based pesticide, liquid, toxic
3013	131	Substituted nitrophenol pesticide, liquid, poisonous, flammable
3013	131	Substituted nitrophenol pesticide, liquid, toxic, flammable
3014	153	Substituted nitrophenol pesticide, liquid, poisonous
3014	153	Substituted nitrophenol pesticide, liquid, toxic
3015	131	Bipyridilium pesticide, liquid, poisonous, flammable
3015	131	Bipyridilium pesticide, liquid, toxic, flammable
3016	151	Bipyridilium pesticide, liquid, poisonous
3016	151	Bipyridilium pesticide, liquid, toxic
3017	131	Organophosphorus pesticide, liquid, poisonous, flammable
3017	131	Organophosphorus pesticide, liquid, toxic, flammable
3018	152	Methyl parathion, liquid
3018	152	Organophosphorus pesticide, liquid, poisonous
3018	152	Organophosphorus pesticide, liquid, toxic
3018	152	Tetraethyl pyrophosphate, liquid
3019	131	Organotin pesticide, liquid, poisonous, flammable
3019	131	Organotin pesticide, liquid, toxic, flammable
3020	153	Organotin pesticide, liquid, poisonous
3020	153	Organotin pesticide, liquid, toxic
3021	131	Pesticide, liquid, flammable, poisonous
3021	131	Pesticide, liquid, flammable, toxic
3022	127P	1,2-Butylene oxide, stabilized
3023	131	2-Methyl-2-hepthanethiol
3023	131	tert-Octyl mercaptan
3024	131	Coumarin derivative pesticide, liquid, flammable, poisonous

ID No.	Guide No.	Name of Material
3024	131	Coumarin derivative pesticide, liquid, flammable, toxic
3025	131	Coumarin derivative pesticide, liquid, poisonous, flammable
3025	131	Coumarin derivative pesticide, liquid, toxic, flammable
3026	151	Coumarin derivative pesticide, liquid, poisonous
3026	151	Coumarin derivative pesticide, liquid, toxic
3027	151	Coumarin derivative pesticide, solid, poisonous
3027	151	Coumarin derivative pesticide, solid, toxic
3028	154	Batteries, dry, containing Potassium hydroxide, solid
3030	150	2,2'-Azodi-(2-methyl-butyronitrile)
3031	149	Self-reactive substances, samples, n.o.s.
3032	149	Self-reactive substances, trial quantities, n.o.s.
3033	149	3-Chloro-4-diethylamino-benzenediazonium zinc chloride
3034	149	4-Dipropylaminobenzene-diazonium zinc chloride
3035	150	3-(2-Hydroxyethoxy)-4-pyrrolidin-1-yl benzene-diazonium zinc chloride
3036	150	2,5-Diethoxy-4-morpholino-benzenediazonium zinc chloride
3037	149	4-[Benzyl(ethyl)amino]-3-ethoxybenzenediazonium zinc chloride
3038	150	4-[Benzyl(methyl)amino]-3-ethoxybenzenediazonium zinc chloride
3039	150	4-Dimethylamino-6-(2-dimethyl-aminoethoxy)toluene-2-diazonium zinc chloride
3040	149	Sodium 2-diazo-1-naphthol-4-sulfonate
3040	149	Sodium 2-diazo-1-naphthol-4-sulphonate
3041	149	Sodium 2-diazo-1-naphthol-5-sulfonate
3041	149	Sodium 2-diazo-1-naphthol-5-sulphonate
3042	149	2-Diazo-1-naphthol-4-sulfochloride
3042	149	2-Diazo-1-naphthol-4-sulphochloride
3043	149	2-Diazo-1-naphthol-5-sulfochloride
3043	149	2-Diazo-1-naphthol-5-sulphochloride
3048	157	Aluminum phosphide pesticide
3049	138	Metal alkyl halides, n.o.s.
3049	138	Metal alkyl halides, water-reactive, n.o.s.
3049	138	Metal aryl halides, n.o.s.
3049	138	Metal aryl halides, water-reactive, n.o.s.
3050	138	Metal alkyl hydrides, n.o.s.
3050	138	Metal alkyl hydrides, water-reactive, n.o.s.
3050	138	Metal aryl hydrides, n.o.s.
3050	138	Metal aryl hydrides, water-reactive, n.o.s.
3051	135	Aluminum alkyls
3052	135	Aluminum alkyl halides
3053	135	Magnesium alkyls
3054	131	Cyclohexanethiol

ID No.	Guide No.	Name of Material
3054	131	Cyclohexyl mercaptan
3055	154	2-(2-Aminoethoxy)ethanol
3056	129	n-Heptaldehyde
3057	125	Trifluoroacetyl chloride
3064	127	Nitroglycerin, solution in alcohol, with more than 1% but not more than 5% Nitroglycerin
3065	127	Alcoholic beverages
3066	153	Paint (corrosive)
3066	153	Paint related material (corrosive)
3070	126	Dichlorodifluoromethane and Ethylene oxide mixture, with not more than 12.5% Ethylene oxide
3070	126	Dichlorodifluoromethane and Ethylene oxide mixtures, with not more than 12% Ethylene oxide
3070	126	Ethylene oxide and Dichlorodifluoromethane mixture, with not more than 12.5% Ethylene oxide
3070	126	Ethylene oxide and Dichlorodifluoromethane mixtures, with not more than 12% Ethylene oxide
3071	131	Mercaptan mixture, liquid, poisonous, flammable, n.o.s.
3071	131	Mercaptan mixture, liquid, toxic, flammable, n.o.s.
3071	131	Mercaptan mixtures, liquid, n.o.s.
3071	131	Mercaptans, liquid, n.o.s.
3071	131	Mercaptans, liquid, poisonous, flammable, n.o.s.
3071	131	Mercaptans, liquid, toxic, flammable, n.o.s.
3072	171	Aircraft survival kits
3072	171	Life-saving appliances, not self-inflating
3073	131P	Vinylpyridines, inhibited
3076	138	Aluminum alkyl hydrides
3077	171	Environmentally hazardous substances, solid, n.o.s.
3077	171	Hazardous waste, solid, n.o.s.
3077	171	Other regulated substances, solid, n.o.s.
3078	138	Cerium, turnings or gritty powder
3079	131P	Methacrylonitrile, inhibited
3080	155	Isocyanate solution, poisonous, flammable, n.o.s.
3080	155	Isocyanate solution, toxic, flammable, n.o.s.
3080	155	Isocyanate solutions, n.o.s.
3080	155	Isocyanates, n.o.s.
3080	155	Isocyanates, poisonous, flammable, n.o.s.
3080	155	Isocyanates, toxic, flammable, n.o.s.
3082	171	Environmentally hazardous substances, liquid, n.o.s.
3082	171	Hazardous waste, liquid, n.o.s.
3082	171	Other regulated substances, liquid, n.o.s.
3083	124	Perchloryl fluoride
3084	140	Corrosive solid, oxidizing, n.o.s.
3085	140	Oxidizing solid, corrosive, n.o.s.
3085	140	Oxidizing substances, solid, corrosive, n.o.s.
3086	141	Poisonous solid, oxidizing, n.o.s.
3086	141	Toxic solid, oxidizing, n.o.s.

ID No.	Guide No.	Name of Material	ID No.	Guide No.	Name of Material
3087	141	Oxidizing solid, poisonous, n.o.s.	3099	142	Oxidizing liquid, toxic, n.o.s.
3087	141	Oxidizing solid, toxic, n.o.s.	3099	142	Oxidizing substances, liquid, poisonous, n.o.s.
3087	141	Oxidizing substances, solid, poisonous, n.o.s.	3099	142	Oxidizing substances, liquid, toxic, n.o.s.
3087	141	Oxidizing substances, solid, toxic, n.o.s.	3100	135	Oxidizing solid, self-heating, n.o.s.
3088	135	Self-heating solid, organic, n.o.s.	3100	135	Oxidizing substances, self-heating, n.o.s.
3088	135	Self-heating substances, solid, n.o.s.	3100	135	Oxidizing substances, solid, self-heating, n.o.s.
3089	170	Metal powder, flammable, n.o.s.	3101	146	Organic peroxide type B, liquid
3090	138	Lithium batteries	3102	146	Organic peroxide type B, solid
3090	138	Lithium batteries, liquid or solid cathode	3103	146	Organic peroxide type C, liquid
3091	138	Lithium batteries contained in equipment	3104	146	Organic peroxide type C, solid
3091	138	Lithium batteries packed with equipment	3105	145	Organic peroxide type D, liquid
			3106	145	Organic peroxide type D, solid
3092	129	1-Methoxy-2-propanol	3107	145	Organic peroxide type E, liquid
3093	140	Corrosive liquid, oxidizing, n.o.s.	3108	145	Organic peroxide type E, solid
3094	138	Corrosive liquid, water-reactive, n.o.s.	3109	145	Organic peroxide type F, liquid
3094	138	Corrosive liquid, which in contact with water emits flammable gases, n.o.s.	3110	145	Organic peroxide type F, solid
			3111	148	Organic peroxide type B, liquid, temperature controlled
3095	136	Corrosive solid, self-heating, n.o.s.	3112	148	Organic peroxide type B, solid, temperature controlled
3096	138	Corrosive solid, water-reactive, n.o.s.	3113	148	Organic peroxide type C, liquid, temperature controlled
3096	138	Corrosive solid, which in contact with water emits flammable gases, n.o.s.	3114	148	Organic peroxide type C, solid, temperature controlled
			3115	148	Organic peroxide type D, liquid, temperature controlled
3097	140	Flammable solid, oxidizing, n.o.s.	3116	148	Organic peroxide type D, solid, temperature controlled
3098	140	Oxidizing liquid, corrosive, n.o.s.			
3098	140	Oxidizing substances, liquid, corrosive, n.o.s.	3117	148	Organic peroxide type E, liquid, temperature controlled
3099	142	Oxidizing liquid, poisonous, n.o.s.			

ID No.	Guide No.	Name of Material
3118	148	Organic peroxide type E, solid, temperature controlled
3119	148	Organic peroxide type F, liquid, temperature controlled
3120	148	Organic peroxide type F, solid, temperature controlled
3121	144	Oxidizing solid, water-reactive, n.o.s.
3121	144	Oxidizing substances, solid, which in contact with water emit flammable gases, n.o.s.
3122	142	Poisonous liquid, oxidizing, n.o.s.
3122	142	Poisonous liquid, oxidizing, n.o.s. (Inhalation Hazard Zone A)
3122	142	Poisonous liquid, oxidizing, n.o.s. (Inhalation Hazard Zone B)
3122	142	Toxic liquid, oxidizing, n.o.s.
3122	142	Toxic liquid, oxidizing, n.o.s. (Inhalation Hazard Zone A)
3122	142	Toxic liquid, oxidizing, n.o.s. (Inhalation Hazard Zone B)
3123	139	Poisonous liquid, water-reactive, n.o.s.
3123	139	Poisonous liquid, water-reactive, n.o.s. (Inhalation Hazard Zone A)
3123	139	Poisonous liquid, water-reactive, n.o.s. (Inhalation Hazard Zone B)
3123	139	Poisonous liquid, which in contact with water emits flammable gases, n.o.s.
3123	139	Poisonous liquid, which in contact with water emits flammable gases, n.o.s. (Inhalation Hazard Zone A)
3123	139	Poisonous liquid, which in contact with water emits flammable gases, n.o.s. (Inhalation Hazard Zone B)
3123	139	Toxic liquid, water-reactive, n.o.s.
3123	139	Toxic liquid, water-reactive, n.o.s. (Inhalation Hazard Zone A)
3123	139	Toxic liquid, water-reactive, n.o.s. (Inhalation Hazard Zone B)
3123	139	Toxic liquid, which in contact with water emits flammable gases, n.o.s.
3123	139	Toxic liquid, which in contact with water emits flammable gases, n.o.s. (Inhalation Hazard Zone A)
3123	139	Toxic liquid, which in contact with water emits flammable gases, n.o.s. (Inhalation Hazard Zone B)
3124	136	Poisonous solid, self-heating, n.o.s.
3124	136	Toxic solid, self-heating, n.o.s.
3125	139	Poisonous solid, water-reactive, n.o.s.
3125	139	Poisonous solid, which in contact with water emits flammable gases, n.o.s.
3125	139	Toxic solid, water-reactive, n.o.s.
3125	139	Toxic solid, which in contact with water emits flammable gases, n.o.s.
3126	136	Self-heating solid, corrosive, organic, n.o.s.

ID No.	Guide No.	Name of Material	ID No.	Guide No.	Name of Material
3126	136	Self-heating substance, solid, corrosive, n.o.s.	3130	139	Water-reactive substances, liquid, toxic, n.o.s.
3127	135	Self-heating solid, oxidizing, n.o.s.	3131	138	Substances, which in contact with water emit flammable gases, solid, corrosive, n.o.s.
3127	135	Self-heating substances, solid, oxidizing, n.o.s.	3131	138	Water-reactive solid, corrosive, n.o.s.
3128	136	Self-heating solid, organic, poisonous, n.o.s.	3131	138	Water-reactive substances, solid, corrosive, n.o.s.
3128	136	Self-heating solid, organic, toxic, n.o.s.	3132	138	Substances, which in contact with water emit flammable gases, solid, flammable, n.o.s.
3128	136	Self-heating solid, poisonous, organic, n.o.s.			
3128	136	Self-heating solid, toxic, organic, n.o.s.	3132	138	Water-reactive solid, flammable, n.o.s.
3128	136	Self-heating substances, solid, poisonous, n.o.s.	3132	138	Water-reactive substances, solid, flammable, n.o.s.
3128	136	Self-heating substances, solid, toxic, n.o.s.	3133	138	Substances, which in contact with water emit flammable gases, solid, oxidizing, n.o.s.
3129	138	Substances, which in contact with water emit flammable gases, liquid, corrosive, n.o.s.	3133	138	Water-reactive solid, oxidizing, n.o.s.
3129	138	Water-reactive liquid, corrosive, n.o.s.	3133	138	Water-reactive substances, solid, oxidizing, n.o.s.
3129	138	Water-reactive substances, liquid, corrosive, n.o.s.	3134	139	Substances, which in contact with water emit flammable gases, solid, poisonous, n.o.s.
3130	139	Substances, which in contact with water emit flammable gases, liquid, poisonous, n.o.s.	3134	139	Substances, which in contact with water emit flammable gases, solid, toxic, n.o.s.
3130	139	Substances, which in contact with water emit flammable gases, liquid, toxic, n.o.s.	3134	139	Water-reactive solid, poisonous, n.o.s.
3130	139	Water-reactive liquid, poisonous, n.o.s.	3134	139	Water-reactive solid, toxic, n.o.s.
3130	139	Water-reactive liquid, toxic, n.o.s.	3134	139	Water-reactive substances, solid, poisonous, n.o.s.
3130	139	Water-reactive substances, liquid, poisonous, n.o.s.	3134	139	Water-reactive substances, solid, toxic, n.o.s.

ID No.	Guide No.	Name of Material	ID No.	Guide No.	Name of Material
3135	138	Substances, which in contact with water emit flammable gases, solid, self-heating, n.o.s.	3141	157	Antimony compound, inorganic, liquid, n.o.s.
3135	138	Water-reactive solid, self-heating, n.o.s.	3142	151	Disinfectant, liquid, poisonous, n.o.s.
3135	138	Water-reactive substances, solid, self-heating, n.o.s.	3142	151	Disinfectant, liquid, toxic, n.o.s.
3136	120	Trifluoromethane, refrigerated liquid	3142	151	Disinfectants, liquid, n.o.s. (poisonous)
3137	140	Oxidizing solid, flammable, n.o.s.	3143	151	Dye, solid, poisonous, n.o.s.
3137	140	Oxidizing substances, solid, flammable, n.o.s.	3143	151	Dye, solid, toxic, n.o.s.
			3143	151	Dye intermediate, solid, poisonous, n.o.s.
3138	116	Acetylene, Ethylene and Propylene in mixture, refrigerated liquid containing at least 71.5% Ethylene with not more than 22.5% Acetylene and not more than 6% Propylene	3143	151	Dye intermediate, solid, toxic, n.o.s.
			3144	151	Nicotine compound, liquid, n.o.s.
			3144	151	Nicotine preparation, liquid, n.o.s.
3138	116	Ethylene, Acetylene and Propylene in mixture, refrigerated liquid containing at least 71.5% Ethylene with not more than 22.5% Acetylene and not more than 6% Propylene	3145	153	Alkyl phenols, liquid, n.o.s. (including C2-C12 homologues)
			3146	153	Organotin compound, solid, n.o.s.
			3147	154	Dye, solid, corrosive, n.o.s.
3138	116	Propylene, Ethylene and Acetylene in mixture, refrigerated liquid containing at least 71.5% Ethylene with not more than 22.5% Acetylene and not more than 6% Propylene	3147	154	Dye intermediate, solid, corrosive, n.o.s.
			3148	138	Substances, which in contact with water emit flammable gases, liquid, n.o.s.
			3148	138	Water-reactive liquid, n.o.s.
3139	140	Oxidizing liquid, n.o.s.	3148	138	Water-reactive substances, liquid, n.o.s.
3139	140	Oxidizing substances, liquid, n.o.s.	3149	140	Hydrogen peroxide and Peroxyacetic acid mixture, with acid(s), water and not more than 5% Peroxyacetic acid, stabilized
3140	151	Alkaloids, liquid, n.o.s. (poisonous)			
3140	151	Alkaloid salts, liquid, n.o.s. (poisonous)	3150	115	Devices, small, hydrocarbon gas powered, with release device

ID No.	Guide No.	Name of Material
3150	115	Hydrocarbon gas refills for small devices, with release device
3151	171	Polyhalogenated biphenyls, liquid
3151	171	Polyhalogenated terphenyls, liquid
3152	171	Polyhalogenated biphenyls, solid
3152	171	Polyhalogenated terphenyls, solid
3153	115	Perfluoromethyl vinyl ether
3153	115	Perfluoro(methyl vinyl ether)
3154	115	Perfluoroethyl vinyl ether
3154	115	Perfluoro(ethyl vinyl ether)
3155	154	Pentachlorophenol
3156	122	Compressed gas, oxidizing, n.o.s.
3157	122	Liquefied gas, oxidizing, n.o.s.
3158	120	Gas, refrigerated liquid, n.o.s.
3159	126	Refrigerant gas R-134a
3159	126	1,1,1,2-Tetrafluoroethane
3160	119	Liquefied gas, poisonous, flammable, n.o.s.
3160	119	Liquefied gas, poisonous, flammable, n.o.s. (Inhalation Hazard Zone A)
3160	119	Liquefied gas, poisonous, flammable, n.o.s. (Inhalation Hazard Zone B)
3160	119	Liquefied gas, poisonous, flammable, n.o.s. (Inhalation Hazard Zone C)
3160	119	Liquefied gas, poisonous, flammable, n.o.s. (Inhalation Hazard Zone D)
3160	119	Liquefied gas, toxic, flammable, n.o.s.
3160	119	Liquefied gas, toxic, flammable, n.o.s. (Inhalation Hazard Zone A)
3160	119	Liquefied gas, toxic, flammable, n.o.s. (Inhalation Hazard Zone B)
3160	119	Liquefied gas, toxic, flammable, n.o.s. (Inhalation Hazard Zone C)
3160	119	Liquefied gas, toxic, flammable, n.o.s. (Inhalation Hazard Zone D)
3161	115	Liquefied gas, flammable, n.o.s.
3162	123	Liquefied gas, poisonous, n.o.s.
3162	123	Liquefied gas, poisonous, n.o.s. (Inhalation Hazard Zone A)
3162	123	Liquefied gas, poisonous, n.o.s. (Inhalation Hazard Zone B)
3162	123	Liquefied gas, poisonous, n.o.s. (Inhalation Hazard Zone C)
3162	123	Liquefied gas, poisonous, n.o.s. (Inhalation Hazard Zone D)
3162	123	Liquefied gas, toxic, n.o.s.
3162	123	Liquefied gas, toxic, n.o.s. (Inhalation Hazard Zone A)
3162	123	Liquefied gas, toxic, n.o.s. (Inhalation Hazard Zone B)
3162	123	Liquefied gas, toxic, n.o.s. (Inhalation Hazard Zone C)
3162	123	Liquefied gas, toxic, n.o.s. (Inhalation Hazard Zone D)
3163	126	Liquefied gas, n.o.s.
3164	126	Articles, pressurized, hydraulic (containing non-flammable gas)
3164	126	Articles, pressurized, pneumatic (containing non-flammable gas)

ID No.	Guide No.	Name of Material
3165	131	Aircraft hydraulic power unit fuel tank
3166	128	Engines, internal combustion, flammable gas powered
3166	128	Engines, internal combustion, flammable liquid powered
3166	128	Engines, internal combustion, including when fitted in machinery or vehicles
3166	128	Vehicle, flammable gas powered
3166	128	Vehicle, flammable liquid powered
3167	115	Gas sample, non-pressurized, flammable, n.o.s., not refrigerated liquid
3168	119	Gas sample, non-pressurized, poisonous, flammable, n.o.s., not refrigerated liquid
3168	119	Gas sample, non-pressurized, toxic, flammable, n.o.s., not refrigerated liquid
3169	123	Gas sample, non-pressurized, poisonous, n.o.s., not refrigerated liquid
3169	123	Gas sample, non-pressurized, toxic, n.o.s., not refrigerated liquid
3170	138	Aluminum dross
3170	138	Aluminum processing by-products
3170	138	Aluminum remelting by-products
3170	138	Aluminum smelting by-products
3171	154	Battery-powered equipment (wet battery)
3171	154	Battery-powered vehicle (wet battery)
3171	154	Wheelchair, electric, with batteries
3172	153	Toxins, extracted from living sources, liquid, n.o.s.
3172	153	Toxins, extracted from living sources, n.o.s.
3172	153	Toxins, extracted from living sources, solid, n.o.s.
3174	135	Titanium disulfide
3174	135	Titanium disulphide
3175	133	Solids containing flammable liquid, n.o.s.
3176	133	Flammable solid, organic, molten, n.o.s.
3178	133	Flammable solid, inorganic, n.o.s.
3178	133	Smokeless powder for small arms
3179	134	Flammable solid, poisonous, inorganic, n.o.s.
3179	134	Flammable solid, toxic, inorganic, n.o.s.
3180	134	Flammable solid, corrosive, inorganic, n.o.s.
3180	134	Flammable solid, inorganic, corrosive, n.o.s.
3181	133	Metal salts of organic compounds, flammable, n.o.s.
3182	170	Metal hydrides, flammable, n.o.s.
3183	135	Self-heating liquid, organic, n.o.s.
3184	136	Self-heating liquid, poisonous, organic, n.o.s.
3184	136	Self-heating liquid, toxic, organic, n.o.s.
3185	136	Self-heating liquid, corrosive, organic, n.o.s.
3186	135	Self-heating liquid, inorganic, n.o.s.
3187	136	Self-heating liquid, poisonous, inorganic, n.o.s.

ID No.	Guide No.	Name of Material
3187	136	Self-heating liquid, toxic, inorganic, n.o.s.
3188	136	Self-heating liquid, corrosive, inorganic, n.o.s.
3189	135	Metal powder, self-heating, n.o.s.
3189	135	Self-heating metal powders, n.o.s.
3190	135	Self-heating solid, inorganic, n.o.s.
3191	136	Self-heating solid, inorganic, poisonous, n.o.s.
3191	136	Self-heating solid, inorganic, toxic, n.o.s.
3191	136	Self-heating solid, poisonous, inorganic, n.o.s.
3191	136	Self-heating solid, toxic, inorganic, n.o.s.
3192	136	Self-heating solid, corrosive, inorganic, n.o.s.
3194	135	Pyrophoric liquid, inorganic, n.o.s.
3200	135	Pyrophoric solid, inorganic, n.o.s.
3203	135	Pyrophoric organometallic compound, n.o.s.
3203	135	Pyrophoric organometallic compound, water-reactive, n.o.s.
3205	135	Alkaline earth metal alcoholates, n.o.s.
3206	136	Alkali metal alcoholates, self-heating, corrosive, n.o.s.
3207	138	Organometallic compound, water-reactive, flammable, n.o.s.
3207	138	Organometallic compound dispersion, water-reactive, flammable, n.o.s.
3207	138	Organometallic compound solution, water-reactive, flammable, n.o.s.
3208	138	Metallic substance, water-reactive, n.o.s.
3209	138	Metallic substance, water-reactive, self-heating, n.o.s.
3210	140	Chlorates, inorganic, aqueous solution, n.o.s.
3211	140	Perchlorates, inorganic, aqueous solution, n.o.s.
3212	140	Hypochlorites, inorganic, n.o.s.
3213	140	Bromates, inorganic, aqueous solution, n.o.s.
3214	140	Permanganates, inorganic, aqueous solution, n.o.s.
3215	140	Persulfates, inorganic, n.o.s.
3215	140	Persulphates, inorganic, n.o.s.
3216	140	Persulfates, inorganic, aqueous solution, n.o.s.
3216	140	Persulphates, inorganic, aqueous solution, n.o.s.
3217	140	Percarbonates, inorganic, n.o.s.
3218	140	Nitrates, inorganic, aqueous solution, n.o.s.
3219	140	Nitrites, inorganic, aqueous solution, n.o.s.
3220	126	Pentafluoroethane
3220	126	Refrigerant gas R-125
3221	149	Self-reactive liquid type B
3222	149	Self-reactive solid type B
3223	149	Self-reactive liquid type C
3224	149	Self-reactive solid type C
3225	149	Self-reactive liquid type D
3226	149	Self-reactive solid type D
3227	149	Self-reactive liquid type E
3228	149	Self-reactive solid type E
3229	149	Self-reactive liquid type F

ID No.	Guide No.	Name of Material
3230	149	Self-reactive solid type F
3231	150	Self-reactive liquid type B, temperature controlled
3232	150	Self-reactive solid type B, temperature controlled
3233	150	Self-reactive liquid type C, temperature controlled
3234	150	Self-reactive solid type C, temperature controlled
3235	150	Self-reactive liquid type D, temperature controlled
3236	150	Self-reactive solid type D, temperature controlled
3237	150	Self-reactive liquid type E, temperature controlled
3238	150	Self-reactive solid type E, temperature controlled
3239	150	Self-reactive liquid type F, temperature controlled
3240	150	Self-reactive solid type F, temperature controlled
3241	133	2-Bromo-2-nitropropane-1,3-diol
3242	149	Azodicarbonamide
3243	151	Solids containing poisonous liquid, n.o.s.
3243	151	Solids containing toxic liquid, n.o.s.
3244	154	Solids containing corrosive liquid, n.o.s.
3245	171	Genetically modified micro-organisms
3246	156	Methanesulfonyl chloride
3246	156	Methanesulphonyl chloride
3247	140	Sodium peroxoborate, anhydrous
3248	131	Medicine, liquid, flammable, poisonous, n.o.s.
3248	131	Medicine, liquid, flammable, toxic, n.o.s.
3249	151	Medicine, solid, poisonous, n.o.s.
3249	151	Medicine, solid, toxic, n.o.s.
3250	153	Chloroacetic acid, molten
3251	133	Isosorbide-5-mononitrate
3252	115	Difluoromethane
3252	115	Refrigerant gas R-32
3253	154	Disodium trioxosilicate
3253	154	Disodium trioxosilicate, pentahydrate
3254	135	Tributylphosphane
3254	135	Tributylphosphine
3255	135	tert-Butyl hypochlorite
3256	128	Elevated temperature liquid, flammable, n.o.s., with flash point above 37.8°C (100°F), at or above its flash point
3256	128	Elevated temperature liquid, flammable, n.o.s., with flash point above 60.5°C (141°F), at or above its flash point
3257	128	Elevated temperature liquid, n.o.s., at or above 100°C (212°F) and below its flash point
3258	171	Elevated temperature solid, n.o.s., at or above 240°C (464°F)
3259	154	Amines, solid, corrosive, n.o.s.
3259	154	Polyamines, solid, corrosive, n.o.s.
3260	154	Corrosive solid, acidic, inorganic, n.o.s.
3261	154	Corrosive solid, acidic, organic, n.o.s.
3262	154	Corrosive solid, basic, inorganic, n.o.s.

3263 **154** Corrosive solid, basic, organic, n.o.s.

3264 **154** Corrosive liquid, acidic, inorganic, n.o.s.

3265 **153** Corrosive liquid, acidic, organic, n.o.s.

3266 **154** Corrosive liquid, basic, inorganic, n.o.s.

3267 **153** Corrosive liquid, basic, organic, n.o.s.

3268 **171** Air bag inflators

3268 **171** Air bag inflators, pyrotechnic

3268 **171** Air bag modules

3268 **171** Air bag modules, pyrotechnic

3268 **171** Seat-belt modules

3268 **171** Seat-belt pre-tensioners

3268 **171** Seat-belt pre-tensioners, pyrotechnic

3269 **127** Polyester resin kit

3270 **133** Nitrocellulose membrane filters

3271 **127** Ethers, n.o.s.

3272 **127** Esters, n.o.s.

3273 **131** Nitriles, flammable, poisonous, n.o.s.

3273 **131** Nitriles, flammable, toxic, n.o.s.

3274 **127** Alcoholates solution, n.o.s., in alcohol

3275 **131** Nitriles, poisonous, flammable, n.o.s.

3275 **131** Nitriles, toxic, flammable, n.o.s.

3276 **151** Nitriles, poisonous, n.o.s.

3276 **151** Nitriles, toxic, n.o.s.

3277 **154** Chloroformates, poisonous, corrosive, n.o.s.

3277 **154** Chloroformates, toxic, corrosive, n.o.s.

3278 **151** Organophosphorus compound, poisonous, n.o.s.

3278 **151** Organophosphorus compound, toxic, n.o.s.

3279 **131** Organophosphorus compound, poisonous, flammable, n.o.s.

3279 **131** Organophosphorus compound, toxic, flammable, n.o.s.

3280 **151** Organoarsenic compound, n.o.s.

3281 **151** Metal carbonyls, n.o.s.

3282 **151** Organometallic compound, poisonous, n.o.s.

3282 **151** Organometallic compound, toxic, n.o.s.

3283 **151** Selenium compound, n.o.s.

3284 **151** Tellurium compound, n.o.s.

3285 **151** Vanadium compound, n.o.s.

3286 **131** Flammable liquid, poisonous, corrosive, n.o.s.

3286 **131** Flammable liquid, toxic, corrosive, n.o.s.

3287 **151** Poisonous liquid, inorganic, n.o.s.

3287 **151** Poisonous liquid, inorganic, n.o.s. (Inhalation Hazard Zone A)

3287 **151** Poisonous liquid, inorganic, n.o.s. (Inhalation Hazard Zone B)

3287 **151** Toxic liquid, inorganic, n.o.s.

3287 **151** Toxic liquid, inorganic, n.o.s. (Inhalation Hazard Zone A)

3287 **151** Toxic liquid, inorganic, n.o.s. (Inhalation Hazard Zone B)

3288 **151** Poisonous solid, inorganic, n.o.s.

3288 **151** Toxic solid, inorganic, n.o.s.

ID No.	Guide No.	Name of Material
3289	154	Poisonous liquid, corrosive, inorganic, n.o.s.
3289	154	Poisonous liquid, corrosive, inorganic, n.o.s. (Inhalation Hazard Zone A)
3289	154	Poisonous liquid, corrosive, inorganic, n.o.s. (Inhalation Hazard Zone B)
3289	154	Toxic liquid, corrosive, inorganic, n.o.s.
3289	154	Toxic liquid, corrosive, inorganic, n.o.s. (Inhalation Hazard Zone A)
3289	154	Toxic liquid, corrosive, inorganic, n.o.s. (Inhalation Hazard Zone B)
3290	154	Poisonous solid, corrosive, inorganic, n.o.s.
3290	154	Toxic solid, corrosive, inorganic, n.o.s.
3291	158	(Bio)Medical waste, n.o.s.
3291	158	Clinical waste, unspecified, n.o.s.
3291	158	Medical waste, n.o.s.
3291	158	Regulated medical waste, n.o.s.
3292	138	Batteries, containing Sodium
3292	138	Cells, containing Sodium
3293	152	Hydrazine, aqueous solution, with not more than 37% Hydrazine
3294	131	Hydrogen cyanide, solution in alcohol, with not more than 45% Hydrogen cyanide
3295	128	Hydrocarbons, liquid, n.o.s.
3296	126	Heptafluoropropane
3296	126	Refrigerant gas R-227
3297	126	Chlorotetrafluoroethane and Ethylene oxide mixture, with not more than 8.8% Ethylene oxide
3297	126	Ethylene oxide and Chlorotetrafluoroethane mixture, with not more than 8.8% Ethylene oxide
3298	126	Ethylene oxide and Pentafluoroethane mixture, with not more than 7.9% Ethylene oxide
3298	126	Pentafluoroethane and Ethylene oxide mixture, with not more than 7.9% Ethylene oxide
3299	126	Ethylene oxide and Tetrafluoroethane mixture, with not more than 5.6% Ethylene oxide
3299	126	Tetrafluoroethane and Ethylene oxide mixture, with not more than 5.6% Ethylene oxide
3300	119P	Carbon dioxide and Ethylene oxide mixture, with more than 87% Ethylene oxide
3300	119P	Ethylene oxide and Carbon dioxide mixture, with more than 87% Ethylene oxide
3301	136	Corrosive liquid, self-heating, n.o.s.
3302	152	2-Dimethylaminoethyl acrylate
3303	124	Compressed gas, poisonous, oxidizing, n.o.s.
3303	124	Compressed gas, poisonous, oxidizing, n.o.s. (Inhalation Hazard Zone A)
3303	124	Compressed gas, poisonous, oxidizing, n.o.s. (Inhalation Hazard Zone B)

ID No.	Guide No.	Name of Material
3303	124	Compressed gas, poisonous, oxidizing, n.o.s. (Inhalation Hazard Zone C)
3303	124	Compressed gas, poisonous, oxidizing, n.o.s. (Inhalation Hazard Zone D)
3303	124	Compressed gas, toxic, oxidizing, n.o.s.
3303	124	Compressed gas, toxic, oxidizing, n.o.s. (Inhalation Hazard Zone A)
3303	124	Compressed gas, toxic, oxidizing, n.o.s. (Inhalation Hazard Zone B)
3303	124	Compressed gas, toxic, oxidizing, n.o.s. (Inhalation Hazard Zone C)
3303	124	Compressed gas, toxic, oxidizing, n.o.s. (Inhalation Hazard Zone D)
3304	123	Compressed gas, poisonous, corrosive, n.o.s.
3304	123	Compressed gas, poisonous, corrosive, n.o.s. (Inhalation Hazard Zone A)
3304	123	Compressed gas, poisonous, corrosive, n.o.s. (Inhalation Hazard Zone B)
3304	123	Compressed gas, poisonous, corrosive, n.o.s. (Inhalation Hazard Zone C)
3304	123	Compressed gas, poisonous, corrosive, n.o.s. (Inhalation Hazard Zone D)
3304	123	Compressed gas, toxic, corrosive, n.o.s.
3304	123	Compressed gas, toxic, corrosive, n.o.s. (Inhalation Hazard Zone A)
3304	123	Compressed gas, toxic, corrosive, n.o.s. (Inhalation Hazard Zone B)
3304	123	Compressed gas, toxic, corrosive, n.o.s. (Inhalation Hazard Zone C)
3304	123	Compressed gas, toxic, corrosive, n.o.s. (Inhalation Hazard Zone D)
3305	119	Compressed gas, poisonous, flammable, corrosive, n.o.s.
3305	119	Compressed gas, poisonous, flammable, corrosive, n.o.s. (Inhalation Hazard Zone A)
3305	119	Compressed gas, poisonous, flammable, corrosive, n.o.s. (Inhalation Hazard Zone B)
3305	119	Compressed gas, poisonous, flammable, corrosive, n.o.s. (Inhalation Hazard Zone C)
3305	119	Compressed gas, poisonous, flammable, corrosive, n.o.s. (Inhalation Hazard Zone D)
3305	119	Compressed gas, toxic, flammable, corrosive, n.o.s.
3305	119	Compressed gas, toxic, flammable, corrosive, n.o.s. (Inhalation Hazard Zone A)
3305	119	Compressed gas, toxic, flammable, corrosive, n.o.s. (Inhalation Hazard Zone B)
3305	119	Compressed gas, toxic, flammable, corrosive, n.o.s. (Inhalation Hazard Zone C)
3305	119	Compressed gas, toxic, flammable, corrosive, n.o.s. (Inhalation Hazard Zone D)
3306	124	Compressed gas, poisonous, oxidizing, corrosive, n.o.s.

ID No.	Guide No.	Name of Material
3306	124	Compressed gas, poisonous, oxidizing, corrosive, n.o.s. (Inhalation Hazard Zone A)
3306	124	Compressed gas, poisonous, oxidizing, corrosive, n.o.s. (Inhalation Hazard Zone B)
3306	124	Compressed gas, poisonous, oxidizing, corrosive, n.o.s. (Inhalation Hazard Zone C)
3306	124	Compressed gas, poisonous, oxidizing, corrosive, n.o.s. (Inhalation Hazard Zone D)
3306	124	Compressed gas, toxic, oxidizing, corrosive, n.o.s.
3306	124	Compressed gas, toxic, oxidizing, corrosive, n.o.s. (Inhalation Hazard Zone A)
3306	124	Compressed gas, toxic, oxidizing, corrosive, n.o.s. (Inhalation Hazard Zone B)
3306	124	Compressed gas, toxic, oxidizing, corrosive, n.o.s. (Inhalation Hazard Zone C)
3306	124	Compressed gas, toxic, oxidizing, corrosive, n.o.s. (Inhalation Hazard Zone D)
3307	124	Liquefied gas, poisonous, oxidizing, n.o.s.
3307	124	Liquefied gas, poisonous, oxidizing, n.o.s. (Inhalation Hazard Zone A)
3307	124	Liquefied gas, poisonous, oxidizing, n.o.s. (Inhalation Hazard Zone B)
3307	124	Liquefied gas, poisonous, oxidizing, n.o.s. (Inhalation Hazard Zone C)
3307	124	Liquefied gas, poisonous, oxidizing, n.o.s. (Inhalation Hazard Zone D)
3307	124	Liquefied gas, toxic, oxidizing, n.o.s.
3307	124	Liquefied gas, toxic, oxidizing, n.o.s. (Inhalation Hazard Zone A)
3307	124	Liquefied gas, toxic, oxidizing, n.o.s. (Inhalation Hazard Zone B)
3307	124	Liquefied gas, toxic, oxidizing, n.o.s. (Inhalation Hazard Zone C)
3307	124	Liquefied gas, toxic, oxidizing, n.o.s. (Inhalation Hazard Zone D)
3308	123	Liquefied gas, poisonous, corrosive, n.o.s.
3308	123	Liquefied gas, poisonous, corrosive, n.o.s. (Inhalation Hazard Zone A)
3308	123	Liquefied gas, poisonous, corrosive, n.o.s. (Inhalation Hazard Zone B)
3308	123	Liquefied gas, poisonous, corrosive, n.o.s. (Inhalation Hazard Zone C)
3308	123	Liquefied gas, poisonous, corrosive, n.o.s. (Inhalation Hazard Zone D)
3308	123	Liquefied gas, toxic, corrosive, n.o.s.
3308	123	Liquefied gas, toxic, corrosive, n.o.s. (Inhalation Hazard Zone A)
3308	123	Liquefied gas, toxic, corrosive, n.o.s. (Inhalation Hazard Zone B)
3308	123	Liquefied gas, toxic, corrosive, n.o.s. (Inhalation Hazard Zone C)

ID No.	Guide No.	Name of Material
3308	123	Liquefied gas, toxic, corrosive, n.o.s. (Inhalation Hazard Zone D)
3309	119	Liquefied gas, poisonous, flammable, corrosive, n.o.s.
3309	119	Liquefied gas, poisonous, flammable, corrosive, n.o.s. (Inhalation Hazard Zone A)
3309	119	Liquefied gas, poisonous, flammable, corrosive, n.o.s. (Inhalation Hazard Zone B)
3309	119	Liquefied gas, poisonous, flammable, corrosive, n.o.s. (Inhalation Hazard Zone C)
3309	119	Liquefied gas, poisonous, flammable, corrosive, n.o.s. (Inhalation Hazard Zone D)
3309	119	Liquefied gas, toxic, flammable, corrosive, n.o.s.
3309	119	Liquefied gas, toxic, flammable, corrosive, n.o.s. (Inhalation Hazard Zone A)
3309	119	Liquefied gas, toxic, flammable, corrosive, n.o.s. (Inhalation Hazard Zone B)
3309	119	Liquefied gas, toxic, flammable, corrosive, n.o.s. (Inhalation Hazard Zone C)
3309	119	Liquefied gas, toxic, flammable, corrosive, n.o.s. (Inhalation Hazard Zone D)
3310	124	Liquefied gas, poisonous, oxidizing, corrosive, n.o.s.
3310	124	Liquefied gas, poisonous, oxidizing, corrosive, n.o.s. (Inhalation Hazard Zone A)
3310	124	Liquefied gas, poisonous, oxidizing, corrosive, n.o.s. (Inhalation Hazard Zone B)
3310	124	Liquefied gas, poisonous, oxidizing, corrosive, n.o.s. (Inhalation Hazard Zone C)
3310	124	Liquefied gas, poisonous, oxidizing, corrosive, n.o.s. (Inhalation Hazard Zone D)
3310	124	Liquefied gas, toxic, oxidizing, corrosive, n.o.s.
3310	124	Liquefied gas, toxic, oxidizing, corrosive, n.o.s. (Inhalation Hazard Zone A)
3310	124	Liquefied gas, toxic, oxidizing, corrosive, n.o.s. (Inhalation Hazard Zone B)
3310	124	Liquefied gas, toxic, oxidizing, corrosive, n.o.s. (Inhalation Hazard Zone C)
3310	124	Liquefied gas, toxic, oxidizing, corrosive, n.o.s. (Inhalation Hazard Zone D)
3311	122	Gas, refrigerated liquid, oxidizing, n.o.s.
3312	115	Gas, refrigerated liquid, flammable, n.o.s.
3313	135	Organic pigments, self-heating
3314	171	Plastic molding compound
3314	171	Plastics moulding compound
3315	151	Chemical sample, poisonous liquid
3315	151	Chemical sample, poisonous solid
3315	151	Chemical sample, toxic liquid
3315	151	Chemical sample, toxic solid
3316	171	Chemical kit
3316	171	First aid kit
3317	113	2-Amino-4,6-dinitrophenol, wetted with not less than 20% water

ID No.	Guide No.	Name of Material
3318	125	Ammonia solution, with more than 50% Ammonia
3319	113	Nitroglycerin mixture, desensitized, solid, n.o.s., with more than 2% but not more than 10% Nitroglycerin
3319	113	Nitroglycerin mixture with more than 2% but not more than 10% Nitroglycerin, desensitized
3320	157	Sodium borohydride and Sodium hydroxide solution, with not more than 12% Sodium borohydride and not more than 40% Sodium hydroxide
3321	162	Radioactive material, low specific activity (LSA-II)
3322	162	Radioactive material, low specific activity (LSA-III)
3323	163	Radioactive material, Type C package
3324	165	Radioactive material, low specific activity (LSA-II), fissile
3325	165	Radioactive material, low specific activity (LSA-III), fissile
3326	165	Radioactive material, surface contaminated objects (SCO-I), fissile
3326	165	Radioactive material, surface contaminated objects (SCO-II), fissile
3327	165	Radioactive material, Type A package, fissile
3328	165	Radioactive material, Type B(U) package, fissile
3329	165	Radioactive material, Type B(M) package, fissile
3330	165	Radioactive material, Type C package, fissile
3331	165	Radioactive material, transported under special arrangement, fissile
3332	164	Radioactive material, Type A package, special form
3333	165	Radioactive material, Type A package, special form, fissile
3334	171	Aviation regulated liquid, n.o.s.
3335	171	Aviation regulated solid, n.o.s.
3336	130	Mercaptan mixture, liquid, flammable, n.o.s.
3336	130	Mercaptans, liquid, flammable, n.o.s.
3337	126	Refrigerant gas R-404A
3338	126	Refrigerant gas R-407A
3339	126	Refrigerant gas R-407B
3340	126	Refrigerant gas R-407C
3341	135	Thiourea dioxide
3342	135	Xanthates
3343	113	Nitroglycerin mixture, desensitized, liquid, flammable, n.o.s., with not more than 30% Nitroglycerin
3344	113	Pentaerythrite tetranitrate mixture, desensitized, solid, n.o.s., with more than 10% but not more than 20% PETN
3345	153	Phenoxyacetic acid derivative pesticide, solid, poisonous
3345	153	Phenoxyacetic acid derivative pesticide, solid, toxic
3346	131	Phenoxyacetic acid derivative pesticide, liquid, flammable, poisonous
3346	131	Phenoxyacetic acid derivative pesticide, liquid, flammable, toxic

ID No.	Guide No.	Name of Material
3347	131	Phenoxyacetic acid derivative pesticide, liquid, poisonous, flammable
3347	131	Phenoxyacetic acid derivative pesticide, liquid, toxic, flammable
3348	153	Phenoxyacetic acid derivative pesticide, liquid, poisonous
3348	153	Phenoxyacetic acid derivative pesticide, liquid, toxic
3349	151	Pyrethroid pesticide, solid, poisonous
3349	151	Pyrethroid pesticide, solid, toxic
3350	131	Pyrethroid pesticide, liquid, flammable, poisonous
3350	131	Pyrethroid pesticide, liquid, flammable, toxic
3351	131	Pyrethroid pesticide, liquid, poisonous, flammable
3351	131	Pyrethroid pesticide, liquid, toxic, flammable
3352	151	Pyrethroid pesticide, liquid, poisonous
3352	151	Pyrethroid pesticide, liquid, toxic
3353	126	Air bag inflators, compressed gas
3353	126	Air bag modules, compressed gas
3353	126	Seat-belt pre-tensioners, compressed gas
3354	115	Insecticide gas, flammable, n.o.s.
3355	119	Insecticide gas, poisonous, flammable, n.o.s.
3355	119	Insecticide gas, poisonous, flammable, n.o.s. (Inhalation Hazard Zone A)
3355	119	Insecticide gas, poisonous, flammable, n.o.s. (Inhalation Hazard Zone B)
3355	119	Insecticide gas, poisonous, flammable, n.o.s. (Inhalation Hazard Zone C)
3355	119	Insecticide gas, poisonous, flammable, n.o.s. (Inhalation Hazard Zone D)
3355	119	Insecticide gas, toxic, flammable, n.o.s.
3355	119	Insecticide gas, toxic, flammable, n.o.s. (Inhalation Hazard Zone A)
3355	119	Insecticide gas, toxic, flammable, n.o.s. (Inhalation Hazard Zone B)
3355	119	Insecticide gas, toxic, flammable, n.o.s. (Inhalation Hazard Zone C)
3355	119	Insecticide gas, toxic, flammable, n.o.s. (Inhalation Hazard Zone D)
3356	140	Oxygen generator, chemical
3357	113	Nitroglycerin mixture, desensitized, liquid, n.o.s., with not more than 30% Nitroglycerin
3358	115	Refrigerating machines containing flammable, non-toxic, liquefied gas
8000	171	Consumer commodity
8001	171	Dangerous goods in apparatus
8001	171	Dangerous goods in machinery
8013	171	Gas generator assemblies
8023	115	Refrigerating machines
8027	171	Other regulated substance
8037	140	Oxygen generators, small
8038	171	Heat producing article
9011	133	Camphene
9018	160	Dichlorodifluoroethylene

ID No.	Guide No.	Name of Material	ID No.	Guide No.	Name of Material
9026	153	Dinitrocyclohexylphenol	9103	171	Cobaltous bromide
9035	123	Gas identification set	9104	171	Cobaltous formate
9037	151	Hexachloroethane	9105	171	Cobaltous sulfamate
9069	132	Tetramethylmethylenediamine	9105	171	Cobaltous sulphamate
9073	113	Trinitroaniline, wetted	9106	171	Cupric acetate
9077	153	Adipic acid	9109	171	Cupric sulfate
9078	171	Aluminum sulfate, solid	9109	171	Cupric sulphate
9078	171	Aluminum sulphate, solid	9110	171	Cupric sulfate, ammoniated
9079	171	Ammonium acetate	9110	171	Cupric sulphate, ammoniated
9080	171	Ammonium benzoate	9111	171	Cupric tartrate
9081	171	Ammonium bicarbonate	9117	171	EDTA
9083	154	Ammonium carbamate	9117	171	Ethylenediaminetetraacetic acid
9084	154	Ammonium carbonate	9118	171	Ferric ammonium citrate
9085	171	Ammonium chloride	9119	171	Ferric ammonium oxalate
9086	143	Ammonium chromate	9120	171	Ferric fluoride
9087	171	Ammonium citrate, dibasic	9121	171	Ferric sulfate
9088	154	Ammonium fluoborate	9121	171	Ferric sulphate
9089	171	Ammonium sulfamate	9122	171	Ferrous ammonium sulfate
9089	171	Ammonium sulphamate	9122	171	Ferrous ammonium sulphate
9090	171	Ammonium sulfite	9125	171	Ferrous sulfate
9090	171	Ammonium sulphite	9125	171	Ferrous sulphate
9091	171	Ammonium tartrate	9126	171	Fumaric acid
9094	153	Benzoic acid	9127	171	Isopropanolamine dodecylbenzenesulfonate
9095	171	n-Butyl phthalate	9127	171	Isopropanolamine dodecylbenzenesulphonate
9096	171	Calcium chromate	9134	171	Lithium chromate
9097	171	Calcium dodecylbenzenesulfonate	9137	171	Naphthenic acid
9097	171	Calcium dodecylbenzenesulphonate	9138	171	Nickel ammonium sulfate
9100	171	Chromic sulfate	9138	171	Nickel ammonium sulphate
9100	171	Chromic sulphate	9139	151	Nickel chloride
9101	171	Chromic acetate	9140	154	Nickel hydroxide
9102	171	Chromous chloride	9141	154	Nickel sulfate

ID No.	Guide No.	Name of Material
9141	154	Nickel sulphate
9142	171	Potassium chromate
9145	171	Sodium chromate
9146	171	Sodium dodecylbenzenesulfonate (branched chain)
9146	171	Sodium dodecylbenzenesulphonate (branched chain)
9147	171	Sodium phosphate, dibasic
9148	171	Sodium phosphate, tribasic
9149	171	Strontium chromate
9151	171	Triethanolamine dodecylbenzenesulfonate
9151	171	Triethanolamine dodecylbenzenesulphonate
9153	171	Zinc acetate
9154	171	Zinc ammonium chloride
9155	171	Zinc borate
9156	171	Zinc bromide
9157	171	Zinc carbonate
9158	151	Zinc fluoride
9159	171	Zinc formate
9160	171	Zinc phenolsulfonate
9160	171	Zinc phenolsulphonate
9161	171	Zinc sulfate
9161	171	Zinc sulphate
9162	171	Zirconium potassium fluoride
9163	171	Zirconium sulfate
9163	171	Zirconium sulphate
9180	162	Uranyl acetate
9183	146	Organic peroxide, liquid, n.o.s.
9183	146	Organic peroxide, solution, n.o.s.
9187	146	Organic peroxide, solid, n.o.s.
9188	171	Hazardous substance, liquid, n.o.s.
9188	171	Hazardous substance, solid, n.o.s.
9188	171	ORM-E, liquid, n.o.s.
9188	171	ORM-E, solid, n.o.s.
9189	171	Hazardous waste, liquid, n.o.s.
9189	171	Hazardous waste, solid, n.o.s.
9190	143	Ammonium permanganate
9191	143	Chlorine dioxide, hydrate, frozen
9192	167	Fluorine, refrigerated liquid (cryogenic liquid)
9193	140	Oxidizer, corrosive, liquid, n.o.s.
9194	140	Oxidizer, corrosive, solid, n.o.s.
9195	135	Metal alkyl, solution, n.o.s.
9199	142	Oxidizer, poisonous, liquid, n.o.s.
9200	141	Oxidizer, poisonous, solid, n.o.s.
9201	171	Antimony trioxide
9202	168	Carbon monoxide, refrigerated liquid (cryogenic liquid)
9206	137	Methyl phosphonic dichloride
9259	128	Elevated temperature material, liquid, n.o.s., (at or above 100°C (212°F) and below its flash point)
9260	169	Aluminum, molten
9263	156	Chloropivaloyl chloride
9264	151	3,5-Dichloro-2,4,6-trifluoropyridine
9269	132	Trimethoxysilane
9274	160	1,1-Dichloro-1-fluoroethane
9275	158	Regulated medical waste
9276	128	Flammable liquids, elevated temperature material, n.o.s.

ID No.	Guide No.	Name of Material
9277	171	Oil, n.o.s., flash point not less than 93°C (200°F)
9278	171	Genetically modified organisms
9301	153	Waste Type 1
9302	153	Waste Type 2
9303	131	Waste Type 3
9304	153	Waste Type 4
9305	131	Waste Type 5
9306	154	Waste Type 6
9307	154	Waste Type 7
9308	153	Waste Type 8
9309	153	Waste Type 9
9310	153	Waste Type 10
9311	153	Waste Type 11
9312	153	Waste Type 12
9313	153	Waste Type 13
9314	153	Waste Type 14
9315	153	Waste Type 15
9316	154	Waste Type 16
9317	154	Waste Type 17
9318	154	Waste Type 18
9319	154	Waste Type 19
9320	154	Waste Type 20
9321	154	Waste Type 21
9322	154	Waste Type 22
9323	154	Waste Type 23
9324	152	Waste Type 24
9325	127	Waste Type 25
9326	152	Waste Type 26
9327	131	Waste Type 27
9328	131	Waste Type 28
9329	153	Waste Type 29
9330	153	Waste Type 30
9331	129	Waste Type 31
9332	129	Waste Type 32
9333	129	Waste Type 33
9334	129	Waste Type 34
9335	153	Waste Type 35
9336	153	Waste Type 36
9337	153	Waste Type 37
9338	153	Waste Type 38
9339	153	Waste Type 39
9340	153	Waste Type 40
9341	132	Waste Type 41
9342	129	Waste Type 42
9343	154	Waste Type 43
9344	132	Waste Type 44
9345	132	Waste Type 45
9346	153	Waste Type 46
9347	132	Waste Type 47
9348	153	Waste Type 48
9349	153	Waste Type 49
9350	153	Waste Type 50
9351	153	Waste Type 51
9352	153	Waste Type 52
9353	153	Waste Type 53
9354	153	Waste Type 54
9355	153	Waste Type 55
9356	153	Waste Type 56
9357	153	Waste Type 57
9358	153	Waste Type 58
9359	151	Waste Type 59
9360	132	Waste Type 60
9361	151	Waste Type 61
9362	151	Waste Type 62
9363	151	Waste Type 63

ID No.	Guide No.	Name of Material	ID No.	Guide No.	Name of Material
9364	151	Waste Type 64	9397	153	Waste Type 97
9365	151	Waste Type 65	9399	137	Waste Type 99
9366	151	Waste Type 66	9400	137	Waste Type 100
9367	152	Waste Type 67	9500	151	Leachable toxic waste
9368	154	Waste Type 68			
9369	151	Waste Type 69			
9370	151	Waste Type 70			
9371	133	Waste Type 71			
9372	151	Waste Type 72			
9373	151	Waste Type 73			
9374	127	Waste Type 74			
9375	153	Waste Type 75			
9376	153	Waste Type 76			
9377	131	Waste Type 77			
9378	153	Waste Type 78			
9379	153	Waste Type 79			
9380	151	Waste Type 80			
9381	154	Waste Type 81			
9382	154	Waste Type 82			
9383	154	Waste Type 83			
9384	151	Waste Type 84			
9385	154	Waste Type 85			
9386	154	Waste Type 86			
9387	154	Waste Type 87			
9388	151	Waste Type 88			
9389	154	Waste Type 89			
9390	154	Waste Type 90			
9391	153	Waste Type 91			
9392	154	Waste Type 92			
9393	153	Waste Type 93			
9394	151	Waste Type 94			
9395	153	Waste Type 95			
9396	151	Waste Type 96			

Note: If an entry is highlighted in either the yellow-bordered or blue-bordered pages AND THERE IS NO FIRE, go directly to the Table of Initial Isolation and Protective Action Distances (green-bordered pages) and look up the ID number and name of material to obtain initial isolation and protective action distances. IF THERE IS A FIRE, or IF A FIRE IS INVOLVED, go directly to the appropriate guide (orange-bordered pages) and use the evacuation information shown under PUBLIC SAFETY.

Name of Material	Guide No.	ID No.
AC	117	1051
Accumulators, pressurized, pneumatic or hydraulic	126	1956
Acetal	127	1088
Acetaldehyde	129	1089
Acetaldehyde ammonia	171	1841
Acetaldehyde oxime	129	2332
Acetic acid, glacial	132	2789
Acetic acid, solution, more than 10% but not more than 80% acid	153	2790
Acetic acid, solution, more than 80% acid	132	2789
Acetic anhydride	137	1715
Acetone	127	1090
Acetone cyanohydrin, stabilized	155	1541
Acetone oils	127	1091
Acetonitrile	131	1648
Acetyl acetone peroxide	145	2080
Acetyl benzoyl peroxide	147	2081
Acetyl bromide	156	1716
Acetyl chloride	132	1717
Acetyl cyclohexanesulfonyl peroxide	148	2082
Acetyl cyclohexanesulfonyl peroxide	148	2083
Acetyl cyclohexanesulphonyl peroxide	148	2082
Acetyl cyclohexanesulphonyl peroxide	148	2083
Acetylene	116	1001
Acetylene, dissolved	116	1001
Acetylene, Ethylene and Propylene in mixture, refrigerated liquid containing at least 71.5% Ethylene with not more than 22.5% Acetylene and not more than 6% Propylene	116	3138
Acetylene tetrabromide	159	2504
Acetyl iodide	156	1898
Acetyl methyl carbinol	127	2621
Acetyl peroxide	148	2084
Acid, liquid, n.o.s.	154	1760
Acid, sludge	153	1906
Acid butyl phosphate	153	1718
Acridine	153	2713
Acrolein, inhibited	131P	1092
Acrolein dimer, stabilized	129P	2607
Acrylamide	153P	2074
Acrylic acid, inhibited	132P	2218
Acrylonitrile, inhibited	131P	1093
Adamsite	154	1698
Adhesives (flammable)	128	1133
Adipic acid	153	9077
Adiponitrile	153	2205
Aerosol dispensers	126	1950
Aerosols	126	1950
Air, compressed	122	1002
Air, refrigerated liquid (cryogenic liquid)	122	1003
Air, refrigerated liquid (cryogenic liquid), non-pressurized	122	1003
Air bag inflators	133	1325
Air bag inflators	171	3268
Air bag inflators, compressed gas	126	3353
Air bag inflators, pyrotechnic	171	3268
Air bag modules	133	1325
Air bag modules	171	3268
Air bag modules, compressed gas	126	3353
Air bag modules, pyrotechnic	171	3268
Aircraft evacuation slides	171	2990
Aircraft hydraulic power unit fuel tank	131	3165

Name of Material	Guide No.	ID No.	Name of Material	Guide No.	ID No.
Aircraft survival kits	171	3072	Alkaline earth metal dispersion	138	1391
Alcoholates solution, n.o.s., in alcohol	127	3274	Alkaline liquid, n.o.s.	154	1719
Alcoholic beverages	127	3065	Alkaloids, liquid, n.o.s. (poisonous)	151	3140
Alcohols, flammable, poisonous, n.o.s.	131	1986	Alkaloids, solid, n.o.s. (poisonous)	151	1544
Alcohols, flammable, toxic, n.o.s.	131	1986	Alkaloid salts, liquid, n.o.s. (poisonous)	151	3140
Alcohols, n.o.s.	127	1987	Alkaloid salts, solid, n.o.s. (poisonous)	151	1544
Alcohols, poisonous, n.o.s.	131	1986	Alkylamines, n.o.s.	132	2733
Alcohols, toxic, n.o.s.	131	1986	Alkylamines, n.o.s.	132	2734
Aldehydes, flammable, poisonous, n.o.s.	131	1988	Alkylamines, n.o.s.	153	2735
Aldehydes, flammable, toxic, n.o.s.	131	1988	Alkyl phenols, liquid, n.o.s. (including C2-C12 homologues)	153	3145
Aldehydes, n.o.s.	129	1989	Alkyl phenols, solid, n.o.s. (including C2-C12 homologues)	153	2430
Aldehydes, poisonous, n.o.s.	131	1988			
Aldehydes, toxic, n.o.s.	131	1988	Alkyl sulfonic acids, liquid, with more than 5% free Sulfuric acid	153	2584
Aldol	153	2839			
Aldrin, liquid	131	2762	Alkyl sulfonic acids, liquid, with not more than 5% free Sulfuric acid	153	2586
Aldrin, solid	151	2761			
Aldrin mixture, dry	151	2761	Alkyl sulfonic acids, solid, with more than 5% free Sulfuric acid	153	2583
Aldrin mixture, liquid	131	2762			
Alkali metal alcoholates, self-heating, corrosive, n.o.s.	136	3206	Alkyl sulfonic acids, solid, with not more than 5% free Sulfuric acid	153	2585
Alkali metal alloy, liquid, n.o.s.	138	1421			
Alkali metal amalgam	138	1389	Alkylsulfuric acids	156	2571
Alkali metal amalgam, liquid	138	1389	Alkyl sulphonic acids, liquid, with more than 5% free Sulphuric acid	153	2584
Alkali metal amalgam, solid	138	1389			
Alkali metal amides	139	1390	Alkyl sulphonic acids, liquid, with not more than 5% free Sulphuric acid	153	2586
Alkali metal dispersion	138	1391			
Alkaline earth metal alcoholates, n.o.s.	135	3205			
Alkaline earth metal alloy, n.o.s.	138	1393			
Alkaline earth metal amalgam	138	1392			

Name of Material	Guide No.	ID No.
Alkyl sulphonic acids, solid, with more than 5% free Sulphuric acid	153	2583
Alkyl sulphonic acids, solid, with not more than 5% free Sulphuric acid	153	2585
Alkylsulphuric acids	156	2571
Allethrin	151	2902
Allyl acetate	131	2333
Allyl alcohol	131	1098
Allylamine	131	2334
Allyl bromide	131	1099
Allyl chloride	131	1100
Allyl chlorocarbonate	155	1722
Allyl chloroformate	155	1722
Allyl ethyl ether	131	2335
Allyl formate	131	2336
Allyl glycidyl ether	129	2219
Allyl iodide	132	1723
Allyl isothiocyanate, inhibited	155	1545
Allyl isothiocyanate, stabilized	155	1545
Allyltrichlorosilane, stabilized	155	1724
Aluminum, molten	169	9260
Aluminum alkyl halides	135	3052
Aluminum alkyl hydrides	138	3076
Aluminum alkyls	135	3051
Aluminum borohydride	135	2870
Aluminum borohydride in devices	135	2870
Aluminum bromide, anhydrous	137	1725
Aluminum bromide, solution	154	2580
Aluminum carbide	138	1394
Aluminum chloride, anhydrous	137	1726
Aluminum chloride, solution	154	2581

Name of Material	Guide No.	ID No.
Aluminum dross	138	3170
Aluminum ferrosilicon powder	139	1395
Aluminum hydride	138	2463
Aluminum nitrate	140	1438
Aluminum phosphate, solution	154	1760
Aluminum phosphide	139	1397
Aluminum phosphide pesticide	157	3048
Aluminum powder, coated	170	1309
Aluminum powder, pyrophoric	135	1383
Aluminum powder, uncoated	138	1396
Aluminum processing by-products	138	3170
Aluminum remelting by-products	138	3170
Aluminum resinate	133	2715
Aluminum silicon powder, uncoated	138	1398
Aluminum smelting by-products	138	3170
Aluminum sulfate, solid	171	9078
Aluminum sulfate, solution	154	1760
Aluminum sulphate, solid	171	9078
Aluminum sulphate, solution	154	1760
Amines, flammable, corrosive, n.o.s.	132	2733
Amines, liquid, corrosive, flammable, n.o.s.	132	2734
Amines, liquid, corrosive, n.o.s.	153	2735
Amines, solid, corrosive, n.o.s.	154	3259
2-Amino-4-chlorophenol	151	2673
2-Amino-5-diethylaminopentane	153	2946
2-Amino-4,6-dinitrophenol, wetted with not less than 20% water	113	3317
2-(2-Aminoethoxy)ethanol	154	1760
2-(2-Aminoethoxy)ethanol	154	3055

Name of Material	Guide No.	ID No.	Name of Material	Guide No.	ID No.
N-Aminoethylpiperazine	153	2815	Ammonium fluoborate	154	9088
Aminophenols	152	2512	Ammonium fluoride	154	2505
Aminopropyldiethanolamine	154	1760	Ammonium fluorosilicate	151	2854
N-Aminopropylmorpholine	154	1760	Ammonium hydrogendifluoride, solid	154	1727
Aminopyridines	153	2671			
Ammonia, anhydrous	125	1005	Ammonium hydrogendifluoride, solution	154	2817
Ammonia, anhydrous, liquefied	125	1005	Ammonium hydrogen fluoride, solid	154	1727
Ammonia, solution, with more than 10% but not more than 35% Ammonia	154	2672			
			Ammonium hydrogen fluoride, solution	154	2817
Ammonia, solution, with more than 35% but not more than 50% Ammonia	125	2073	Ammonium hydrogen sulfate	154	2506
			Ammonium hydrogen sulphate	154	2506
Ammonia solution, with more than 50% Ammonia	125	1005	Ammonium hydrosulfide, solution	132	2683
Ammonia solution, with more than 50% Ammonia	125	3318	Ammonium hydrosulphide, solution	132	2683
Ammonium acetate	171	9079	Ammonium hydroxide	154	2672
Ammonium arsenate	151	1546	Ammonium hydroxide, with more than 10% but not more than 35% Ammonia	154	2672
Ammonium benzoate	171	9080			
Ammonium bicarbonate	171	9081			
Ammonium bifluoride, solid	154	1727	Ammonium metavanadate	154	2859
Ammonium bifluoride, solution	154	2817	Ammonium nitrate, liquid (hot concentrated solution)	140	2426
Ammonium bisulfite, solid	154	2693			
Ammonium bisulfite, solution	154	2693	Ammonium nitrate, with not more than 0.2% combustible substances	140	1942
Ammonium bisulphite, solid	154	2693			
Ammonium bisulphite, solution	154	2693	Ammonium nitrate, with organic coating	140	1942
Ammonium carbamate	154	9083			
Ammonium carbonate	154	9084	Ammonium nitrate fertilizer, n.o.s.	140	2072
Ammonium chloride	171	9085			
Ammonium chromate	143	9086	Ammonium nitrate fertilizer, with not more than 0.4% combustible material	140	2071
Ammonium citrate, dibasic	171	9087			
Ammonium dichromate	141	1439	Ammonium nitrate fertilizers	140	2067
Ammonium dinitro-o-cresolate	141	1843	Ammonium nitrate fertilizers	140	2071
			Ammonium nitrate fertilizers	140	2072

Name of Material	Guide No.	ID No.	Name of Material	Guide No.	ID No.
Ammonium nitrate fertilizers, with Ammonium sulfate	140	2069	Ammunition, tear-producing, non-explosive	159	2017
Ammonium nitrate fertilizers, with Ammonium sulphate	140	2069	Ammunition, toxic, non-explosive	151	2016
Ammonium nitrate fertilizers, with Calcium carbonate	140	2068	Amyl acetates	129	1104
			Amyl acid phosphate	153	2819
Ammonium nitrate fertilizers, with Phosphate or Potash	143	2070	Amyl alcohols	129	1105
Ammonium nitrate-fuel oil mixtures	112	——	Amylamines	132	1106
			Amyl butyrates	130	2620
Ammonium nitrate mixed fertilizers	140	2069	Amyl chloride	129	1107
			n-Amylene	127	1108
Ammonium oxalate	154	2449	Amyl formates	129	1109
Ammonium perchlorate	143	1442	Amyl mercaptan	130	1111
Ammonium permanganate	143	9190	n-Amyl methyl ketone	127	1110
Ammonium persulfate	140	1444	Amyl methyl ketone	127	1110
Ammonium persulphate	140	1444	Amyl nitrate	140	1112
Ammonium picrate, wetted with not less than 10% water	113	1310	Amyl nitrite	129	1113
			tert-Amyl peroxy-2-ethylhexanoate	148	2898
Ammonium polysulfide, solution	154	2818	tert-Amyl peroxyneodecanoate	148	2891
Ammonium polysulphide, solution	154	2818	Amyltrichlorosilane	155	1728
Ammonium polyvanadate	151	2861	Anhydrous ammonia	125	1005
Ammonium silicofluoride	151	2854	Anhydrous ammonia, liquefied	125	1005
Ammonium sulfamate	171	9089	Aniline	153	1547
Ammonium sulfate nitrate	140	1477	Aniline hydrochloride	153	1548
Ammonium sulfide, solution	132	2683	Anisidines	153	2431
Ammonium sulfite	171	9090	Anisidines, liquid	153	2431
Ammonium sulphamate	171	9089	Anisidines, solid	153	2431
Ammonium sulphate nitrate	140	1477	Anisole	127	2222
Ammonium sulphide, solution	132	2683	Anisoyl chloride	156	1729
Ammonium sulphite	171	9090	Antimony compound, inorganic, liquid, n.o.s.	157	3141
Ammonium tartrate	171	9091			
Ammonium picrate, poisonous, non-explosive					
Ammunition, poisonous, non-explosive	151	2016	Antimony compound, inorganic, n.o.s.	157	1549

Name of Material	Guide No.	ID No.	Name of Material	Guide No.	ID No.
Antimony compound, inorganic, solid, n.o.s.	157	1549	Arsenical pesticide, liquid, poisonous, flammable	131	2993
Antimony lactate	151	1550	Arsenical pesticide, liquid, toxic	151	2994
Antimony pentachloride, liquid	157	1730	Arsenical pesticide, liquid, toxic, flammable	131	2993
Antimony pentachloride, solution	157	1731	Arsenical pesticide, solid, poisonous	151	2759
Antimony pentafluoride	157	1732	Arsenical pesticide, solid, toxic	151	2759
Antimony potassium tartrate	151	1551	Arsenic bromide	151	1555
Antimony powder	170	2871	Arsenic chloride	157	1560
Antimony sulfide, solid	133	1325	Arsenic compound, liquid, n.o.s.	152	1556
Antimony sulphide, solid	133	1325	Arsenic compound, liquid, n.o.s., inorganic	152	1556
Antimony tribromide, solid	157	1549	Arsenic compound, solid, n.o.s.	152	1557
Antimony tribromide, solution	157	1549	Arsenic compound, solid, n.o.s., inorganic	152	1557
Antimony trichloride	157	1733	Arsenic iodide, solid	152	1557
Antimony trichloride, liquid	157	1733	Arsenic pentoxide	151	1559
Antimony trichloride, solid	157	1733	Arsenic sulfide	152	1557
Antimony trichloride, solution	157	1733	Arsenic sulphide	152	1557
Antimony trifluoride, solid	157	1549	Arsenic trichloride	157	1560
Antimony trifluoride, solution	157	1549	Arsenic trioxide	151	1561
Antimony trioxide	171	9201	Arsenic trisulfide	152	1557
Aqua regia	157	1798	Arsenic trisulphide	152	1557
Argon	121	1006	Arsine	119	2188
Argon, compressed	121	1006	Articles containing Polychlorinated biphenyls (PCB)	171	2315
Argon, refrigerated liquid (cryogenic liquid)	120	1951	Articles, pressurized, hydraulic (containing non-flammable gas)	126	3164
Arsenic	152	1558	Articles, pressurized, pneumatic (containing non-flammable gas)	126	3164
Arsenic acid, liquid	154	1553			
Arsenic acid, solid	154	1554			
Arsenical dust	152	1562			
Arsenical pesticide, liquid, flammable, poisonous	131	2760	Aryl sulfonic acids, liquid, with more than 5% free Sulfuric acid	153	2584
Arsenical pesticide, liquid, flammable, toxic	131	2760			
Arsenical pesticide, liquid, poisonous	151	2994			

Name of Material	Guide No.	ID No.
Aryl sulfonic acids, liquid, with not more than 5% free Sulfuric acid	153	2586
Aryl sulfonic acids, solid, with more than 5% free Sulfuric acid	153	2583
Aryl sulfonic acids, solid, with not more than 5% free Sulfuric acid	153	2585
Aryl sulphonic acids, liquid, with more than 5% free Sulphuric acid	153	2584
Aryl sulphonic acids, liquid, with not more than 5% free Sulphuric acid	153	2586
Aryl sulphonic acids, solid, with more than 5% free Sulphuric acid	153	2583
Aryl sulphonic acids, solid, with not more than 5% free Sulphuric acid	153	2585
Asbestos	171	2212
Asbestos, blue	171	2212
Asbestos, brown	171	2212
Asbestos, white	171	2590
Asphalt	130	1999
Asphalt, cut back	130	1999
Aviation regulated liquid, n.o.s.	171	3334
Aviation regulated solid, n.o.s.	171	3335
Azinphos methyl	152	2783
1-Aziridinyl phosphine oxide (Tris)	152	2501
Azodicarbonamide	149	3242
2,2'-Azodi-(2,4-dimethyl-4-methoxyvaleronitrile)	150	2955
2,2'-Azodi-(2,4-dimethylvaleronitrile)	150	2953
1,1'-Azodi-(hexahydrobenzonitrile)	149	2954
Azodiisobutyronitrile	150	2952
2,2'-Azodi-(2-methyl-butyronitrile)	150	3030
Barium	138	1400
Barium alloys, pyrophoric	135	1854
Barium azide, wetted with not less than 50% water	113	1571
Barium bromate	141	2719
Barium chlorate	141	1445
Barium chlorate, wet	141	1445
Barium compound, n.o.s.	154	1564
Barium cyanide	157	1565
Barium hypochlorite, with more than 22% available Chlorine	141	2741
Barium nitrate	141	1446
Barium oxide	157	1884
Barium perchlorate	141	1447
Barium permanganate	141	1448
Barium peroxide	141	1449
Barium selenate	151	2630
Barium selenite	151	2630
Batteries, containing Sodium	138	3292
Batteries, dry, containing Potassium hydroxide, solid	154	3028
Batteries, wet, filled with acid	154	2794
Batteries, wet, filled with alkali	154	2795
Batteries, wet, non-spillable	154	2800
Battery	154	1813
Battery	154	2794
Battery	154	2795
Battery fluid, acid	157	2796
Battery fluid, acid, with battery	157	2796

Name of Material	Guide No.	ID No.
Battery fluid, acid, with electronic equipment or actuating device	157	2796
Battery fluid, alkali	154	2797
Battery fluid, alkali, with battery	154	2797
Battery fluid, alkali, with electronic equipment or actuating device	154	2797
Battery-powered equipment (wet battery)	154	3171
Battery-powered vehicle (wet battery)	154	3171
Benzaldehyde	129	1989
Benzaldehyde	129	1990
Benzene	130	1114
Benzene-1,3-disulfohydrazide	149	2971
Benzene-1,3-disulphohydrazide	149	2971
Benzene phosphorus dichloride	137	2798
Benzene phosphorus thiodichloride	137	2799
Benzene sulfohydrazide	149	2970
Benzenesulfonyl chloride	156	2225
Benzene sulphohydrazide	149	2970
Benzenesulphonyl chloride	156	2225
Benzidine	153	1885
Benzoic acid	153	9094
Benzoic derivative pesticide, liquid, flammable, poisonous	131	2770
Benzoic derivative pesticide, liquid, flammable, toxic	131	2770
Benzoic derivative pesticide, liquid, poisonous	151	3004
Benzoic derivative pesticide, liquid, poisonous, flammable	131	3003
Benzoic derivative pesticide, liquid, toxic	151	3004
Benzoic derivative pesticide, liquid, toxic, flammable	131	3003
Benzoic derivative pesticide, solid, poisonous	151	2769
Benzoic derivative pesticide, solid, toxic	151	2769
Benzonitrile	152	2224
Benzoquinone	153	2587
Benzotrichloride	156	2226
Benzotrifluoride	131	2338
Benzoyl chloride	137	1736
Benzoyl peroxide	146	2085
Benzoyl peroxide	146	2087
Benzoyl peroxide	146	2088
Benzoyl peroxide	145	2089
Benzoyl peroxide	146	2090
Benzyl bromide	156	1737
Benzyl chloride	156	1738
Benzyl chloroformate	137	1739
Benzyldimethylamine	132	2619
4-[Benzyl(ethyl)amino]-3-ethoxybenzenediazonium zinc chloride	149	3037
Benzylidene chloride	156	1886
Benzyl iodide	156	2653
4-[Benzyl(methyl)amino]-3-ethoxybenzenediazonium zinc chloride	150	3038
Beryllium chloride	154	1566
Beryllium compound, n.o.s.	154	1566
Beryllium fluoride	154	1566
Beryllium nitrate	141	2464
Beryllium powder	134	1567
Bhusa, wet, damp or contaminated with oil	133	1327

Name of Material	Guide No.	ID No.
Bicyclo[2.2.1]hepta-2,5-diene	127P	2251
Bicyclo[2.2.1]hepta-2,5-diene, inhibited	127P	2251
Bifluorides, n.o.s.	154	1740
Biological agents	158	——
(Bio)Medical waste, n.o.s.	158	3291
Bipyridilium pesticide, liquid, flammable, poisonous	131	2782
Bipyridilium pesticide, liquid, flammable, toxic	131	2782
Bipyridilium pesticide, liquid, poisonous	151	3016
Bipyridilium pesticide, liquid, poisonous, flammable	131	3015
Bipyridilium pesticide, liquid, toxic	151	3016
Bipyridilium pesticide, liquid, toxic, flammable	131	3015
Bipyridilium pesticide, solid, poisonous	151	2781
Bipyridilium pesticide, solid, toxic	151	2781
Bis-(2-chloroethyl) ethylamine	153	2810
Bis-(2-chloroethyl) methylamine	153	2810
Bis-(2-chloroethyl) sulfide	153	2810
Bis-(2-chloroethyl) sulphide	153	2810
Bisulfates, aqueous solution	154	2837
Bisulfites, aqueous solution, n.o.s.	154	2693
Bisulfites, inorganic, aqueous solutions, n.o.s.	154	2693
Bisulphates, aqueous solution	154	2837
Bisulphites, aqueous solution, n.o.s.	154	2693
Bisulphites, inorganic, aqueous solutions, n.o.s.	154	2693

Name of Material	Guide No.	ID No.
Blasting agent, n.o.s.	112	——
Bleaching powder	140	2208
Blue asbestos	171	2212
Bombs, smoke, non-explosive, with corrosive liquid, without initiating device	153	2028
Borate and Chlorate mixtures	140	1458
Borneol	133	1312
Boron tribromide	157	2692
Boron trichloride	125	1741
Boron trifluoride	125	1008
Boron trifluoride, compressed	125	1008
Boron trifluoride, dihydrate	157	2851
Boron trifluoride acetic acid complex	157	1742
Boron trifluoride diethyl etherate	132	2604
Boron trifluoride dimethyl etherate	139	2965
Boron trifluoride propionic acid complex	157	1743
Brake fluid, hydraulic	130	1118
Bromates, inorganic, aqueous solution, n.o.s.	140	3213
Bromates, inorganic, n.o.s.	141	1450
Bromine	154	1744
Bromine, solution	154	1744
Bromine chloride	124	2901
Bromine pentafluoride	144	1745
Bromine trifluoride	144	1746
Bromoacetic acid	156	1938
Bromoacetic acid, solid	156	1938
Bromoacetic acid, solution	156	1938
Bromoacetone	131	1569
Bromoacetyl bromide	156	2513

Name of Material	Guide No.	ID No.	Name of Material	Guide No.	ID No.
Bromobenzene	129	2514	Butyl alcohol	129	1120
Bromobenzyl cyanides	159	1694	n-Butylamine	132	1125
1-Bromobutane	129	1126	N-Butylaniline	153	2738
2-Bromobutane	130	2339	Butylbenzenes	128	2709
Bromochlorodifluoromethane	126	1974	n-Butyl bromide	129	1126
Bromochloromethane	160	1887	Butyl chloride	130	1127
1-Bromo-3-chloropropane	159	2688	n-Butyl chloroformate	155	2743
2-Bromoethyl ethyl ether	130	2340	sec-Butyl chloroformate	155	2742
Bromoform	159	2515	tert-Butyl cumene peroxide	145	2091
1-Bromo-3-methylbutane	130	2341	tert-Butyl cumyl peroxide	145	2091
Bromomethylpropanes	130	2342	tert-Butylcyclohexyl chloroformate	156	2747
2-Bromo-2-nitropropane-1,3-diol	133	3241			
2-Bromopentane	130	2343	n-Butyl-4,4-di-(tert-butylperoxy)valerate	146	2140
2-Bromopropane	130	2344			
Bromopropanes	130	2344	n-Butyl-4,4-di-(tert-butylperoxy)valerate	145	2141
3-Bromopropyne	129	2345			
Bromotrifluoroethylene	116	2419	Butylene	115	1012
Bromotrifluoromethane	126	1009	Butylene	115	1075
Brown asbestos	171	2212	1,2-Butylene oxide, stabilized	127P	3022
Brucine	152	1570	Butyl ethers	127	1149
Burnt cotton, not picked	133	1325	n-Butyl formate	129	1128
Butadienes, inhibited	116P	1010	tert-Butyl hydroperoxide	147	2093
Butane	115	1011	tert-Butyl hydroperoxide	147	2094
Butane	115	1075	tert-Butyl hydroperoxide, not more than 80% in Di-tert-butyl peroxide and/or solvent	147	2092
Butanedione	127	2346			
Butane mixture	115	1011			
Butane mixture	115	1075	tert-Butyl hypochlorite	135	3255
Butanols	129	1120	N,n-Butylimidazole	152	2690
Butoxyl	127	2708	n-Butyl isocyanate	155	2485
Butyl acetates	129	1123	tert-Butyl isocyanate	155	2484
Butyl acid phosphate	153	1718	tert-Butyl isopropyl benzene hydroperoxide	145	2091
Butyl acrylate	129P	2348	Butyl mercaptan	130	2347
Butyl acrylates, inhibited	129P	2348	n-Butyl methacrylate	129P	2227

Name of Material	Guide No.	ID No.	Name of Material	Guide No.	ID No.
n-Butyl methacrylate, inhibited	129P	2227	tert-Butyl peroxypivalate	148	2110
Butyl methyl ether	127	2350	tert-Butyl peroxy-3,5,5-trimethylhexanoate	145	2104
tert-Butyl monoperoxymaleate	146	2099	Butylphenols, liquid	153	2228
Butyl nitrites	129	2351	Butylphenols, solid	153	2229
tert-Butyl peroxyacetate	146	2095	n-Butyl phthalate	171	9095
tert-Butyl peroxyacetate	146	2096	Butyl propionates	130	1914
tert-Butyl peroxybenzoate	146	2097	Butyltoluenes	131	2667
tert-Butyl peroxybenzoate	145	2098	Butyltrichlorosilane	155	1747
tert-Butyl peroxybenzoate	145	2890	5-tert-Butyl-2,4,6-trinitro-m-xylene	149	2956
tert-Butyl peroxycrotonate	145	2183	Butyl vinyl ether, inhibited	127P	2352
Butyl peroxydicarbonate	148	2169	1,4-Butynediol	153	2716
Butyl peroxydicarbonate	148	2170	Butyraldehyde	129	1129
tert-Butyl peroxydiethylacetate	148	2144	Butyraldoxime	129	2840
tert-Butyl peroxydiethylacetate, with tert-Butyl peroxybenzoate	145	2551	Butyric acid	153	2820
			Butyric anhydride	156	2739
tert-Butyl peroxy-2-ethylhexanoate	148	2143	Butyronitrile	131	2411
tert-Butyl peroxy-2-ethylhexanoate, not more than 50%, with phlegmatizer	148	2888	Butyryl chloride	132	2353
			Buzz	153	2810
			BZ	153	2810
tert-Butyl peroxy-2-ethylhexanoate, with 2,2-Di-(tert-butylperoxy)butane	148	2886	CA	159	1694
			Cacodylic acid	151	1572
			Cadmium compound	154	2570
tert-Butyl peroxy-2-ethylhexanoate, with 2,2-Di-(tert-butylperoxy)butane	145	2887	Caesium	138	1407
			Caesium hydroxide	157	2682
tert-Butyl peroxyisobutyrate	148	2142	Caesium hydroxide, solution	154	2681
tert-Butyl peroxyisobutyrate	148	2562	Caesium nitrate	140	1451
tert-Butyl peroxyisononanoate	145	2104	Calcium	138	1401
tert-Butyl peroxyisopropyl carbonate	146	2103	Calcium, metal and alloys, pyrophoric	135	1855
tert-Butyl peroxyneodecanoate	148	2177	Calcium, pyrophoric	135	1855
tert-Butyl peroxyneodecanoate	148	2594	Calcium alloys, pyrophoric	135	1855
tert-Butyl peroxy-3-phenylphthalide	145	2596	Calcium arsenate	151	1573

Name of Material	Guide No.	ID No.	Name of Material	Guide No.	ID No.
Calcium arsenate and Calcium arsenite mixture, solid	151	1574	Calcium hypochlorite mixture, dry, with more than 10% but not more than 39% available Chlorine	140	2208
Calcium arsenite, solid	151	1574			
Calcium arsenite and Calcium arsenate mixture, solid	151	1574	Calcium hypochlorite mixture, dry, with more than 39% available Chlorine (8.8% available Oxygen)	140	1748
Calcium carbide	138	1402			
Calcium chlorate	140	1452			
Calcium chlorate, aqueous solution	140	2429	Calcium manganese silicon	138	2844
Calcium chlorate, solution	140	2429	Calcium metal, crystalline	138	1401
Calcium chlorite	140	1453	Calcium nitrate	140	1454
Calcium chromate	171	9096	Calcium oxide	157	1910
Calcium cyanamide, with more than 0.1% Calcium carbide	138	1403	Calcium perchlorate	140	1455
			Calcium permanganate	140	1456
Calcium cyanide	157	1575	Calcium peroxide	140	1457
Calcium dithionite	135	1923	Calcium phosphide	139	1360
Calcium dodecylbenzenesulfonate	171	9097	Calcium resinate	133	1313
			Calcium resinate, fused	133	1314
Calcium dodecylbenzenesulphonate	171	9097	Calcium selenate	151	2630
			Calcium silicide	138	1405
Calcium hydride	138	1404	Calcium silicon	138	1406
Calcium hydrogen sulfite, solution	154	2693	Camphene	133	9011
			Camphor	133	2717
Calcium hydrogen sulphite, solution	154	2693	Camphor, synthetic	133	2717
			Camphor oil	128	1130
Calcium hydrosulfite	135	1923	Caproic acid	153	2829
Calcium hydrosulphite	135	1923	Caprylyl peroxide	148	2129
Calcium hypochlorite, dry	140	1748	Caprylyl peroxide, solution	148	2129
Calcium hypochlorite, hydrated, with not less than 5.5% but not more than 10% water	140	2880	Carbamate pesticide, liquid, flammable, poisonous	131	2758
			Carbamate pesticide, liquid, flammable, toxic	131	2758
Calcium hypochlorite, hydrated mixture, with not less than 5.5% but not more than 10% water	140	2880	Carbamate pesticide, liquid, poisonous	151	2992
			Carbamate pesticide, liquid, poisonous, flammable	131	2991

Name of Material	Guide No.	ID No.
Carbamate pesticide, liquid, toxic	151	2992
Carbamate pesticide, liquid, toxic, flammable	131	2991
Carbamate pesticide, solid, poisonous	151	2757
Carbamate pesticide, solid, toxic	151	2757
Carbaryl	151	2757
Carbofuran	151	2757
Carbon, activated	133	1362
Carbon, animal or vegetable origin	133	1361
Carbon bisulfide	131	1131
Carbon bisulphide	131	1131
Carbon dioxide	120	1013
Carbon dioxide, compressed	120	1013
Carbon dioxide, refrigerated liquid	120	2187
Carbon dioxide, solid	120	1845
Carbon dioxide and Ethylene oxide mixture, with more than 9% but not more than 87% Ethylene oxide	115	1041
Carbon dioxide and Ethylene oxide mixture, with more than 87% Ethylene oxide	119P	3300
Carbon dioxide and Ethylene oxide mixtures, with more than 6% Ethylene oxide	115	1041
Carbon dioxide and Ethylene oxide mixtures, with not more than 6% Ethylene oxide	126	1952
Carbon dioxide and Ethylene oxide mixtures, with not more than 9% Ethylene oxide	126	1952
Carbon dioxide and Nitrous oxide mixture	126	1015
Carbon dioxide and Oxygen mixture	122	1014
Carbon dioxide and Oxygen mixture, compressed	122	1014
Carbon disulfide	131	1131
Carbon disulphide	131	1131
Carbon monoxide	119	1016
Carbon monoxide, compressed	119	1016
Carbon monoxide and Hydrogen mixture	119	2600
Carbon monoxide and Hydrogen mixture, compressed	119	2600
Carbon monoxide, refrigerated liquid (cryogenic liquid)	168	9202
Carbon tetrabromide	151	2516
Carbon tetrachloride	151	1846
Carbonyl fluoride	125	2417
Carbonyl fluoride, compressed	125	2417
Carbonyl sulfide	119	2204
Carbonyl sulphide	119	2204
Cargo transport unit under fumigation	171	——
Castor beans, meal, pomace or flake	171	2969
Caustic alkali liquid, n.o.s.	154	1719
Caustic potash, dry, solid	154	1813
Caustic potash, liquid	154	1814
Caustic potash, solution	154	1814
Caustic soda, bead	154	1823
Caustic soda, flake	154	1823
Caustic soda, granular	154	1823
Caustic soda, solid	154	1823
Caustic soda, solution	154	1824
Cells, containing Sodium	138	3292

Name of Material	Guide No.	ID No.
Celluloid, in blocks, rods, rolls, sheets, tubes, etc., except scrap	133	2000
Celluloid, scrap	135	2002
Cement (flammable)	128	1133
Cement, container, linoleum, tile or wallboard, liquid	128	1133
Cement, leather	128	1133
Cement, liquid, n.o.s.	128	1133
Cement, pyroxylin	128	1133
Cement, roofing, liquid	128	1133
Cement, rubber	128	1133
Cerium, slabs, ingots or rods	170	1333
Cerium, turnings or gritty powder	138	3078
Cesium	138	1407
Cesium hydroxide	157	2682
Cesium hydroxide, solution	154	2681
Cesium nitrate	140	1451
CG	125	1076
Charcoal	133	1361
Charcoal, briquettes	133	1361
Charcoal, shell	133	1361
Charcoal, wood, ground, crushed, granulated or pulverized	133	1361
Charcoal screenings, made from "Pinon" wood	133	1361
Charcoal screenings, other than "Pinon" wood screenings	133	1361
Chemical kit	154	1760
Chemical kit	171	3316
Chemical kits (containing corrosive substances)	154	——
Chemical kits (containing flammable liquids)	128	——
Chemical kits (containing flammable solids)	133	——
Chemical kits (containing oxidizing substances)	140	——
Chemical kits (containing poisonous liquids)	153	——
Chemical kits (containing poisonous solids)	154	——
Chemical kits (containing toxic liquids)	153	——
Chemical kits (containing toxic solids)	154	——
Chemical sample, poisonous liquid	151	3315
Chemical sample, poisonous solid	151	3315
Chemical sample, toxic liquid	151	3315
Chemical sample, toxic solid	151	3315
Chloral, anhydrous, inhibited	153	2075
Chlorate, n.o.s., wet	140	1461
Chlorate and Borate mixtures	140	1458
Chlorate and Magnesium chloride mixture	140	1459
Chlorates, inorganic, aqueous solution, n.o.s.	140	3210
Chlorates, inorganic, n.o.s.	140	1461
Chloric acid	140	2626
Chloric acid, aqueous solution, with not more than 10% Chloric acid	140	2626
Chlorine	124	1017
Chlorine dioxide, hydrate, frozen	143	9191
Chlorine pentafluoride	124	2548
Chlorine trifluoride	124	1749
Chlorite solution	154	1908

Name of Material	Guide No.	ID No.
Chlorite solution, with more than 5% available Chlorine	154	1908
Chlorites, inorganic, n.o.s.	143	1462
Chloroacetaldehyde	153	2232
Chloroacetic acid, liquid	153	1750
Chloroacetic acid, molten	153	3250
Chloroacetic acid, solid	153	1751
Chloroacetic acid, solution	153	1750
Chloroacetone, stabilized	131	1695
Chloroacetonitrile	131	2668
Chloroacetophenone	153	1697
Chloroacetophenone, liquid	153	1697
Chloroacetophenone, solid	153	1697
Chloroacetyl chloride	156	1752
Chloroanilines, liquid	152	2019
Chloroanilines, solid	152	2018
Chloroanisidines	152	2233
Chlorobenzene	130	1134
Chlorobenzotrifluorides	130	2234
p-Chlorobenzoyl peroxide	146	2113
p-Chlorobenzoyl peroxide	145	2114
p-Chlorobenzoyl peroxide	145	2115
Chlorobenzyl chlorides	153	2235
o-Chlorobenzylidene malononitrile	153	2810
1-Chloro-3-bromopropane	159	2688
Chlorobutanes	130	1127
Chlorocresols	152	2669
Chlorocresols, liquid	152	2669
Chlorocresols, solid	152	2669
3-Chloro-4-diethylamino-benzenediazonium zinc chloride	149	3033
Chlorodifluorobromomethane	126	1974
1-Chloro-1,1-difluoroethane	115	2517
Chlorodifluoroethanes	115	2517
Chlorodifluoromethane	126	1018
Chlorodifluoromethane and Chloropentafluoroethane mixture	126	1973
Chlorodinitrobenzenes	153	1577
1-Chloro-2,3-epoxypropane	131P	2023
2-Chloroethanal	153	2232
Chloroform	151	1888
Chloroformates, n.o.s.	155	2742
Chloroformates, poisonous, corrosive, flammable, n.o.s.	155	2742
Chloroformates, poisonous, corrosive, n.o.s.	154	3277
Chloroformates, toxic, corrosive, flammable, n.o.s.	155	2742
Chloroformates, toxic, corrosive, n.o.s.	154	3277
1-Chloroheptane	129	—
1-Chlorohexane	129	—
Chloromethyl chloroformate	157	2745
Chloromethyl ethyl ether	131	2354
3-Chloro-4-methylphenyl isocyanate	156	2236
Chloronitroanilines	153	2237
Chloronitrobenzenes	152	1578
Chloronitrobenzenes, liquid	152	1578
Chloronitrobenzenes, solid	152	1578
Chloronitrotoluenes	152	2433
Chloronitrotoluenes, liquid	152	2433
Chloronitrotoluenes, solid	152	2433
Chloropentafluoroethane	126	1020
Chloropentafluoroethane and Chlorodifluoromethane mixture	126	1973

Name of Material	Guide No.	ID No.
3-Chloroperoxybenzoic acid	146	2755
Chlorophenates, liquid	154	2904
Chlorophenates, solid	154	2905
Chlorophenolates, liquid	154	2904
Chlorophenolates, solid	154	2905
Chlorophenols, liquid	153	2021
Chlorophenols, solid	153	2020
Chlorophenyltrichlorosilane	156	1753
Chloropicrin	154	1580
Chloropicrin, absorbed	154	1583
Chloropicrin and Methyl bromide mixture	123	1581
Chloropicrin and Methyl chloride mixture	119	1582
Chloropicrin and non-flammable, non-liquefied compressed gas mixture	123	1955
Chloropicrin mixture, flammable	131	2929
Chloropicrin mixture, n.o.s.	154	1583
Chloropivaloyl chloride	156	9263
Chloroplatinic acid, solid	154	2507
Chloroprene, inhibited	131P	1991
1-Chloropropane	129	1278
2-Chloropropane	129	2356
3-Chloropropanol-1	153	2849
2-Chloropropene	130P	2456
2-Chloropropionic acid	153	2511
alpha-Chloropropionic acid	153	2511
2-Chloropyridine	153	2822
Chlorosilanes, corrosive, flammable, n.o.s.	155	2986
Chlorosilanes, corrosive, n.o.s.	156	2987
Chlorosilanes, flammable, corrosive, n.o.s.	155	2985
Chlorosilanes, n.o.s.	155	2985
Chlorosilanes, n.o.s.	155	2986
Chlorosilanes, n.o.s.	156	2987
Chlorosilanes, n.o.s.	139	2988
Chlorosilanes, water-reactive, flammable, corrosive, n.o.s.	139	2988
Chlorosulfonic acid	137	1754
Chlorosulfonic acid and Sulfur trioxide mixture	137	1754
Chlorosulphonic acid	137	1754
Chlorosulphonic acid and Sulphur trioxide mixture	137	1754
1-Chloro-1,2,2,2-tetrafluoroethane	126	1021
Chlorotetrafluoroethane	126	1021
Chlorotetrafluoroethane and Ethylene oxide mixture, with not more than 8.8% Ethylene oxide	126	3297
Chlorotoluenes	130	2238
4-Chloro-o-toluidine hydrochloride	153	1579
Chlorotoluidines	153	2239
Chlorotoluidines, liquid	153	2239
Chlorotoluidines, solid	153	2239
1-Chloro-2,2,2-trifluoroethane	126	1983
Chlorotrifluoroethane	126	1983
Chlorotrifluoromethane	126	1022
Chlorotrifluoromethane and Trifluoromethane azeotropic mixture with approximately 60% Chlorotrifluoromethane	126	2599
Chlorpyrifos	152	2783
Chromic acetate	171	9101
Chromic acid, solid	141	1463
Chromic acid, solution	154	1755

Name of Material	Guide No.	ID No.
Chromic acid mixture, dry	141	1463
Chromic fluoride, solid	154	1756
Chromic fluoride, solution	154	1757
Chromic sulfate	171	9100
Chromic sulphate	171	9100
Chromium nitrate	141	2720
Chromium oxychloride	137	1758
Chromium trioxide, anhydrous	141	1463
Chromosulfuric acid	154	2240
Chromosulphuric acid	154	2240
Chromous chloride	171	9102
Cigarette lighter, with flammable gas	115	1057
Cigarette lighter, with flammable liquid	127	1226
Cigarettes, self-lighting	133	1867
CK	125	1589
Clinical waste, unspecified, n.o.s.	158	3291
CN	153	1697
Coal gas	119	1023
Coal gas, compressed	119	1023
Coal tar distillate	128	1137
Coal tar distillates, flammable	128	1136
Coal tar dye, liquid	154	2801
Coating solution	127	1139
Cobalt naphthenates, powder	133	2001
Cobaltous bromide	171	9103
Cobaltous formate	171	9104
Cobaltous sulfamate	171	9105
Cobaltous sulphamate	171	9105
Cobalt resinate, precipitated	133	1318
Cocculus	151	1584
Collodion	127	2059

Name of Material	Guide No.	ID No.
Combustible liquid, n.o.s.	128	1993
Compound, cleaning liquid (containing Hydrochloric (muriatic) acid)	157	1789
Compound, cleaning liquid (containing Hydrofluoric acid)	157	1790
Compound, rust preventing (corrosive)	154	1760
Compound, rust removing (corrosive)	154	1760
Compound, tree or weed killing, liquid (corrosive)	154	1760
Compound, tree or weed killing, liquid (flammable)	128	1993
Compound, tree or weed killing, liquid (toxic)	153	2810
Compound, tree or weed killing, solid (oxidizer)	140	1479
Compound, vulcanizing, liquid (corrosive)	154	1760
Compound, vulcanizing, liquid (flammable)	127	1142
Compounds, cleaning, liquid (corrosive)	154	1760
Compounds, cleaning, liquid (flammable)	128	1993
Compounds, polishing, liquid, etc. (flammable)	127	1142
Compressed gas, flammable, n.o.s.	115	1954
Compressed gas, flammable, poisonous, n.o.s. (Inhalation Hazard Zone A)	119	1953
Compressed gas, flammable, poisonous, n.o.s. (Inhalation Hazard Zone B)	119	1953
Compressed gas, flammable, poisonous, n.o.s. (Inhalation Hazard Zone C)	119	1953

Name of Material	Guide No.	ID No.
Compressed gas, flammable, poisonous, n.o.s. (Inhalation Hazard Zone D)	119	1953
Compressed gas, flammable, toxic, n.o.s. (Inhalation Hazard Zone A)	119	1953
Compressed gas, flammable, toxic, n.o.s. (Inhalation Hazard Zone B)	119	1953
Compressed gas, flammable, toxic, n.o.s. (Inhalation Hazard Zone C)	119	1953
Compressed gas, flammable, toxic, n.o.s. (Inhalation Hazard Zone D)	119	1953
Compressed gas, n.o.s.	126	1956
Compressed gas, oxidizing, n.o.s.	122	3156
Compressed gas, poisonous, corrosive, n.o.s.	123	3304
Compressed gas, poisonous, corrosive, n.o.s. (Inhalation Hazard Zone A)	123	3304
Compressed gas, poisonous, corrosive, n.o.s. (Inhalation Hazard Zone B)	123	3304
Compressed gas, poisonous, corrosive, n.o.s. (Inhalation Hazard Zone C)	123	3304
Compressed gas, poisonous, corrosive, n.o.s. (Inhalation Hazard Zone D)	123	3304
Compressed gas, poisonous, flammable, corrosive, n.o.s.	119	3305
Compressed gas, poisonous, flammable, corrosive, n.o.s. (Inhalation Hazard Zone A)	119	3305
Compressed gas, poisonous, flammable, corrosive, n.o.s. (Inhalation Hazard Zone B)	119	3305
Compressed gas, poisonous, flammable, corrosive, n.o.s. (Inhalation Hazard Zone C)	119	3305
Compressed gas, poisonous, flammable, corrosive, n.o.s. (Inhalation Hazard Zone D)	119	3305
Compressed gas, poisonous, flammable, n.o.s.	119	1953
Compressed gas, poisonous, flammable, n.o.s. (Inhalation Hazard Zone A)	119	1953
Compressed gas, poisonous, flammable, n.o.s. (Inhalation Hazard Zone B)	119	1953
Compressed gas, poisonous, flammable, n.o.s. (Inhalation Hazard Zone C)	119	1953
Compressed gas, poisonous, flammable, n.o.s. (Inhalation Hazard Zone D)	119	1953
Compressed gas, poisonous, n.o.s.	123	1955
Compressed gas, poisonous, n.o.s. (Inhalation Hazard Zone A)	123	1955
Compressed gas, poisonous, n.o.s. (Inhalation Hazard Zone B)	123	1955
Compressed gas, poisonous, n.o.s. (Inhalation Hazard Zone C)	123	1955
Compressed gas, poisonous, n.o.s. (Inhalation Hazard Zone D)	123	1955
Compressed gas, poisonous, oxidizing, corrosive, n.o.s.	124	3306
Compressed gas, poisonous, oxidizing, corrosive, n.o.s. (Inhalation Hazard Zone A)	124	3306

Name of Material	Guide No.	ID No.
Compressed gas, poisonous, oxidizing, corrosive, n.o.s. (Inhalation Hazard Zone B)	124	3306
Compressed gas, poisonous, oxidizing, corrosive, n.o.s. (Inhalation Hazard Zone C)	124	3306
Compressed gas, poisonous, oxidizing, corrosive, n.o.s. (Inhalation Hazard Zone D)	124	3306
Compressed gas, poisonous, oxidizing, n.o.s.	124	3303
Compressed gas, poisonous, oxidizing, n.o.s. (Inhalation Hazard Zone A)	124	3303
Compressed gas, poisonous, oxidizing, n.o.s. (Inhalation Hazard Zone B)	124	3303
Compressed gas, poisonous, oxidizing, n.o.s. (Inhalation Hazard Zone C)	124	3303
Compressed gas, poisonous, oxidizing, n.o.s. (Inhalation Hazard Zone D)	124	3303
Compressed gas, toxic, corrosive, n.o.s.	123	3304
Compressed gas, toxic, corrosive, n.o.s. (Inhalation Hazard Zone A)	123	3304
Compressed gas, toxic, corrosive, n.o.s. (Inhalation Hazard Zone B)	123	3304
Compressed gas, toxic, corrosive, n.o.s. (Inhalation Hazard Zone C)	123	3304
Compressed gas, toxic, corrosive, n.o.s. (Inhalation Hazard Zone D)	123	3304
Compressed gas, toxic, flammable, corrosive, n.o.s.	119	3305
Compressed gas, toxic, flammable, corrosive, n.o.s. (Inhalation Hazard Zone A)	119	3305
Compressed gas, toxic, flammable, corrosive, n.o.s. (Inhalation Hazard Zone B)	119	3305
Compressed gas, toxic, flammable, corrosive, n.o.s. (Inhalation Hazard Zone C)	119	3305
Compressed gas, toxic, flammable, corrosive, n.o.s. (Inhalation Hazard Zone D)	119	3305
Compressed gas, toxic, flammable, n.o.s.	119	1953
Compressed gas, toxic, flammable, n.o.s. (Inhalation Hazard Zone A)	119	1953
Compressed gas, toxic, flammable, n.o.s. (Inhalation Hazard Zone B)	119	1953
Compressed gas, toxic, flammable, n.o.s. (Inhalation Hazard Zone C)	119	1953
Compressed gas, toxic, flammable, n.o.s. (Inhalation Hazard Zone D)	119	1953
Compressed gas, toxic, n.o.s.	123	1955
Compressed gas, toxic, n.o.s. (Inhalation Hazard Zone A)	123	1955
Compressed gas, toxic, n.o.s. (Inhalation Hazard Zone B)	123	1955
Compressed gas, toxic, n.o.s. (Inhalation Hazard Zone C)	123	1955
Compressed gas, toxic, n.o.s. (Inhalation Hazard Zone D)	123	1955
Compressed gas, toxic, oxidizing, corrosive, n.o.s.	124	3306

Name of Material	Guide No.	ID No.
Compressed gas, toxic, oxidizing, corrosive, n.o.s. (Inhalation Hazard Zone A)	124	3306
Compressed gas, toxic, oxidizing, corrosive, n.o.s. (Inhalation Hazard Zone B)	124	3306
Compressed gas, toxic, oxidizing, corrosive, n.o.s. (Inhalation Hazard Zone C)	124	3306
Compressed gas, toxic, oxidizing, corrosive, n.o.s. (Inhalation Hazard Zone D)	124	3306
Compressed gas, toxic, oxidizing, n.o.s.	124	3303
Compressed gas, toxic, oxidizing, n.o.s. (Inhalation Hazard Zone A)	124	3303
Compressed gas, toxic, oxidizing, n.o.s. (Inhalation Hazard Zone B)	124	3303
Compressed gas, toxic, oxidizing, n.o.s. (Inhalation Hazard Zone C)	124	3303
Compressed gas, toxic, oxidizing, n.o.s. (Inhalation Hazard Zone D)	124	3303
Consumer commodity	171	8000
Copper acetoarsenite	151	1585
Copper arsenite	151	1586
Copper based pesticide, liquid, flammable, poisonous	131	2776
Copper based pesticide, liquid, flammable, toxic	131	2776
Copper based pesticide, liquid, poisonous	151	3010
Copper based pesticide, liquid, poisonous, flammable	131	3009
Copper based pesticide, liquid, toxic	151	3010
Copper based pesticide, liquid, toxic, flammable	131	3009
Copper based pesticide, solid, poisonous	151	2775
Copper based pesticide, solid, toxic	151	2775
Copper chlorate	141	2721
Copper chloride	154	2802
Copper cyanide	151	1587
Copra	135	1363
Corrosive liquid, acidic, inorganic, n.o.s.	154	3264
Corrosive liquid, acidic, organic, n.o.s.	153	3265
Corrosive liquid, basic, inorganic, n.o.s.	154	3266
Corrosive liquid, basic, organic, n.o.s.	153	3267
Corrosive liquid, flammable, n.o.s.	132	2920
Corrosive liquid, n.o.s.	154	1760
Corrosive liquid, oxidizing, n.o.s.	140	3093
Corrosive liquid, poisonous, n.o.s.	154	2922
Corrosive liquid, self-heating, n.o.s.	136	3301
Corrosive liquid, toxic, n.o.s.	154	2922
Corrosive liquid, water-reactive, n.o.s.	138	3094
Corrosive liquid, which in contact with water emits flammable gases, n.o.s.	138	3094
Corrosive solid, acidic, inorganic, n.o.s.	154	3260
Corrosive solid, acidic, organic, n.o.s.	154	3261

Name of Material	Guide No.	ID No.
Corrosive solid, basic, inorganic, n.o.s.	154	3262
Corrosive solid, basic, organic, n.o.s.	154	3263
Corrosive solid, flammable, n.o.s.	134	2921
Corrosive solid, n.o.s.	154	1759
Corrosive solid, oxidizing, n.o.s.	140	3084
Corrosive solid, poisonous, n.o.s.	154	2923
Corrosive solid, self-heating, n.o.s.	136	3095
Corrosive solid, toxic, n.o.s.	154	2923
Corrosive solid, water-reactive, n.o.s.	138	3096
Corrosive solid, which in contact with water emits flammable gases, n.o.s.	138	3096
Cosmetics, liquid, n.o.s.	154	1760
Cosmetics, n.o.s.	133	1325
Cosmetics, n.o.s.	140	1479
Cosmetics, n.o.s.	128	1993
Cosmetics, solid, n.o.s.	154	1759
Cotton	133	1365
Cotton, wet	133	1365
Cotton waste, oily	133	1364
Coumaphos	152	2783
Coumarin derivative pesticide, liquid, flammable, poisonous	131	3024
Coumarin derivative pesticide, liquid, flammable, toxic	131	3024
Coumarin derivative pesticide, liquid, poisonous	151	3026
Coumarin derivative pesticide, liquid, poisonous, flammable	131	3025
Coumarin derivative pesticide, liquid, toxic	151	3026
Coumarin derivative pesticide, liquid, toxic, flammable	131	3025
Coumarin derivative pesticide, solid, poisonous	151	3027
Coumarin derivative pesticide, solid, toxic	151	3027
Cresols	153	2076
Cresylic acid	153	2022
Crotonaldehyde, inhibited	131P	1143
Crotonaldehyde, stabilized	131P	1143
Crotonic acid	153	2823
Crotonic acid, liquid	153	2823
Crotonic acid, solid	153	2823
Crotonylene	128	1144
CS	153	2810
Cumene	130	1918
Cumene hydroperoxide	147	2116
Cupric acetate	171	9106
Cupric sulfate	171	9109
Cupric sulfate, ammoniated	171	9110
Cupric sulphate	171	9109
Cupric sulphate, ammoniated	171	9110
Cupric tartrate	171	9111
Cupriethylenediamine, solution	154	1761
CX	154	2811
Cyanide solution, n.o.s.	157	1935
Cyanides, inorganic, n.o.s.	157	1588
Cyanides, inorganic, solid, n.o.s.	157	1588
Cyanogen	119	1026
Cyanogen, liquefied	119	1026
Cyanogen bromide	157	1889
Cyanogen chloride, inhibited	125	1589
Cyanogen gas	119	1026

Name of Material	Guide No.	ID No.	Name of Material	Guide No.	ID No.
Cyanuric chloride	157	2670	DA	151	1699
Cyclobutane	115	2601	Dangerous goods in apparatus	171	8001
Cyclobutyl chloroformate	155	2744	Dangerous goods in machinery	171	8001
1,5,9-Cyclododecatriene	153	2518	DC	153	2810
Cycloheptane	128	2241	DDT	151	2761
Cycloheptatriene	131	2603	Decaborane	134	1868
Cycloheptene	128	2242	Decahydronaphthalene	130	1147
Cyclohexane	128	1145	n-Decane	128	2247
Cyclohexanethiol	131	3054	Decanoyl peroxide	148	2120
Cyclohexanone	127	1915	Denatured alcohol	127	1987
Cyclohexanone peroxide, not more than 72% as a paste	147	2896	Denatured alcohol (toxic)	131	1986
Cyclohexanone peroxide, not more than 72% in solution	147	2118	Deuterium	115	1957
			Deuterium, compressed	115	1957
Cyclohexanone peroxide, not more than 90%, with not less than 10% water	147	2119	Devices, small, hydrocarbon gas powered, with release device	115	3150
			Diacetone alcohol	129	1148
Cyclohexene	130	2256	Diacetone alcohol peroxides	148	2163
Cyclohexenyltrichlorosilane	156	1762	Diacetyl	127	2346
Cyclohexyl acetate	130	2243	Diallylamine	132	2359
Cyclohexylamine	132	2357	Diallyl ether	131P	2360
Cyclohexyl isocyanate	155	2488	4,4'-Diaminodiphenylmethane	153	2651
Cyclohexyl mercaptan	131	3054	Di-n-amylamine	131	2841
Cyclohexyltrichlorosilane	156	1763	Diazinon	152	2783
Cyclooctadiene phosphines	135	2940	2-Diazo-1-naphthol-4-sulfochloride	149	3042
Cyclooctadienes	130P	2520			
Cyclooctatetraene	128P	2358	2-Diazo-1-naphthol-4-sulphochloride	149	3042
Cyclopentane	128	1146	2-Diazo-1-naphthol-5-sulfochloride	149	3043
Cyclopentanol	129	2244			
Cyclopentanone	127	2245	2-Diazo-1-naphthol-5-sulphochloride	149	3043
Cyclopentene	128	2246			
Cyclopropane	115	1027	Dibenzyldichlorosilane	156	2434
Cyclopropane, liquefied	115	1027	Dibenzyl peroxydicarbonate	148	2149
Cymenes	130	2046	Diborane	119	1911

Name of Material	Guide No.	ID No.
Diborane, compressed	119	1911
Diborane mixtures	119	1911
Dibromobenzene	129	2711
1,2-Dibromobutan-3-one	154	2648
Dibromochloropropanes	159	2872
Dibromodifluoromethane	171	1941
Dibromomethane	160	2664
Di-n-butylamine	132	2248
Dibutylaminoethanol	153	2873
Di-(4-tert-butylcyclohexyl)-peroxydicarbonate	148	2154
Di-(4-tert-butylcyclohexyl)-peroxydicarbonate	148	2894
Dibutyl ethers	127	1149
Di-tert-butyl peroxide	145	2102
2,2-Di-(tert-butylperoxy)butane	146	2111
1,1-Di-(tert-butylperoxy)-cyclohexane	146	2179
1,1-Di-(tert-butylperoxy)-cyclohexane	146	2180
1,1-Di-(tert-butylperoxy)-cyclohexane	145	2885
1,1-Di-(tert-butylperoxy)-cyclohexane	145	2897
Di-(sec-butyl)peroxydicarbonate	148	2150
Di-(sec-butyl)peroxydicarbonate	148	2151
1,3-Di-(2-tert-butylperoxy-isopropyl)benzene and 1,4-Di-(2-tert-butylperoxy-isopropyl)benzene mixtures	145	2112
1,4-Di-(2-tert-butylperoxy-isopropyl)benzene and 1,3-Di-(2-tert-butylperoxy-isopropyl)benzene mixtures	145	2112
Di-(tert-butylperoxy)phthalate	146	2106
Di-(tert-butylperoxy)phthalate	145	2107
Di-(tert-butylperoxy)phthalate	145	2108
2,2-Di-(tert-butylperoxy)-propane	145	2883
2,2-Di-(tert-butylperoxy)-propane	145	2884
1,1-Di-(tert-butylperoxy)-3,3,5-trimethyl cyclohexane	146	2145
1,1-Di-(tert-butylperoxy)-3,3,5-trimethyl cyclohexane	145	2146
1,1-Di-(tert-butylperoxy)-3,3,5-trimethyl cyclohexane	145	2147
Dicetyl peroxydicarbonate	148	2164
Dicetyl peroxydicarbonate, not more than 42%, in water	148	2895
Dichloroacetic acid	153	1764
1,3-Dichloroacetone	153	2649
Dichloroacetyl chloride	156	1765
Dichloroanilines	153	1590
Dichloroanilines, liquid	153	1590
Dichloroanilines, solid	153	1590
m-Dichlorobenzene	152	——
o-Dichlorobenzene	152	1591
p-Dichlorobenzene	152	1592
2,4-Dichlorobenzoyl peroxide	146	2137
2,4-Dichlorobenzoyl peroxide	145	2138
2,4-Dichlorobenzoyl peroxide	145	2139
Dichlorobutene	132	2920
Dichlorobutene	132	2924
Dichloro-(2-chlorovinyl) arsine	153	2810
2,2'-Dichlorodiethyl ether	152	1916
Dichlorodifluoroethylene	160	9018
Dichlorodifluoromethane	126	1028
Dichlorodifluoromethane and Difluoroethane azeotropic mixture with approximately 74% Dichlorodifluoromethane	126	2602

Name of Material	Guide No.	ID No.	Name of Material	Guide No.	ID No.
Dichlorodifluoromethane and Ethylene oxide mixture, with not more than 12.5% Ethylene oxide	126	3070	Dichlorotetrafluoroethane	126	1958
			3,5-Dichloro-2,4,6-trifluoropyridine	151	9264
Dichlorodifluoromethane and Ethylene oxide mixtures, with not more than 12% Ethylene oxide	126	3070	Dichlorvos	152	2783
			Dicumyl peroxide	145	2121
			Dicycloheptadiene	127P	2251
Dichlorodimethyl ether, symmetrical	153	2249	Dicyclohexylamine	153	2565
			Dicyclohexylammonium nitrite	133	2687
Dichlorodiphenyltrichloroethane (DDT)	151	2761	Dicyclohexyl peroxydicarbonate	148	2152
			Dicyclohexyl peroxydicarbonate	148	2153
1,1-Dichloroethane	130	2362	Dicyclopentadiene	129	2048
1,2-Dichloroethylene	130P	1150	2,2-Di-(4,4-di-tert-butyl-peroxycyclohexyl)propane	145	2168
Dichloroethylene	130P	1150	1,2-Di-(dimethylamino)ethane	129	2372
Dichloroethyl ether	152	1916	Didymium nitrate	140	1465
1,1-Dichloro-1-fluoroethane	160	9274	Dieldrin	151	2761
Dichlorofluoromethane	126	1029	Diesel fuel	128	1202
Dichloroisocyanuric acid, dry	140	2465	Diesel fuel	128	1993
Dichloroisocyanuric acid salts	140	2465	Diethoxymethane	127	2373
Dichloroisopropyl ether	153	2490	2,5-Diethoxy-4-morpholino-benzenediazonium zinc chloride	150	3036
Dichloromethane	160	1593			
1,1-Dichloro-1-nitroethane	153	2650	3,3-Diethoxypropene	127	2374
Dichloropentanes	130	1152	Diethylamine	132	1154
2,4-Dichlorophenoxyacetic acid	152	2765	2-Diethylaminoethanol	132	2686
Dichlorophenyl isocyanates	156	2250	Diethylaminoethanol	132	2686
Dichlorophenyltrichlorosilane	156	1766	3-Diethylaminopropylamine	132	2684
1,2-Dichloropropane	130	1279	Diethylaminopropylamine	132	2684
Dichloropropane	130	1279	N,N-Diethylaniline	153	2432
1,3-Dichloropropanol-2	153	2750	Diethylbenzene	130	2049
Dichloropropenes	132	2047	Diethyl carbonate	127	2366
2,2-Dichloropropionic acid	154	1760	Diethyldichlorosilane	155	1767
Dichlorosilane	119	2189	Diethylenetriamine	154	2079
1,2-Dichloro-1,1,2,2-tetrafluoroethane	126	1958	Diethyl ether	127	1155

Name of Material	Guide No.	ID No.	Name of Material	Guide No.	ID No.
N,N-Diethylethylenediamine	132	2685	Diisobutyl ketone	127	1157
Di-(2-ethylhexyl)-peroxydicarbonate	148	2122	Diisobutyryl peroxide	148	2182
			Diisooctyl acid phosphate	153	1902
Di-(2-ethylhexyl)-peroxydicarbonate	148	2123	Diisopropylamine	132	1158
Di-(2-ethylhexyl)phosphoric acid	153	1902	Diisopropylbenzene hydroperoxide	145	2171
Diethyl ketone	127	1156	Diisopropyl ether	127	1159
p-Diethylnitrosoaniline	136	——	Diisotridecyl peroxydicarbonate	148	2889
Diethyl peroxydicarbonate	148	2175	Diketene, inhibited	131P	2521
Diethyl sulfate	152	1594	1,1-Dimethoxyethane	127	2377
Diethyl sulfide	129	2375	1,2-Dimethoxyethane	127	2252
Diethyl sulphate	152	1594	Dimethylamine, anhydrous	118	1032
Diethyl sulphide	129	2375	Dimethylamine, aqueous solution	129	1160
Diethylthiophosphoryl chloride	155	2751	Dimethylamine, solution	129	1160
Diethylzinc	135	1366	2-Dimethylaminoacetonitrile	131	2378
Difluorochloroethanes	115	2517	4-Dimethylamino-6-(2-dimethyl-aminoethoxy)toluene-2-diazonium zinc chloride	150	3039
1,1-Difluoroethane	115	1030			
Difluoroethane	115	1030	2-Dimethylaminoethanol	132	2051
Difluoroethane and Dichlorodifluoromethane azeotropic mixture with approximately 74% dichlorodifluoromethane	126	2602	2-Dimethylaminoethyl acrylate	152	3302
			2-Dimethylaminoethyl methacrylate	153P	2522
1,1-Difluoroethylene	116P	1959	Dimethylaminoethyl methacrylate	153P	2522
Difluoromethane	115	3252	N,N-Dimethylaniline	153	2253
Difluorophosphoric acid, anhydrous	154	1768	Di-(2-methylbenzoyl)peroxide	148	2593
2,2-Dihydroperoxypropane	146	2178	2,3-Dimethylbutane	128	2457
2,3-Dihydropyran	127	2376	1,3-Dimethylbutylamine	132	2379
Di-(1-hydroxycyclohexyl)-peroxide	145	2148	Dimethylcarbamoyl chloride	156	2262
Diisobutylamine	132	2361	Dimethyl carbonate	129	1161
Diisobutylene, isomeric compounds	127	2050	Dimethyl chlorothiophosphate	156	2267
			Dimethylcyclohexanes	128	2263
			Dimethylcyclohexylamine	132	2264

Name of Material	Guide No.	ID No.	Name of Material	Guide No.	ID No.
2,5-Dimethyl-2,5-di-(benzoylperoxy)hexane	146	2172	2,2-Dimethylpropane	115	2044
2,5-Dimethyl-2,5-di-(benzoylperoxy)hexane	145	2173	Dimethyl-N-propylamine	132	2266
2,5-Dimethyl-2,5-di-(tert-butylperoxy)hexane	145	2155	Dimethyl sulfate	156	1595
2,5-Dimethyl-2,5-di-(tert-butylperoxy)hexane	145	2156	Dimethyl sulfide	130	1164
2,5-Dimethyl-2,5-di-(tert-butylperoxy)hexyne-3	146	2158	Dimethyl sulphate	156	1595
2,5-Dimethyl-2,5-di-(tert-butylperoxy)hexyne-3, with not more than 52% Peroxide in inert solid	145	2159	Dimethyl sulphide	130	1164
			Dimethyl thiophosphoryl chloride	156	2267
			Dimethylzinc	135	1370
Dimethyldichlorosilane	155	1162	Dimyristyl peroxydicarbonate	148	2595
Dimethyldiethoxysilane	127	2380	Dimyristyl peroxydicarbonate, not more than 42%, in water	148	2892
2,5-Dimethyl-2,5-di-(2-ethyl-hexanoylperoxy)hexane	148	2157	Dinitroanilines	153	1596
2,5-Dimethyl-2,5-dihydroperoxy hexane, not more than 82% with water	146	2174	Dinitrobenzenes	152	1597
			Dinitrochlorobenzene	153	1577
Dimethyldioxanes	128	2707	Dinitro-o-cresol	153	1598
Dimethyl disulfide	130	2381	Dinitrocyclohexylphenol	153	9026
Dimethyl disulphide	130	2381	Dinitrogen tetroxide	124	1067
Dimethylethanolamine	132	2051	Dinitrogen tetroxide, liquefied	124	1067
Dimethyl ether	115	1033	Dinitrogen tetroxide and Nitric oxide mixture	124	1975
N,N-Dimethylformamide	129	2265			
Dimethylhexane dihydroperoxide, with 18% or more water	146	2174	Dinitrophenol, solution	153	1599
			Dinitrophenol, wetted with not less than 15% water	113	1320
1,1-Dimethylhydrazine	131	1163	Dinitrophenolates, wetted with not less than 15% water	113	1321
1,2-Dimethylhydrazine	131	2382	Dinitroresorcinol, wetted with not less than 15% water	113	1322
Dimethylhydrazine, symmetrical	131	2382			
Dimethylhydrazine, unsymmetrical	131	1163	N,N'-Dinitroso-N,N'-dimethyl terephthalamide	149	2973
Dimethyl phosphorochloridothioate	156	2267	N,N'-Dinitrosopentamethylene tetramine	149	2972
			Dinitrotoluenes	152	2038
			Dinitrotoluenes, liquid	152	2038
			Dinitrotoluenes, molten	152	1600
			Dinitrotoluenes, solid	152	2038

Name of Material	Guide No.	ID No.
Dioxane	127	1165
Dioxolane	127	1166
Dipentene	128	2052
Diphenylamine chloroarsine	154	1698
Diphenylchloroarsine	151	1699
Diphenylchloroarsine, liquid	151	1699
Diphenylchloroarsine, solid	151	1699
Diphenylcyanoarsine	153	2810
Diphenyldichlorosilane	156	1769
Diphenylmethane-4,4'-diisocyanate	156	2489
Diphenylmethyl bromide	153	1770
Diphenyloxide-4,4'-disulfohydrazide	149	2951
Diphenyloxide-4,4'-disulphohydrazide	149	2951
Diphosgene	125	1076
Dipicryl sulfide, wetted with not less than 10% water	113	2852
Dipicryl sulphide, wetted with not less than 10% water	113	2852
Dipropylamine	132	2383
4-Dipropylaminobenzene-diazonium zinc chloride	149	3034
Di-n-propyl ether	127	2384
Dipropyl ether	127	2384
Dipropyl ketone	127	2710
Di-n-propyl peroxydicarbonate	148	2176
Disinfectant, liquid, corrosive, n.o.s.	153	1903
Disinfectant, liquid, n.o.s.	128	1993
Disinfectant, liquid, poisonous, n.o.s.	151	3142
Disinfectant, liquid, toxic, n.o.s.	151	3142
Disinfectant, solid, poisonous,n.o.s.	151	1601
Disinfectant, solid, toxic, n.o.s.	151	1601
Disinfectants, corrosive, liquid, n.o.s.	153	1903
Disinfectants, liquid, n.o.s. (poisonous)	151	3142
Disinfectants, solid, n.o.s. (poisonous)	151	1601
Disodium trioxosilicate	154	3253
Disodium trioxosilicate, pentahydrate	154	3253
Dispersant gas, n.o.s.	126	1078
Dispersant gas, n.o.s. (flammable)	115	1954
Distearyl peroxydicarbonate	145	2592
Disulfoton	152	2783
Dithiocarbamate pesticide, liquid, flammable, poisonous	131	2772
Dithiocarbamate pesticide, liquid, flammable, toxic	131	2772
Dithiocarbamate pesticide, liquid, poisonous	151	3006
Dithiocarbamate pesticide, liquid, poisonous, flammable	131	3005
Dithiocarbamate pesticide, liquid, toxic	151	3006
Dithiocarbamate pesticide, liquid, toxic, flammable	131	3005
Dithiocarbamate pesticide, solid, poisonous	151	2771
Dithiocarbamate pesticide, solid, toxic	151	2771
Di-(3,5,5-trimethyl-1,2-dioxolanyl-3)peroxide	148	2597
Divinyl ether, inhibited	131P	1167
DM	154	1698
Dodecylbenzenesulfonic acid	153	2584
Dodecylbenzenesulphonic acid	153	2584

Name of Material	Guide No.	ID No.
Dodecyltrichlorosilane	156	1771
DP	125	1076
Driers, paint or varnish, liquid, n.o.s.	127	1168
Drugs, liquid, n.o.s.	154	1760
Drugs, liquid, n.o.s.	153	2810
Drugs, n.o.s.	133	1325
Drugs, n.o.s.	140	1479
Drugs, n.o.s.	128	1993
Drugs, solid, n.o.s.	154	1759
Drugs, solid, n.o.s.	154	2811
Dry ice	120	1845
Dye, liquid, corrosive, n.o.s.	154	2801
Dye, liquid, poisonous, n.o.s.	151	1602
Dye, liquid, toxic, n.o.s.	151	1602
Dye, solid, corrosive, n.o.s.	154	3147
Dye, solid, poisonous, n.o.s.	151	3143
Dye, solid, toxic, n.o.s.	151	3143
Dye intermediate, liquid, corrosive, n.o.s.	154	2801
Dye intermediate, liquid, poisonous, n.o.s.	151	1602
Dye intermediate, liquid, toxic, n.o.s.	151	1602
Dye intermediate, solid, corrosive, n.o.s.	154	3147
Dye intermediate, solid, poisonous, n.o.s.	151	3143
Dye intermediate, solid, toxic, n.o.s.	151	3143
ED	151	1892
EDTA	171	9117
Elevated temperature liquid, flammable, n.o.s., with flash point above 37.8°C (100°F), at or above its flash point	128	3256
Elevated temperature liquid, flammable, n.o.s., with flash point above 60.5°C (141°F), at or above its flash point	128	3256
Elevated temperature liquid, n.o.s., at or above 100°C (212°F) and below its flash point	128	3257
Elevated temperature material, liquid, n.o.s., (at or above 100°C (212°F) and below its flash point)	128	9259
Elevated temperature solid, n.o.s., at or above 240°C (464°F)	171	3258
Endosulfan	151	2761
Engine starting fluid	115	1960
Engines, internal combustion, flammable gas powered	128	3166
Engines, internal combustion, flammable liquid powered	128	3166
Engines, internal combustion, including when fitted in machinery or vehicles	128	3166
Environmentally hazardous substances, liquid, n.o.s.	171	3082
Environmentally hazardous substances, solid, n.o.s.	171	3077
Epibromohydrin	131	2558
Epichlorohydrin	131P	2023
1,2-Epoxy-3-ethoxypropane	127	2752
Esters, n.o.s.	127	3272
Etching acid, liquid, n.o.s.	157	1790
Ethane	115	1035
Ethane, compressed	115	1035
Ethane, refrigerated liquid	115	1961
Ethane-Propane mixture, refrigerated liquid	115	1961

Name of Material	Guide No.	ID No.	Name of Material	Guide No.	ID No.
Ethanol	127	1170	Ethyl 2-chloropropionate	132	2935
Ethanol, solution	127	1170	Ethyl chlorothioformate	155	2826
Ethanolamine	153	2491	Ethyl crotonate	129	1862
Ethanolamine, solution	153	2491	Ethyl cyanoacetate	156	2666
Ethers, n.o.s.	127	3271	Ethyl-3,3-di-(tert-butyl-peroxy)butyrate	146	2184
Ethion	152	2783	Ethyl-3,3-di-(tert-butylperoxy)butyrate	145	2598
Ethyl acetate	129	1173	Ethyl-3,3-di-(tert-butyl-peroxy)butyrate, not more than 77% in solution	145	2185
Ethylacetylene, inhibited	116P	2452			
Ethyl acrylate, inhibited	129P	1917			
Ethyl alcohol	127	1170	Ethyldichloroarsine	151	1892
Ethyl alcohol, solution	127	1170	Ethyldichlorosilane	139	1183
Ethylamine	118	1036	O-Ethyl S-(2-diisopropylamino-ethyl) methylphosphonothiolate	153	2810
Ethylamine, aqueous solution, with not less than 50% but not more than 70% Ethylamine	132	2270	Ethyl N,N-dimethylphosphor-amidocyanidate	153	2810
Ethyl amyl ketone	127	2271	Ethylene	116P	1962
2-Ethylaniline	153	2273	Ethylene, Acetylene and Propylene in mixture, refrigerated liquid containing at least 71.5% Ethylene with not more than 22.5% Acetylene and not more than 6% Propylene	116	3138
N-Ethylaniline	153	2272			
Ethylbenzene	129	1175			
N-Ethyl-N-benzylaniline	153	2274			
N-Ethylbenzyltoluidines	153	2753			
Ethyl borate	129	1176			
Ethyl bromide	131	1891	Ethylene, compressed	116P	1962
Ethyl bromoacetate	155	1603	Ethylene, refrigerated liquid (cryogenic liquid)	115	1038
2-Ethylbutanol	129	2275			
2-Ethylbutyl acetate	129	1177	Ethylene chlorohydrin	131	1135
Ethylbutyl acetate	129	1177	Ethylenediamine	132	1604
Ethyl butyl ether	127	1179	Ethylenediaminetetraacetic acid	171	9117
2-Ethylbutyraldehyde	129	1178	Ethylene dibromide	154	1605
Ethyl butyrate	129	1180	Ethylene dibromide and Methyl bromide mixture, liquid	151	1647
Ethyl chloride	115	1037			
Ethyl chloroacetate	155	1181	Ethylene dichloride	129	1184
Ethyl chloroformate	155	1182	Ethylene glycol diethyl ether	127	1153
			Ethylene glycol monobutyl ether	152	2369

Name of Material	Guide No.	ID No.
Ethylene glycol monoethyl ether	127	1171
Ethylene glycol monoethyl ether acetate	129	1172
Ethylene glycol monomethyl ether	127	1188
Ethylene glycol monomethyl ether acetate	129	1189
Ethyleneimine, inhibited	131P	1185
Ethylene oxide	119P	1040
Ethylene oxide and Carbon dioxide mixture, with more than 9% but not more than 87% Ethylene oxide	115	1041
Ethylene oxide and Carbon dioxide mixture, with more than 87% Ethylene oxide	119P	3300
Ethylene oxide and Carbon dioxide mixtures, with more than 6 % Ethylene oxide	115	1041
Ethylene oxide and Carbon dioxide mixtures, with not more than 6% Ethylene oxide	126	1952
Ethylene oxide and Carbon dioxide mixtures, with not more than 9% Ethylene oxide	126	1952
Ethylene oxide and Chlorotetrafluoroethane mixture, with not more than 8.8% Ethylene oxide	126	3297
Ethylene oxide and Dichlorodifluoromethane mixture, with not more than 12.5% Ethylene oxide	126	3070
Ethylene oxide and Dichlorodifluoromethane mixtures, with not more than 12% Ethylene oxide	126	3070
Ethylene oxide and Pentafluoroethane mixture, with not more than 7.9% Ethylene oxide	126	3298
Ethylene oxide and Propylene oxide mixture, with not more than 30% Ethylene oxide	129P	2983
Ethylene oxide and Tetrafluoroethane mixture, with not more than 5.6% Ethylene oxide	126	3299
Ethylene oxide with Nitrogen	119P	1040
Ethyl ether	127	1155
Ethyl fluoride	115	2453
Ethyl formate	129	1190
Ethylhexaldehydes	129	1191
2-Ethylhexylamine	132	2276
2-Ethylhexyl chloroformate	156	2748
Ethyl isobutyrate	129	2385
Ethyl isocyanate	155	2481
Ethyl lactate	129	1192
Ethyl mercaptan	130	2363
Ethyl methacrylate	129P	2277
Ethyl methacrylate, inhibited	129P	2277
Ethyl methyl ether	115	1039
Ethyl methyl ketone	127	1193
Ethyl nitrate	128	1993
Ethyl nitrite, solution	131	1194
Ethyl orthoformate	129	2524
Ethyl oxalate	156	2525
Ethylphenyldichlorosilane	156	2435
Ethyl phosphonothioic dichloride, anhydrous	154	2927
Ethyl phosphonous dichloride, anhydrous	135	2845
Ethyl phosphorodichloridate	154	2927
1-Ethylpiperidine	132	2386
Ethyl propionate	129	1195
2-Ethyl-3-propylacrolein	153	—

Name of Material	Guide No.	ID No.	Name of Material	Guide No.	ID No.
Ethyl propyl ether	127	2615	Ferrous ammonium sulphate	171	9122
Ethyl silicate	132	1292	Ferrous arsenate	151	1608
Ethylsulfuric acid	156	2571	Ferrous chloride, solid	154	1759
Ethylsulphuric acid	156	2571	Ferrous chloride, solution	154	1760
N-Ethyltoluidines	153	2754	Ferrous metal borings, shavings, turnings or cuttings	170	2793
Ethyltrichlorosilane	155	1196			
Etiologic agent, n.o.s.	158	2814	Ferrous sulfate	171	9125
Explosive A	112	——	Ferrous sulphate	171	9125
Explosive B	112	——	Fertilizer, ammoniating solution, with free Ammonia	125	1043
Explosive C	114	——			
Explosives, division 1.1, 1.2, 1.3, 1.5 or 1.6	112	——	Fiber, animal, synthetic or vegetable, n.o.s., with oil	133	1373
Explosives, division 1.4	114	——	Fiber, animal or vegetable, n.o.s., burnt, wet or damp	133	1372
Extracts, aromatic, liquid	127	1169			
Extracts, flavoring, liquid	127	1197	Fibers	133	1372
Extracts, flavouring, liquid	127	1197	Fibers impregnated with weakly nitrated Nitrocellulose, n.o.s.	133	1353
Fabrics, animal, synthetic or vegetable, n.o.s., with oil	133	1373			
Fabrics impregnated with weakly nitrated Nitrocellulose, n.o.s.	133	1353	Fibres, animal, synthetic or vegetable, n.o.s., with oil	133	1373
			Fibres, animal or vegetable, burnt, wet or damp	133	——
Ferric ammonium citrate	171	9118			
Ferric ammonium oxalate	171	9119	Fibres, vegetable, dry	133	——
Ferric arsenate	151	1606	Fibres impregnated with weakly nitrated Nitrocellulose, n.o.s.	133	1353
Ferric arsenite	151	1607			
Ferric chloride	157	1773	Film	133	1324
Ferric chloride, anhydrous	157	1773	Films, nitrocellulose base	133	1324
Ferric chloride, solution	154	2582	Fire extinguisher charges, corrosive liquid	154	1774
Ferric fluoride	171	9120			
Ferric nitrate	140	1466	Fire extinguishers with compressed gas	126	1044
Ferric sulfate	171	9121			
Ferric sulphate	171	9121	Fire extinguishers with liquefied gas	126	1044
Ferrocerium	170	1323			
Ferrosilicon	139	1408	Firelighters, solid, with flammable liquid	133	2623
Ferrous ammonium sulfate	171	9122	First aid kit	171	3316
			Fish meal, stabilized	171	2216

Name of Material	Guide No.	ID No.
Fish meal, unstabilized	133	1374
Fish meal containing 6% to 12% water	171	2216
Fish meal containing less than 6% or more than 12% water	133	1374
Fish scrap, stabilized	171	2216
Fish scrap, unstabilized	133	1374
Fish scrap containing 6% to 12% water	171	2216
Fish scrap containing less than 6% or more than 12% water	133	1374
Flame retardant compound, liquid (corrosive)	154	1760
Flammable gas in lighter for cigars, cigarettes, etc.	115	1057
Flammable liquid, corrosive, n.o.s	132	2924
Flammable liquid, n.o.s.	128	1993
Flammable liquid, poisonous, corrosive, n.o.s.	131	3286
Flammable liquid, poisonous, n.o.s.	131	1992
Flammable liquid, toxic, corrosive, n.o.s.	131	3286
Flammable liquid, toxic, n.o.s.	131	1992
Flammable liquid preparations, n.o.s.	127	1142
Flammable liquids, elevated temperature material, n.o.s.	128	9276
Flammable solid, corrosive, inorganic, n.o.s.	134	3180
Flammable solid, corrosive, n.o.s.	134	2925
Flammable solid, corrosive, organic, n.o.s.	134	2925
Flammable solid, inorganic, corrosive, n.o.s.	134	3180
Flammable solid, inorganic, n.o.s.	133	3178
Flammable solid, n.o.s.	133	1325
Flammable solid, organic, molten, n.o.s.	133	3176
Flammable solid, organic, n.o.s.	133	1325
Flammable solid, oxidizing, n.o.s.	140	3097
Flammable solid, poisonous, inorganic, n.o.s.	134	3179
Flammable solid, poisonous, n.o.s.	134	2926
Flammable solid, poisonous, organic, n.o.s.	134	2926
Flammable solid, toxic, inorganic, n.o.s.	134	3179
Flammable solid, toxic, organic, n.o.s.	134	2926
Flue dust, poisonous	154	2811
Fluoboric acid	154	1775
Fluorine	124	1045
Fluorine, compressed	124	1045
Fluorine, refrigerated liquid (cryogenic liquid)	167	9192
Fluoroacetic acid	154	2642
Fluoroanilines	153	2941
Fluorobenzene	130	2387
Fluoroboric acid	154	1775
Fluorophosphoric acid, anhydrous	154	1776
Fluorosilicates, n.o.s.	151	2856
Fluorosilicic acid	154	1778
Fluorosulfonic acid	137	1777
Fluorosulphonic acid	137	1777
Fluorotoluenes	130	2388

Name of Material	Guide No.	ID No.	Name of Material	Guide No.	ID No.
Fluosilicic acid	154	1778	Gas oil	128	1202
Formaldehyde, solution, flammable	132	1198	Gasoline	128	1203
Formaldehyde, solutions (Formalin)	132	1198	Gas sample, non-pressurized, flammable, n.o.s., not refrigerated liquid	115	3167
Formaldehyde, solutions (Formalin) (corrosive)	132	2209	Gas sample, non-pressurized, poisonous, flammable, n.o.s., not refrigerated liquid	119	3168
Formic acid	153	1779	Gas sample, non-pressurized, poisonous, n.o.s., not refrigerated liquid	123	3169
Fuel, aviation, turbine engine	128	1863			
Fuel oil	128	1202			
Fuel oil	128	1993	Gas sample, non-pressurized, toxic, flammable, n.o.s., not refrigerated liquid	119	3168
Fuel oil, no. 1,2,4,5,6	128	1202			
Fumaric acid	171	9126	Gas sample, non-pressurized, toxic, n.o.s., not refrigerated liquid	123	3169
Fumaryl chloride	156	1780			
Furaldehydes	132P	1199	GB	153	2810
Furan	127	2389	GD	153	2810
Furfural	132P	1199	Genetically modified micro-organisms	171	3245
Furfuraldehydes	132P	1199			
Furfuryl alcohol	153	2874	Genetically modified organisms	171	9278
Furfurylamine	132	2526	Germane	119	2192
Fusee (rail or highway)	133	1325	GF	153	2810
Fusel oil	127	1201	Glycerol alpha-monochlorohydrin	153	2689
GA	153	2810			
Gallium	172	2803	Glycidaldehyde	131P	2622
Gas, refrigerated liquid, flammable, n.o.s.	115	3312	Grenade, tear gas	159	2017
			Guanidine nitrate	143	1467
Gas, refrigerated liquid, n.o.s.	120	3158	H	153	2810
Gas, refrigerated liquid, oxidizing, n.o.s.	122	3311	Hafnium powder, dry	135	2545
			Hafnium powder, wetted with not less than 25% water	170	1326
Gas cartridges	115	2037			
Gas drips, hydrocarbon	128	1864	Halogenated irritating liquid, n.o.s.	159	1610
Gas generator assemblies	171	8013			
Gas identification set	123	9035	Hay, wet, damp or contaminated with oil	133	1327
Gasohol	128	1203			

Name of Material	Guide No.	ID No.	Name of Material	Guide No.	ID No.
Hazardous substance, liquid, n.o.s.	171	9188	Hexaethyl tetraphosphate and compressed gas mixture	123	1612
Hazardous substance, solid, n.o.s.	171	9188	Hexaethyl tetraphosphate mixture, liquid	152	2783
Hazardous waste, liquid, n.o.s.	171	3082	Hexafluoroacetone	125	2420
Hazardous waste, liquid, n.o.s.	171	9189	Hexafluoroacetone hydrate	151	2552
Hazardous waste, solid, n.o.s.	171	3077	Hexafluoroethane	126	2193
Hazardous waste, solid, n.o.s.	171	9189	Hexafluoroethane, compressed	126	2193
HD	153	2810	Hexafluorophosphoric acid	154	1782
Heater for refrigerator car, liquid fuel type	128	1993	Hexafluoropropylene	126	1858
Heating oil, light	128	1202	Hexafluoropropylene oxide	126	1956
Heat producing article	171	8038	Hexaldehyde	129	1207
Helium	121	1046	Hexamethylenediamine, solid	153	2280
Helium, compressed	121	1046	Hexamethylenediamine, solution	153	1783
Helium, refrigerated liquid (cryogenic liquid)	120	1963	Hexamethylene diisocyanate	156	2281
Helium-Oxygen mixture	122	1980	Hexamethyleneimine	132	2493
Heptafluoropropane	126	3296	Hexamethylenetetramine	133	1328
n-Heptaldehyde	129	3056	3,3,6,6,9,9-Hexamethyl-1,2,4,5-tetraoxacyclononane	146	2165
Heptanes	128	1206	3,3,6,6,9,9-Hexamethyl-1,2,4,5-tetraoxacyclononane	145	2166
n-Heptene	128	2278	3,3,6,6,9,9-Hexamethyl-1,2,4,5-tetraoxacyclononane	145	2167
Hexachloroacetone	153	2661			
Hexachlorobenzene	152	2729	Hexamine	133	1328
Hexachlorobutadiene	151	2279	Hexanes	128	1208
Hexachlorocyclopentadiene	151	2646	Hexanoic acid	154	1760
Hexachloroethane	151	9037	Hexanoic acid	153	2829
Hexachlorophene	151	2875	Hexanols	129	2282
Hexadecyltrichlorosilane	156	1781	1-Hexene	128	2370
Hexadiene	130	2458	Hexyltrichlorosilane	156	1784
Hexaethyl tetraphosphate	151	1611	HL	153	2810
Hexaethyl tetraphosphate, liquid	151	1611	HN-1 (nitrogen mustard)	153	2810
Hexaethyl tetraphosphate, solid	151	1611	HN-2	153	2810

Name of Material	Guide No.	ID No.
HN-3	153	2810
Hydrazine, anhydrous	132	2029
Hydrazine, aqueous solution, with not less than 37% but not more than 64% Hydrazine	153	2030
Hydrazine, aqueous solution, with not more than 37% Hydrazine	152	3293
Hydrazine, aqueous solutions, with more than 64% Hydrazine	132	2029
Hydrazine, aqueous solutions, with not more than 64% Hydrazine	153	2030
Hydrazine hydrate	153	2030
Hydrides, metal, n.o.s.	138	1409
Hydriodic acid	154	1787
Hydriodic acid, solution	154	1787
Hydrobromic acid	154	1788
Hydrobromic acid, solution	154	1788
Hydrocarbon gas, compressed, n.o.s.	115	1964
Hydrocarbon gas, liquefied, n.o.s.	115	1965
Hydrocarbon gas mixture, compressed, n.o.s.	115	1964
Hydrocarbon gas mixture, liquefied, n.o.s.	115	1965
Hydrocarbon gas refills for small devices, with release device	115	3150
Hydrocarbons, liquid, n.o.s.	128	3295
Hydrochloric acid	157	1789
Hydrochloric acid, mixture	157	1789
Hydrochloric acid, solution	157	1789
Hydrocyanic acid, aqueous solution, with less than 5% Hydrogen cyanide	154	1613
Hydrocyanic acid, aqueous solution, with not more than 20% Hydrogen cyanide	154	1613
Hydrocyanic acid, aqueous solutions, with more than 20% Hydrogen cyanide	117	1051
Hydrocyanic acid, liquefied	117	1051
Hydrofluoric acid	157	1790
Hydrofluoric acid, solution	157	1790
Hydrofluoric acid and Sulfuric acid mixture	157	1786
Hydrofluoric acid and Sulphuric acid mixture	157	1786
Hydrofluorosilicic acid	154	1778
Hydrofluosilicic acid	154	1778
Hydrogen	115	1049
Hydrogen, compressed	115	1049
Hydrogen, refrigerated liquid (cryogenic liquid)	115	1966
Hydrogen and Carbon monoxide mixture	119	2600
Hydrogen and Carbon monoxide mixture, compressed	119	2600
Hydrogen and Methane mixture, compressed	115	2034
Hydrogen bromide, anhydrous	125	1048
Hydrogen chloride, anhydrous	125	1050
Hydrogen chloride, refrigerated liquid	125	2186
Hydrogen cyanide, anhydrous, stabilized	117	1051
Hydrogen cyanide, anhydrous, stabilized (absorbed)	131	1614
Hydrogen cyanide, aqueous solution, with not more than 20% Hydrogen cyanide	154	1613

Name of Material	Guide No.	ID No.
Hydrogen cyanide, solution in alcohol, with not more than 45% Hydrogen cyanide	131	3294
Hydrogen cyanide, stabilized	117	1051
Hydrogen cyanide, stabilized (absorbed)	131	1614
Hydrogendifluorides, n.o.s.	154	1740
Hydrogen fluoride, anhydrous	125	1052
Hydrogen iodide, anhydrous	125	2197
Hydrogen peroxide, aqueous solution, stabilized, with more than 60% Hydrogen peroxide	143	2015
Hydrogen peroxide, aqueous solution, with not less than 8% but less than 20% Hydrogen peroxide	140	2984
Hydrogen peroxide, aqueous solution, with not less than 20% but not more than 60% Hydrogen peroxide (stabilized as necessary)	140	2014
Hydrogen peroxide, stabilized	143	2015
Hydrogen peroxide and Peroxyacetic acid mixture, with acid(s), water and not more than 5% Peroxyacetic acid, stabilized	140	3149
Hydrogen selenide, anhydrous	117	2202
Hydrogen sulfide	117	1053
Hydrogen sulfide, liquefied	117	1053
Hydrogen sulphide	117	1053
Hydrogen sulphide, liquefied	117	1053
Hydroquinone	153	2662
3-(2-Hydroxyethoxy)-4-pyrrolidin-1-yl benzene-diazonium zinc chloride	150	3035
Hydroxylamine sulfate	154	2865
Hydroxylamine sulphate	154	2865

Name of Material	Guide No.	ID No.
Hypochlorite solution	154	1791
Hypochlorite solution, with more than 5% available Chlorine	154	1791
Hypochlorites, inorganic, n.o.s.	140	3212
3,3'-Iminodipropylamine	153	2269
Infectious substance, affecting animals only	158	2900
Infectious substance, affecting humans	158	2814
Ink, printer's, flammable	129	1210
Insecticide, dry, n.o.s.	151	2588
Insecticide, liquefied gas	126	1968
Insecticide, liquefied gas, containing Poison A or Poison B material	123	1967
Insecticide, liquid, poisonous, n.o.s.	151	2902
Insecticide gas, flammable, n.o.s.	115	1954
Insecticide gas, flammable, n.o.s.	115	3354
Insecticide gas, n.o.s.	126	1968
Insecticide gas, poisonous, flammable, n.o.s.	119	3355
Insecticide gas, poisonous, flammable, n.o.s. (Inhalation Hazard Zone A)	119	3355
Insecticide gas, poisonous, flammable, n.o.s. (Inhalation Hazard Zone B)	119	3355
Insecticide gas, poisonous, flammable, n.o.s. (Inhalation Hazard Zone C)	119	3355
Insecticide gas, poisonous, flammable, n.o.s. (Inhalation Hazard Zone D)	119	3355
Insecticide gas, poisonous, n.o.s.	123	1967
Insecticide gas, toxic, flammable, n.o.s.	119	3355

Name of Material	Guide No.	ID No.	Name of Material	Guide No.	ID No.
Insecticide gas, toxic, flammable, n.o.s. (Inhalation Hazard Zone A)	119	3355	Isobutylene	115	1055
			Isobutylene	115	1075
			Isobutyl formate	132	2393
Insecticide gas, toxic, flammable, n.o.s. (Inhalation Hazard Zone B)	119	3355	Isobutyl isobutyrate	129	2528
			Isobutyl isocyanate	155	2486
Insecticide gas, toxic, flammable, n.o.s. (Inhalation Hazard Zone C)	119	3355	Isobutyl methacrylate	130P	2283
			Isobutyl methacrylate, inhibited	130P	2283
Insecticide gas, toxic, flammable, n.o.s. (Inhalation Hazard Zone D)	119	3355	Isobutyl propionate	129	2394
			Isobutyraldehyde	129	2045
Insecticide gas, toxic, n.o.s.	123	1967	Isobutyric acid	132	2529
Iodine monochloride	157	1792	Isobutyric anhydride	132	2530
Iodine pentafluoride	144	2495	Isobutyronitrile	131	2284
2-Iodobutane	129	2390	Isobutyryl chloride	132	2395
Iodomethylpropanes	129	2391	Isocyanate solution, flammable, poisonous, n.o.s.	155	2478
Iodopropanes	129	2392			
IPDI	156	2290	Isocyanate solution, flammable, toxic, n.o.s.	155	2478
Iron oxide, spent	135	1376			
Iron pentacarbonyl	131	1994	Isocyanate solution, poisonous, flammable, n.o.s.	155	3080
Iron sponge, spent	135	1376			
Irritating agent, n.o.s.	159	1693	Isocyanate solution, poisonous, n.o.s.	155	2206
Isobutane	115	1075			
Isobutane	115	1969	Isocyanate solution, toxic, flammable, n.o.s.	155	3080
Isobutane mixture	115	1075			
Isobutane mixture	115	1969	Isocyanate solution, toxic, n.o.s.	155	2206
Isobutanol	129	1212	Isocyanate solutions, n.o.s.	155	2206
Isobutyl acetate	129	1213	Isocyanate solutions, n.o.s.	155	2478
Isobutyl acrylate	130P	2527	Isocyanate solutions, n.o.s.	155	3080
Isobutyl acrylate, inhibited	130P	2527	Isocyanate solutions, n.o.s. (toxic)	155	2207
Isobutyl alcohol	129	1212			
Isobutyl aldehyde	129	2045	Isocyanates, flammable, poisonous, n.o.s.	155	2478
Isobutylamine	132	1214			
Isobutyl chloroformate	155	2742	Isocyanates, flammable, toxic, n.o.s.	155	2478
			Isocyanates, n.o.s.	155	2206
			Isocyanates, n.o.s.	155	2478

Name of Material	Guide No.	ID No.
Isocyanates, n.o.s.	155	3080
Isocyanates, n.o.s. (toxic)	155	2207
Isocyanates, poisonous, flammable, n.o.s.	155	3080
Isocyanates, poisonous, n.o.s.	155	2206
Isocyanates, toxic, flammable, n.o.s.	155	3080
Isocyanates, toxic, n.o.s.	155	2206
Isocyanatobenzotrifluorides	156	2285
Isoheptene	128	2287
Isohexene	128	2288
Isononanoyl peroxide	148	2128
Isooctane	128	1262
Isooctene	128	1216
Isopentane	128	1265
Isopentanoic acid	154	1760
Isopentenes	128	2371
Isophoronediamine	153	2289
Isophorone diisocyanate	156	2290
Isoprene, inhibited	130P	1218
Isopropanol	129	1219
Isopropanolamine dodecylbenzenesulfonate	171	9127
Isopropanolamine dodecylbenzenesulphonate	171	9127
Isopropenyl acetate	129P	2403
Isopropenylbenzene	128	2303
Isopropyl acetate	129	1220
Isopropyl acid phosphate	153	1793
Isopropyl alcohol	129	1219
Isopropylamine	132	1221
Isopropylbenzene	130	1918
Isopropyl butyrate	129	2405
Isopropyl chloroacetate	155	2947

Name of Material	Guide No.	ID No.
Isopropyl chloroformate	155	2407
Isopropyl 2-chloropropionate	132	2934
Isopropyl isobutyrate	131	2406
Isopropyl isocyanate	155	2483
Isopropyl mercaptan	130	2402
Isopropyl methylphosphono-fluoridate	153	2810
Isopropyl nitrate	130	1222
Isopropyl percarbonate, unstabilized	148	2133
Isopropyl peroxydicarbonate	148	2133
Isopropyl peroxydicarbonate	148	2134
Isopropyl propionate	129	2409
Isosorbide dinitrate mixture	133	2907
Isosorbide-5-mononitrate	133	3251
Kerosene	128	1223
Ketones, liquid, n.o.s.	127	1224
Krypton	121	1056
Krypton, compressed	121	1056
Krypton, refrigerated liquid (cryogenic liquid)	120	1970
L (Lewisite)	153	2810
Lacquer chips, dry	133	2557
Lauroyl peroxide	145	2124
Lauroyl peroxide, not more than 42%, stable dispersion, in water	145	2893
Leachable toxic waste	151	9500
Lead acetate	151	1616
Lead arsenates	151	1617
Lead arsenites	151	1618
Lead chloride	151	2291
Lead compound, soluble, n.o.s.	151	2291
Lead cyanide	151	1620
Lead dioxide	141	1872

Name of Material	Guide No.	ID No.
Lead fluoborate	151	2291
Lead fluoride	154	2811
Lead nitrate	141	1469
Lead perchlorate	141	1470
Lead perchlorate, solid	141	1470
Lead perchlorate, solution	141	1470
Lead peroxide	141	1872
Lead phosphite, dibasic	133	2989
Lead sulfate, with more than 3% free acid	154	1794
Lead sulphate, with more than 3% free acid	154	1794
Lewisite	153	2810
Life-saving appliances, not self-inflating	171	3072
Life-saving appliances, self-inflating	171	2990
Lighter refills (cigarettes) (flammable gas)	115	1057
Lighters (cigarettes) (flammable gas)	115	1057
Lighters for cigars, cigarettes etc. with lighter fluid	127	1226
Lighters for cigars, cigarettes (flammable liquid)	127	1226
Lindane	151	2761
Liquefied gas (nonflammable)	121	1058
Liquefied gas, flammable, n.o.s.	115	1954
Liquefied gas, flammable, n.o.s.	115	3161
Liquefied gas, flammable, poisonous, n.o.s.	119	1953
Liquefied gas, flammable, poisonous, n.o.s. (Inhalation Hazard Zone A)	119	1953
Liquefied gas, flammable, poisonous, n.o.s. (Inhalation Hazard Zone B)	119	1953
Liquefied gas, flammable, poisonous, n.o.s. (Inhalation Hazard Zone C)	119	1953
Liquefied gas, flammable, poisonous, n.o.s. (Inhalation Hazard Zone D)	119	1953
Liquefied gas, flammable, toxic, n.o.s.	119	1953
Liquefied gas, flammable, toxic, n.o.s. (Inhalation Hazard Zone A)	119	1953
Liquefied gas, flammable, toxic, n.o.s. (Inhalation Hazard Zone B)	119	1953
Liquefied gas, flammable, toxic, n.o.s. (Inhalation Hazard Zone C)	119	1953
Liquefied gas, flammable, toxic, n.o.s. (Inhalation Hazard Zone D)	119	1953
Liquefied gas, n.o.s.	126	1956
Liquefied gas, n.o.s.	126	3163
Liquefied gas, oxidizing, n.o.s.	122	3157
Liquefied gas, poisonous, corrosive, n.o.s.	123	3308
Liquefied gas, poisonous, corrosive, n.o.s. (Inhalation Hazard Zone A)	123	3308
Liquefied gas, poisonous, corrosive, n.o.s. (Inhalation Hazard Zone B)	123	3308
Liquefied gas, poisonous, corrosive, n.o.s. (Inhalation Hazard Zone C)	123	3308
Liquefied gas, poisonous, corrosive, n.o.s. (Inhalation Hazard Zone D)	123	3308
Liquefied gas, poisonous, flammable, corrosive, n.o.s.	119	3309

Name of Material	Guide No.	ID No.
Liquefied gas, poisonous, flammable, corrosive, n.o.s. (Inhalation Hazard Zone A)	119	3309
Liquefied gas, poisonous, flammable, corrosive, n.o.s. (Inhalation Hazard Zone B)	119	3309
Liquefied gas, poisonous, flammable, corrosive, n.o.s. (Inhalation Hazard Zone C)	119	3309
Liquefied gas, poisonous, flammable, corrosive, n.o.s. (Inhalation Hazard Zone D)	119	3309
Liquefied gas, poisonous, flammable, n.o.s.	119	3160
Liquefied gas, poisonous, flammable, n.o.s. (Inhalation Hazard Zone A)	119	3160
Liquefied gas, poisonous, flammable, n.o.s. (Inhalation Hazard Zone B)	119	3160
Liquefied gas, poisonous, flammable, n.o.s. (Inhalation Hazard Zone C)	119	3160
Liquefied gas, poisonous, flammable, n.o.s. (Inhalation Hazard Zone D)	119	3160
Liquefied gas, poisonous, n.o.s.	123	1955
Liquefied gas, poisonous, n.o.s.	123	3162
Liquefied gas, poisonous, n.o.s. (Inhalation Hazard Zone A)	123	1955
Liquefied gas, poisonous, n.o.s. (Inhalation Hazard Zone A)	123	3162
Liquefied gas, poisonous, n.o.s. (Inhalation Hazard Zone B)	123	1955
Liquefied gas, poisonous, n.o.s. (Inhalation Hazard Zone B)	123	3162
Liquefied gas, poisonous, n.o.s. (Inhalation Hazard Zone C)	123	1955
Liquefied gas, poisonous, n.o.s. (Inhalation Hazard Zone C)	123	3162
Liquefied gas, poisonous, n.o.s. (Inhalation Hazard Zone D)	123	1955
Liquefied gas, poisonous, n.o.s. (Inhalation Hazard Zone D)	123	3162
Liquefied gas, poisonous, oxidizing, corrosive, n.o.s.	124	3310
Liquefied gas, poisonous, oxidizing, corrosive, n.o.s. (Inhalation Hazard Zone A)	124	3310
Liquefied gas, poisonous, oxidizing, corrosive, n.o.s. (Inhalation Hazard Zone B)	124	3310
Liquefied gas, poisonous, oxidizing, corrosive, n.o.s. (Inhalation Hazard Zone C)	124	3310
Liquefied gas, poisonous, oxidizing, corrosive, n.o.s. (Inhalation Hazard Zone D)	124	3310
Liquefied gas, poisonous, oxidizing, n.o.s.	124	3307
Liquefied gas, poisonous, oxidizing, n.o.s. (Inhalation Hazard Zone A)	124	3307
Liquefied gas, poisonous, oxidizing, n.o.s. (Inhalation Hazard Zone B)	124	3307
Liquefied gas, poisonous, oxidizing, n.o.s. (Inhalation Hazard Zone C)	124	3307
Liquefied gas, poisonous, oxidizing, n.o.s. (Inhalation Hazard Zone D)	124	3307
Liquefied gas, toxic, corrosive, n.o.s.	123	3308
Liquefied gas, toxic, corrosive, n.o.s. (Inhalation Hazard Zone A)	123	3308

Name of Material	Guide No.	ID No.
Liquefied gas, toxic, corrosive, n.o.s. (Inhalation Hazard Zone B)	123	3308
Liquefied gas, toxic, corrosive, n.o.s. (Inhalation Hazard Zone C)	123	3308
Liquefied gas, toxic, corrosive, n.o.s. (Inhalation Hazard Zone D)	123	3308
Liquefied gas, toxic, flammable, corrosive, n.o.s.	119	3309
Liquefied gas, toxic, flammable, corrosive, n.o.s. (Inhalation Hazard Zone A)	119	3309
Liquefied gas, toxic, flammable, corrosive, n.o.s. (Inhalation Hazard Zone B)	119	3309
Liquefied gas, toxic, flammable, corrosive, n.o.s. (Inhalation Hazard Zone C)	119	3309
Liquefied gas, toxic, flammable, corrosive, n.o.s. (Inhalation Hazard Zone D)	119	3309
Liquefied gas, toxic, flammable, n.o.s.	119	3160
Liquefied gas, toxic, flammable, n.o.s. (Inhalation Hazard Zone A)	119	3160
Liquefied gas, toxic, flammable, n.o.s. (Inhalation Hazard Zone B)	119	3160
Liquefied gas, toxic, flammable, n.o.s. (Inhalation Hazard Zone C)	119	3160
Liquefied gas, toxic, flammable, n.o.s. (Inhalation Hazard Zone D)	119	3160
Liquefied gas, toxic, n.o.s.	123	1955
Liquefied gas, toxic, n.o.s.	123	3162
Liquefied gas, toxic, n.o.s. (Inhalation Hazard Zone A)	123	1955
Liquefied gas, toxic, n.o.s. (Inhalation Hazard Zone A)	123	3162
Liquefied gas, toxic, n.o.s. (Inhalation Hazard Zone B)	123	1955
Liquefied gas, toxic, n.o.s. (Inhalation Hazard Zone B)	123	3162
Liquefied gas, toxic, n.o.s. (Inhalation Hazard Zone C)	123	1955
Liquefied gas, toxic, n.o.s. (Inhalation Hazard Zone C)	123	3162
Liquefied gas, toxic, n.o.s. (Inhalation Hazard Zone D)	123	1955
Liquefied gas, toxic, n.o.s. (Inhalation Hazard Zone D)	123	3162
Liquefied gas, toxic, oxidizing, corrosive, n.o.s.	124	3310
Liquefied gas, toxic, oxidizing, corrosive, n.o.s. (Inhalation Hazard Zone A)	124	3310
Liquefied gas, toxic, oxidizing, corrosive, n.o.s. (Inhalation Hazard Zone B)	124	3310
Liquefied gas, toxic, oxidizing, corrosive, n.o.s. (Inhalation Hazard Zone C)	124	3310
Liquefied gas, toxic, oxidizing, corrosive, n.o.s. (Inhalation Hazard Zone D)	124	3310
Liquefied gas, toxic, oxidizing, n.o.s.	124	3307
Liquefied gas, toxic, oxidizing, n.o.s. (Inhalation Hazard Zone A)	124	3307
Liquefied gas, toxic, oxidizing, n.o.s. (Inhalation Hazard Zone B)	124	3307

Name of Material	Guide No.	ID No.
Liquefied gas, toxic, oxidizing, n.o.s. (Inhalation Hazard Zone C)	124	3307
Liquefied gas, toxic, oxidizing, n.o.s. (Inhalation Hazard Zone D)	124	3307
Liquefied gases, non-flammable, charged with Nitrogen, Carbon dioxide or Air	121	1058
Liquefied natural gas (cryogenic liquid)	115	1972
Liquefied petroleum gas	115	1075
Lithium	138	1415
Lithium acetylide-Ethylenediamine complex	138	2813
Lithium alkyls	135	2445
Lithium aluminum hydride	138	1410
Lithium aluminum hydride, ethereal	138	1411
Lithium amide	139	1412
Lithium batteries	138	3090
Lithium batteries, liquid or solid cathode	138	3090
Lithium batteries contained in equipment	138	3091
Lithium batteries packed with equipment	138	3091
Lithium borohydride	138	1413
Lithium chromate	171	9134
Lithium ferrosilicon	139	2830
Lithium hydride	138	1414
Lithium hydride, fused solid	138	2805
Lithium hydroxide, monohydrate	154	2680
Lithium hydroxide, solid	154	2680
Lithium hydroxide, solution	154	2679
Lithium hypochlorite, dry	140	1471

Name of Material	Guide No.	ID No.
Lithium hypochlorite mixture	140	1471
Lithium hypochlorite mixtures, dry	140	1471
Lithium nitrate	140	2722
Lithium nitride	138	2806
Lithium peroxide	143	1472
Lithium silicon	138	1417
LNG (cryogenic liquid)	115	1972
London purple	151	1621
LPG	115	1075
Magnesium	138	1869
Magnesium, in pellets, turnings or ribbons	138	1869
Magnesium alkyls	135	3053
Magnesium alloys, with more than 50% Magnesium, in pellets, turnings or ribbons	138	1869
Magnesium alloys powder	138	1418
Magnesium aluminum phosphide	139	1419
Magnesium arsenate	151	1622
Magnesium bisulfite solution	154	2693
Magnesium bisulphite solution	154	2693
Magnesium bromate	140	1473
Magnesium chlorate	140	2723
Magnesium chloride and Chlorate mixture	140	1459
Magnesium diamide	135	2004
Magnesium diphenyl	135	2005
Magnesium fluorosilicate	151	2853
Magnesium granules, coated	138	2950
Magnesium hydride	138	2010
Magnesium nitrate	140	1474
Magnesium perchlorate	140	1475
Magnesium peroxide	140	1476

Name of Material	Guide No.	ID No.	Name of Material	Guide No.	ID No.
Magnesium phosphide	139	2011	Medicines, corrosive, solid, n.o.s.	154	1759
Magnesium powder	138	1418	Medicines, flammable, liquid, n.o.s.	128	1993
Magnesium scrap	138	1869			
Magnesium silicide	138	2624	Medicines, flammable, solid, n.o.s.	133	1325
Magnesium silicofluoride	151	2853	Medicines, oxidizing substances, solid, n.o.s.	140	1479
Magnetized material	171	2807			
Maleic acid	156	2215	Medicines, poisonous, liquid, n.o.s.	153	2810
Maleic anhydride	156	2215	Medicines, poisonous, solid, n.o.s.	154	2811
Malononitrile	153	2647			
Maneb	135	2210	Medicines, toxic, liquid, n.o.s.	153	2810
Maneb, stabilized	135	2968	Medicines, toxic, solid, n.o.s.	154	2811
Maneb preparation, stabilized	135	2968	p-Menthane hydroperoxide	147	2125
Maneb preparation, with not less than 60% Maneb	135	2210	Mercaptan mixture, aliphatic	131	1228
Manganese nitrate	140	2724	Mercaptan mixture, liquid, flammable, n.o.s.	130	3336
Manganese resinate	133	1330	Mercaptan mixture, liquid, flammable, poisonous, n.o.s.	131	1228
Matches, fusee	133	2254			
Matches, safety	133	1944	Mercaptan mixture, liquid, flammable, toxic, n.o.s.	131	1228
Matches, "strike anywhere"	133	1331	Mercaptan mixture, liquid, poisonous, flammable, n.o.s.	131	3071
Matches, wax "vesta"	133	1945			
MD	152	1556	Mercaptan mixture, liquid, toxic, flammable, n.o.s.	131	3071
Medical waste, n.o.s.	158	3291	Mercaptan mixtures, liquid, n.o.s.	131	1228
Medicine, liquid, flammable, poisonous, n.o.s.	131	3248			
Medicine, liquid, flammable, toxic, n.o.s.	131	3248	Mercaptan mixtures, liquid, n.o.s.	131	3071
Medicine, liquid, poisonous, n.o.s.	151	1851	Mercaptans, liquid, flammable, n.o.s.	130	3336
Medicine, liquid, toxic, n.o.s.	151	1851	Mercaptans, liquid, flammable, poisonous, n.o.s.	131	1228
Medicine, solid, poisonous, n.o.s.	151	3249	Mercaptans, liquid, flammable, toxic, n.o.s.	131	1228
Medicine, solid, toxic, n.o.s.	151	3249			
Medicines, corrosive, liquid, n.o.s.	154	1760	Mercaptans, liquid, n.o.s.	131	3071

Name of Material	Guide No.	ID No.
Mercaptans, liquid, poisonous, flammable, n.o.s.	131	3071
Mercaptans, liquid, toxic, flammable, n.o.s.	131	3071
Mercuric arsenate	151	1623
Mercuric bromide	154	1634
Mercuric chloride	154	1624
Mercuric cyanide	154	1636
Mercuric nitrate	141	1625
Mercuric oxycyanide	151	1642
Mercuric potassium cyanide	157	1626
Mercuric sulfate	151	1645
Mercuric sulphate	151	1645
Mercurous bromide	154	1634
Mercurous nitrate	141	1627
Mercurous sulfate	151	1628
Mercurous sulphate	151	1628
Mercury	172	2809
Mercury, metallic	172	2809
Mercury acetate	151	1629
Mercury ammonium chloride	151	1630
Mercury based pesticide, liquid, flammable, poisonous	131	2778
Mercury based pesticide, liquid, flammable, toxic	131	2778
Mercury based pesticide, liquid, poisonous	151	3012
Mercury based pesticide, liquid, poisonous, flammable	131	3011
Mercury based pesticide, liquid, toxic	151	3012
Mercury based pesticide, liquid, toxic, flammable	131	3011
Mercury based pesticide, solid, poisonous	151	2777
Mercury based pesticide, solid, toxic	151	2777
Mercury benzoate	154	1631
Mercury bisulfate	151	1633
Mercury bisulphate	151	1633
Mercury bromides	154	1634
Mercury compound, liquid, n.o.s.	151	2024
Mercury compound, solid, n.o.s.	151	2025
Mercury cyanide	154	1636
Mercury gluconate	151	1637
Mercury iodide	151	1638
Mercury metal	172	2809
Mercury nucleate	151	1639
Mercury oleate	151	1640
Mercury oxide	151	1641
Mercury oxycyanide, desensitized	151	1642
Mercury potassium iodide	151	1643
Mercury salicylate	151	1644
Mercury sulfate	151	1645
Mercury sulphate	151	1645
Mercury thiocyanate	151	1646
Mesityl oxide	129	1229
Metal alkyl, solution, n.o.s.	135	9195
Metal alkyl halides, n.o.s.	138	3049
Metal alkyl halides, water-reactive, n.o.s.	138	3049
Metal alkyl hydrides, n.o.s.	138	3050
Metal alkyl hydrides, water-reactive, n.o.s.	138	3050
Metal alkyls, n.o.s.	135	2003
Metal alkyls, water-reactive, n.o.s.	135	2003
Metal aryl halides, n.o.s.	138	3049

Name of Material	Guide No.	ID No.
Metal aryl halides, water-reactive, n.o.s.	138	3049
Metal aryl hydrides, n.o.s.	138	3050
Metal aryl hydrides, water-reactive, n.o.s.	138	3050
Metal aryls, n.o.s	135	2003
Metal aryls, water-reactive, n.o.s.	135	2003
Metal carbonyls, n.o.s.	151	3281
Metal catalyst, dry	135	2881
Metal catalyst, wetted	170	1378
Metaldehyde	133	1332
Metal hydrides, flammable, n.o.s.	170	3182
Metal hydrides, water-reactive, n.o.s.	138	1409
Metallic substance, water-reactive, n.o.s.	138	3208
Metallic substance, water-reactive, self-heating, n.o.s.	138	3209
Metal powder, flammable, n.o.s.	170	3089
Metal powder, self-heating, n.o.s.	135	3189
Metal salts of organic compounds, flammable, n.o.s.	133	3181
Methacrylaldehyde	131P	2396
Methacrylaldehyde, inhibited	131P	2396
Methacrylic acid, inhibited	153P	2531
Methacrylonitrile, inhibited	131P	3079
Methallyl alcohol	129	2614
Methane	115	1971
Methane, compressed	115	1971
Methane, refrigerated liquid (cryogenic liquid)	115	1972
Methane and Hydrogen mixture, compressed	115	2034
Methanesulfonyl chloride	156	3246

Name of Material	Guide No.	ID No.
Methanesulphonyl chloride	156	3246
Methanol	131	1230
Methoxymethyl isocyanate	155	2605
4-Methoxy-4-methyl-pentan-2-one	127	2293
1-Methoxy-2-propanol	129	3092
Methyl acetate	129	1231
Methyl acetone	127	1232
Methylacetylene and Propadiene mixture, stabilized	116P	1060
Methyl acrylate, inhibited	129P	1919
Methylal	127	1234
Methyl alcohol	131	1230
Methylallyl chloride	129P	2554
Methylamine, anhydrous	118	1061
Methylamine, aqueous solution	132	1235
Methylamyl acetate	129	1233
Methylamyl alcohol	129	2053
Methyl amyl ketone	127	1110
N-Methylaniline	153	2294
Methyl benzoate	152	2938
alpha-Methylbenzyl alcohol	153	2937
Methylbenzyl alcohol (alpha)	153	2937
Methyl bromide	123	1062
Methyl bromide and Chloropicrin mixtures	123	1581
Methyl bromide and Ethylene dibromide mixture, liquid	151	1647
Methyl bromide and more than 2% Chloropicrin mixture, liquid	123	1581
Methyl bromide and nonflammable, nonliquefied compressed gas mixture	123	1955

Name of Material	Guide No.	ID No.
Methyl bromoacetate	155	2643
Methylbromoacetone	159	—
3-Methylbutan-2-one	127	2397
2-Methyl-1-butene	127	2459
2-Methyl-2-butene	127	2460
3-Methyl-1-butene	127	2561
N-Methylbutylamine	132	2945
Methyl tert-butyl ether	127	2398
Methyl butyrate	129	1237
Methyl chloride	115	1063
Methyl chloride and Chloropicrin mixtures	119	1582
Methyl chloride and Methylene chloride mixture	115	1912
Methyl chloroacetate	155	2295
Methyl chloroformate	155	1238
Methyl chloromethyl ether	131	1239
Methyl 2-chloropropionate	132	2933
Methylchlorosilane	119	2534
Methyl cyanide	131	1648
Methylcyclohexane	128	2296
Methylcyclohexanols	129	2617
Methylcyclohexanone	127	2297
Methylcyclopentane	128	2298
Methyl dichloroacetate	155	2299
Methyldichloroarsine	152	1556
Methyldichlorosilane	139	1242
Methylene chloride	160	1593
Methylene chloride and Methyl chloride mixture	115	1912
Methyl ethyl ether	115	1039
Methyl ethyl ketone	127	1193
Methyl ethyl ketone peroxide	147	2550
2-Methyl-5-ethylpyridine	153	2300
Methyl fluoride	115	2454
Methyl formate	129	1243
2-Methylfuran	127	2301
2-Methyl-2-heptanethiol	131	3023
5-Methylhexan-2-one	127	2302
Methylhydrazine	131	1244
Methyl iodide	151	2644
Methyl isobutyl carbinol	129	2053
Methyl isobutyl ketone	127	1245
Methyl isobutyl ketone peroxide	147	2126
Methyl isocyanate	155	2480
Methyl isopropenyl ketone, inhibited	127P	1246
Methyl isothiocyanate	131	2477
Methyl isovalerate	130	2400
Methyl magnesium bromide in Ethyl ether	135	1928
Methyl mercaptan	117	1064
Methyl methacrylate monomer, inhibited	129P	1247
Methyl methacrylate monomer, uninhibited	129P	1247
4-Methylmorpholine	132	2535
N-Methylmorpholine	132	2535
Methylmorpholine	132	2535
Methyl nitrite	116	2455
N-Methyl-N'-Nitro-N-Nitrosoguanidine	133	1325
Methyl orthosilicate	155	2606
Methyl parathion, liquid	152	2783
Methyl parathion, liquid	152	3018
Methyl parathion, mixture, dry	152	2783
Methyl parathion, solid	152	2783
Methylpentadiene	127	2461

Name of Material	Guide No.	ID No.	Name of Material	Guide No.	ID No.
Methyl pentane	128	2462	Mustard Lewisite	153	2810
2-Methylpentan-2-ol	129	2560	Naphtha	128	2553
Methylphenyldichlorosilane	156	2437	Naphtha, petroleum	128	1255
Methyl phosphonic dichloride	137	9206	Naphtha, solvent	128	1256
Methyl phosphonous dichloride	135	2845	Naphthalene, crude	133	1334
1-Methylpiperidine	132	2399	Naphthalene, molten	133	2304
Methyl propionate	129	1248	Naphthalene, refined	133	1334
Methyl propyl ether	127	2612	Naphthenic acid	171	9137
Methyl propyl ketone	127	1249	alpha-Naphthylamine	153	2077
Methyltetrahydrofuran	127	2536	Naphthylamine (alpha)	153	2077
Methyl trichloroacetate	156	2533	beta-Naphthylamine	153	1650
Methyltrichlorosilane	155	1250	Naphthylamine (beta)	153	1650
alpha-Methylvaleraldehyde	130	2367	Naphthylthiourea	153	1651
Methyl valeraldehyde (alpha)	130	2367	Naphthylurea	153	1652
Methyl vinyl ketone	131P	1251	Natural gas, compressed	115	1971
Methyl vinyl ketone, stabilized	131P	1251	Natural gas, refrigerated liquid (cryogenic liquid)	115	1972
Mevinphos	152	2783	Natural gasoline	128	1257
Mexacarbate	151	2757	Neohexane	128	1208
M.I.B.C.	129	2053	Neon	121	1065
Mining reagent, liquid	153	2022	Neon, compressed	121	1065
Molybdenum pentachloride	156	2508	Neon, refrigerated liquid (cryogenic liquid)	120	1913
Monoethanolamine	153	2491	Nickel ammonium sulfate	171	9138
Mononitrotoluidines	153	2660	Nickel ammonium sulphate	171	9138
Monopropylamine	132	1277	Nickel carbonyl	131	1259
Morpholine	132	2054	Nickel catalyst, dry	135	2881
Morpholine, aqueous mixture	154	1760	Nickel chloride	151	9139
Morpholine, aqueous mixture	132	2054	Nickel cyanide	151	1653
Motor fuel anti-knock compound	131	1649	Nickel hydroxide	154	9140
Motor fuel anti-knock mixture	131	1649	Nickel nitrate	140	2725
Motor spirit	128	1203	Nickel nitrite	140	2726
Muriatic acid	157	1789	Nickel sulfate	154	9141
Musk xylene	149	2956			
Mustard	153	2810			

Name of Material	Guide No.	ID No.
Nickel sulphate	154	9141
Nicotine	151	1654
Nicotine compound, liquid, n.o.s.	151	3144
Nicotine compound, solid, n.o.s.	151	1655
Nicotine hydrochloride	151	1656
Nicotine hydrochloride, solution	151	1656
Nicotine preparation, liquid, n.o.s.	151	3144
Nicotine preparation, solid, n.o.s.	151	1655
Nicotine salicylate	151	1657
Nicotine sulfate, solid	151	1658
Nicotine sulfate, solution	151	1658
Nicotine sulphate, solid	151	1658
Nicotine sulphate, solution	151	1658
Nicotine tartrate	151	1659
Nitrate, n.o.s.	140	1477
Nitrates, inorganic, aqueous solution, n.o.s.	140	3218
Nitrates, inorganic, n.o.s.	140	1477
Nitrating acid, spent	157	1826
Nitrating acid mixture	157	1796
Nitrating acid mixture, spent	157	1826
Nitric acid, 40% or less	154	1760
Nitric acid, fuming	157	2032
Nitric acid, other than red fuming	157	2031
Nitric acid, red fuming	157	2032
Nitric oxide	124	1660
Nitric oxide, compressed	124	1660
Nitric oxide and Dinitrogen tetroxide mixture	124	1975
Nitric oxide and Nitrogen dioxide mixture	124	1975
Nitric oxide and Nitrogen tetroxide mixture	124	1975
Nitriles, flammable, poisonous, n.o.s.	131	3273
Nitriles, flammable, toxic, n.o.s.	131	3273
Nitriles, poisonous, flammable, n.o.s.	131	3275
Nitriles, poisonous, n.o.s.	151	3276
Nitriles, toxic, flammable, n.o.s.	131	3275
Nitriles, toxic, n.o.s.	151	3276
Nitrites, inorganic, aqueous solution, n.o.s.	140	3219
Nitrites, inorganic, n.o.s.	140	2627
Nitroanilines	153	1661
Nitroanisole	152	2730
Nitroanisole, liquid	152	2730
Nitroanisole, solid	152	2730
Nitrobenzene	152	1662
Nitrobenzenesulfonic acid	153	2305
Nitrobenzenesulphonic acid	153	2305
Nitrobenzotrifluorides	152	2306
Nitrobromobenzene	152	2732
Nitrobromobenzene, liquid	152	2732
Nitrobromobenzene, solid	152	2732
Nitrocellulose, block, wet, with not less than 25% alcohol	127	2059
Nitrocellulose, colloided, granular or flake, wet, with not less than 20% alcohol or solvent	127	2059
Nitrocellulose, colloided, granular or flake, wet, with not less than 20% water	113	2555
Nitrocellulose, solution, flammable	127	2059
Nitrocellulose, solution, in a flammable liquid	127	2059

Name of Material	Guide No.	ID No.
Nitrocellulose, wet, with not less than 30% alcohol or solvent	113	2556
Nitrocellulose membrane filters	133	3270
Nitrocellulose mixture, without plasticizer, without pigment	133	2557
Nitrocellulose mixture, without plasticizer, with pigment	133	2557
Nitrocellulose mixture, with plasticizer, without pigment	133	2557
Nitrocellulose mixture, with plasticizer, with pigment	133	2557
Nitrocellulose with alcohol	113	2556
Nitrocellulose with not less than 25% alcohol	113	2556
Nitrocellulose with plasticizing substance	133	2557
Nitrocellulose with water, not less than 25% water	113	2555
Nitrochlorobenzenes, liquid	152	1578
Nitrochlorobenzenes, solid	152	1578
3-Nitro-4-chlorobenzotrifluoride	152	2307
Nitrocresols	153	2446
Nitroethane	129	2842
Nitrogen	121	1066
Nitrogen, compressed	121	1066
Nitrogen, refrigerated liquid (cryogenic liquid)	120	1977
Nitrogen and Rare gases mixture	121	1981
Nitrogen and Rare gases mixture, compressed	121	1981
Nitrogen dioxide	124	1067
Nitrogen dioxide, liquefied	124	1067
Nitrogen dioxide and Nitric oxide mixture	124	1975
Nitrogen peroxide, liquid	124	1067
Nitrogen tetroxide, liquid	124	1067
Nitrogen tetroxide and Nitric oxide mixture	124	1975
Nitrogen trifluoride	122	2451
Nitrogen trifluoride, compressed	122	2451
Nitrogen trioxide	124	2421
Nitroglycerin, solution in alcohol, with more than 1% but not more than 5% Nitroglycerin	127	3064
Nitroglycerin, solution in alcohol, with not more than 1% Nitroglycerin	127	1204
Nitroglycerin mixture, desensitized, liquid, flammable, n.o.s., with not more than 30% Nitroglycerin	113	3343
Nitroglycerin mixture, desensitized, liquid, n.o.s., with not more than 30% Nitroglycerin	113	3357
Nitroglycerin mixture, desensitized, solid, n.o.s., with more than 2% but not more than 10% Nitroglycerin	113	3319
Nitroglycerin mixture with more than 2% but not more than 10% Nitroglycerin, desensitized	113	3319
Nitroguanidine (Picrite), wetted with not less than 20% water	113	1336
Nitroguanidine, wetted with not less than 20% water	113	1336
Nitrohydrochloric acid	157	1798
Nitromethane	129	1261
Nitronaphthalene	133	2538
Nitrophenols	153	1663
Nitropropanes	129	2608

Name of Material	Guide No.	ID No.	Name of Material	Guide No.	ID No.
p-Nitrosodiethylaniline	135	——	tert-Octyl mercaptan	131	3023
p-Nitrosodimethylaniline	135	1369	Octyltrichlorosilane	156	1801
Nitrostarch, wet, with not less than 30% alcohol or solvent	113	1337	Oil, n.o.s., flash point not less than 93°C (200°F)	171	9277
Nitrostarch, wetted with not less than 20% water	113	1337	Oil, petroleum, n.o.s.	128	1270
Nitrostarch, wetted with not less than 30% solvent	113	1337	Oil gas	119	1071
Nitrosyl chloride	125	1069	Oil gas, compressed	119	1071
Nitrosylsulfuric acid	157	2308	Oleum	137	1831
Nitrosylsulphuric acid	157	2308	Oleum, with less than 30% free Sulfur trioxide	137	1831
Nitrotoluenes	152	1664	Oleum, with less than 30% free Sulphur trioxide	137	1831
Nitrotoluenes, liquid	152	1664	Oleum, with not less than 30% free Sulfur trioxide	137	1831
Nitrotoluenes, solid	152	1664	Oleum, with not less than 30% free Sulphur trioxide	137	1831
Nitrotoluidines (mono)	153	2660	Organic peroxide, liquid, n.o.s.	146	9183
Nitrous oxide	122	1070	Organic peroxide, solution, n.o.s.	146	9183
Nitrous oxide, compressed	122	1070	Organic peroxide, solid, n.o.s.	146	9187
Nitrous oxide, refrigerated liquid	122	2201	Organic peroxides, mixtures	146	2756
Nitrous oxide and Carbon dioxide mixture	126	1015	Organic peroxides, n.o.s. (including trial quantities)	148	2899
Nitroxylenes	152	1665	Organic peroxides, samples, n.o.s	146	2255
Nitroxylol	152	1665	Organic peroxide type B, liquid	146	3101
Nonanes	128	1920	Organic peroxide type B, liquid, temperature controlled	148	3111
Nonyltrichlorosilane	156	1799	Organic peroxide type B, solid	146	3102
2,5-Norbornadiene	127P	2251	Organic peroxide type B, solid, temperature controlled	148	3112
2,5-Norbornadiene, inhibited	127P	2251	Organic peroxide type C, liquid	146	3103
Octadecyltrichlorosilane	156	1800	Organic peroxide type C, liquid, temperature controlled	148	3113
Octadiene	128P	2309	Organic peroxide type C, solid	146	3104
Octafluorobut-2-ene	126	2422	Organic peroxide type C, solid, temperature controlled	148	3114
Octafluorocyclobutane	126	1976			
Octafluoropropane	126	2424			
Octanes	128	1262			
Octanoyl peroxide	148	2129			
Octyl aldehydes	129	1191			

Name of Material	Guide No.	ID No.
Organic peroxide type D, liquid	145	3105
Organic peroxide type D, liquid, temperature controlled	148	3115
Organic peroxide type D, solid	145	3106
Organic peroxide type D, solid, temperature controlled	148	3116
Organic peroxide type E, liquid	145	3107
Organic peroxide type E, liquid, temperature controlled	148	3117
Organic peroxide type E, solid	145	3108
Organic peroxide type E, solid, temperature controlled	148	3118
Organic peroxide type F, liquid	145	3109
Organic peroxide type F, liquid, temperature controlled	148	3119
Organic peroxide type F, solid	145	3110
Organic peroxide type F, solid, temperature controlled	148	3120
Organic phosphate, dry	152	2783
Organic phosphate, solid	152	2783
Organic phosphate compound, dry	152	2783
Organic phosphate compound, solid	152	2783
Organic phosphate compound mixed with compressed gas	123	1955
Organic phosphate mixed with compressed gas	123	1955
Organic phosphorus compound, dry	152	2783
Organic phosphorus compound, solid	152	2783
Organic phosphorus compound mixed with compressed gas	123	1955
Organic pigments, self-heating	135	3313
Organoarsenic compound, n.o.s.	151	3280
Organochlorine pesticide, liquid, flammable, poisonous	131	2762
Organochlorine pesticide, liquid, flammable, toxic	131	2762
Organochlorine pesticide, liquid, poisonous	151	2996
Organochlorine pesticide, liquid, poisonous, flammable	131	2995
Organochlorine pesticide, liquid, toxic	151	2996
Organochlorine pesticide, liquid, toxic, flammable	131	2995
Organochlorine pesticide, solid, poisonous	151	2761
Organochlorine pesticide, solid, toxic	151	2761
Organometallic compound, poisonous, n.o.s.	151	3282
Organometallic compound, toxic, n.o.s.	151	3282
Organometallic compound, water-reactive, flammable, n.o.s.	138	3207
Organometallic compound dispersion, water-reactive, flammable, n.o.s.	138	3207
Organometallic compound solution, water-reactive, flammable, n.o.s.	138	3207
Organophosphorus compound, poisonous, flammable, n.o.s.	131	3279
Organophosphorus compound, poisonous, n.o.s.	151	3278
Organophosphorus compound, toxic, flammable, n.o.s.	131	3279
Organophosphorus compound, toxic, n.o.s.	151	3278
Organophosphorus pesticide, liquid, flammable, poisonous	131	2784

Name of Material	Guide No.	ID No.
Organophosphorus pesticide, liquid, flammable, toxic	131	2784
Organophosphorus pesticide, liquid, poisonous	152	3018
Organophosphorus pesticide, liquid, poisonous, flammable	131	3017
Organophosphorus pesticide, liquid, toxic	152	3018
Organophosphorus pesticide, liquid, toxic, flammable	131	3017
Organophosphorus pesticide, solid, poisonous	152	2783
Organophosphorus pesticide, solid, toxic	152	2783
Organotin compound, liquid, n.o.s.	153	2788
Organotin compound, solid, n.o.s.	153	3146
Organotin pesticide, liquid, flammable, poisonous	131	2787
Organotin pesticide, liquid, flammable, toxic	131	2787
Organotin pesticide, liquid, poisonous	153	3020
Organotin pesticide, liquid, poisonous, flammable	131	3019
Organotin pesticide, liquid, toxic	153	3020
Organotin pesticide, liquid, toxic, flammable	131	3019
Organotin pesticide, solid, poisonous	153	2786
Organotin pesticide, solid, toxic	153	2786
ORM-A, n.o.s.	159	1693
ORM-B, n.o.s.	154	1760
ORM-E, liquid, n.o.s.	171	9188
ORM-E, solid, n.o.s.	171	9188
Osmium tetroxide	154	2471

Name of Material	Guide No.	ID No.
Other regulated substance	171	8027
Other regulated substances, liquid, n.o.s.	171	3082
Other regulated substances, solid, n.o.s.	171	3077
Oxalates, water soluble	154	2449
Oxidizer, corrosive, liquid, n.o.s.	140	9193
Oxidizer, corrosive, solid, n.o.s.	140	9194
Oxidizer, poisonous, liquid, n.o.s.	142	9199
Oxidizer, poisonous, solid, n.o.s.	141	9200
Oxidizing liquid, corrosive, n.o.s.	140	3098
Oxidizing liquid, n.o.s.	140	3139
Oxidizing liquid, poisonous, n.o.s.	142	3099
Oxidizing liquid, toxic, n.o.s.	142	3099
Oxidizing solid, corrosive, n.o.s.	140	3085
Oxidizing solid, flammable, n.o.s.	140	3137
Oxidizing solid, n.o.s.	140	1479
Oxidizing solid, poisonous, n.o.s.	141	3087
Oxidizing solid, self-heating, n.o.s.	135	3100
Oxidizing solid, toxic, n.o.s.	141	3087
Oxidizing solid, water-reactive, n.o.s.	144	3121
Oxidizing substances, liquid, corrosive, n.o.s.	140	3098
Oxidizing substances, liquid, n.o.s.	140	3139
Oxidizing substances, liquid, poisonous, n.o.s.	142	3099
Oxidizing substances, liquid, toxic, n.o.s.	142	3099

Name of Material	Guide No.	ID No.
Oxidizing substances, self-heating, n.o.s.	135	3100
Oxidizing substances, solid, corrosive, n.o.s.	140	3085
Oxidizing substances, solid, flammable, n.o.s.	140	3137
Oxidizing substances, solid, n.o.s.	140	1479
Oxidizing substances, solid, poisonous, n.o.s.	141	3087
Oxidizing substances, solid, self-heating, n.o.s.	135	3100
Oxidizing substances, solid, toxic, n.o.s.	141	3087
Oxidizing substances, solid, which in contact with water emit flammable gases, n.o.s.	144	3121
Oxygen	122	1072
Oxygen, compressed	122	1072
Oxygen, refrigerated liquid (cryogenic liquid)	122	1073
Oxygen and Carbon dioxide mixture	122	1014
Oxygen and Carbon dioxide mixture, compressed	122	1014
Oxygen and Rare gases mixture	122	1980
Oxygen and Rare gases mixture, compressed	122	1980
Oxygen difluoride	124	2190
Oxygen difluoride, compressed	124	2190
Oxygen generator, chemical	140	3356
Oxygen generators, small	140	8037
Paint (corrosive)	154	1760
Paint (corrosive)	153	3066
Paint (flammable)	128	1263
Paint related material (corrosive)	154	1760

Name of Material	Guide No.	ID No.
Paint related material (corrosive)	153	3066
Paint related material (flammable)	128	1263
Paper, unsaturated oil treated	133	1379
Paraformaldehyde	133	2213
Paraldehyde	129	1264
Parathion	152	2783
Parathion and compressed gas mixture	123	1967
Parathion mixture, dry	152	2783
Parathion mixture, liquid	152	2783
PCB	171	2315
PD	152	1556
Pelargonyl peroxide	148	2130
Pentaborane	135	1380
Pentachloroethane	151	1669
Pentachlorophenol	154	3155
Pentaerythrite tetranitrate mixture,desensitized, solid, n.o.s., with more than 10% but not more than 20% PETN	113	3344
Pentafluoroethane	126	3220
Pentafluoroethane and Ethylene oxide mixture, with not more than 7.9% Ethylene oxide	126	3298
Pentamethylheptane	128	2286
Pentan-2,4-dione	131	2310
n-Pentane	128	1265
2,4-Pentanedione	131	2310
Pentane-2,4-dione	131	2310
Pentanes	128	1265
Pentanols	129	1105
1-Pentene	127	1108
1-Pentol	153P	2705

Name of Material	Guide No.	ID No.
Peracetic acid, solution	147	2131
Percarbonates, inorganic, n.o.s.	140	3217
Perchlorate, n.o.s.	140	1481
Perchlorates, inorganic, aqueous solution, n.o.s.	140	3211
Perchlorates, inorganic, n.o.s.	140	1481
Perchloric acid, with more than 50% but not more than 72% acid	143	1873
Perchloric acid, with not more than 50% acid	140	1802
Perchloroethylene	160	1897
Perchloromethyl mercaptan	157	1670
Perchloryl fluoride	124	3083
Perfluoroethyl vinyl ether	115	3154
Perfluoro(ethyl vinyl ether)	115	3154
Perfluoromethyl vinyl ether	115	3153
Perfluoro(methyl vinyl ether)	115	3153
Perfumery products, with flammable solvents	127	1266
Permanganate, n.o.s.	140	1482
Permanganates, inorganic, aqueous solution, n.o.s.	140	3214
Permanganates, inorganic, n.o.s.	140	1482
Peroxides, inorganic, n.o.s.	140	1483
Peroxyacetic acid, solution	147	2131
Persulfates, inorganic, aqueous solution, n.o.s.	140	3216
Persulfates, inorganic, n.o.s.	140	3215
Persulphates, inorganic, aqueous solution, n.o.s.	140	3216
Persulphates, inorganic, n.o.s.	140	3215
Pesticide, liquid, flammable, poisonous	131	3021
Pesticide, liquid, flammable, toxic	131	3021
Pesticide, liquid, poisonous, flammable, n.o.s.	131	2903
Pesticide, liquid, poisonous, n.o.s.	151	2902
Pesticide, liquid, toxic, flammable, n.o.s.	131	2903
Pesticide, liquid, toxic, n.o.s.	151	2902
Pesticide, solid, poisonous	151	2588
Pesticide, solid, poisonous, n.o.s.	151	2588
Pesticide, solid, toxic, n.o.s.	151	2588
Pesticide, water-reactive	135	2210
Petrol	128	1203
Petroleum crude oil	128	1267
Petroleum distillates, n.o.s.	128	1268
Petroleum ether	128	1271
Petroleum gases, liquefied	115	1075
Petroleum naphtha	128	1255
Petroleum oil	128	1270
Petroleum products, n.o.s.	128	1268
Petroleum spirit	128	1271
Phenacyl bromide	153	2645
Phenetidines	153	2311
Phenol, liquid	153	2821
Phenol, molten	153	2312
Phenol, solid	153	1671
Phenol solution	153	2821
Phenolates, liquid	154	2904
Phenolates, solid	154	2905
Phenolsulfonic acid, liquid	153	1803
Phenolsulphonic acid, liquid	153	1803

Name of Material	Guide No.	ID No.
Phenoxyacetic acid derivative pesticide, liquid, flammable, poisonous	131	3346
Phenoxyacetic acid derivative pesticide, liquid, flammable, toxic	131	3346
Phenoxyacetic acid derivative pesticide, liquid, poisonous	153	3348
Phenoxyacetic acid derivative pesticide, liquid, poisonous, flammable	131	3347
Phenoxyacetic acid derivative pesticide, liquid, toxic	153	3348
Phenoxyacetic acid derivative pesticide, liquid, toxic, flammable	131	3347
Phenoxyacetic acid derivative pesticide, solid, poisonous	153	3345
Phenoxyacetic acid derivative pesticide, solid, toxic	153	3345
Phenoxy pesticide, liquid, flammable, poisonous	131	2766
Phenoxy pesticide, liquid, flammable, toxic	131	2766
Phenoxy pesticide, liquid, poisonous	152	3000
Phenoxy pesticide, liquid, poisonous, flammable	131	2999
Phenoxy pesticide, liquid, toxic	152	3000
Phenoxy pesticide, liquid, toxic, flammable	131	2999
Phenoxy pesticide, solid, poisonous	152	2765
Phenoxy pesticide, solid, toxic	152	2765
Phenylacetonitrile, liquid	152	2470
Phenylacetyl chloride	156	2577
Phenylcarbylamine chloride	151	1672
Phenyl chloroformate	156	2746

Name of Material	Guide No.	ID No.
Phenyldichloroarsine	152	1556
Phenylenediamines	153	1673
Phenylhydrazine	153	2572
Phenyl isocyanate	155	2487
Phenyl mercaptan	131	2337
Phenylmercuric acetate	151	1674
Phenylmercuric compound, n.o.s.	151	2026
Phenylmercuric hydroxide	151	1894
Phenylmercuric nitrate	151	1895
Phenylphosphorus dichloride	137	2798
Phenylphosphorus thiodichloride	137	2799
Phenyltrichlorosilane	156	1804
Phenyl urea pesticide, liquid, flammable, poisonous	131	2768
Phenyl urea pesticide, liquid, flammable, toxic	131	2768
Phenyl urea pesticide, liquid, poisonous	151	3002
Phenyl urea pesticide, liquid, poisonous, flammable	131	3001
Phenyl urea pesticide, liquid, toxic	151	3002
Phenyl urea pesticide, liquid, toxic, flammable	131	3001
Phenyl urea pesticide, solid, poisonous	151	2767
Phenyl urea pesticide, solid, toxic	151	2767
Phosgene	125	1076
Phosgene oxime	154	2811
9-Phosphabicyclononanes	135	2940
Phosphine	119	2199
Phosphoric acid	154	1805

Name of Material	Guide No.	ID No.
Phosphoric anhydride	137	1807
Phosphorous acid	154	2834
Phosphorous acid, ortho	154	2834
Phosphorus, amorphous	133	1338
Phosphorus, amorphous, red	133	1338
Phosphorus, white, dry or under water or in solution	136	1381
Phosphorus, white, molten	136	2447
Phosphorus, yellow, dry or under water or in solution	136	1381
Phosphorus heptasulfide, free from yellow and white Phosphorus	139	1339
Phosphorus heptasulphide, free from yellow and white Phosphorus	139	1339
Phosphorus oxybromide	137	1939
Phosphorus oxybromide, molten	137	2576
Phosphorus oxybromide, solid	137	1939
Phosphorus oxychloride	137	1810
Phosphorus pentabromide	137	2691
Phosphorus pentachloride	137	1806
Phosphorus pentafluoride	125	2198
Phosphorus pentafluoride, compressed	125	2198
Phosphorus pentasulfide, free from yellow and white Phosphorus	139	1340
Phosphorus pentasulphide, free from yellow and white Phosphorus	139	1340
Phosphorus pentoxide	137	1807
Phosphorus sesquisulfide, free from yellow and white Phosphorus	139	1341
Phosphorus sesquisulphide, free from yellow and white Phosphorus	139	1341
Phosphorus tribromide	137	1808
Phosphorus trichloride	137	1809
Phosphorus trioxide	157	2578
Phosphorus trisulfide, free from yellow and white Phosphorus	139	1343
Phosphorus trisulphide, free from yellow and white Phosphorus	139	1343
Phthalic anhydride	156	2214
Phthalimide derivative pesticide, liquid, flammable, poisonous	131	2774
Phthalimide derivative pesticide, liquid, flammable, toxic	131	2774
Phthalimide derivative pesticide, liquid, poisonous	151	3008
Phthalimide derivative pesticide, liquid, poisonous, flammable	131	3007
Phthalimide derivative pesticide, liquid, toxic	151	3008
Phthalimide derivative pesticide, liquid, toxic, flammable	131	3007
Phthalimide derivative pesticide, solid, poisonous	151	2773
Phthalimide derivative pesticide, solid, toxic	151	2773
Picolines	130	2313
Picric acid, wet, with not less than 10% water	113	1344
Picrite, wetted	113	1336
Pinacolyl methylphosphonofluoridate	153	2810

Name of Material	Guide No.	ID No.
Pinane hydroperoxide	147	2162
alpha-Pinene	127	2368
Pinene (alpha)	127	2368
Pine oil	129	1272
Piperazine	153	2579
Piperidine	132	2401
Plastic molding compound	171	3314
Plastic molding material	171	—
Plastic, nitrocellulose-based, spontaneously combustible, n.o.s.	135	2006
Plastics moulding compound	171	3314
Plastics, nitrocellulose-based, self-heating, n.o.s.	135	2006
Poison B, liquid, n.o.s.	153	2810
Poison B, solid, n.o.s.	154	2811
Poisonous gas, flammable, n.o.s.	119	1953
Poisonous gas, n.o.s.	123	1955
Poisonous liquid, corrosive, inorganic, n.o.s.	154	3289
Poisonous liquid, corrosive, inorganic, n.o.s. (Inhalation Hazard Zone A)	154	3289
Poisonous liquid, corrosive, inorganic, n.o.s. (Inhalation Hazard Zone B)	154	3289
Poisonous liquid, corrosive, n.o.s.	154	2927
Poisonous liquid, corrosive, n.o.s. (Inhalation Hazard Zone A)	154	2927
Poisonous liquid, corrosive, n.o.s. (Inhalation Hazard Zone B)	154	2927
Poisonous liquid, flammable, n.o.s.	119	1953
Poisonous liquid, flammable, n.o.s.	131	2929
Poisonous liquid, flammable, n.o.s. (Inhalation Hazard Zone A)	131	2929
Poisonous liquid, flammable, n.o.s. (Inhalation Hazard Zone B)	131	2929
Poisonous liquid, flammable, organic, n.o.s.	131	2929
Poisonous liquid, flammable, organic, n.o.s. (Inhalation Hazard Zone A)	131	2929
Poisonous liquid, flammable, organic, n.o.s. (Inhalation Hazard Zone B)	131	2929
Poisonous liquid, inorganic, n.o.s.	151	3287
Poisonous liquid, inorganic, n.o.s. (Inhalation Hazard Zone A)	151	3287
Poisonous liquid, inorganic, n.o.s. (Inhalation Hazard Zone B)	151	3287
Poisonous liquid, n.o.s.	123	1955
Poisonous liquid, n.o.s.	153	2810
Poisonous liquid, n.o.s. (Inhalation Hazard Zone A)	153	2810
Poisonous liquid, n.o.s. (Inhalation Hazard Zone B)	153	2810
Poisonous liquid, organic, n.o.s.	153	2810
Poisonous liquid, organic, n.o.s. (Inhalation Hazard Zone A)	153	2810
Poisonous liquid, organic, n.o.s. (Inhalation Hazard Zone B)	153	2810
Poisonous liquid, oxidizing, n.o.s.	142	3122

Name of Material	Guide No.	ID No.
Poisonous liquid, oxidizing, n.o.s. (Inhalation Hazard Zone A)	142	3122
Poisonous liquid, oxidizing, n.o.s. (Inhalation Hazard Zone B)	142	3122
Poisonous liquid, water-reactive, n.o.s.	139	3123
Poisonous liquid, water-reactive, n.o.s. (Inhalation Hazard Zone A)	139	3123
Poisonous liquid, water-reactive, n.o.s. (Inhalation Hazard Zone B)	139	3123
Poisonous liquid, which in contact with water emits flammable gases, n.o.s.	139	3123
Poisonous liquid, which in contact with water emits flammable gases, n.o.s. (Inhalation Hazard Zone A)	139	3123
Poisonous liquid, which in contact with water emits flammable gases, n.o.s. (Inhalation Hazard Zone B)	139	3123
Poisonous solid, corrosive, inorganic, n.o.s.	154	3290
Poisonous solid, corrosive, n.o.s.	154	2928
Poisonous solid, flammable, n.o.s.	134	2930
Poisonous solid, flammable, organic, n.o.s.	134	2930
Poisonous solid, inorganic, n.o.s.	151	3288
Poisonous solid, n.o.s.	154	2811
Poisonous solid, organic, n.o.s.	154	2811
Poisonous solid, oxidizing, n.o.s.	141	3086
Poisonous solid, self-heating, n.o.s.	136	3124
Poisonous solid, water-reactive, n.o.s.	139	3125
Poisonous solid, which in contact with water emits flammable gases, n.o.s.	139	3125
Polyalkylamines, n.o.s.	132	2733
Polyalkylamines, n.o.s.	132	2734
Polyalkylamines, n.o.s.	153	2735
Polyamines, flammable, corrosive, n.o.s.	132	2733
Polyamines, liquid, corrosive, flammable, n.o.s.	132	2734
Polyamines, liquid, corrosive, n.o.s.	153	2735
Polyamines, solid, corrosive, n.o.s.	154	3259
Polychlorinated biphenyls	171	2315
Polychlorinated biphenyls, liquid	171	2315
Polychlorinated biphenyls, solid	171	2315
Polyester resin kit	146	2255
Polyester resin kit	127	3269
Polyhalogenated biphenyls, liquid	171	3151
Polyhalogenated biphenyls, solid	171	3152
Polyhalogenated terphenyls, liquid	171	3151
Polyhalogenated terphenyls, solid	171	3152
Polymeric beads, expandable	133	2211
Polymerizable material, stabilized with dry ice	171P	——
Polystyrene beads, expandable	133	2211
Potassium	138	2257

Name of Material	Guide No.	ID No.	Name of Material	Guide No.	ID No.
Potassium, metal	138	2257	Potassium metavanadate	151	2864
Potassium, metal alloys	138	1420	Potassium monoxide	154	2033
Potassium, metal liquid alloy	138	1420	Potassium nitrate	140	1486
Potassium arsenate	151	1677	Potassium nitrate and Sodium nitrate mixture	140	1499
Potassium arsenite	154	1678	Potassium nitrate and Sodium nitrite mixture	140	1487
Potassium bifluoride	154	1811			
Potassium bisulfite solution	154	2693	Potassium nitrite	140	1488
Potassium bisulphite solution	154	2693	Potassium perchlorate	140	1489
Potassium borohydride	138	1870	Potassium permanganate	140	1490
Potassium bromate	140	1484	Potassium peroxide	144	1491
Potassium chlorate	140	1485	Potassium persulfate	140	1492
Potassium chlorate, aqueous solution	140	2427	Potassium persulphate	140	1492
			Potassium phosphide	139	2012
Potassium chlorate, solution	140	2427	Potassium selenate	151	2630
Potassium chromate	171	9142	Potassium selenite	151	2630
Potassium cuprocyanide	157	1679	Potassium silicofluoride	151	2655
Potassium cyanide	157	1680	Potassium sodium alloys	138	1422
Potassium dichloro-s-triazinetrione, dry	140	2465	Potassium sulfide, anhydrous	135	1382
			Potassium sulfide, hydrated, with not less than 30% water of crystallization	153	1847
Potassium dithionite	135	1929			
Potassium fluoride	154	1812			
Potassium fluoroacetate	151	2628	Potassium sulfide, hydrated, with not less than 30% water of hydration	153	1847
Potassium fluorosilicate	151	2655			
Potassium hydrogendifluoride	154	1811			
Potassium hydrogen fluoride, solution	154	1811	Potassium sulfide, with less than 30% water of crystallization	135	1382
Potassium hydrogen sulfate	154	2509	Potassium sulfide, with less than 30% water of hydration	135	1382
Potassium hydrogen sulphate	154	2509	Potassium sulphide, anhydrous	135	1382
Potassium hydrosulfite	135	1929	Potassium sulphide, hydrated, with not less than 30% water of crystallization	153	1847
Potassium hydrosulphite	135	1929			
Potassium hydroxide, dry, solid	154	1813			
Potassium hydroxide, flake	154	1813	Potassium sulphide, hydrated, with not less than 30% water of hydration	153	1847
Potassium hydroxide, solid	154	1813			
Potassium hydroxide, solution	154	1814			

Name of Material	Guide No.	ID No.
Potassium sulphide, with less than 30% water of crystallization	135	1382
Potassium sulphide, with less than 30% water of hydration	135	1382
Potassium superoxide	143	2466
Printing ink, flammable	129	1210
Printing ink related material	129	1210
Propadiene, inhibited	116P	2200
Propadiene and Methylacetylene mixture, stabilized	116P	1060
Propane	115	1075
Propane	115	1978
Propane-Ethane mixture, refrigerated liquid	115	1961
Propane mixture	115	1075
Propane mixture	115	1978
Propanethiols	130	2402
n-Propanol	129	1274
Propargyl alcohol	131	1986
Propionaldehyde	129	1275
Propionic acid	132	1848
Propionic anhydride	156	2496
Propionitrile	131	2404
Propionyl chloride	132	1815
Propionyl peroxide	148	2132
n-Propyl acetate	129	1276
normal Propyl alcohol	129	1274
Propyl alcohol, normal	129	1274
Propylamine	132	1277
n-Propyl benzene	127	2364
Propyl chloride	129	1278
n-Propyl chloroformate	155	2740

Name of Material	Guide No.	ID No.
Propylene	115	1075
Propylene	115	1077
Propylene, Ethylene and Acetylene in mixture, refrigerated liquid containing at least 71.5% Ethylene with not more than 22.5% Acetylene and not more than 6% Propylene	116	3138
Propylene chlorohydrin	131	2611
1,2-Propylenediamine	132	2258
1,3-Propylenediamine	132	2258
Propylene dichloride	130	1279
Propyleneimine, inhibited	131P	1921
Propylene oxide	127P	1280
Propylene oxide and Ethylene oxide mixture, with not more than 30% Ethylene oxide	129P	2983
Propylene tetramer	128	2850
Propyl formates	129	1281
n-Propyl isocyanate	155	2482
Propyl mercaptan	130	2402
n-Propyl nitrate	131	1865
Propyltrichlorosilane	155	1816
Pyrethroid pesticide, liquid, flammable, poisonous	131	3350
Pyrethroid pesticide, liquid, flammable, toxic	131	3350
Pyrethroid pesticide, liquid, poisonous	151	3352
Pyrethroid pesticide, liquid, poisonous, flammable	131	3351
Pyrethroid pesticide, liquid, toxic	151	3352
Pyrethroid pesticide, liquid, toxic, flammable	131	3351
Pyrethroid pesticide, solid, poisonous	151	3349

Name of Material	Guide No.	ID No.
Pyrethroid pesticide, solid, toxic	151	3349
Pyridine	129	1282
Pyrophoric alloy, n.o.s.	135	1383
Pyrophoric liquid, inorganic, n.o.s.	135	3194
Pyrophoric liquid, n.o.s.	135	2845
Pyrophoric liquid, organic, n.o.s.	135	2845
Pyrophoric metal, n.o.s.	135	1383
Pyrophoric organometallic compound, n.o.s.	135	3203
Pyrophoric organometallic compound, water-reactive, n.o.s.	135	3203
Pyrophoric solid, inorganic, n.o.s.	135	3200
Pyrophoric solid, n.o.s.	135	2846
Pyrophoric solid, organic, n.o.s.	135	2846
Pyrosulfuryl chloride	137	1817
Pyrosulphuryl chloride	137	1817
Pyroxylin plastic, rod, sheet, roll, tube or scrap	133	1325
Pyrrolidine	132	1922
Quinoline	154	2656
Radioactive material, articles manufactured from depleted Uranium	161	2909
Radioactive material, articles manufactured from natural Thorium	161	2909
Radioactive material, articles manufactured from natural Uranium	161	2909
Radioactive material, empty packages	161	2908
Radioactive material, excepted package, articles manufactured from depleted Uranium	161	2909
Radioactive material, excepted package, articles manufactured from depleted Uranium	161	2910
Radioactive material, excepted package, articles manufactured from natural Thorium	161	2909
Radioactive material, excepted package, articles manufactured from natural Thorium	161	2910
Radioactive material, excepted package, articles manufactured from natural Uranium	161	2909
Radioactive material, excepted package, articles manufactured from natural Uranium	161	2910
Radioactive material, excepted package, empty packaging	161	2908
Radioactive material, excepted package, empty packaging	161	2910
Radioactive material, excepted package, instruments or articles	161	2910
Radioactive material, excepted package, instruments or articles	161	2911
Radioactive material, excepted package, limited quantity of material	161	2910
Radioactive material, fissile, n.o.s.	165	2918
Radioactive material, instruments or articles	161	2911
Radioactive material, limited quantity, n.o.s.	161	2910
Radioactive material, low specific activity (LSA), n.o.s.	162	2912
Radioactive material, low specific activity (LSA-I)	162	2912

Name of Material	Guide No.	ID No.	Name of Material	Guide No.	ID No.
Radioactive material, low specific activity (LSA-II)	162	3321	Radioactive material, Type B(M) package	163	2917
Radioactive material, low specific activity (LSA-II), fissile	165	3324	Radioactive material, Type B(M) package, fissile	165	3329
Radioactive material, low specific activity (LSA-III)	162	3322	Radioactive material, Type B(U) package	163	2916
Radioactive material, low specific activity (LSA-III), fissile	165	3325	Radioactive material, Type B(U) package, fissile	165	3328
Radioactive material, n.o.s.	163	2982	Radioactive material, Type C package	163	3323
Radioactive material, special form, n.o.s.	164	2974	Radioactive material, Type C package, fissile	165	3330
Radioactive material, surface contaminated objects (SCO)	162	2913	Radioactive material, Uranium hexafluoride, fissile	166	2977
Radioactive material, surface contaminated objects (SCO-I)	162	2913	Radioactive material, Uranium hexafluoride, non-fissile or fissile-excepted	166	2978
Radioactive material, surface contaminated objects (SCO-I), fissile	165	3326	Rags, oily	133	1856
Radioactive material, surface contaminated objects (SCO-II)	162	2913	Rare gases and Nitrogen mixture	121	1981
Radioactive material, surface contaminated objects (SCO-II), fissile	165	3326	Rare gases and Nitrogen mixture, compressed	121	1981
Radioactive material, transported under special arrangement	163	2919	Rare gases and Oxygen mixture	122	1980
Radioactive material, transported under special arrangement, fissile	165	3331	Rare gases and Oxygen mixture, compressed	122	1980
Radioactive material, Type A package	163	2915	Rare gases mixture	121	1979
			Rare gases mixture, compressed	121	1979
Radioactive material, Type A package, fissile	165	3327	Receptacles, small, containing gas	115	2037
Radioactive material, Type A package, special form	164	3332	Red phosphorus	133	1338
			Red phosphorus, amorphous	133	1338
Radioactive material, Type A package, special form, fissile	165	3333	Refrigerant gas, n.o.s.	126	1078
			Refrigerant gas, n.o.s. (flammable)	115	1954
			Refrigerant gas R-12	126	1028
			Refrigerant gas R-12 and Refrigerant gas R-152a azeotropic mixture with 74% Refrigerant gas R-12	126	2602

Name of Material	Guide No.	ID No.	Name of Material	Guide No.	ID No.
Refrigerant gas R-12B1	126	1974	Refrigerant gas R-227	126	3296
Refrigerant gas R-13	126	1022	Refrigerant gas R-404A	126	3337
Refrigerant gas R-13 and Refrigerant gas R-23 azeotropic mixture with 60% Refrigerant gas R-13	126	2599	Refrigerant gas R-407A	126	3338
			Refrigerant gas R-407B	126	3339
			Refrigerant gas R-407C	126	3340
Refrigerant gas R-13B1	126	1009	Refrigerant gas R-500 (azeotropic mixture of Refrigerant gas R-12 and Refrigerant gas R-152a with approximately 74% Refrigerant gas R-12)	126	2602
Refrigerant gas R-14, compressed	126	1982			
Refrigerant gas R-21	126	1029			
Refrigerant gas R-22	126	1018			
Refrigerant gas R-23	126	1984	Refrigerant gas R-502	126	1973
Refrigerant gas R-23 and Refrigerant gas R-13 azeotropic mixture with 60% Refrigerant gas R-13	126	2599	Refrigerant gas R-503 (azeotropic mixture of Refrigerant gas R-13 and Refrigerant gas R-23 with approximately 60% Refrigerant gas R-13)	126	2599
Refrigerant gas R-32	115	3252			
Refrigerant gas R-40	115	1063	Refrigerant gas R-1216	126	1858
Refrigerant gas R-41	115	2454	Refrigerant gas R-1132a	116P	1959
Refrigerant gas R-114	126	1958	Refrigerant gas R-1318	126	2422
Refrigerant gas R-115	126	1020	Refrigerant gas RC-318	126	1976
Refrigerant gas R-116, compressed	126	2193	Refrigerating machine	128	1993
			Refrigerating machines	115	8023
Refrigerant gas R-124	126	1021	Refrigerating machines, containing Ammonia solutions (UN2073)	126	2857
Refrigerant gas R-125	126	3220			
Refrigerant gas R-133a	126	1983	Refrigerating machines, containing Ammonia solutions (UN2672)	126	2857
Refrigerant gas R-134a	126	3159			
Refrigerant gas R-143a	115	2035	Refrigerating machines, containing flammable, liquefied gas	115	1954
Refrigerant gas R-142b	115	2517			
Refrigerant gas R-152a	115	1030			
Refrigerant gas R-152a and Refrigerant gas R-12 azeotropic mixture with 74% Refrigerant gas R-12	126	2602	Refrigerating machines, containing flammable, non-poisonous, non-corrosive, liquefied gas	115	1954
Refrigerant gas R-161	115	2453			
Refrigerant gas R-218	126	2424			

Name of Material	Guide No.	ID No.
Refrigerating machines, containing flammable, non-toxic, liquefied gas	115	3358
Refrigerating machines, containing non-flammable, liquefied gas	126	2857
Refrigerating machines, containing non-flammable, non-poisonous, liquefied gas	126	2857
Refrigerating machines, containing non-flammable, non-poisonous, non-corrosive, liquefied gas	126	2857
Refrigerating machines, containing non-flammable, non-toxic, liquefied gas	126	2857
Refrigerating machines, containing non-flammable, non-toxic, non-corrosive, liquefied gas	126	2857
Regulated medical waste, n.o.s.	158	3291
Regulated medical waste	158	9275
Resin solution	127	1866
Resorcinol	153	2876
Rosin oil	127	1286
Rubber scrap, powdered or granulated	133	1345
Rubber shoddy, powdered or granulated	133	1345
Rubber solution	127	1287
Rubidium	138	1423
Rubidium hydroxide	154	2678
Rubidium hydroxide, solid	154	2678
Rubidium hydroxide, solution	154	2677
Rubidium metal	138	1423
SA	119	2188
Sarin	153	2810
Seat-belt modules	171	3268

Name of Material	Guide No.	ID No.
Seat-belt pre-tensioners	171	3268
Seat-belt pre-tensioners, compressed gas	126	3353
Seat-belt pre-tensioners, pyrotechnic	171	3268
Seed cake, with more than 1.5% oil and not more than 11% moisture	135	1386
Seed cake, with not more than 1.5% oil and not more than 11% moisture	135	2217
Selenates	151	2630
Selenic acid	154	1905
Selenites	151	2630
Selenium compound, n.o.s.	151	3283
Selenium disulfide	153	2657
Selenium disulphide	153	2657
Selenium hexafluoride	125	2194
Selenium oxide	154	2811
Selenium oxychloride	157	2879
Selenium powder	152	2658
Self-heating liquid, corrosive, inorganic, n.o.s.	136	3188
Self-heating liquid, corrosive, organic, n.o.s.	136	3185
Self-heating liquid, inorganic, n.o.s.	135	3186
Self-heating liquid, organic, n.o.s.	135	3183
Self-heating liquid, poisonous, inorganic, n.o.s.	136	3187
Self-heating liquid, poisonous, organic, n.o.s.	136	3184
Self-heating liquid, toxic, inorganic, n.o.s.	136	3187
Self-heating liquid, toxic, organic, n.o.s.	136	3184

Name of Material	Guide No.	ID No.
Self-heating metal powders, n.o.s.	135	3189
Self-heating solid, corrosive, inorganic, n.o.s.	136	3192
Self-heating solid, corrosive, organic, n.o.s.	136	3126
Self-heating solid, inorganic, n.o.s.	135	3190
Self-heating solid, inorganic, poisonous, n.o.s.	136	3191
Self-heating solid, inorganic, toxic, n.o.s.	136	3191
Self-heating solid, organic, n.o.s.	135	3088
Self-heating solid, organic, poisonous, n.o.s.	136	3128
Self-heating solid, organic, toxic, n.o.s.	136	3128
Self-heating solid, oxidizing, n.o.s.	135	3127
Self-heating solid, poisonous, inorganic, n.o.s.	136	3191
Self-heating solid, poisonous, organic, n.o.s.	136	3128
Self-heating solid, toxic, inorganic, n.o.s.	136	3191
Self-heating solid, toxic, organic, n.o.s.	136	3128
Self-heating substance, solid, corrosive, n.o.s.	136	3126
Self-heating substances, solid, n.o.s.	135	3088
Self-heating substances, solid, oxidizing, n.o.s.	135	3127
Self-heating substances, solid, poisonous, n.o.s.	136	3128
Self-heating substances, solid, toxic, n.o.s.	136	3128
Self-reactive liquid type B	149	3221
Self-reactive liquid type B, temperature controlled	150	3231
Self-reactive liquid type C	149	3223
Self-reactive liquid type C, temperature controlled	150	3233
Self-reactive liquid type D	149	3225
Self-reactive liquid type D, temperature controlled	150	3235
Self-reactive liquid type E	149	3227
Self-reactive liquid type E, temperature controlled	150	3237
Self-reactive liquid type F	149	3229
Self-reactive liquid type F, temperature controlled	150	3239
Self-reactive solid type B	149	3222
Self-reactive solid type B, temperature controlled	150	3232
Self-reactive solid type C	149	3224
Self-reactive solid type C, temperature controlled	150	3234
Self-reactive solid type D	149	3226
Self-reactive solid type D, temperature controlled	150	3236
Self-reactive solid type E	149	3228
Self-reactive solid type E, temperature controlled	150	3238
Self-reactive solid type F	149	3230
Self-reactive solid type F, temperature controlled	150	3240
Self-reactive substances, samples, n.o.s.	149	3031
Self-reactive substances, trial quantities, n.o.s.	149	3032
Shale oil	128	1288
Silane	116	2203
Silicofluorides, n.o.s.	151	2856

Name of Material	Guide No.	ID No.
Silane, compressed	116	2203
Silicon powder, amorphous	170	1346
Silicon tetrachloride	157	1818
Silicon tetrafluoride	125	1859
Silicon tetrafluoride, compressed	125	1859
Silver arsenite	151	1683
Silver cyanide	151	1684
Silver nitrate	140	1493
Silver picrate, wetted with not less than 30% water	113	1347
Sludge acid	153	1906
Smokeless powder for small arms	133	1325
Smokeless powder for small arms	133	3178
Soda lime, with more than 4% Sodium hydroxide	154	1907
Sodium	138	1428
Sodium aluminate, solid	154	2812
Sodium aluminate, solution	154	1819
Sodium aluminum hydride	138	2835
Sodium ammonium vanadate	154	2863
Sodium arsanilate	154	2473
Sodium arsenate	151	1685
Sodium arsenite, aqueous solution	154	1686
Sodium arsenite, solid	151	2027
Sodium azide	153	1687
Sodium bifluoride, solid	154	2439
Sodium bifluoride, solution	154	2439
Sodium bisulfate, solid	154	1821
Sodium bisulfate, solution	154	2837
Sodium bisulphate, solid	154	1821

Name of Material	Guide No.	ID No.
Sodium bisulphate, solution	154	2837
Sodium borohydride	138	1426
Sodium borohydride and Sodium hydroxide solution, with not more than 12% Sodium borohydride and not more than 40% Sodium hydroxide	157	3320
Sodium bromate	141	1494
Sodium cacodylate	152	1688
Sodium chlorate	140	1495
Sodium chlorate, aqueous solution	140	2428
Sodium chlorite	143	1496
Sodium chlorite, solution, with more than 5% available Chlorine	154	1908
Sodium chloroacetate	151	2659
Sodium chromate	171	9145
Sodium cuprocyanide, solid	157	2316
Sodium cuprocyanide, solution	157	2317
Sodium cyanide	157	1689
Sodium 2-diazo-1-naphthol-4-sulfonate	149	3040
Sodium 2-diazo-1-naphthol-4-sulphonate	149	3040
Sodium 2-diazo-1-naphthol-5-sulfonate	149	3041
Sodium 2-diazo-1-naphthol-5-sulphonate	149	3041
Sodium dichloroisocyanurate	140	2465
Sodium dichloro-s-triazinetrione	140	2465
Sodium dinitro-o-cresolate, wetted with not less than 15% water	113	1348
Sodium dinitro-ortho-cresolate, wetted	113	1348
Sodium dithionite	135	1384

Name of Material	Guide No.	ID No.
Sodium dodecylbenzenesulfonate (branched chain)	171	9146
Sodium dodecylbenzenesulphonate (branched chain)	171	9146
Sodium fluoride	154	1690
Sodium fluoride, solid	154	1690
Sodium fluoride, solution	154	1690
Sodium fluoroacetate	151	2629
Sodium fluorosilicate	154	2674
Sodium hydride	138	1427
Sodium hydrogendifluoride	154	2439
Sodium hydrogen fluoride	154	2439
Sodium hydrogen sulfate, solid	154	1821
Sodium hydrogen sulfate, solution	154	2837
Sodium hydrogen sulphate, solid	154	1821
Sodium hydrogen sulphate, solution	154	2837
Sodium hydrosulfide, solid	154	2923
Sodium hydrosulfide, solid, with less than 25% water of crystallization	135	2318
Sodium hydrosulfide, solution	154	2922
Sodium hydrosulfide, with less than 25% water of crystallization	135	2318
Sodium hydrosulfide, with not less than 25% water of crystallization	154	2949
Sodium hydrosulfite	135	1384
Sodium hydrosulphide, solid	154	2923
Sodium hydrosulphide, solid, with less than 25% water of crystallization	135	2318
Sodium hydrosulphide, solution	154	2922
Sodium hydrosulphide, with less than 25% water of crystallization	135	2318
Sodium hydrosulphide, with not less than 25% water of crystallization	154	2949
Sodium hydrosulphite	135	1384
Sodium hydroxide, dry	154	1823
Sodium hydroxide, bead	154	1823
Sodium hydroxide, flake	154	1823
Sodium hydroxide, granular	154	1823
Sodium hydroxide, solid	154	1823
Sodium hydroxide, solution	154	1824
Sodium methylate	138	1431
Sodium methylate, alcohol mixture	132	1289
Sodium methylate, dry	138	1431
Sodium methylate, solution in alcohol	132	1289
Sodium monoxide	157	1825
Sodium nitrate	140	1498
Sodium nitrate and Potassium nitrate mixture	140	1499
Sodium nitrite	140	1500
Sodium nitrite and Potassium nitrate mixtures	140	1487
Sodium nitrite mixture	140	1487
Sodium pentachlorophenate	154	2567
Sodium percarbonates	140	2467
Sodium perchlorate	140	1502
Sodium permanganate	140	1503
Sodium peroxide	144	1504
Sodium peroxoborate, anhydrous	140	3247

Name of Material	Guide No.	ID No.	Name of Material	Guide No.	ID No.
Sodium persulfate	140	1505	Stannic phosphides	139	1433
Sodium persulphate	140	1505	Stannous chloride, solid	154	1759
Sodium phenolate, solid	153	2497	Steel swarf	170	2793
Sodium phosphate, dibasic	171	9147	Stibine	119	2676
Sodium phosphate, tribasic	171	9148	Straw, wet, damp or contaminated with oil	133	1327
Sodium phosphide	139	1432			
Sodium picramate, wetted with not less than 20% water	113	1349	Strontium arsenite	151	1691
			Strontium chlorate	143	1506
Sodium potassium alloys	138	1422	Strontium chlorate, solid	143	1506
Sodium selenite	151	2630	Strontium chlorate, solution	143	1506
Sodium silicofluoride	154	2674	Strontium chromate	171	9149
Sodium sulfide, anhydrous	135	1385	Strontium nitrate	140	1507
Sodium sulfide, hydrated, with not less than 30% water	153	1849	Strontium perchlorate	140	1508
			Strontium peroxide	143	1509
Sodium sulfide, with less than 30% water of crystallization	135	1385	Strontium phosphide	139	2013
			Strychnine	151	1692
Sodium sulphide, anhydrous	135	1385	Strychnine salts	151	1692
Sodium sulphide, hydrated, with not less than 30% water	153	1849	Styrene monomer, inhibited	128P	2055
			Substances, which in contact with water emit flammable gases, liquid, corrosive, n.o.s.	138	3129
Sodium sulphide, with less than 30% water of crystallization	135	1385			
Sodium superoxide	143	2547	Substances, which in contact with water emit flammable gases, liquid, n.o.s.	138	3148
Solids containing corrosive liquid, n.o.s.	154	3244			
Solids containing flammable liquid, n.o.s.	133	3175	Substances, which in contact with water emit flammable gases, liquid, poisonous, n.o.s.	139	3130
Solids containing poisonous liquid, n.o.s.	151	3243			
Solids containing toxic liquid, n.o.s.	151	3243	Substances, which in contact with water emit flammable gases, liquid, toxic, n.o.s.	139	3130
Soman	153	2810			
Spirits of Nitroglycerin, not exceeding 1% Nitroglycerin	127	1204	Substances, which in contact with water emit flammable gases, solid, corrosive, n.o.s.	138	3131
Stannic chloride, anhydrous	137	1827			
Stannic chloride, pentahydrate	154	2440	Substances, which in contact with water emit flammable gases, solid, flammable, n.o.s.	138	3132

Name of Material	Guide No.	ID No.
Substances, which in contact with water emit flammable gases, solid, n.o.s.	138	2813
Substances, which in contact with water emit flammable gases, solid, oxidizing, n.o.s.	138	3133
Substances, which in contact with water emit flammable gases, solid, poisonous, n.o.s.	139	3134
Substances, which in contact with water emit flammable gases, solid, self-heating, n.o.s.	138	3135
Substances, which in contact with water emit flammable gases, solid, toxic, n.o.s.	139	3134
Substituted nitrophenol pesticide, liquid, flammable, poisonous	131	2780
Substituted nitrophenol pesticide, liquid, flammable, toxic	131	2780
Substituted nitrophenol pesticide, liquid, poisonous	153	3014
Substituted nitrophenol pesticide, liquid, poisonous, flammable	131	3013
Substituted nitrophenol pesticide, liquid, toxic	153	3014
Substituted nitrophenol pesticide, liquid, toxic, flammable	131	3013
Substituted nitrophenol pesticide, solid, poisonous	153	2779
Substituted nitrophenol pesticide, solid, toxic	153	2779
Succinic acid peroxide	146	2135
Sulfamic acid	154	2967

Name of Material	Guide No.	ID No.
Sulfur	133	1350
Sulfur, molten	133	2448
Sulfur chlorides	137	1828
Sulfur dioxide	125	1079
Sulfur dioxide, liquefied	125	1079
Sulfur hexafluoride	126	1080
Sulfuric acid	137	1830
Sulfuric acid, fuming	137	1831
Sulfuric acid, fuming, with less than 30% free Sulfur trioxide	137	1831
Sulfuric acid, fuming, with not less than 30% free Sulfur trioxide	137	1831
Sulfuric acid, spent	137	1832
Sulfuric acid, with more than 51% acid	137	1830
Sulfuric acid, with not more than 51% acid	157	2796
Sulfuric acid and Hydrofluoric acid mixtures	157	1786
Sulfurous acid	154	1833
Sulfur tetrafluoride	125	2418
Sulfur trioxide	137	1829
Sulfur trioxide, inhibited	137	1829
Sulfur trioxide, stabilized	137	1829
Sulfur trioxide, uninhibited	137	1829
Sulfur trioxide and Chlorosulfonic acid mixture	137	1754
Sulfuryl chloride	137	1834
Sulfuryl fluoride	123	2191
Sulphamic acid	154	2967
Sulphur	133	1350
Sulphur, molten	133	2448
Sulphur chlorides	137	1828
Sulphur dioxide	125	1079

Name of Material	Guide No.	ID No.
Sulphur dioxide, liquefied	125	1079
Sulphur hexafluoride	126	1080
Sulphuric acid	137	1830
Sulphuric acid, fuming	137	1831
Sulphuric acid, fuming, with less than 30% free Sulphur trioxide	137	1831
Sulphuric acid, fuming, with not less than 30% free Sulphur trioxide	137	1831
Sulphuric acid, spent	137	1832
Sulphuric acid, with more than 51% acid	137	1830
Sulphuric acid, with not more than 51% acid	157	2796
Sulphuric acid and Hydrofluoric acid mixtures	157	1786
Sulphurous acid	154	1833
Sulphur tetrafluoride	125	2418
Sulphur trioxide	137	1829
Sulphur trioxide, inhibited	137	1829
Sulphur trioxide, stabilized	137	1829
Sulphur trioxide, uninhibited	137	1829
Sulphur trioxide and Chlorosulphonic acid mixture	137	1754
Sulphuryl chloride	137	1834
Sulphuryl fluoride	123	2191
Tabun	153	2810
Tars, liquid	130	1999
TDE (1,1-Dichloro-2,2-bis (p-chlorophenyl)ethane)	151	2761
Tear gas candles	159	1700
Tear gas devices	159	1693
Tear gas grenades	159	1700
Tear gas substance, liquid, n.o.s.	159	1693

Name of Material	Guide No.	ID No.
Tear gas substance, solid, n.o.s.	159	1693
Tellurium compound, n.o.s.	151	3284
Tellurium hexafluoride	125	2195
Terpene hydrocarbons, n.o.s.	128	2319
Terpinolene	128	2541
Tetrabromoethane	159	2504
1,1,2,2-Tetrachloroethane	151	1702
Tetrachloroethane	151	1702
Tetrachloroethylene	160	1897
Tetraethyl dithiopyrophosphate	153	1704
Tetraethyl dithiopyrophosphate, mixture, dry or liquid	153	1704
Tetraethyl dithiopyrophosphate and gases, in solution	123	1703
Tetraethyl dithiopyrophosphate and gases, mixtures	123	1703
Tetraethyl dithiopyrophosphate and gases, mixtures, or in solution (LC50 more than 200 ppm but not more than 5000 ppm)	123	1703
Tetraethyl dithiopyrophosphate and gases, mixtures, or in solution (LC50 not more than 200 ppm)	123	1703
Tetraethylenepentamine	153	2320
Tetraethyl lead, liquid	131	1649
Tetraethyl pyrophosphate, liquid	152	2783
Tetraethyl pyrophosphate, liquid	152	3018
Tetraethyl pyrophosphate, solid	152	2783
Tetraethyl pyrophosphate and compressed gas mixtures	123	1705
Tetraethyl pyrophosphate and compressed gas mixtures (LC50 more than 200 ppm but not more than 5000 ppm)	123	1705

Name of Material	Guide No.	ID No.	Name of Material	Guide No.	ID No.
Tetraethyl pyrophosphate and compressed gas mixtures (LC50 not more than 200 ppm)	123	1705	Thallium compound, n.o.s.	151	1707
			Thallium nitrate	141	2727
Tetraethyl pyrophosphate mixture, dry	152	2783	Thallium sulfate, solid	151	1707
			Thallium sulphate, solid	151	1707
Tetraethyl silicate	132	1292	4-Thiapentanal	152	2785
1,1,1,2-Tetrafluoroethane	126	3159	Thia-4-pentanal	152	2785
Tetrafluoroethane and Ethylene oxide mixture, with not more than 5.6% Ethylene oxide	126	3299	Thickened GD	153	2810
			Thioacetic acid	129	2436
Tetrafluoroethylene, inhibited	116P	1081	Thiocarbamate pesticide, liquid, flammable, poisonous	131	2772
Tetrafluoromethane	126	1982	Thiocarbamate pesticide, liquid, flammable, toxic	131	2772
Tetrafluoromethane, compressed	126	1982	Thiocarbamate pesticide, liquid, poisonous	151	3006
1,2,3,6-Tetrahydro-benzaldehyde	132	2498	Thiocarbamate pesticide, liquid, poisonous, flammable	131	3005
Tetrahydrofuran	127	2056	Thiocarbamate pesticide, liquid, toxic	151	3006
Tetrahydrofurfurylamine	129	2943			
Tetrahydrophthalic anhydrides	156	2698	Thiocarbamate pesticide, liquid, toxic, flammable	131	3005
1,2,3,6-Tetrahydropyridine	129	2410	Thiocarbamate pesticide, solid, poisonous	151	2771
1,2,5,6-Tetrahydropyridine	129	2410			
Tetrahydrothiophene	129	2412	Thiocarbamate pesticide, solid, toxic	151	2771
Tetralin hydroperoxide	145	2136			
Tetramethylammonium hydroxide	153	1835	Thioglycol	153	2966
			Thioglycolic acid	153	1940
1,1,3,3-Tetramethylbutyl hydroperoxide	145	2160	Thiolactic acid	153	2936
			Thionyl chloride	137	1836
1,1,3,3-Tetramethylbutyl peroxy-2-ethylhexanoate	148	2161	Thiophene	130	2414
			Thiophosgene	157	2474
Tetramethylmethylenediamine	132	9069	Thiophosphoryl chloride	157	1837
Tetramethylsilane	130	2749	Thiourea dioxide	135	3341
Tetranitromethane	143	1510	Thiram	151	2771
Tetrapropyl orthotitanate	128	2413	Thorium metal, pyrophoric	162	2975
Textile treating compound or mixture, liquid (corrosive)	154	1760	Thorium nitrate, solid	162	2976
Thallium chlorate	141	2573			

Name of Material	Guide No.	ID No.
Tinctures, medicinal	127	1293
Tin tetrachloride	137	1827
Tin tetrachloride, pentahydrate	154	2440
Titanium disulfide	135	3174
Titanium disulphide	135	3174
Titanium hydride	170	1871
Titanium powder, dry	135	2546
Titanium powder, wetted with not less than 25% water	170	1352
Titanium sponge granules	170	2878
Titanium sponge powders	170	2878
Titanium sulfate, solution	154	1760
Titanium sulphate, solution	154	1760
Titanium tetrachloride	137	1838
Titanium tetrachloride and Vanadium oxytrichloride, mixture	137	2443
Titanium trichloride, pyrophoric	135	2441
Titanium trichloride mixture	157	2869
Titanium trichloride mixture, pyrophoric	135	2441
TNT, wetted with not less than 30% water	113	1356
Toe puffs, nitrocellulose base	133	1353
Toluene	130	1294
2,4-Toluenediamine	151	1709
Toluenediamine	151	1709
Toluene diisocyanate	156	2078
Toluene sulfonic acid, liquid, with more than 5% free Sulfuric acid	153	2584
Toluene sulfonic acid, liquid, with not more than 5% free Sulfuric acid	153	2586

Name of Material	Guide No.	ID No.
Toluene sulfonic acid, solid, with more than 5% free Sulfuric acid	153	2583
Toluene sulfonic acid, solid, with not more than 5% free Sulfuric acid	153	2585
Toluene sulphonic acid, liquid, with more than 5% free Sulphuric acid	153	2584
Toluene sulphonic acid, liquid, with not more than 5% free Sulphuric acid	153	2586
Toluene sulphonic acid, solid, with more than 5% free Sulphuric acid	153	2583
Toluene sulphonic acid, solid, with not more than 5% free Sulphuric acid	153	2585
Toluidines	153	1708
Toluidines, liquid	153	1708
Toluidines, solid	153	1708
2,4-Toluylenediamine	151	1709
Toxaphene	151	2761
Toxic liquid, corrosive, inorganic, n.o.s.	154	3289
Toxic liquid, corrosive, inorganic, n.o.s. (Inhalation Hazard Zone A)	154	3289
Toxic liquid, corrosive, inorganic, n.o.s. (Inhalation Hazard Zone B)	154	3289
Toxic liquid, corrosive, organic, n.o.s.	154	2927
Toxic liquid, corrosive, organic, n.o.s. (Inhalation Hazard Zone A)	154	2927
Toxic liquid, corrosive, organic, n.o.s. (Inhalation Hazard Zone B)	154	2927

Name of Material	Guide No.	ID No.
Toxic liquid, flammable, n.o.s.	131	2929
Toxic liquid, flammable, n.o.s. (Inhalation Hazard Zone A)	131	2929
Toxic liquid, flammable, n.o.s. (Inhalation Hazard Zone B)	131	2929
Toxic liquid, flammable, organic, n.o.s.	131	2929
Toxic liquid, flammable, organic, n.o.s. (Inhalation Hazard Zone A)	131	2929
Toxic liquid, flammable, organic, n.o.s. (Inhalation Hazard Zone B)	131	2929
Toxic liquid, inorganic, n.o.s.	151	3287
Toxic liquid, inorganic, n.o.s. (Inhalation Hazard Zone A)	151	3287
Toxic liquid, inorganic, n.o.s. (Inhalation Hazard Zone B)	151	3287
Toxic liquid, n.o.s.	153	2810
Toxic liquid, n.o.s. (Inhalation Hazard Zone A)	153	2810
Toxic liquid, n.o.s. (Inhalation Hazard Zone B)	153	2810
Toxic liquid, organic, n.o.s.	153	2810
Toxic liquid, organic, n.o.s. (Inhalation Hazard Zone A)	153	2810
Toxic liquid, organic, n.o.s. (Inhalation Hazard Zone B)	153	2810
Toxic liquid, oxidizing, n.o.s.	142	3122
Toxic liquid, oxidizing, n.o.s. (Inhalation Hazard Zone A)	142	3122
Toxic liquid, oxidizing, n.o.s. (Inhalation Hazard Zone B)	142	3122
Toxic liquid, water-reactive, n.o.s.	139	3123
Toxic liquid, water-reactive, n.o.s. (Inhalation Hazard Zone A)	139	3123
Toxic liquid, water-reactive, n.o.s. (Inhalation Hazard Zone B)	139	3123
Toxic liquid, which in contact with water emits flammable gases, n.o.s.	139	3123
Toxic liquid, which in contact with water emits flammable gases, n.o.s. (Inhalation Hazard Zone A)	139	3123
Toxic liquid, which in contact with water emits flammable gases, n.o.s. (Inhalation Hazard Zone B)	139	3123
Toxic solid, corrosive, inorganic, n.o.s.	154	3290
Toxic solid, corrosive, organic, n.o.s.	154	2928
Toxic solid, flammable, n.o.s.	134	2930
Toxic solid, flammable, organic, n.o.s.	134	2930
Toxic solid, inorganic, n.o.s.	151	3288
Toxic solid, n.o.s.	154	2811
Toxic solid, organic, n.o.s.	154	2811
Toxic solid, oxidizing, n.o.s.	141	3086
Toxic solid, self-heating, n.o.s.	136	3124
Toxic solid, water-reactive, n.o.s.	139	3125
Toxic solid, which in contact with water emits flammable gases, n.o.s.	139	3125
Toxins	153	—
Toxins, extracted from living sources, liquid, n.o.s.	153	3172
Toxins, extracted from living sources, n.o.s.	153	3172
Toxins, extracted from living sources, solid, n.o.s.	153	3172

Name of Material	Guide No.	ID No.	Name of Material	Guide No.	ID No.
Triallylamine	132	2610	Trichlorosilane	139	1295
Triallyl borate	156	2609	Trichloro-s-triazinetrione, dry	140	2468
Triazine pesticide, liquid, flammable, poisonous	131	2764	(mono)-(Trichloro)-tetra-(monopotassium dichloro)-penta-s-triazinetrione, dry	140	2468
Triazine pesticide, liquid, flammable, toxic	131	2764	Tricresyl phosphate	151	2574
Triazine pesticide, liquid, poisonous	151	2998	Triethanolamine dodecylbenzenesulfonate	171	9151
Triazine pesticide, liquid, poisonous, flammable	131	2997	Triethanolamine dodecylbenzenesulphonate	171	9151
Triazine pesticide, liquid, toxic	151	2998	Triethylamine	132	1296
Triazine pesticide, liquid, toxic, flammable	131	2997	Triethylenetetramine	153	2259
Triazine pesticide, solid, poisonous	151	2763	Triethyl phosphite	129	2323
Triazine pesticide, solid, toxic	151	2763	Trifluoroacetic acid	154	2699
Tri-(1-aziridinyl)phosphine oxide, solution	152	2501	Trifluoroacetyl chloride	125	3057
Tributylamine	153	2542	Trifluorochloroethylene	119P	1082
Tributylphosphane	135	3254	Trifluorochloroethylene, inhibited	119P	1082
Tributylphosphine	135	3254	1,1,1-Trifluoroethane	115	2035
Trichlorfon	152	2783	Trifluoroethane, compressed	115	2035
Trichloroacetic acid	153	1839	Trifluoromethane	126	1984
Trichloroacetic acid, solution	153	2564	Trifluoromethane, refrigerated liquid	120	3136
Trichloroacetyl chloride	156	2442	Trifluoromethane and Chlorotrifluoromethane azeotropic mixture with approximately 60% Chlorotrifluoromethane	126	2599
Trichlorobenzenes, liquid	153	2321			
Trichlorobutene	152	2322			
1,1,1-Trichloroethane	160	2831	2-Trifluoromethylaniline	153	2942
Trichloroethylene	160	1710	3-Trifluoromethylaniline	153	2948
Trichloroisocyanuric acid, dry	140	2468	Triisobutylene	128	2324
Trichlorophenol	153	2020	Triisocyanatoisocyanurate of Isophoronediisocyanate, solution (70%)	127	2906
2,4,5-Trichlorophenoxyacetic acid	152	2765			
2,4,5-Trichlorophenoxy-propionic acid	152	2765	Triisopropyl borate	129	2616
			Trimethoxysilane	132	9269

Name of Material	Guide No.	ID No.	Name of Material	Guide No.	ID No.
Trimethylacetyl chloride	132	2438	Uranium hexafluoride, low specific activity	166	2978
Trimethylamine, anhydrous	118	1083	Uranium hexafluoride, non-fissile	166	2978
Trimethylamine, aqueous solution	132	1297	Uranium metal, pyrophoric	162	2979
1,3,5-Trimethylbenzene	129	2325	Uranyl acetate	162	9180
Trimethyl borate	129	2416	Uranyl nitrate, hexahydrate, solution	162	2980
Trimethylchlorosilane	155	1298	Uranyl nitrate, solid	162	2981
Trimethylcyclohexylamine	153	2326	Urea hydrogen peroxide	140	1511
Trimethylhexamethylenediamines	153	2327	Urea nitrate, wetted with not less than 20% water	113	1357
Trimethylhexamethylene diisocyanate	156	2328	Urea peroxide	140	1511
Trimethyl phosphite	129	2329	Valeraldehyde	129	2058
Trinitroaniline, wetted	113	9073	Valeryl chloride	132	2502
Trinitrobenzene, wetted with not less than 30% water	113	1354	Vanadium compound, n.o.s.	151	3285
Trinitrobenzoic acid, wetted with not less than 30% water	113	1355	Vanadium oxytrichloride	137	2443
Trinitrophenol, wetted with not less than 30% water	113	1344	Vanadium oxytrichloride and Titanium tetrachloride, mixture	137	2443
Trinitrotoluene, wetted with not less than 30% water	113	1356	Vanadium pentoxide	151	2862
Tripropylamine	132	2260	Vanadium tetrachloride	137	2444
Tripropylene	128	2057	Vanadium trichloride	157	2475
Tris-(1-aziridinyl)phosphine oxide, solution	152	2501	Vanadium trioxide	154	2860
Tris-(2-chloroethyl) amine	153	2810	Vanadyl sulfate	151	2931
Tungsten hexafluoride	125	2196	Vanadyl sulphate	151	2931
Turpentine	128	1299	Vehicle, flammable gas powered	128	3166
Turpentine substitute	128	1300	Vehicle, flammable liquid powered	128	3166
Undecane	128	2330	Vinyl acetate	129P	1301
Uranium hexafluoride, fissile containing more than 1% Uranium-235	166	2977	Vinyl acetate, inhibited	129P	1301
Uranium hexafluoride, fissile-excepted	166	2978	Vinyl bromide, inhibited	116P	1085
			Vinyl butyrate, inhibited	129P	2838
			Vinyl chloride	116P	1086
			Vinyl chloride, inhibited	116P	1086

Name of Material	Guide No.	ID No.	Name of Material	Guide No.	ID No.
Vinyl chloride, stabilized	116P	1086	Waste Type 19	154	9319
Vinyl chloroacetate	155	2589	Waste Type 20	154	9320
Vinyl ethyl ether	127P	1302	Waste Type 21	154	9321
Vinyl ethyl ether, inhibited	127P	1302	Waste Type 22	154	9322
Vinyl fluoride, inhibited	116P	1860	Waste Type 23	154	9323
Vinylidene chloride, inhibited	129P	1303	Waste Type 24	152	9324
Vinyl isobutyl ether	127P	1304	Waste Type 25	127	9325
Vinyl isobutyl ether, inhibited	127P	1304	Waste Type 26	152	9326
Vinyl methyl ether	116P	1087	Waste Type 27	131	9327
Vinyl methyl ether, inhibited	116P	1087	Waste Type 28	131	9328
Vinylpyridines, inhibited	131P	3073	Waste Type 29	153	9329
Vinyltoluenes, inhibited	130P	2618	Waste Type 30	153	9330
Vinyltrichlorosilane	155	1305	Waste Type 31	129	9331
Vinyltrichlorosilane, inhibited	155	1305	Waste Type 32	129	9332
VX	153	2810	Waste Type 33	129	9333
Waste Type 1	153	9301	Waste Type 34	129	9334
Waste Type 2	153	9302	Waste Type 35	153	9335
Waste Type 3	131	9303	Waste Type 36	153	9336
Waste Type 4	153	9304	Waste Type 37	153	9337
Waste Type 5	131	9305	Waste Type 38	153	9338
Waste Type 6	154	9306	Waste Type 39	153	9339
Waste Type 7	154	9307	Waste Type 40	153	9340
Waste Type 8	153	9308	Waste Type 41	132	9341
Waste Type 9	153	9309	Waste Type 42	129	9342
Waste Type 10	153	9310	Waste Type 43	154	9343
Waste Type 11	153	9311	Waste Type 44	132	9344
Waste Type 12	153	9312	Waste Type 45	132	9345
Waste Type 13	153	9313	Waste Type 46	153	9346
Waste Type 14	153	9314	Waste Type 47	132	9347
Waste Type 15	153	9315	Waste Type 48	153	9348
Waste Type 16	154	9316	Waste Type 49	153	9349
Waste Type 17	154	9317	Waste Type 50	153	9350
Waste Type 18	154	9318	Waste Type 51	153	9351

Name of Material	Guide No.	ID No.	Name of Material	Guide No.	ID No.
Waste Type 52	153	9352	Waste Type 85	154	9385
Waste Type 53	153	9353	Waste Type 86	154	9386
Waste Type 54	153	9354	Waste Type 87	154	9387
Waste Type 55	153	9355	Waste Type 88	151	9388
Waste Type 56	153	9356	Waste Type 89	154	9389
Waste Type 57	153	9357	Waste Type 90	154	9390
Waste Type 58	153	9358	Waste Type 91	153	9391
Waste Type 59	151	9359	Waste Type 92	154	9392
Waste Type 60	132	9360	Waste Type 93	153	9393
Waste Type 61	151	9361	Waste Type 94	151	9394
Waste Type 62	151	9362	Waste Type 95	153	9395
Waste Type 63	151	9363	Waste Type 96	151	9396
Waste Type 64	151	9364	Waste Type 97	153	9397
Waste Type 65	151	9365	Waste Type 99	137	9399
Waste Type 66	151	9366	Waste Type 100	137	9400
Waste Type 67	152	9367	Water pump system	126	1956
Waste Type 68	154	9368	Water-reactive liquid, corrosive, n.o.s.	138	3129
Waste Type 69	151	9369	Water-reactive liquid, n.o.s.	138	3148
Waste Type 70	151	9370	Water-reactive liquid, poisonous, n.o.s.	139	3130
Waste Type 71	133	9371	Water-reactive liquid, toxic, n.o.s.	139	3130
Waste Type 72	151	9372			
Waste Type 73	151	9373	Water-reactive solid, corrosive, n.o.s.	138	3131
Waste Type 74	127	9374			
Waste Type 75	153	9375	Water-reactive solid, flammable, n.o.s.	138	3132
Waste Type 76	153	9376			
Waste Type 77	131	9377	Water-reactive solid, n.o.s.	138	2813
Waste Type 78	153	9378	Water-reactive solid, oxidizing, n.o.s.	138	3133
Waste Type 79	153	9379			
Waste Type 80	151	9380	Water-reactive solid, poisonous, n.o.s.	139	3134
Waste Type 81	154	9381			
Waste Type 82	154	9382	Water-reactive solid, self-heating, n.o.s.	138	3135
Waste Type 83	154	9383			
Waste Type 84	151	9384	Water-reactive solid, toxic, n.o.s.	139	3134

Name of Material	Guide No.	ID No.	Name of Material	Guide No.	ID No.
Water-reactive substances, liquid, corrosive, n.o.s.	138	3129	Xylenes	130	1307
Water-reactive substances, liquid, n.o.s.	138	3148	Xylenols	153	2261
			Xylidines	153	1711
Water-reactive substances, liquid, poisonous, n.o.s.	139	3130	Xylyl bromide	152	1701
Water-reactive substances, liquid, toxic, n.o.s.	139	3130	Yellow phosphorus, dry	136	1381
			Yellow phosphorus, in solution	136	1381
Water-reactive substances, solid, corrosive, n.o.s.	138	3131	Yellow phosphorus, molten	136	2447
			Yellow phosphorus, under water	136	1381
Water-reactive substances, solid, flammable, n.o.s.	138	3132	Zinc acetate	171	9153
			Zinc ammonium chloride	171	9154
Water-reactive substances, solid, n.o.s.	138	2813	Zinc ammonium nitrite	140	1512
Water-reactive substances, solid, oxidizing, n.o.s.	138	3133	Zinc arsenate	151	1712
			Zinc arsenate and Zinc arsenite mixture	151	1712
Water-reactive substances, solid, poisonous, n.o.s.	139	3134	Zinc arsenite	151	1712
Water-reactive substances, solid, self-heating, n.o.s.	138	3135	Zinc arsenite and Zinc arsenate mixture	151	1712
Water-reactive substances, solid, toxic, n.o.s.	139	3134	Zinc ashes	138	1435
			Zinc bisulfite solution	154	2693
Wheelchair, electric, with batteries	154	3171	Zinc bisulphite solution	154	2693
White asbestos	171	2590	Zinc borate	171	9155
White phosphorus, dry	136	1381	Zinc bromate	140	2469
			Zinc bromide	171	9156
White phosphorus, in solution	136	1381	Zinc carbonate	171	9157
White phosphorus, molten	136	2447	Zinc chlorate	140	1513
White phosphorus, under water	136	1381	Zinc chloride, anhydrous	154	2331
Wood preservatives, liquid	129	1306	Zinc chloride, solution	154	1840
Wool waste, wet	133	—	Zinc cyanide	151	1713
Xanthates	135	3342	Zinc dithionite	171	1931
Xenon	121	2036	Zinc dross	138	1435
Xenon, compressed	121	2036	Zinc dust	138	1436
Xenon, refrigerated liquid (cryogenic liquid)	120	2591	Zinc fluoride	151	9158
			Zinc fluorosilicate	151	2855

Name of Material	Guide No.	ID No.
Zinc formate	171	9159
Zinc hydrosulfite	171	1931
Zinc hydrosulphite	171	1931
Zinc nitrate	140	1514
Zinc permanganate	140	1515
Zinc peroxide	143	1516
Zinc phenolsulfonate	171	9160
Zinc phenolsulphonate	171	9160
Zinc phosphide	139	1714
Zinc powder	138	1436
Zinc residue	138	1435
Zinc resinate	133	2714
Zinc selenate	151	2630
Zinc selenite	151	2630
Zinc silicofluoride	151	2855
Zinc skimmings	138	1435
Zinc sulfate	171	9161
Zinc sulphate	171	9161
Zirconium, dry, coiled wire, finished metal sheets or strips	170	2858
Zirconium, dry, finished sheets, strips or coiled wire	135	2009
Zirconium hydride	138	1437
Zirconium metal, liquid, suspension	170	1308
Zirconium metal, powder, wet	170	1358
Zirconium nitrate	140	2728
Zirconium picramate, wetted with not less than 20% water	113	1517
Zirconium potassium fluoride	171	9162
Zirconium powder, dry	135	2008
Zirconium powder, wetted with not less than 25% water	170	1358
Zirconium scrap	135	1932

Name of Material	Guide No.	ID No.
Zirconium sulfate	171	9163
Zirconium sulphate	171	9163
Zirconium suspended in a flammable liquid	170	1308
Zirconium suspended in a liquid (flammable)	170	1308
Zirconium tetrachloride	137	2503

GUIDES

POTENTIAL HAZARDS

FIRE OR EXPLOSION

- May explode from heat, shock, friction or contamination.
- May react violently or explosively on contact with air, water or foam.
- May be ignited by heat, sparks or flames.
- Vapors may travel to source of ignition and flash back.
- Containers may explode when heated.
- Ruptured cylinders may rocket.

HEALTH

- Inhalation, ingestion or contact with substance may cause severe injury, infection, disease or death.
- High concentration of gas may cause asphyxiation without warning.
- Contact may cause burns to skin and eyes.
- Fire or contact with water may produce irritating, toxic and/or corrosive gases.
- Runoff from fire control may cause pollution.

PUBLIC SAFETY

- **CALL Emergency Response Telephone Number on Shipping Paper first. If Shipping Paper not available or no answer, refer to appropriate telephone number listed on the inside back cover.**
- Isolate spill or leak area immediately for at least 100 to 200 meters (330 to 660 feet) in all directions.
- Keep unauthorized personnel away.
- Stay upwind.
- Keep out of low areas.

PROTECTIVE CLOTHING

- Wear positive pressure self-contained breathing apparatus (SCBA).
- Structural firefighters' protective clothing provides limited protection in fire situations ONLY; it may not be effective in spill situations.

EVACUATION

Fire

- If tank, rail car or tank truck is involved in a fire, ISOLATE for 800 meters (1/2 mile) in all directions; also, consider initial evacuation for 800 meters (1/2 mile) in all directions.

EMERGENCY RESPONSE

FIRE
CAUTION: Material may react with extinguishing agent.

Small Fires
- Dry chemical, CO_2, water spray or regular foam.

Large Fires
- Water spray, fog or regular foam.
- Move containers from fire area if you can do it without risk.

Fire involving Tanks
- Cool containers with flooding quantities of water until well after fire is out.
- Do not get water inside containers.
- Withdraw immediately in case of rising sound from venting safety devices or discoloration of tank.
- ALWAYS stay away from tanks engulfed in fire.

SPILL OR LEAK
- Do not touch or walk through spilled material.
- ELIMINATE all ignition sources (no smoking, flares, sparks or flames in immediate area).
- All equipment used when handling the product must be grounded.
- Keep combustibles (wood, paper, oil, etc.) away from spilled material.
- Use water spray to reduce vapors or divert vapor cloud drift. Avoid allowing water runoff to contact spilled material.
- Prevent entry into waterways, sewers, basements or confined areas.

Small Spills · Take up with sand or other noncombustible absorbent material and place into containers for later disposal.

Large Spills · Dike far ahead of liquid spill for later disposal.

FIRST AID
- Move victim to fresh air.　　· Call 911 or emergency medical service.
- Apply artificial respiration if victim is not breathing.
- **Do not use mouth-to-mouth method if victim ingested or inhaled the substance; induce artificial respiration with the aid of a pocket mask equipped with a one-way valve or other proper respiratory medical device.**
- Administer oxygen if breathing is difficult.
- Remove and isolate contaminated clothing and shoes.
- In case of contact with substance, immediately flush skin or eyes with running water for at least 20 minutes.
- Shower and wash with soap and water.
- Keep victim warm and quiet.
- Effects of exposure (inhalation, ingestion or skin contact) to substance may be delayed.
- Ensure that medical personnel are aware of the material(s) involved, and take precautions to protect themselves.

POTENTIAL HAZARDS

FIRE OR EXPLOSION
- MAY EXPLODE AND THROW FRAGMENTS 1600 meters (1 MILE) OR MORE IF FIRE REACHES CARGO.
- For information on *Compatibility Group* letters, refer to Glossary section.

HEALTH
- Fire may produce irritating, corrosive and/or toxic gases.

PUBLIC SAFETY
- CALL Emergency Response Telephone Number on Shipping Paper first. If Shipping Paper not available or no answer, refer to appropriate telephone number listed on the inside back cover.
- Isolate spill or leak area immediately for at least 500 meters (1/3 mile) in all directions.
- Move people out of line of sight of the scene and away from windows.
- Keep unauthorized personnel away.
- Stay upwind.
- Ventilate closed spaces before entering.

PROTECTIVE CLOTHING
- Wear positive pressure self-contained breathing apparatus (SCBA).
- Structural firefighters' protective clothing will only provide limited protection.

EVACUATION
Large Spill
- Consider initial evacuation for 800 meters (1/2 mile) in all directions.
Fire
- If rail car or trailer is involved in a fire and heavily encased explosives such as bombs or artillery projectiles are suspected, ISOLATE for 1600 m (1 mile) in all directions; also, initiate evacuation including emergency responders for 1600 m (1 mile) in all directions.
- When heavily encased explosives are not involved, evacuate the area for 800 meters (1/2 mile) in all directions.

* For information on *Compatibility Group* letters, refer to the Glossary section.

EMERGENCY RESPONSE

FIRE

CARGO Fires

- **DO NOT fight fire when fire reaches cargo! Cargo may EXPLODE!**
- Stop all traffic and clear the area for at least 1600 meters (1 mile) in all directions and let burn.
- Do not move cargo or vehicle if cargo has been exposed to heat.

TIRE or VEHICLE Fires

- **Use plenty of water - FLOOD it! If water is not available, use CO_2, dry chemical or dirt.**
- If possible, and WITHOUT RISK, use unmanned hose holders or monitor nozzles from maximum distance to prevent fire from spreading to cargo area.
- Pay special attention to tire fires as re-ignition may occur. Stand by with extinguisher ready.

SPILL OR LEAK

- ELIMINATE all ignition sources (no smoking, flares, sparks or flames in immediate area).
- All equipment used when handling the product must be grounded.
- Do not touch or walk through spilled material.
- DO NOT OPERATE RADIO TRANSMITTERS WITHIN 100 meters (330 feet) OF ELECTRIC DETONATORS.
- **DO NOT CLEAN-UP OR DISPOSE OF, EXCEPT UNDER SUPERVISION OF A SPECIALIST.**

FIRST AID

- Move victim to fresh air.   • Call 911 or emergency medical service.
- Apply artificial respiration if victim is not breathing.
- Administer oxygen if breathing is difficult.
- Remove and isolate contaminated clothing and shoes.
- In case of contact with substance, immediately flush skin or eyes with running water for at least 20 minutes.
- Ensure that medical personnel are aware of the material(s) involved, and take precautions to protect themselves.

* For information on "Compatibility Group" letters, refer to the Glossary section.

POTENTIAL HAZARDS

FIRE OR EXPLOSION

- Flammable/combustible material.
- May be ignited by heat, sparks or flames.
- **DRIED OUT material may explode if exposed to heat, flame, friction or shock; Treat as an explosive (GUIDE 112).**
- **Keep material wet with water or treat as an explosive (Guide 112).**
- Runoff to sewer may create fire or explosion hazard.

HEALTH

- Some are toxic and may be fatal if inhaled, swallowed or absorbed through skin.
- Contact may cause burns to skin and eyes.
- Fire may produce irritating, corrosive and/or toxic gases.
- Runoff from fire control or dilution water may cause pollution.

PUBLIC SAFETY

- **CALL Emergency Response Telephone Number on Shipping Paper first. If Shipping Paper not available or no answer, refer to appropriate telephone number listed on the inside back cover.**
- Isolate spill or leak area immediately for at least 100 meters (330 feet) in all directions.
- Keep unauthorized personnel away.
- Stay upwind.
- Ventilate closed spaces before entering.

PROTECTIVE CLOTHING

- Wear positive pressure self-contained breathing apparatus (SCBA).
- Structural firefighters' protective clothing will only provide limited protection.

EVACUATION

Large Spill

- **Consider initial evacuation for 500 meters (1/3 mile) in all directions.**

Fire

- If tank, rail car or tank truck is involved in a fire, ISOLATE for 800 meters (1/2 mile) in all directions; also, consider initial evacuation for 800 meters (1/2 mile) in all directions.

EMERGENCY RESPONSE

FIRE

CARGO Fires
- **DO NOT fight fire when fire reaches cargo! Cargo may EXPLODE!**
- Stop all traffic and clear the area for at least 800 meters (1/2 mile) in all directions and let burn.
- **Do not move cargo or vehicle if cargo has been exposed to heat.**

TIRE or VEHICLE Fires
- **Use plenty of water - FLOOD it! If water is not available, use CO$_2$, dry chemical or dirt.**
- If possible, and WITHOUT RISK, use unmanned hose holders or monitor nozzles from maximum distance to prevent fire from spreading to cargo area.
- Pay special attention to tire fires as re-ignition may occur. Stand by with extinguisher ready.

SPILL OR LEAK

- ELIMINATE all ignition sources (no smoking, flares, sparks or flames in immediate area).
- All equipment used when handling the product must be grounded.
- Do not touch or walk through spilled material.

Small Spills
- Flush area with flooding quantities of water.

Large Spills
- Wet down with water and dike for later disposal.
- KEEP "WETTED" PRODUCT WET BY SLOWLY ADDING FLOODING QUANTITIES OF WATER.

FIRST AID

- Move victim to fresh air.   • Call 911 or emergency medical service.
- Apply artificial respiration if victim is not breathing.
- Administer oxygen if breathing is difficult.
- Remove and isolate contaminated clothing and shoes.
- In case of contact with substance, immediately flush skin or eyes with running water for at least 20 minutes.
- Ensure that medical personnel are aware of the material(s) involved, and take precautions to protect themselves.

POTENTIAL HAZARDS

FIRE OR EXPLOSION
- MAY EXPLODE AND THROW FRAGMENTS 500 meters (1/3 MILE) OR MORE IF FIRE REACHES CARGO.
- For information on "Compatibility Group" letters, refer to Glossary section.

HEALTH
- Fire may produce irritating, corrosive and/or toxic gases.

PUBLIC SAFETY

- CALL Emergency Response Telephone Number on Shipping Paper first. If Shipping Paper not available or no answer, refer to appropriate telephone number listed on the inside back cover.
- Isolate spill or leak area immediately for at least 100 meters (330 feet) in all directions.
- Move people out of line of sight of the scene and away from windows.
- Keep unauthorized personnel away.
- Stay upwind.
- Ventilate closed spaces before entering.

PROTECTIVE CLOTHING
- Wear positive pressure self-contained breathing apparatus (SCBA).
- Structural firefighters' protective clothing will only provide limited protection.

EVACUATION
Large Spill
- Consider initial evacuation for 250 meters (800 feet) in all directions.
Fire
- If rail car or trailer is involved in a fire, ISOLATE for 500 meters (1/3 mile) in all directions; also initiate evacuation including emergency responders for 500 meters (1/3 mile) in all directions.

* For information on "Compatibility Group" letters, refer to the Glossary section.

EMERGENCY RESPONSE

FIRE

CARGO Fires

- **DO NOT fight fire when fire reaches cargo! Cargo may EXPLODE!**
- Stop all traffic and clear the area for at least 500 meters (1/3 mile) in all directions and let burn.
- **Do not move cargo or vehicle if cargo has been exposed to heat.**

TIRE or VEHICLE Fires

- **Use plenty of water - FLOOD it! If water is not available, use CO_2, dry chemical or dirt.**
- If possible, and WITHOUT RISK, use unmanned hose holders or monitor nozzles from maximum distance to prevent fire from spreading to cargo area.
- Pay special attention to tire fires as re-ignition may occur. Stand by with extinguisher ready.

SPILL OR LEAK

- ELIMINATE all ignition sources (no smoking, flares, sparks or flames in immediate area).
- All equipment used when handling the product must be grounded.
- Do not touch or walk through spilled material.
- DO NOT OPERATE RADIO TRANSMITTERS WITHIN 100 meters (330 feet) OF ELECTRIC DETONATORS.
- **DO NOT CLEAN-UP OR DISPOSE OF, EXCEPT UNDER SUPERVISION OF A SPECIALIST.**

FIRST AID

- Move victim to fresh air.   • Call 911 or emergency medical service.
- Apply artificial respiration if victim is not breathing.
- Administer oxygen if breathing is difficult.
- Remove and isolate contaminated clothing and shoes.
- In case of contact with substance, immediately flush skin or eyes with running water for at least 20 minutes.
- Ensure that medical personnel are aware of the material(s) involved, and take precautions to protect themselves.

SUPPLEMENTAL INFORMATION

- Packages bearing the 1.4S label or packages containing material classified as 1.4S are designed or packaged in such a manner that when involved in a fire, may burn vigorously with localized detonations and projection of fragments.
- Effects are usually confined to immediate vicinity of packages.
- If fire threatens cargo area containing packages bearing the 1.4S label or packages containing material classified as 1.4S, consider isolating at least 15 meters (50 feet) in all directions. Fight fire with normal precautions from a reasonable distance.

---

* **For information on "Compatibility Group" letters, refer to the Glossary section.**

POTENTIAL HAZARDS

FIRE OR EXPLOSION
- **EXTREMELY FLAMMABLE.**
- Will be easily ignited by heat, sparks or flames.
- Will form explosive mixtures with air.
- Vapors from liquefied gas are initially heavier than air and spread along ground.
- Vapors may travel to source of ignition and flash back.
- Containers may explode when heated.
- Ruptured cylinders may rocket.

HEALTH
- Vapors may cause dizziness or asphyxiation without warning.
- Some may be irritating if inhaled at high concentrations.
- Contact with gas or liquefied gas may cause burns, severe injury and/or frostbite.
- Fire may produce irritating and/or toxic gases.

PUBLIC SAFETY
- **CALL Emergency Response Telephone Number on Shipping Paper first. If Shipping Paper not available or no answer, refer to appropriate telephone number listed on the inside back cover.**
- Isolate spill or leak area immediately for at least 50 to 100 meters (160 to 330 feet) in all directions.
- Keep unauthorized personnel away.
- Stay upwind.
- Many gases are heavier than air and will spread along ground and collect in low or confined areas (sewers, basements, tanks).
- Keep out of low areas.

PROTECTIVE CLOTHING
- Wear positive pressure self-contained breathing apparatus (SCBA).
- Structural firefighters' protective clothing will only provide limited protection.
- Always wear thermal protective clothing when handling refrigerated/cryogenic liquids.

EVACUATION
Large Spill
- Consider initial downwind evacuation for at least 800 meters (1/2 mile).

Fire
- If tank, rail car or tank truck is involved in a fire, ISOLATE for 1600 meters (1 mile) in all directions; also, consider initial evacuation for 1600 meters (1 mile) in all directions.

EMERGENCY RESPONSE

FIRE
• **DO NOT EXTINGUISH A LEAKING GAS FIRE UNLESS LEAK CAN BE STOPPED.**

Small Fires
• Dry chemical or CO_2.

Large Fires
• Water spray or fog.
• Move containers from fire area if you can do it without risk.

Fire involving Tanks
• Fight fire from maximum distance or use unmanned hose holders or monitor nozzles.
• Cool containers with flooding quantities of water until well after fire is out.
• Do not direct water at source of leak or safety devices; icing may occur.
• Withdraw immediately in case of rising sound from venting safety devices or discoloration of tank.
• ALWAYS stay away from tanks engulfed in fire.
• For massive fire, use unmanned hose holders or monitor nozzles; if this is impossible, withdraw from area and let fire burn.

SPILL OR LEAK
• ELIMINATE all ignition sources (no smoking, flares, sparks or flames in immediate area).
• All equipment used when handling the product must be grounded.
• Do not touch or walk through spilled material.
• Stop leak if you can do it without risk.
• If possible, turn leaking containers so that gas escapes rather than liquid.
• Use water spray to reduce vapors or divert vapor cloud drift. Avoid allowing water runoff to contact spilled material.
• Do not direct water at spill or source of leak.
• Prevent spreading of vapors through sewers, ventilation systems and confined areas.
• Isolate area until gas has dispersed.
CAUTION: When in contact with refrigerated/cryogenic liquids, many materials become brittle and are likely to break without warning.

FIRST AID
• Move victim to fresh air.   • Call 911 or emergency medical service.
• Apply artificial respiration if victim is not breathing.
• Administer oxygen if breathing is difficult.
• Remove and isolate contaminated clothing and shoes.
• Clothing frozen to the skin should be thawed before being removed.
• In case of contact with liquefied gas, thaw frosted parts with lukewarm water.
• Keep victim warm and quiet.
• Ensure that medical personnel are aware of the material(s) involved, and take precautions to protect themselves.

POTENTIAL HAZARDS

FIRE OR EXPLOSION

- **EXTREMELY FLAMMABLE.**
- Will be easily ignited by heat, sparks or flames.
- Will form explosive mixtures with air.
- Silane will ignite spontaneously in air.
- Those substances designated with a **"P"** may polymerize explosively when heated or involved in a fire.
- Vapors from liquefied gas are initially heavier than air and spread along ground.
- Vapors may travel to source of ignition and flash back.
- Containers may explode when heated.
- Ruptured cylinders may rocket.

HEALTH

- Vapors may cause dizziness or asphyxiation without warning.
- Some may be toxic if inhaled at high concentrations.
- Contact with gas or liquefied gas may cause burns, severe injury and/or frostbite.
- Fire may produce irritating and/or toxic gases.

PUBLIC SAFETY

- **CALL Emergency Response Telephone Number on Shipping Paper first. If Shipping Paper not available or no answer, refer to appropriate telephone number listed on the inside back cover.**
- Isolate spill or leak area immediately for at least 100 meters (330 feet) in all directions.
- Keep unauthorized personnel away.
- Stay upwind.
- Many gases are heavier than air and will spread along ground and collect in low or confined areas (sewers, basements, tanks).
- Keep out of low areas.

PROTECTIVE CLOTHING

- Wear positive pressure self-contained breathing apparatus (SCBA).
- Structural firefighters' protective clothing will only provide limited protection.

EVACUATION

Large Spill

- Consider initial downwind evacuation for at least 800 meters (1/2 mile).

Fire

- If tank, rail car or tank truck is involved in a fire, ISOLATE for 1600 meters (1 mile) in all directions; also, consider initial evacuation for 1600 meters (1 mile) in all directions.

EMERGENCY RESPONSE

FIRE
- **DO NOT EXTINGUISH A LEAKING GAS FIRE UNLESS LEAK CAN BE STOPPED.**

Small Fires
- Dry chemical or CO_2.

Large Fires
- Water spray or fog.
- Move containers from fire area if you can do it without risk.

Fire involving Tanks
- Fight fire from maximum distance or use unmanned hose holders or monitor nozzles.
- Cool containers with flooding quantities of water until well after fire is out.
- Do not direct water at source of leak or safety devices; icing may occur.
- Withdraw immediately in case of rising sound from venting safety devices or discoloration of tank.
- ALWAYS stay away from tanks engulfed in fire.
- For massive fire, use unmanned hose holders or monitor nozzles; if this is impossible, withdraw from area and let fire burn.

SPILL OR LEAK
- ELIMINATE all ignition sources (no smoking, flares, sparks or flames in immediate area).
- All equipment used when handling the product must be grounded.
- Stop leak if you can do it without risk.
- Do not touch or walk through spilled material.
- Do not direct water at spill or source of leak.
- Use water spray to reduce vapors or divert vapor cloud drift. Avoid allowing water runoff to contact spilled material.
- If possible, turn leaking containers so that gas escapes rather than liquid.
- Prevent entry into waterways, sewers, basements or confined areas.
- Isolate area until gas has dispersed.

FIRST AID
- Move victim to fresh air.   • Call 911 or emergency medical service.
- Apply artificial respiration if victim is not breathing.
- Administer oxygen if breathing is difficult.
- Remove and isolate contaminated clothing and shoes.
- In case of contact with liquefied gas, thaw frosted parts with lukewarm water.
- Keep victim warm and quiet.
- Ensure that medical personnel are aware of the material(s) involved, and take precautions to protect themselves.

POTENTIAL HAZARDS

HEALTH

- **TOXIC; Extremely Hazardous.**
- May be fatal if inhaled or absorbed through skin.
- Initial odor may be irritating or foul and may deaden your sense of smell.
- Contact with gas or liquefied gas may cause burns, severe injury and/or frostbite.
- Fire will produce irritating, corrosive and/or toxic gases.
- Runoff from fire control may cause pollution.

FIRE OR EXPLOSION

- These materials are extremely flammable.
- May form explosive mixtures with air.
- May be ignited by heat, sparks or flames.
- Vapors from liquefied gas are initially heavier than air and spread along ground.
- Vapors may travel to source of ignition and flash back.
- Runoff may create fire or explosion hazard.
- Containers may explode when heated.
- Ruptured cylinders may rocket.

PUBLIC SAFETY

- **CALL Emergency Response Telephone Number on Shipping Paper first. If Shipping Paper not available or no answer, refer to appropriate telephone number listed on the inside back cover.**
- Isolate spill or leak area immediately for at least 100 to 200 meters (330 to 660 feet) in all directions.
- Keep unauthorized personnel away.
- Stay upwind.
- Many gases are heavier than air and will spread along ground and collect in low or confined areas (sewers, basements, tanks).
- Keep out of low areas.
- Ventilate closed spaces before entering.

PROTECTIVE CLOTHING

- Wear positive pressure self-contained breathing apparatus (SCBA).
- Wear chemical protective clothing which is specifically recommended by the manufacturer. It may provide little or no thermal protection.
- Structural firefighters' protective clothing provides limited protection in fire situations ONLY; it is not effective in spill situations.

EVACUATION

Spill

- See the Table of Initial Isolation and Protective Action Distances for highlighted substances. For non-highlighted substances, increase, in the downwind direction, as necessary, the isolation distance shown under "PUBLIC SAFETY".

Fire

- If tank, rail car or tank truck is involved in a fire, ISOLATE for 1600 meters (1 mile) in all directions; also, consider initial evacuation for 1600 meters (1 mile) in all directions.

EMERGENCY RESPONSE

FIRE
- **DO NOT EXTINGUISH A LEAKING GAS FIRE UNLESS LEAK CAN BE STOPPED.**

Small Fires
- Dry chemical, CO_2, water spray or regular foam.

Large Fires
- Water spray, fog or regular foam.
- Move containers from fire area if you can do it without risk.
- Damaged cylinders should be handled only by specialists.

Fire involving Tanks
- Fight fire from maximum distance or use unmanned hose holders or monitor nozzles.
- Cool containers with flooding quantities of water until well after fire is out.
- Do not direct water at source of leak or safety devices; icing may occur.
- Withdraw immediately in case of rising sound from venting safety devices or discoloration of tank.
- ALWAYS stay away from tanks engulfed in fire.

SPILL OR LEAK
- ELIMINATE all ignition sources (no smoking, flares, sparks or flames in immediate area).
- All equipment used when handling the product must be grounded.
- Fully encapsulating, vapor protective clothing should be worn for spills and leaks with no fire.
- Do not touch or walk through spilled material.
- Stop leak if you can do it without risk.
- Use water spray to reduce vapors or divert vapor cloud drift. Avoid allowing water runoff to contact spilled material.
- Do not direct water at spill or source of leak.
- If possible, turn leaking containers so that gas escapes rather than liquid.
- Prevent entry into waterways, sewers, basements or confined areas.
- Isolate area until gas has dispersed.
- Consider igniting spill or leak to eliminate toxic gas concerns.

FIRST AID
- Move victim to fresh air.   • Call 911 or emergency medical service.
- Apply artificial respiration if victim is not breathing.
- **Do not use mouth-to-mouth method if victim ingested or inhaled the substance; induce artificial respiration with the aid of a pocket mask equipped with a one-way valve or other proper respiratory medical device.**
- Administer oxygen if breathing is difficult.
- Remove and isolate contaminated clothing and shoes.
- In case of contact with substance, immediately flush skin or eyes with running water for at least 20 minutes.
- In case of contact with liquefied gas, thaw frosted parts with lukewarm water.
- Keep victim warm and quiet.   • Keep victim under observation.
- Effects of contact or inhalation may be delayed.
- Ensure that medical personnel are aware of the material(s) involved, and take precautions to protect themselves.

POTENTIAL HAZARDS

FIRE OR EXPLOSION
- **EXTREMELY FLAMMABLE.**
- May be ignited by heat, sparks or flames.
- May form explosive mixtures with air.
- Vapors from liquefied gas are initially heavier than air and spread along ground.
- Vapors may travel to source of ignition and flash back.
- Some of these materials may react violently with water.
- Containers may explode when heated.
- Ruptured cylinders may rocket.

HEALTH
- May cause toxic effects if inhaled.
- Vapors are extremely irritating.
- Contact with gas or liquefied gas may cause burns, severe injury and/or frostbite.
- Fire will produce irritating, corrosive and/or toxic gases.
- Runoff from fire control may cause pollution.

PUBLIC SAFETY

- **CALL Emergency Response Telephone Number on Shipping Paper first. If Shipping Paper not available or no answer, refer to appropriate telephone number listed on the inside back cover.**
- Isolate spill or leak area immediately for at least 100 to 200 meters (330 to 660 feet) in all directions.
- Keep unauthorized personnel away.
- Stay upwind.
- Many gases are heavier than air and will spread along ground and collect in low or confined areas (sewers, basements, tanks).
- Keep out of low areas.
- Ventilate closed spaces before entering.

PROTECTIVE CLOTHING
- Wear positive pressure self-contained breathing apparatus (SCBA).
- Wear chemical protective clothing which is specifically recommended by the manufacturer. It may provide little or no thermal protection.
- Structural firefighters' protective clothing provides limited protection in fire situations ONLY; it is not effective in spill situations.

EVACUATION
Large Spill
- Consider initial downwind evacuation for at least 800 meters (1/2 mile).
Fire
- If tank, rail car or tank truck is involved in a fire, ISOLATE for 1600 meters (1 mile) in all directions; also, consider initial evacuation for 1600 meters (1 mile) in all directions.

EMERGENCY RESPONSE

FIRE
- **DO NOT EXTINGUISH A LEAKING GAS FIRE UNLESS LEAK CAN BE STOPPED.**

Small Fires
- Dry chemical or CO_2.

Large Fires
- Water spray, fog or regular foam.
- Move containers from fire area if you can do it without risk.
- Damaged cylinders should be handled only by specialists.

Fire involving Tanks
- Fight fire from maximum distance or use unmanned hose holders or monitor nozzles.
- Cool containers with flooding quantities of water until well after fire is out.
- Do not direct water at source of leak or safety devices; icing may occur.
- Withdraw immediately in case of rising sound from venting safety devices or discoloration of tank.
- ALWAYS stay away from tanks engulfed in fire.

SPILL OR LEAK
- ELIMINATE all ignition sources (no smoking, flares, sparks or flames in immediate area).
- All equipment used when handling the product must be grounded.
- Fully encapsulating, vapor protective clothing should be worn for spills and leaks with no fire.
- Do not touch or walk through spilled material.
- Stop leak if you can do it without risk.
- If possible, turn leaking containers so that gas escapes rather than liquid.
- Use water spray to reduce vapors or divert vapor cloud drift. Avoid allowing water runoff to contact spilled material.
- Do not direct water at spill or source of leak.

FIRST AID
- Move victim to fresh air.   • Call 911 or emergency medical service.
- Apply artificial respiration if victim is not breathing.
- **Do not use mouth-to-mouth method if victim ingested or inhaled the substance; induce artificial respiration with the aid of a pocket mask equipped with a one-way valve or other proper respiratory medical device.**
- Administer oxygen if breathing is difficult.
- Remove and isolate contaminated clothing and shoes.
- In case of contact with liquefied gas, thaw frosted parts with lukewarm water.
- Keep victim warm and quiet.   • Keep victim under observation.
- Effects of contact or inhalation may be delayed.
- Ensure that medical personnel are aware of the material(s) involved, and take precautions to protect themselves.

POTENTIAL HAZARDS

HEALTH

- **TOXIC; may be fatal if inhaled or absorbed through skin.**
- Contact with gas or liquefied gas may cause burns, severe injury and/or frostbite.
- Fire will produce irritating, corrosive and/or toxic gases.
- Runoff from fire control may cause pollution.

FIRE OR EXPLOSION

- Flammable; may be ignited by heat, sparks or flames.
- May form explosive mixtures with air.
- Those substances designated with a **"P"** may polymerize explosively when heated or involved in a fire.
- Vapors from liquefied gas are initially heavier than air and spread along ground.
- Vapors may travel to source of ignition and flash back.
- Some of these materials may react violently with water.
- Containers may explode when heated.
- Ruptured cylinders may rocket.
- Runoff may create fire or explosion hazard.

PUBLIC SAFETY

- **CALL Emergency Response Telephone Number on Shipping Paper first. If Shipping Paper not available or no answer, refer to appropriate telephone number listed on the inside back cover.**
- Isolate spill or leak area immediately for at least 100 to 200 meters (330 to 660 feet) in all directions.
- Keep unauthorized personnel away.
- Stay upwind.
- Many gases are heavier than air and will spread along ground and collect in low or confined areas (sewers, basements, tanks).
- Keep out of low areas.
- Ventilate closed spaces before entering.

PROTECTIVE CLOTHING

- Wear positive pressure self-contained breathing apparatus (SCBA).
- Wear chemical protective clothing which is specifically recommended by the manufacturer. It may provide little or no thermal protection.
- Structural firefighters' protective clothing provides limited protection in fire situations ONLY; it is not effective in spill situations.

EVACUATION

Spill

- See the Table of Initial Isolation and Protective Action Distances for highlighted substances. For non-highlighted substances, increase, in the downwind direction, as necessary, the isolation distance shown under "PUBLIC SAFETY".

Fire

- If tank, rail car or tank truck is involved in a fire, ISOLATE for 1600 meters (1 mile) in all directions; also, consider initial evacuation for 1600 meters (1 mile) in all directions.

EMERGENCY RESPONSE

FIRE
- **DO NOT EXTINGUISH A LEAKING GAS FIRE UNLESS LEAK CAN BE STOPPED.**

Small Fires
- Dry chemical, CO_2, water spray or alcohol-resistant foam.

Large Fires
- Water spray, fog or alcohol-resistant foam.
- **FOR CHLOROSILANES, DO NOT USE WATER**; use AFFF alcohol-resistant medium expansion foam.
- Move containers from fire area if you can do it without risk.
- Damaged cylinders should be handled only by specialists.

Fire involving Tanks
- Fight fire from maximum distance or use unmanned hose holders or monitor nozzles.
- Cool containers with flooding quantities of water until well after fire is out.
- Do not direct water at source of leak or safety devices; icing may occur.
- Withdraw immediately in case of rising sound from venting safety devices or discoloration of tank.
- ALWAYS stay away from tanks engulfed in fire.

SPILL OR LEAK
- ELIMINATE all ignition sources (no smoking, flares, sparks or flames in immediate area).
- All equipment used when handling the product must be grounded.
- Fully encapsulating, vapor protective clothing should be worn for spills and leaks with no fire.
- Do not touch or walk through spilled material.
- Stop leak if you can do it without risk.
- Do not direct water at spill or source of leak.
- Use water spray to reduce vapors or divert vapor cloud drift. Avoid allowing water runoff to contact spilled material.
- **FOR CHLOROSILANES, use AFFF alcohol-resistant medium expansion foam to reduce vapors.**
- If possible, turn leaking containers so that gas escapes rather than liquid.
- Prevent entry into waterways, sewers, basements or confined areas.
- Isolate area until gas has dispersed.

FIRST AID
- Move victim to fresh air.   • Call 911 or emergency medical service.
- Apply artificial respiration if victim is not breathing.
- **Do not use mouth-to-mouth method if victim ingested or inhaled the substance; induce artificial respiration with the aid of a pocket mask equipped with a one-way valve or other proper respiratory medical device.**
- Administer oxygen if breathing is difficult.
- Remove and isolate contaminated clothing and shoes.
- In case of contact with substance, immediately flush skin or eyes with running water for at least 20 minutes.
- In case of contact with liquefied gas, thaw frosted parts with lukewarm water.
- Keep victim warm and quiet.   • Keep victim under observation.
- Effects of contact or inhalation may be delayed.
- Ensure that medical personnel are aware of the material(s) involved, and take precautions to protect themselves.

POTENTIAL HAZARDS

HEALTH

- Vapors may cause dizziness or asphyxiation without warning.
- Vapors from liquefied gas are initially heavier than air and spread along ground.
- Contact with gas or liquefied gas may cause burns, severe injury and/or frostbite.

FIRE OR EXPLOSION

- **Non-flammable gases.**
- Containers may explode when heated.
- Ruptured cylinders may rocket.

PUBLIC SAFETY

- **CALL Emergency Response Telephone Number on Shipping Paper first. If Shipping Paper not available or no answer, refer to appropriate telephone number listed on the inside back cover.**
- Isolate spill or leak area immediately for at least 25 meters (80 feet) in all directions.
- Keep unauthorized personnel away.
- Stay upwind.
- Many gases are heavier than air and will spread along ground and collect in low or confined areas (sewers, basements, tanks).
- Keep out of low areas.
- Ventilate closed spaces before entering.

PROTECTIVE CLOTHING

- Wear positive pressure self-contained breathing apparatus (SCBA).
- Structural firefighters' protective clothing will only provide limited protection.
- Always wear thermal protective clothing when handling refrigerated/cryogenic liquids or solids.

EVACUATION

Large Spill

- Consider initial downwind evacuation for at least 100 meters (330 feet).

Fire

- If tank, rail car or tank truck is involved in a fire, ISOLATE for 800 meters (1/2 mile) in all directions; also, consider initial evacuation for 800 meters (1/2 mile) in all directions.

EMERGENCY RESPONSE

FIRE
- Use extinguishing agent suitable for type of surrounding fire.
- Move containers from fire area if you can do it without risk.
- Damaged cylinders should be handled only by specialists.

Fire involving Tanks
- Fight fire from maximum distance or use unmanned hose holders or monitor nozzles.
- Cool containers with flooding quantities of water until well after fire is out.
- Do not direct water at source of leak or safety devices; icing may occur.
- Withdraw immediately in case of rising sound from venting safety devices or discoloration of tank.
- ALWAYS stay away from tanks engulfed in fire.

SPILL OR LEAK
- Do not touch or walk through spilled material.
- Stop leak if you can do it without risk.
- Use water spray to reduce vapors or divert vapor cloud drift. Avoid allowing water runoff to contact spilled material.
- Do not direct water at spill or source of leak.
- If possible, turn leaking containers so that gas escapes rather than liquid.
- Prevent entry into waterways, sewers, basements or confined areas.
- Allow substance to evaporate.
- Ventilate the area.

CAUTION: When in contact with refrigerated/cryogenic liquids, many materials become brittle and are likely to break without warning.

FIRST AID
- Move victim to fresh air. • Call 911 or emergency medical service.
- Apply artificial respiration if victim is not breathing.
- Administer oxygen if breathing is difficult.
- Clothing frozen to the skin should be thawed before being removed.
- In case of contact with liquefied gas, thaw frosted parts with lukewarm water.
- Keep victim warm and quiet.
- Ensure that medical personnel are aware of the material(s) involved, and take precautions to protect themselves.

POTENTIAL HAZARDS

HEALTH

- Vapors may cause dizziness or asphyxiation without warning.
- Vapors from liquefied gas are initially heavier than air and spread along ground.
- Contact with liquefied gas may cause frostbite.

FIRE OR EXPLOSION

- **Non-flammable gases.**
- Containers may explode when heated.
- Ruptured cylinders may rocket.

PUBLIC SAFETY

- **CALL Emergency Response Telephone Number on Shipping Paper first. If Shipping Paper not available or no answer, refer to appropriate telephone number listed on the inside back cover.**
- Isolate spill or leak area immediately for at least 10 to 25 meters (30 to 80 feet) in all directions.
- Keep unauthorized personnel away.
- Stay upwind.
- Many gases are heavier than air and will spread along ground and collect in low or confined areas (sewers, basements, tanks).
- Keep out of low areas.
- Ventilate closed spaces before entering.

PROTECTIVE CLOTHING

- Wear positive pressure self-contained breathing apparatus (SCBA).
- Structural firefighters' protective clothing will only provide limited protection.

EVACUATION

Large Spill

- Consider initial downwind evacuation for at least 100 meters (330 feet).

Fire

- If tank, rail car or tank truck is involved in a fire, ISOLATE for 800 meters (1/2 mile) in all directions; also, consider initial evacuation for 800 meters (1/2 mile) in all directions.

EMERGENCY RESPONSE

FIRE
- Use extinguishing agent suitable for type of surrounding fire.
- Move containers from fire area if you can do it without risk.
- Damaged cylinders should be handled only by specialists.

Fire involving Tanks
- Fight fire from maximum distance or use unmanned hose holders or monitor nozzles.
- Cool containers with flooding quantities of water until well after fire is out.
- Do not direct water at source of leak or safety devices; icing may occur.
- Withdraw immediately in case of rising sound from venting safety devices or discoloration of tank.
- ALWAYS stay away from tanks engulfed in fire.

SPILL OR LEAK
- Do not touch or walk through spilled material.
- Stop leak if you can do it without risk.
- Use water spray to reduce vapors or divert vapor cloud drift. Avoid allowing water runoff to contact spilled material.
- Do not direct water at spill or source of leak.
- If possible, turn leaking containers so that gas escapes rather than liquid.
- Prevent entry into waterways, sewers, basements or confined areas.
- Allow substance to evaporate.
- Ventilate the area.

FIRST AID
- Move victim to fresh air.   • Call 911 or emergency medical service.
- Apply artificial respiration if victim is not breathing.
- Administer oxygen if breathing is difficult.
- Clothing frozen to the skin should be thawed before being removed.
- In case of contact with liquefied gas, thaw frosted parts with lukewarm water.
- Keep victim warm and quiet.
- Ensure that medical personnel are aware of the material(s) involved, and take precautions to protect themselves.

POTENTIAL HAZARDS

FIRE OR EXPLOSION

- Substance does not burn but will support combustion.
- Some may react explosively with fuels.
- May ignite combustibles (wood, paper, oil, clothing, etc.).
- Vapors from liquefied gas are initially heavier than air and spread along ground.
- Runoff may create fire or explosion hazard.
- Containers may explode when heated.
- Ruptured cylinders may rocket.

HEALTH

- Vapors may cause dizziness or asphyxiation without warning.
- Contact with gas or liquefied gas may cause burns, severe injury and/or frostbite.
- Fire may produce irritating and/or toxic gases.

PUBLIC SAFETY

- **CALL Emergency Response Telephone Number on Shipping Paper first. If Shipping Paper not available or no answer, refer to appropriate telephone number listed on the inside back cover.**
- Isolate spill or leak area immediately for at least 25 to 50 meters (80 to 160 feet) in all directions.
- Keep unauthorized personnel away.
- Stay upwind.
- Many gases are heavier than air and will spread along ground and collect in low or confined areas (sewers, basements, tanks).
- Keep out of low areas.
- Ventilate closed spaces before entering.

PROTECTIVE CLOTHING

- Wear positive pressure self-contained breathing apparatus (SCBA).
- Wear chemical protective clothing which is specifically recommended by the manufacturer. It may provide little or no thermal protection.
- Structural firefighters' protective clothing provides limited protection in fire situations ONLY; it is not effective in spill situations.
- Always wear thermal protective clothing when handling refrigerated/cryogenic liquids.

EVACUATION

Large Spill

- Consider initial downwind evacuation for at least 500 meters (1/3 mile).

Fire

- If tank, rail car or tank truck is involved in a fire, ISOLATE for 800 meters (1/2 mile) in all directions; also, consider initial evacuation for 800 meters (1/2 mile) in all directions.

EMERGENCY RESPONSE

FIRE
- Use extinguishing agent suitable for type of surrounding fire.

Small Fires
- Dry chemical or CO_2.

Large Fires
- Water spray, fog or regular foam.
- Move containers from fire area if you can do it without risk.
- Damaged cylinders should be handled only by specialists.

Fire involving Tanks
- Fight fire from maximum distance or use unmanned hose holders or monitor nozzles.
- Cool containers with flooding quantities of water until well after fire is out.
- Do not direct water at source of leak or safety devices; icing may occur.
- Withdraw immediately in case of rising sound from venting safety devices or discoloration of tank.
- ALWAYS stay away from tanks engulfed in fire.
- For massive fire, use unmanned hose holders or monitor nozzles; if this is impossible, withdraw from area and let fire burn.

SPILL OR LEAK
- Keep combustibles (wood, paper, oil, etc.) away from spilled material.
- Do not touch or walk through spilled material.
- Stop leak if you can do it without risk.
- If possible, turn leaking containers so that gas escapes rather than liquid.
- Do not direct water at spill or source of leak.
- Use water spray to reduce vapors or divert vapor cloud drift. Avoid allowing water runoff to contact spilled material.
- Prevent entry into waterways, sewers, basements or confined areas.
- Allow substance to evaporate.
- Isolate area until gas has dispersed.

CAUTION: When in contact with refrigerated/cryogenic liquids, many materials become brittle and are likely to break without warning.

FIRST AID
- Move victim to fresh air.   • Call 911 or emergency medical service.
- Apply artificial respiration if victim is not breathing.
- Administer oxygen if breathing is difficult.
- Remove and isolate contaminated clothing and shoes.
- Clothing frozen to the skin should be thawed before being removed.
- In case of contact with liquefied gas, thaw frosted parts with lukewarm water.
- Keep victim warm and quiet.
- Ensure that medical personnel are aware of the material(s) involved, and take precautions to protect themselves.

POTENTIAL HAZARDS

HEALTH

- **TOXIC; may be fatal if inhaled or absorbed through skin.**
- Vapors may be irritating.
- Contact with gas or liquefied gas may cause burns, severe injury and/or frostbite.
- Fire will produce irritating, corrosive and/or toxic gases.
- Runoff from fire control may cause pollution.

FIRE OR EXPLOSION

- Some may burn, but none ignite readily.
- Vapors from liquefied gas are initially heavier than air and spread along ground.
- Containers may explode when heated.
- Ruptured cylinders may rocket.

PUBLIC SAFETY

- **CALL Emergency Response Telephone Number on Shipping Paper first. If Shipping Paper not available or no answer, refer to appropriate telephone number listed on the inside back cover.**
- Isolate spill or leak area immediately for at least 100 to 200 meters (330 to 660 feet) in all directions.
- Keep unauthorized personnel away.
- Stay upwind.
- Many gases are heavier than air and will spread along ground and collect in low or confined areas (sewers, basements, tanks).
- Keep out of low areas.
- Ventilate closed spaces before entering.

PROTECTIVE CLOTHING

- Wear positive pressure self-contained breathing apparatus (SCBA).
- Wear chemical protective clothing which is specifically recommended by the manufacturer. It may provide little or no thermal protection.
- Structural firefighters' protective clothing provides limited protection in fire situations ONLY; it is not effective in spill situations.

EVACUATION

Spill

- See the Table of Initial Isolation and Protective Action Distances for highlighted substances. For non-highlighted substances, increase, in the downwind direction, as necessary, the isolation distance shown under "PUBLIC SAFETY".

Fire

- If tank, rail car or tank truck is involved in a fire, ISOLATE for 800 meters (1/2 mile) in all directions; also, consider initial evacuation for 800 meters (1/2 mile) in all directions.

EMERGENCY RESPONSE

FIRE

Small Fires
- Dry chemical or CO_2.

Large Fires
- Water spray, fog or regular foam.
- Do not get water inside containers.
- Move containers from fire area if you can do it without risk.
- Damaged cylinders should be handled only by specialists.

Fire involving Tanks
- Fight fire from maximum distance or use unmanned hose holders or monitor nozzles.
- Cool containers with flooding quantities of water until well after fire is out.
- Do not direct water at source of leak or safety devices; icing may occur.
- Withdraw immediately in case of rising sound from venting safety devices or discoloration of tank.
- ALWAYS stay away from tanks engulfed in fire.

SPILL OR LEAK
- Fully encapsulating, vapor protective clothing should be worn for spills and leaks with no fire.
- Do not touch or walk through spilled material.
- Stop leak if you can do it without risk.
- If possible, turn leaking containers so that gas escapes rather than liquid.
- Prevent entry into waterways, sewers, basements or confined areas.
- Use water spray to reduce vapors or divert vapor cloud drift. Avoid allowing water runoff to contact spilled material.
- Do not direct water at spill or source of leak.
- Isolate area until gas has dispersed.

FIRST AID
- Move victim to fresh air.   • Call 911 or emergency medical service.
- Apply artificial respiration if victim is not breathing.
- **Do not use mouth-to-mouth method if victim ingested or inhaled the substance; induce artificial respiration with the aid of a pocket mask equipped with a one-way valve or other proper respiratory medical device.**
- Administer oxygen if breathing is difficult.
- Remove and isolate contaminated clothing and shoes.
- In case of contact with liquefied gas, thaw frosted parts with lukewarm water.
- In case of contact with substance, immediately flush skin or eyes with running water for at least 20 minutes.
- Keep victim warm and quiet.   • Keep victim under observation.
- Effects of contact or inhalation may be delayed.
- Ensure that medical personnel are aware of the material(s) involved, and take precautions to protect themselves.

POTENTIAL HAZARDS

HEALTH

- **TOXIC; may be fatal if inhaled or absorbed through skin.**
- Fire will produce irritating, corrosive and/or toxic gases.
- Contact with gas or liquefied gas may cause burns, severe injury and/or frostbite.
- Runoff from fire control may cause pollution.

FIRE OR EXPLOSION

- Substance does not burn but will support combustion.
- Vapors from liquefied gas are initially heavier than air and spread along ground.
- These are strong oxidizers and will react vigorously or explosively with many materials including fuels.
- May ignite combustibles (wood, paper, oil, clothing, etc.).
- Some will react violently with air, moist air and/or water.
- Containers may explode when heated.
- Ruptured cylinders may rocket.

PUBLIC SAFETY

- **CALL Emergency Response Telephone Number on Shipping Paper first. If Shipping Paper not available or no answer, refer to appropriate telephone number listed on the inside back cover.**
- Isolate spill or leak area immediately for at least 100 to 200 meters (330 to 660 feet) in all directions.
- Keep unauthorized personnel away.
- Stay upwind.
- Many gases are heavier than air and will spread along ground and collect in low or confined areas (sewers, basements, tanks).
- Keep out of low areas.
- Ventilate closed spaces before entering.

PROTECTIVE CLOTHING

- Wear positive pressure self-contained breathing apparatus (SCBA).
- Wear chemical protective clothing which is specifically recommended by the manufacturer. It may provide little or no thermal protection.
- Structural firefighters' protective clothing provides limited protection in fire situations ONLY; it is not effective in spill situations.

EVACUATION

Spill

- See the Table of Initial Isolation and Protective Action Distances for highlighted substances. For non-highlighted substances, increase, in the downwind direction, as necessary, the isolation distance shown under "PUBLIC SAFETY".

Fire

- If tank, rail car or tank truck is involved in a fire, ISOLATE for 800 meters (1/2 mile) in all directions; also, consider initial evacuation for 800 meters (1/2 mile) in all directions.

EMERGENCY RESPONSE

FIRE

Small Fires: Water only; no dry chemical, CO_2 or Halon®.

- Contain fire and let burn. If fire must be fought, water spray or fog is recommended.
- Do not get water inside containers.
- Move containers from fire area if you can do it without risk.
- Damaged cylinders should be handled only by specialists.

Fire involving Tanks

- Fight fire from maximum distance or use unmanned hose holders or monitor nozzles.
- Cool containers with flooding quantities of water until well after fire is out.
- Do not direct water at source of leak or safety devices; icing may occur.
- Withdraw immediately in case of rising sound from venting safety devices or discoloration of tank.
- ALWAYS stay away from tanks engulfed in fire.
- For massive fire, use unmanned hose holders or monitor nozzles; if this is impossible, withdraw from area and let fire burn.

SPILL OR LEAK

- Fully encapsulating, vapor protective clothing should be worn for spills and leaks with no fire.
- Do not touch or walk through spilled material.
- Keep combustibles (wood, paper, oil, etc.) away from spilled material.
- Stop leak if you can do it without risk.
- Use water spray to reduce vapors or divert vapor cloud drift. Avoid allowing water runoff to contact spilled material.
- Do not direct water at spill or source of leak.
- If possible, turn leaking containers so that gas escapes rather than liquid.
- Prevent entry into waterways, sewers, basements or confined areas.
- Isolate area until gas has dispersed.
- Ventilate the area.

FIRST AID

- Move victim to fresh air. • Call 911 or emergency medical service.
- Apply artificial respiration if victim is not breathing.
- Do not use mouth-to-mouth method if victim ingested or inhaled the substance; induce artificial respiration with the aid of a pocket mask equipped with a one-way valve or other proper respiratory medical device.
- Administer oxygen if breathing is difficult.
- Clothing frozen to the skin should be thawed before being removed.
- Remove and isolate contaminated clothing and shoes.
- In case of contact with substance, immediately flush skin or eyes with running water for at least 20 minutes.
- Keep victim warm and quiet. • Keep victim under observation.
- Effects of contact or inhalation may be delayed.
- Ensure that medical personnel are aware of the material(s) involved, and take precautions to protect themselves.

POTENTIAL HAZARDS

HEALTH

- **TOXIC; may be fatal if inhaled.**
- Vapors are extremely irritating and corrosive.
- Contact with gas or liquefied gas may cause burns, severe injury and/or frostbite.
- Fire will produce irritating, corrosive and/or toxic gases.
- Runoff from fire control may cause pollution.

FIRE OR EXPLOSION

- Some may burn, but none ignite readily.
- Vapors from liquefied gas are initially heavier than air and spread along ground.
- Some of these materials may react violently with water.
- Containers may explode when heated.
- Ruptured cylinders may rocket.

PUBLIC SAFETY

- **CALL Emergency Response Telephone Number on Shipping Paper first. If Shipping Paper not available or no answer, refer to appropriate telephone number listed on the inside back cover.**
- Isolate spill or leak area immediately for at least 100 to 200 meters (330 to 660 feet) in all directions.
- Keep unauthorized personnel away.
- Stay upwind.
- Many gases are heavier than air and will spread along ground and collect in low or confined areas (sewers, basements, tanks).
- Keep out of low areas.
- Ventilate closed spaces before entering.

PROTECTIVE CLOTHING

- Wear positive pressure self-contained breathing apparatus (SCBA).
- Wear chemical protective clothing which is specifically recommended by the manufacturer. It may provide little or no thermal protection.
- Structural firefighters' protective clothing provides limited protection in fire situations ONLY; it is not effective in spill situations.

EVACUATION

Spill

- See the Table of Initial Isolation and Protective Action Distances for highlighted substances. For non-highlighted substances, increase, in the downwind direction, as necessary, the isolation distance shown under "PUBLIC SAFETY".

Fire

- If tank, rail car or tank truck is involved in a fire, ISOLATE for 1600 meters (1 mile) in all directions; also, consider initial evacuation for 1600 meters (1 mile) in all directions.

EMERGENCY RESPONSE

FIRE

Small Fires

- Dry chemical or CO_2.

Large Fires

- Water spray, fog or regular foam.
- Move containers from fire area if you can do it without risk.
- Do not get water inside containers.
- Damaged cylinders should be handled only by specialists.

Fire involving Tanks

- Fight fire from maximum distance or use unmanned hose holders or monitor nozzles.
- Cool containers with flooding quantities of water until well after fire is out.
- Do not direct water at source of leak or safety devices; icing may occur.
- Withdraw immediately in case of rising sound from venting safety devices or discoloration of tank.
- ALWAYS stay away from tanks engulfed in fire.

SPILL OR LEAK

- Fully encapsulating, vapor protective clothing should be worn for spills and leaks with no fire.
- Do not touch or walk through spilled material.
- Stop leak if you can do it without risk.
- If possible, turn leaking containers so that gas escapes rather than liquid.
- Prevent entry into waterways, sewers, basements or confined areas.
- Do not direct water at spill or source of leak.
- Use water spray to reduce vapors or divert vapor cloud drift. Avoid allowing water runoff to contact spilled material.
- Isolate area until gas has dispersed.

FIRST AID

- Move victim to fresh air.   • Call 911 or emergency medical service.
- Apply artificial respiration if victim is not breathing.
- **Do not use mouth-to-mouth method if victim ingested or inhaled the substance; induce artificial respiration with the aid of a pocket mask equipped with a one-way valve or other proper respiratory medical device.**
- Administer oxygen if breathing is difficult.
- Remove and isolate contaminated clothing and shoes.
- In case of contact with liquefied gas, thaw frosted parts with lukewarm water.
- In case of contact with substance, immediately flush skin or eyes with running water for at least 20 minutes.
- Keep victim warm and quiet.   • Keep victim under observation.
- Effects of contact or inhalation may be delayed.
- Ensure that medical personnel are aware of the material(s) involved, and take precautions to protect themselves.

POTENTIAL HAZARDS

FIRE OR EXPLOSION
- Some may burn, but none ignite readily.
- Containers may explode when heated.
- Ruptured cylinders may rocket.

HEALTH
- Vapors may cause dizziness or asphyxiation without warning.
- Vapors from liquefied gas are initially heavier than air and spread along ground.
- Contact with gas or liquefied gas may cause burns, severe injury and/or frostbite.
- Fire may produce irritating, corrosive and/or toxic gases.

PUBLIC SAFETY
- **CALL Emergency Response Telephone Number on Shipping Paper first. If Shipping Paper not available or no answer, refer to appropriate telephone number listed on the inside back cover.**
- Isolate spill or leak area immediately for at least 100 meters (330 feet) in all directions.
- Keep unauthorized personnel away.
- Stay upwind.
- Many gases are heavier than air and will spread along ground and collect in low or confined areas (sewers, basements, tanks).
- Keep out of low areas.
- Ventilate closed spaces before entering.

PROTECTIVE CLOTHING
- Wear positive pressure self-contained breathing apparatus (SCBA).
- Structural firefighters' protective clothing will only provide limited protection.

EVACUATION
Large Spill
- Consider initial downwind evacuation for at least 500 meters (1/3 mile).

Fire
- If tank, rail car or tank truck is involved in a fire, ISOLATE for 800 meters (1/2 mile) in all directions; also, consider initial evacuation for 800 meters (1/2 mile) in all directions.

EMERGENCY RESPONSE

FIRE
- Use extinguishing agent suitable for type of surrounding fire.

Small Fires
- Dry chemical or CO_2.

Large Fires
- Water spray, fog or regular foam.
- Move containers from fire area if you can do it without risk.
- Damaged cylinders should be handled only by specialists.

Fire involving Tanks
- Fight fire from maximum distance or use unmanned hose holders or monitor nozzles.
- Cool containers with flooding quantities of water until well after fire is out.
- Do not direct water at source of leak or safety devices; icing may occur.
- Withdraw immediately in case of rising sound from venting safety devices or discoloration of tank.
- ALWAYS stay away from tanks engulfed in fire.
- Some of these materials, if spilled, may evaporate leaving a flammable residue.

SPILL OR LEAK
- Do not touch or walk through spilled material.
- Stop leak if you can do it without risk.
- Do not direct water at spill or source of leak.
- Use water spray to reduce vapors or divert vapor cloud drift. Avoid allowing water runoff to contact spilled material.
- If possible, turn leaking containers so that gas escapes rather than liquid.
- Prevent entry into waterways, sewers, basements or confined areas.
- Allow substance to evaporate.
- Ventilate the area.

FIRST AID
- Move victim to fresh air.   • Call 911 or emergency medical service.
- Apply artificial respiration if victim is not breathing.
- Administer oxygen if breathing is difficult.
- Remove and isolate contaminated clothing and shoes.
- In case of contact with liquefied gas, thaw frosted parts with lukewarm water.
- Keep victim warm and quiet.
- Ensure that medical personnel are aware of the material(s) involved, and take precautions to protect themselves.

POTENTIAL HAZARDS

FIRE OR EXPLOSION
- **HIGHLY FLAMMABLE: Will be easily ignited by heat, sparks or flames.**
- Vapors may form explosive mixtures with air.
- Vapors may travel to source of ignition and flash back.
- Most vapors are heavier than air. They will spread along ground and collect in low or confined areas (sewers, basements, tanks).
- Vapor explosion hazard indoors, outdoors or in sewers.
- Those substances designated with a "P" may polymerize explosively when heated or involved in a fire.
- Runoff to sewer may create fire or explosion hazard.
- Containers may explode when heated.
- Many liquids are lighter than water.

HEALTH
- Inhalation or contact with material may irritate or burn skin and eyes.
- Fire may produce irritating, corrosive and/or toxic gases.
- Vapors may cause dizziness or suffocation.
- Runoff from fire control may cause pollution.

PUBLIC SAFETY
- **CALL Emergency Response Telephone Number on Shipping Paper first. If Shipping Paper not available or no answer, refer to appropriate telephone number listed on the inside back cover.**
- Isolate spill or leak area immediately for at least 25 to 50 meters (80 to 160 feet) in all directions.
- Keep unauthorized personnel away.
- Stay upwind.
- Keep out of low areas.
- Ventilate closed spaces before entering.

PROTECTIVE CLOTHING
- Wear positive pressure self-contained breathing apparatus (SCBA).
- Structural firefighters' protective clothing will only provide limited protection.

EVACUATION
Large Spill
- Consider initial downwind evacuation for at least 300 meters (1000 feet).

Fire
- If tank, rail car or tank truck is involved in a fire, ISOLATE for 800 meters (1/2 mile) in all directions; also, consider initial evacuation for 800 meters (1/2 mile) in all directions.

EMERGENCY RESPONSE

FIRE

CAUTION: All these products have a very low flash point: Use of water spray when fighting fire may be inefficient.

Small Fires

• Dry chemical, CO_2, water spray or alcohol-resistant foam.

Large Fires

• Water spray, fog or alcohol-resistant foam.
• Use water spray or fog; do not use straight streams.
• Move containers from fire area if you can do it without risk.

Fire involving Tanks or Car/Trailer Loads

• Fight fire from maximum distance or use unmanned hose holders or monitor nozzles.
• Cool containers with flooding quantities of water until well after fire is out.
• Withdraw immediately in case of rising sound from venting safety devices or discoloration of tank.
• ALWAYS stay away from tanks engulfed in fire.
• For massive fire, use unmanned hose holders or monitor nozzles; if this is impossible, withdraw from area and let fire burn.

SPILL OR LEAK

• ELIMINATE all ignition sources (no smoking, flares, sparks or flames in immediate area).
• All equipment used when handling the product must be grounded.
• Do not touch or walk through spilled material.
• Stop leak if you can do it without risk.
• Prevent entry into waterways, sewers, basements or confined areas.
• A vapor suppressing foam may be used to reduce vapors.
• Absorb or cover with dry earth, sand or other non-combustible material and transfer to containers.
• Use clean non-sparking tools to collect absorbed material.

Large Spills

• Dike far ahead of liquid spill for later disposal.
• Water spray may reduce vapor; but may not prevent ignition in closed spaces.

FIRST AID

• Move victim to fresh air. • Call 911 or emergency medical service.
• Apply artificial respiration if victim is not breathing.
• Administer oxygen if breathing is difficult.
• Remove and isolate contaminated clothing and shoes.
• In case of contact with substance, immediately flush skin or eyes with running water for at least 20 minutes.
• Wash skin with soap and water.
• Keep victim warm and quiet.
• Ensure that medical personnel are aware of the material(s) involved, and take precautions to protect themselves.

POTENTIAL HAZARDS

FIRE OR EXPLOSION

- **HIGHLY FLAMMABLE: Will be easily ignited by heat, sparks or flames.**
- Vapors may form explosive mixtures with air.
- Vapors may travel to source of ignition and flash back.
- Most vapors are heavier than air. They will spread along ground and collect in low or confined areas (sewers, basements, tanks).
- Vapor explosion hazard indoors, outdoors or in sewers.
- Those substances designated with a "**P**" may polymerize explosively when heated or involved in a fire.
- Runoff to sewer may create fire or explosion hazard.
- Containers may explode when heated.
- Many liquids are lighter than water.
- Substance may be transported hot.

HEALTH

- Inhalation or contact with material may irritate or burn skin and eyes.
- Fire may produce irritating, corrosive and/or toxic gases.
- Vapors may cause dizziness or suffocation.
- Runoff from fire control or dilution water may cause pollution.

PUBLIC SAFETY

- **CALL Emergency Response Telephone Number on Shipping Paper first. If Shipping Paper not available or no answer, refer to appropriate telephone number listed on the inside back cover.**
- Isolate spill or leak area immediately for at least 25 to 50 meters (80 to 160 feet) in all directions.
- Keep unauthorized personnel away.
- Stay upwind.
- Keep out of low areas.
- Ventilate closed spaces before entering.

PROTECTIVE CLOTHING

- Wear positive pressure self-contained breathing apparatus (SCBA).
- Structural firefighters' protective clothing will only provide limited protection.

EVACUATION

Large Spill

- Consider initial downwind evacuation for at least 300 meters (1000 feet).

Fire

- If tank, rail car or tank truck is involved in a fire, ISOLATE for 800 meters (1/2 mile) in all directions; also, consider initial evacuation for 800 meters (1/2 mile) in all directions.

EMERGENCY RESPONSE

FIRE

CAUTION: All these products have a very low flash point: Use of water spray when fighting fire may be inefficient.

Small Fires

• Dry chemical, CO_2, water spray or regular foam.

Large Fires

• Water spray, fog or regular foam.
• Use water spray or fog; do not use straight streams.
• Move containers from fire area if you can do it without risk.

Fire involving Tanks or Car/Trailer Loads

• Fight fire from maximum distance or use unmanned hose holders or monitor nozzles.
• Cool containers with flooding quantities of water until well after fire is out.
• Withdraw immediately in case of rising sound from venting safety devices or discoloration of tank.
• ALWAYS stay away from tanks engulfed in fire.
• For massive fire, use unmanned hose holders or monitor nozzles; if this is impossible, withdraw from area and let fire burn.

SPILL OR LEAK

• ELIMINATE all ignition sources (no smoking, flares, sparks or flames in immediate area).
• All equipment used when handling the product must be grounded.
• Do not touch or walk through spilled material.
• Stop leak if you can do it without risk.
• Prevent entry into waterways, sewers, basements or confined areas.
• A vapor suppressing foam may be used to reduce vapors.
• Absorb or cover with dry earth, sand or other non-combustible material and transfer to containers.
• Use clean non-sparking tools to collect absorbed material.

Large Spills

• Dike far ahead of liquid spill for later disposal.
• Water spray may reduce vapor; but may not prevent ignition in closed spaces.

FIRST AID

• Move victim to fresh air.   • Call 911 or emergency medical service.
• Apply artificial respiration if victim is not breathing.
• Administer oxygen if breathing is difficult.
• Remove and isolate contaminated clothing and shoes.
• In case of contact with substance, immediately flush skin or eyes with running water for at least 20 minutes.
• Wash skin with soap and water.
• Keep victim warm and quiet.
• Ensure that medical personnel are aware of the material(s) involved, and take precautions to protect themselves.

POTENTIAL HAZARDS

FIRE OR EXPLOSION

- **HIGHLY FLAMMABLE: Will be easily ignited by heat, sparks or flames.**
- Vapors may form explosive mixtures with air.
- Vapors may travel to source of ignition and flash back.
- Most vapors are heavier than air. They will spread along ground and collect in low or confined areas (sewers, basements, tanks).
- Vapor explosion hazard indoors, outdoors or in sewers.
- Those substances designated with a "P" may polymerize explosively when heated or involved in a fire.
- Runoff to sewer may create fire or explosion hazard.
- Containers may explode when heated.
- Many liquids are lighter than water.

HEALTH

- May cause toxic effects if inhaled or absorbed through skin.
- Inhalation or contact with material may irritate or burn skin and eyes.
- Fire will produce irritating, corrosive and/or toxic gases.
- Vapors may cause dizziness or suffocation.
- Runoff from fire control or dilution water may cause pollution.

PUBLIC SAFETY

- **CALL Emergency Response Telephone Number on Shipping Paper first. If Shipping Paper not available or no answer, refer to appropriate telephone number listed on the inside back cover.**
- Isolate spill or leak area immediately for at least 50 to 100 meters (160 to 330 feet) in all directions.
- Keep unauthorized personnel away.
- Stay upwind.
- Keep out of low areas.
- Ventilate closed spaces before entering.

PROTECTIVE CLOTHING

- Wear positive pressure self-contained breathing apparatus (SCBA).
- Structural firefighters' protective clothing will only provide limited protection.

EVACUATION

Large Spill

- Consider initial downwind evacuation for at least 300 meters (1000 feet).

Fire

- If tank, rail car or tank truck is involved in a fire, ISOLATE for 800 meters (1/2 mile) in all directions; also, consider initial evacuation for 800 meters (1/2 mile) in all directions.

EMERGENCY RESPONSE

FIRE

CAUTION: All these products have a very low flash point: Use of water spray when fighting fire may be inefficient.

Small Fires • Dry chemical, CO_2, water spray or alcohol-resistant foam.

- **Do not use dry chemical extinguishers to control fires involving nitromethane or nitroethane.**

Large Fires

- Water spray, fog or alcohol-resistant foam.
- **Do not use straight streams.**
- Move containers from fire area if you can do it without risk.

Fire involving Tanks or Car/Trailer Loads

- Fight fire from maximum distance or use unmanned hose holders or monitor nozzles.
- Cool containers with flooding quantities of water until well after fire is out.
- Withdraw immediately in case of rising sound from venting safety devices or discoloration of tank.
- ALWAYS stay away from tanks engulfed in fire.
- For massive fire, use unmanned hose holders or monitor nozzles; if this is impossible, withdraw from area and let fire burn.

SPILL OR LEAK

- ELIMINATE all ignition sources (no smoking, flares, sparks or flames in immediate area).
- All equipment used when handling the product must be grounded.
- Do not touch or walk through spilled material.
- Stop leak if you can do it without risk.
- Prevent entry into waterways, sewers, basements or confined areas.
- A vapor suppressing foam may be used to reduce vapors.
- Absorb or cover with dry earth, sand or other non-combustible material and transfer to containers.
- Use clean non-sparking tools to collect absorbed material.

Large Spills • Dike far ahead of liquid spill for later disposal.

- Water spray may reduce vapor; but may not prevent ignition in closed spaces.

FIRST AID

- Move victim to fresh air.   • Call 911 or emergency medical service.
- Apply artificial respiration if victim is not breathing.
- Administer oxygen if breathing is difficult.
- Remove and isolate contaminated clothing and shoes.
- In case of contact with substance, immediately flush skin or eyes with running water for at least 20 minutes.
- Wash skin with soap and water.
- Keep victim warm and quiet.
- Effects of exposure (inhalation, ingestion or skin contact) to substance may be delayed.
- Ensure that medical personnel are aware of the material(s) involved, and take precautions to protect themselves.

POTENTIAL HAZARDS

FIRE OR EXPLOSION

- **HIGHLY FLAMMABLE: Will be easily ignited by heat, sparks or flames.**
- Vapors may form explosive mixtures with air.
- Vapors may travel to source of ignition and flash back.
- Most vapors are heavier than air. They will spread along ground and collect in low or confined areas (sewers, basements, tanks).
- Vapor explosion hazard indoors, outdoors or in sewers.
- Those substances designated with a "**P**" may polymerize explosively when heated or involved in a fire.
- Runoff to sewer may create fire or explosion hazard.
- Containers may explode when heated.
- Many liquids are lighter than water.

HEALTH

- May cause toxic effects if inhaled or absorbed through skin.
- Inhalation or contact with material may irritate or burn skin and eyes.
- Fire will produce irritating, corrosive and/or toxic gases.
- Vapors may cause dizziness or suffocation.
- Runoff from fire control or dilution water may cause pollution.

PUBLIC SAFETY

- **CALL Emergency Response Telephone Number on Shipping Paper first. If Shipping Paper not available or no answer, refer to appropriate telephone number listed on the inside back cover.**
- Isolate spill or leak area immediately for at least 50 to 100 meters (160 to 330 feet) in all directions.
- Keep unauthorized personnel away.
- Stay upwind.
- Keep out of low areas.
- Ventilate closed spaces before entering.

PROTECTIVE CLOTHING

- Wear positive pressure self-contained breathing apparatus (SCBA).
- Structural firefighters' protective clothing will only provide limited protection.

EVACUATION

Large Spill

- Consider initial downwind evacuation for at least 300 meters (1000 feet).

Fire

- If tank, rail car or tank truck is involved in a fire, ISOLATE for 800 meters (1/2 mile) in all directions; also, consider initial evacuation for 800 meters (1/2 mile) in all directions.

EMERGENCY RESPONSE

FIRE

CAUTION: All these products have a very low flash point: Use of water spray when fighting fire may be inefficient.

Small Fires
- Dry chemical, CO_2, water spray or regular foam.

Large Fires
- Water spray, fog or regular foam.
- **Do not use straight streams.**
- Move containers from fire area if you can do it without risk.

Fire involving Tanks or Car/Trailer Loads
- Fight fire from maximum distance or use unmanned hose holders or monitor nozzles.
- Cool containers with flooding quantities of water until well after fire is out.
- Withdraw immediately in case of rising sound from venting safety devices or discoloration of tank.
- ALWAYS stay away from tanks engulfed in fire.
- For massive fire, use unmanned hose holders or monitor nozzles; if this is impossible, withdraw from area and let fire burn.

SPILL OR LEAK
- ELIMINATE all ignition sources (no smoking, flares, sparks or flames in immediate area).
- All equipment used when handling the product must be grounded.
- Do not touch or walk through spilled material.
- Stop leak if you can do it without risk.
- Prevent entry into waterways, sewers, basements or confined areas.
- A vapor suppressing foam may be used to reduce vapors.
- Absorb or cover with dry earth, sand or other non-combustible material and transfer to containers.
- Use clean non-sparking tools to collect absorbed material.

Large Spills • Dike far ahead of liquid spill for later disposal.
- Water spray may reduce vapor; but may not prevent ignition in closed spaces.

FIRST AID
- Move victim to fresh air.   • Call 911 or emergency medical service.
- Apply artificial respiration if victim is not breathing.
- Administer oxygen if breathing is difficult.
- Remove and isolate contaminated clothing and shoes.
- In case of contact with substance, immediately flush skin or eyes with running water for at least 20 minutes.
- Wash skin with soap and water.
- Keep victim warm and quiet.
- Effects of exposure (inhalation, ingestion or skin contact) to substance may be delayed.
- Ensure that medical personnel are aware of the material(s) involved, and take precautions to protect themselves.

POTENTIAL HAZARDS

HEALTH

- **TOXIC; may be fatal if inhaled, ingested or absorbed through skin.**
- Inhalation or contact with some of these materials will irritate or burn skin and eyes.
- Fire will produce irritating, corrosive and/or toxic gases.
- Vapors may cause dizziness or suffocation.
- Runoff from fire control or dilution water may cause pollution.

FIRE OR EXPLOSION

- **HIGHLY FLAMMABLE: Will be easily ignited by heat, sparks or flames.**
- Vapors may form explosive mixtures with air.
- Vapors may travel to source of ignition and flash back.
- Most vapors are heavier than air. They will spread along ground and collect in low or confined areas (sewers, basements, tanks).
- Vapor explosion and poison hazard indoors, outdoors or in sewers.
- Those substances designated with a **"P"** may polymerize explosively when heated or involved in a fire.
- Runoff to sewer may create fire or explosion hazard.
- Containers may explode when heated.
- Many liquids are lighter than water.

PUBLIC SAFETY

- **CALL Emergency Response Telephone Number on Shipping Paper first. If Shipping Paper not available or no answer, refer to appropriate telephone number listed on the inside back cover.**
- Isolate spill or leak area immediately for at least 100 to 200 meters (330 to 660 feet) in all directions.
- Keep unauthorized personnel away.
- Stay upwind.
- Keep out of low areas.
- Ventilate closed spaces before entering.

PROTECTIVE CLOTHING

- Wear positive pressure self-contained breathing apparatus (SCBA).
- Wear chemical protective clothing which is specifically recommended by the manufacturer. It may provide little or no thermal protection.
- Structural firefighters' protective clothing provides limited protection in fire situations ONLY; it is not effective in spill situations.

EVACUATION

Spill

- See the Table of Initial Isolation and Protective Action Distances for highlighted substances. For non-highlighted substances, increase, in the downwind direction, as necessary, the isolation distance shown under "PUBLIC SAFETY".

Fire

- If tank, rail car or tank truck is involved in a fire, ISOLATE for 800 meters (1/2 mile) in all directions; also, consider initial evacuation for 800 meters (1/2 mile) in all directions.

EMERGENCY RESPONSE

FIRE

CAUTION: All these products have a very low flash point: Use of water spray when fighting fire may be inefficient.

Small Fires • Dry chemical, CO_2, water spray or alcohol-resistant foam.

Large Fires
- Water spray, fog or alcohol-resistant foam.
- Move containers from fire area if you can do it without risk.
- Dike fire control water for later disposal; do not scatter the material.
- Use water spray or fog; do not use straight streams.

Fire involving Tanks or Car/Trailer Loads
- Fight fire from maximum distance or use unmanned hose holders or monitor nozzles.
- Cool containers with flooding quantities of water until well after fire is out.
- Withdraw immediately in case of rising sound from venting safety devices or discoloration of tank.
- ALWAYS stay away from tanks engulfed in fire.
- For massive fire, use unmanned hose holders or monitor nozzles; if this is impossible, withdraw from area and let fire burn.

SPILL OR LEAK
- Fully encapsulating, vapor protective clothing should be worn for spills and leaks with no fire.
- ELIMINATE all ignition sources (no smoking, flares, sparks or flames in immediate area).
- All equipment used when handling the product must be grounded.
- Do not touch or walk through spilled material.
- Stop leak if you can do it without risk.
- Prevent entry into waterways, sewers, basements or confined areas.
- A vapor suppressing foam may be used to reduce vapors.

Small Spills • Absorb with earth, sand or other non-combustible material and transfer to containers for later disposal.
- Use clean non-sparking tools to collect absorbed material.

Large Spills • Dike far ahead of liquid spill for later disposal.
- Water spray may reduce vapor; but may not prevent ignition in closed spaces.

FIRST AID
- Move victim to fresh air.   • Call 911 or emergency medical service.
- Apply artificial respiration if victim is not breathing.
- **Do not use mouth-to-mouth method if victim ingested or inhaled the substance; induce artificial respiration with the aid of a pocket mask equipped with a one-way valve or other proper respiratory medical device.**
- Administer oxygen if breathing is difficult.
- Remove and isolate contaminated clothing and shoes.
- In case of contact with substance, immediately flush skin or eyes with running water for at least 20 minutes.
- Wash skin with soap and water.
- Keep victim warm and quiet.
- Effects of exposure (inhalation, ingestion or skin contact) to substance may be delayed.
- Ensure that medical personnel are aware of the material(s) involved, and take precautions to protect themselves.

POTENTIAL HAZARDS

FIRE OR EXPLOSION

- **Flammable/combustible materials.**
- May be ignited by heat, sparks or flames.
- Vapors may form explosive mixtures with air.
- Vapors may travel to source of ignition and flash back.
- Most vapors are heavier than air. They will spread along ground and collect in low or confined areas (sewers, basements, tanks).
- Vapor explosion hazard indoors, outdoors or in sewers.
- Those substances designated with a **"P"** may polymerize explosively when heated or involved in a fire.
- Runoff to sewer may create fire or explosion hazard.
- Containers may explode when heated.
- Many liquids are lighter than water.

HEALTH

- May cause toxic effects if inhaled or ingested/swallowed.
- Contact with substance may cause severe burns to skin and eyes.
- Fire will produce irritating, corrosive and/or toxic gases.
- Vapors may cause dizziness or suffocation.
- Runoff from fire control or dilution water may cause pollution.

PUBLIC SAFETY

- **CALL Emergency Response Telephone Number on Shipping Paper first. If Shipping Paper not available or no answer, refer to appropriate telephone number listed on the inside back cover.**
- Isolate spill or leak area immediately for at least 50 to 100 meters (160 to 330 feet) in all directions.
- Keep unauthorized personnel away.
- Stay upwind.
- Keep out of low areas.
- Ventilate closed spaces before entering.

PROTECTIVE CLOTHING

- Wear positive pressure self-contained breathing apparatus (SCBA).
- Wear chemical protective clothing which is specifically recommended by the manufacturer. It may provide little or no thermal protection.
- Structural firefighters' protective clothing provides limited protection in fire situations ONLY; it is not effective in spill situations.

EVACUATION

Large Spill

- See the Table of Initial Isolation and Protective Action Distances for highlighted substances. For non-highlighted substances, increase, in the downwind direction, as necessary, the isolation distance shown under "PUBLIC SAFETY".

Fire

- If tank, rail car or tank truck is involved in a fire, ISOLATE for 800 meters (1/2 mile) in all directions; also, consider initial evacuation for 800 meters (1/2 mile) in all directions.

EMERGENCY RESPONSE

FIRE
- **Some of these materials may react violently with water.**
- **Small Fires** • Dry chemical, CO_2, water spray or alcohol-resistant foam.

Large Fires
- Water spray, fog or alcohol-resistant foam.
- Move containers from fire area if you can do it without risk.
- Dike fire control water for later disposal; do not scatter the material.
- Do not get water inside containers.

Fire involving Tanks or Car/Trailer Loads
- Fight fire from maximum distance or use unmanned hose holders or monitor nozzles.
- Cool containers with flooding quantities of water until well after fire is out.
- Withdraw immediately in case of rising sound from venting safety devices or discoloration of tank.
- ALWAYS stay away from tanks engulfed in fire.
- For massive fire, use unmanned hose holders or monitor nozzles; if this is impossible, withdraw from area and let fire burn.

SPILL OR LEAK
- Fully encapsulating, vapor protective clothing should be worn for spills and leaks with no fire.
- ELIMINATE all ignition sources (no smoking, flares, sparks or flames in immediate area).
- All equipment used when handling the product must be grounded.
- Do not touch or walk through spilled material.
- Stop leak if you can do it without risk.
- Prevent entry into waterways, sewers, basements or confined areas.
- A vapor suppressing foam may be used to reduce vapors.
- Absorb with earth, sand or other non-combustible material and transfer to containers (except for Hydrazine).
- Use clean non-sparking tools to collect absorbed material.

Large Spills • Dike far ahead of liquid spill for later disposal.
- Water spray may reduce vapor; but may not prevent ignition in closed spaces.

FIRST AID
- Move victim to fresh air.　　• Call 911 or emergency medical service.
- Apply artificial respiration if victim is not breathing.
- **Do not use mouth-to-mouth method if victim ingested or inhaled the substance; induce artificial respiration with the aid of a pocket mask equipped with a one-way valve or other proper respiratory medical device.**
- Administer oxygen if breathing is difficult.
- Remove and isolate contaminated clothing and shoes.
- In case of contact with substance, immediately flush skin or eyes with running water for at least 20 minutes.
- Keep victim warm and quiet.
- Effects of exposure (inhalation, ingestion or skin contact) to substance may be delayed.
- Ensure that medical personnel are aware of the material(s) involved, and take precautions to protect themselves.

POTENTIAL HAZARDS

FIRE OR EXPLOSION

- Flammable/combustible material.
- May be ignited by friction, heat, sparks or flames.
- Some may burn rapidly with flare burning effect.
- Powders, dusts, shavings, borings, turnings or cuttings may explode or burn with explosive violence.
- Substance may be transported in a molten form.
- May re-ignite after fire is extinguished.

HEALTH

- Fire may produce irritating and/or toxic gases.
- Contact may cause burns to skin and eyes.
- Contact with molten substance may cause severe burns to skin and eyes.
- Runoff from fire control may cause pollution.

PUBLIC SAFETY

- **CALL Emergency Response Telephone Number on Shipping Paper first. If Shipping Paper not available or no answer, refer to appropriate telephone number listed on the inside back cover.**
- Isolate spill or leak area immediately for at least 10 to 25 meters (30 to 80 feet) in all directions.
- Keep unauthorized personnel away.
- Stay upwind.
- Keep out of low areas.

PROTECTIVE CLOTHING

- Wear positive pressure self-contained breathing apparatus (SCBA).
- Structural firefighters' protective clothing will only provide limited protection.

EVACUATION

Large Spill

- Consider initial downwind evacuation for at least 100 meters (330 feet).

Fire

- If tank, rail car or tank truck is involved in a fire, ISOLATE for 800 meters (1/2 mile) in all directions; also, consider initial evacuation for 800 meters (1/2 mile) in all directions.

EMERGENCY RESPONSE

FIRE
Small Fires
- Dry chemical, CO_2, sand, earth, water spray or regular foam.

Large Fires
- Water spray, fog or regular foam.
- Move containers from fire area if you can do it without risk.

Fire involving Tanks or Car/Trailer Loads
- Cool containers with flooding quantities of water until well after fire is out.
- For massive fire, use unmanned hose holders or monitor nozzles; if this is impossible, withdraw from area and let fire burn.
- Withdraw immediately in case of rising sound from venting safety devices or discoloration of tank.
- ALWAYS stay away from tanks engulfed in fire.

SPILL OR LEAK
- ELIMINATE all ignition sources (no smoking, flares, sparks or flames in immediate area).
- Do not touch or walk through spilled material.

Small Dry Spills
- With clean shovel place material into clean, dry container and cover loosely; move containers from spill area.

Large Spills
- Wet down with water and dike for later disposal.
- Prevent entry into waterways, sewers, basements or confined areas.

FIRST AID
- Move victim to fresh air.   • Call 911 or emergency medical service.
- Apply artificial respiration if victim is not breathing.
- Administer oxygen if breathing is difficult.
- Remove and isolate contaminated clothing and shoes.
- In case of contact with substance, immediately flush skin or eyes with running water for at least 20 minutes.
- Removal of solidified molten material from skin requires medical assistance.
- Keep victim warm and quiet.
- Ensure that medical personnel are aware of the material(s) involved, and take precautions to protect themselves.

POTENTIAL HAZARDS

FIRE OR EXPLOSION
- Flammable/combustible material.
- May be ignited by heat, sparks or flames.
- When heated, vapors may form explosive mixtures with air: indoors, outdoors, and sewers explosion hazards.
- Contact with metals may evolve flammable hydrogen gas.
- Containers may explode when heated.

HEALTH
- TOXIC; inhalation, ingestion, or skin contact with material may cause severe injury or death.
- Fire will produce irritating, corrosive and/or toxic gases.
- Runoff from fire control or dilution water may be corrosive and/or toxic and cause pollution.

PUBLIC SAFETY
- **CALL Emergency Response Telephone Number on Shipping Paper first. If Shipping Paper not available or no answer, refer to appropriate telephone number listed on the inside back cover.**
- Isolate spill or leak area immediately for at least 25 to 50 meters (80 to 160 feet) in all directions.
- Stay upwind.
- Keep unauthorized personnel away.
- Keep out of low areas.
- Ventilate enclosed areas.

PROTECTIVE CLOTHING
- Wear positive pressure self-contained breathing apparatus (SCBA).
- Wear chemical protective clothing which is specifically recommended by the manufacturer. It may provide little or no thermal protection.
- Structural firefighters' protective clothing provides limited protection in fire situations ONLY; it is not effective in spill situations.

EVACUATION
Large Spill
- Consider initial downwind evacuation for at least 100 meters (330 feet).

Fire
- If tank, rail car or tank truck is involved in a fire, ISOLATE for 800 meters (1/2 mile) in all directions; also, consider initial evacuation for 800 meters (1/2 mile) in all directions.

EMERGENCY RESPONSE

FIRE

Small Fires

- Dry chemical, CO_2, water spray or alcohol-resistant foam.

Large Fires

- Water spray, fog or alcohol-resistant foam.
- Move containers from fire area if you can do it without risk.
- Use water spray or fog; do not use straight streams.
- Do not get water inside containers.
- Dike fire control water for later disposal; do not scatter the material.

Fire involving Tanks or Car/Trailer Loads

- Fight fire from maximum distance or use unmanned hose holders or monitor nozzles.
- Cool containers with flooding quantities of water until well after fire is out.
- Withdraw immediately in case of rising sound from venting safety devices or discoloration of tank.
- ALWAYS stay away from tanks engulfed in fire.

SPILL OR LEAK

- Fully encapsulating, vapor protective clothing should be worn for spills and leaks with no fire.
- ELIMINATE all ignition sources (no smoking, flares, sparks or flames in immediate area).
- Stop leak if you can do it without risk.
- Do not touch damaged containers or spilled material unless wearing appropriate protective clothing.
- Prevent entry into waterways, sewers, basements or confined areas.
- Use clean non-sparking tools to collect material and place it into loosely covered plastic containers for later disposal.

FIRST AID

- Move victim to fresh air.   • Call 911 or emergency medical service.
- Apply artificial respiration if victim is not breathing.
- **Do not use mouth-to-mouth method if victim ingested or inhaled the substance; induce artificial respiration with the aid of a pocket mask equipped with a one-way valve or other proper respiratory medical device.**
- Administer oxygen if breathing is difficult.
- Remove and isolate contaminated clothing and shoes.
- In case of contact with substance, immediately flush skin or eyes with running water for at least 20 minutes.
- For minor skin contact, avoid spreading material on unaffected skin.
- Keep victim warm and quiet.
- Effects of exposure (inhalation, ingestion or skin contact) to substance may be delayed.
- Ensure that medical personnel are aware of the material(s) involved, and take precautions to protect themselves.

POTENTIAL HAZARDS

FIRE OR EXPLOSION

- Flammable/combustible material.
- May ignite on contact with moist air or moisture.
- May burn rapidly with flare-burning effect.
- Some react vigorously or explosively on contact with water.
- Some may decompose explosively when heated or involved in a fire.
- May re-ignite after fire is extinguished.
- Runoff may create fire or explosion hazard.

HEALTH

- Fire will produce irritating, corrosive and/or toxic gases.
- Inhalation of decomposition products may cause severe injury or death.
- Contact with substance may cause severe burns to skin and eyes.
- Runoff from fire control may cause pollution.

PUBLIC SAFETY

- **CALL Emergency Response Telephone Number on Shipping Paper first. If Shipping Paper not available or no answer, refer to appropriate telephone number listed on the inside back cover.**
- Isolate spill or leak area immediately for at least 100 to 150 meters (330 to 490 feet) in all directions.
- Stay upwind.
- Keep unauthorized personnel away.
- Keep out of low areas.

PROTECTIVE CLOTHING

- Wear positive pressure self-contained breathing apparatus (SCBA).
- Wear chemical protective clothing which is specifically recommended by the manufacturer. It may provide little or no thermal protection.
- Structural firefighters' protective clothing will only provide limited protection.

EVACUATION

Spill

- See the Table of Initial Isolation and Protective Action Distances for highlighted substances. For non-highlighted substances, increase, in the downwind direction, as necessary, the isolation distance shown under "PUBLIC SAFETY".

Fire

- If tank, rail car or tank truck is involved in a fire, ISOLATE for 800 meters (1/2 mile) in all directions; also, consider initial evacuation for 800 meters (1/2 mile) in all directions.

EMERGENCY RESPONSE

FIRE
- DO NOT USE WATER, CO_2 OR FOAM ON MATERIAL ITSELF.
- Some of these materials may react violently with water.

EXCEPTION: For Dithionite (Hydrosulfite/Hydrosulphite) UN1384, UN1923 and UN1929, USE FLOODING AMOUNTS OF WATER for SMALL AND LARGE fires to stop the reaction. Smothering will not work for these materials. They do not need air to burn.

Small Fires
- Dry chemical, soda ash, lime or DRY sand, EXCEPT for UN1384, UN1923 and UN1929.

Large Fires
- DRY sand, dry chemical, soda ash or lime, EXCEPT for UN1384, UN1923 and UN1929, or withdraw from area and let fire burn.
- Move containers from fire area if you can do it without risk.

Fire involving Tanks or Car/Trailer Loads
- Fight fire from maximum distance or use unmanned hose holders or monitor nozzles.
- Do not get water inside containers or in contact with substance.
- Cool containers with flooding quantities of water until well after fire is out.
- Withdraw immediately in case of rising sound from venting safety devices or discoloration of tank.
- ALWAYS stay away from tanks engulfed in fire.

SPILL OR LEAK
- Fully encapsulating, vapor protective clothing should be worn for spills and leak with no fire.
- ELIMINATE all ignition sources (no smoking, flares, sparks or flames in immediate area).
- Do not touch or walk through spilled material.
- Stop leak if you can do it without risk.

Small Spills
EXCEPTION: For Dithionite (Hydrosulfite/Hydrosulphite) spills, UN1384, UN1923 and UN1929, dissolve with 5 parts water and collect for proper disposal.
- Cover with DRY earth, DRY sand, or other non-combustible material followed with plastic sheet to minimize spreading or contact with rain.
- Use clean non-sparking tools to collect material and place it into loosely covered plastic containers for later disposal.
- Prevent entry into waterways, sewers, basements or confined areas.

FIRST AID
- Move victim to fresh air.   • Call 911 or emergency medical service.
- Apply artificial respiration if victim is not breathing.
- Administer oxygen if breathing is difficult.
- Remove and isolate contaminated clothing and shoes.
- In case of contact with substance, immediately flush skin or eyes with running water for at least 20 minutes.
- Keep victim warm and quiet.
- Ensure that medical personnel are aware of the material(s) involved, and take precautions to protect themselves.

POTENTIAL HAZARDS

FIRE OR EXPLOSION

- Extremely flammable; will ignite itself if exposed to air.
- Burns rapidly, releasing dense, irritating fumes.
- Substance may be transported in a molten form.
- May re-ignite after fire is extinguished.

HEALTH

- Fire will produce irritating, corrosive and/or toxic gases.
- TOXIC; ingestion of substance or inhalation of decomposition products will cause severe injury or death.
- Contact with substance may cause severe burns to skin and eyes.
- Some effects may be experienced due to skin absorption.
- Runoff from fire control may be corrosive and/or toxic and cause pollution.

PUBLIC SAFETY

- CALL Emergency Response Telephone Number on Shipping Paper first. If Shipping Paper not available or no answer, refer to appropriate telephone number listed on the inside back cover.
- Isolate spill or leak area immediately for at least 100 to 150 meters (330 to 490 feet) in all directions.
- Stay upwind.
- Keep unauthorized personnel away.
- Keep out of low areas.

PROTECTIVE CLOTHING

- Wear positive pressure self-contained breathing apparatus (SCBA).
- Wear chemical protective clothing which is specifically recommended by the manufacturer. It may provide little or no thermal protection.
- Structural firefighters' protective clothing provides limited protection in fire situations ONLY; it is not effective in spill situations.

EVACUATION

Spill

- Consider initial downwind evacuation for at least 300 meters (1000 feet).

Fire

- If tank, rail car or tank truck is involved in a fire, ISOLATE for 800 meters (1/2 mile) in all directions; also, consider initial evacuation for 800 meters (1/2 mile) in all directions.

EMERGENCY RESPONSE

FIRE

Small Fires
- Water spray, wet sand or wet earth.

Large Fires
- Water spray or fog.
- **Do not scatter spilled material with high pressure water streams.**
- Move containers from fire area if you can do it without risk.

Fire involving Tanks or Car/Trailer Loads
- Fight fire from maximum distance or use unmanned hose holders or monitor nozzles.
- Cool containers with flooding quantities of water until well after fire is out.
- Withdraw immediately in case of rising sound from venting safety devices or discoloration of tank.
- ALWAYS stay away from tanks engulfed in fire.

SPILL OR LEAK

- Fully encapsulating, vapor protective clothing should be worn for spills and leaks with no fire.
- ELIMINATE all ignition sources (no smoking, flares, sparks or flames in immediate area).
- Do not touch or walk through spilled material.
- Do not touch damaged containers or spilled material unless wearing appropriate protective clothing.
- Stop leak if you can do it without risk.

Small Spills
- Cover with water, sand or earth. Shovel into metal container and keep material under water.

Large Spills
- Dike for later disposal and cover with wet sand or earth.
- Prevent entry into waterways, sewers, basements or confined areas.

FIRST AID

- Move victim to fresh air.   • Call 911 or emergency medical service.
- Apply artificial respiration if victim is not breathing.
- Administer oxygen if breathing is difficult.
- In case of contact with substance, keep exposed skin areas immersed in water or covered with wet bandages until medical attention is received.
- Removal of solidified molten material from skin requires medical assistance.
- Remove and isolate contaminated clothing and shoes at the site and place in metal container filled with water. Fire hazard if allowed to dry.
- Effects of exposure (inhalation, ingestion or skin contact) to substance may be delayed.
- Keep victim warm and quiet.
- Ensure that medical personnel are aware of the material(s) involved, and take precautions to protect themselves.

POTENTIAL HAZARDS

HEALTH

- TOXIC; inhalation, ingestion or contact (skin, eyes) with vapors, dusts or substance may cause severe injury, burns, or death.
- Fire will produce irritating, corrosive and/or toxic gases.
- Reaction with water may generate much heat which will increase the concentration of fumes in the air.
- Contact with molten substance may cause severe burns to skin and eyes.
- Runoff from fire control or dilution water may cause pollution.

FIRE OR EXPLOSION

- Some of these materials may burn, but none ignite readily.
- May ignite combustibles (wood, paper, oil, clothing, etc.).
- Substance will react with water (some violently), releasing corrosive and/or toxic gases.
- Flammable/toxic gases may accumulate in confined areas (basement, tanks, hopper/tank cars etc.)
- Contact with metals may evolve flammable hydrogen gas.
- Containers may explode when heated or if contaminated with water.
- Substance may be transported in a molten form.

PUBLIC SAFETY

- CALL Emergency Response Telephone Number on Shipping Paper first. If Shipping Paper not available or no answer, refer to appropriate telephone number listed on the inside back cover.
- Isolate spill or leak area immediately for at least 50 to 100 meters (160 to 330 feet) in all directions.
- Keep unauthorized personnel away.
- Stay upwind.
- Keep out of low areas.
- Ventilate enclosed areas.

PROTECTIVE CLOTHING

- Wear positive pressure self-contained breathing apparatus (SCBA).
- Wear chemical protective clothing which is specifically recommended by the manufacturer. It may provide little or no thermal protection.
- Structural firefighters' protective clothing provides limited protection in fire situations ONLY; it is not effective in spill situations.

EVACUATION

Spill

- See the Table of Initial Isolation and Protective Action Distances for highlighted substances. For non-highlighted substances, increase, in the downwind direction, as necessary, the isolation distance shown under "PUBLIC SAFETY".

Fire

- If tank, rail car or tank truck is involved in a fire, ISOLATE for 800 meters (1/2 mile) in all directions; also, consider initial evacuation for 800 meters (1/2 mile) in all directions.

EMERGENCY RESPONSE

FIRE
- **When material is not involved in fire: do not use water on material itself.**

Small Fires
- Dry chemical or CO_2.
- Move containers from fire area if you can do it without risk.

Large Fires
- Flood fire area with large quantities of water, while knocking down vapors with water fog. If insufficient water supply: knock down vapors only.

Fire involving Tanks or Car/Trailer Loads
- Cool containers with flooding quantities of water until well after fire is out.
- Do not get water inside containers.
- Withdraw immediately in case of rising sound from venting safety devices or discoloration of tank.
- ALWAYS stay away from tanks engulfed in fire.

SPILL OR LEAK
- Fully encapsulating, vapor protective clothing should be worn for spills and leaks with no fire.
- Do not touch damaged containers or spilled material unless wearing appropriate protective clothing.
- Stop leak if you can do it without risk.
- Use water spray to reduce vapors; do not put water directly on leak, spill area or inside container.
- Keep combustibles (wood, paper, oil, etc.) away from spilled material.

Small Spills • Cover with DRY earth, DRY sand, or other non-combustible material followed with plastic sheet to minimize spreading or contact with rain.
- Use clean non-sparking tools to collect material and place it into loosely covered plastic containers for later disposal.
- Prevent entry into waterways, sewers, basements or confined areas.

FIRST AID
- Move victim to fresh air.   • Call 911 or emergency medical service.
- Apply artificial respiration if victim is not breathing.
- **Do not use mouth-to-mouth method if victim ingested or inhaled the substance; induce artificial respiration with the aid of a pocket mask equipped with a one-way valve or other proper respiratory medical device.**
- Administer oxygen if breathing is difficult.
- Remove and isolate contaminated clothing and shoes.
- In case of contact with substance, immediately flush skin or eyes with running water for at least 20 minutes.
- For minor skin contact, avoid spreading material on unaffected skin.
- Removal of solidified molten material from skin requires medical assistance.
- Keep victim warm and quiet.
- Effects of exposure (inhalation, ingestion or skin contact) to substance may be delayed.
- Ensure that medical personnel are aware of the material(s) involved, and take precautions to protect themselves.

POTENTIAL HAZARDS

FIRE OR EXPLOSION

- Produce flammable gases on contact with water.
- May ignite on contact with water or moist air.
- Some react vigorously or explosively on contact with water.
- May be ignited by heat, sparks or flames.
- May re-ignite after fire is extinguished.
- Some are transported in highly flammable liquids.
- Runoff may create fire or explosion hazard.

HEALTH

- Inhalation or contact with vapors, substance, or decomposition products may cause severe injury or death.
- May produce corrosive solutions on contact with water.
- Fire will produce irritating, corrosive and/or toxic gases.
- Runoff from fire control may cause pollution.

PUBLIC SAFETY

- **CALL Emergency Response Telephone Number on Shipping Paper first. If Shipping Paper not available or no answer, refer to appropriate telephone number listed on the inside back cover.**
- Isolate spill or leak area immediately for at least 50 to 100 meters (160 to 330 feet) in all directions.
- Keep unauthorized personnel away.
- Stay upwind.
- Keep out of low areas.
- Ventilate the area before entry.

PROTECTIVE CLOTHING

- Wear positive pressure self-contained breathing apparatus (SCBA).
- Structural firefighters' protective clothing will only provide limited protection.

EVACUATION

Large Spill

- Consider initial downwind evacuation for at least 250 meters (800 feet).

Fire

- If tank, rail car or tank truck is involved in a fire, ISOLATE for 800 meters (1/2 mile) in all directions; also, consider initial evacuation for 800 meters (1/2 mile) in all directions.

EMERGENCY RESPONSE

FIRE
- **DO NOT USE WATER OR FOAM.**

Small Fires
- Dry chemical, soda ash, lime or sand.

Large Fires
- DRY sand, dry chemical, soda ash or lime or withdraw from area and let fire burn.
- Move containers from fire area if you can do it without risk.

Magnesium Fires
- DRY sand, sodium chloride powder, graphite powder or Met-L-X® powder.

Lithium Fires
- DRY sand, sodium chloride powder, graphite powder, copper powder or Lith-X® powder.

Fire involving Tanks or Car/Trailer Loads
- Fight fire from maximum distance or use unmanned hose holders or monitor nozzles.
- Do not get water inside containers.
- Cool containers with flooding quantities of water until well after fire is out.
- Withdraw immediately in case of rising sound from venting safety devices or discoloration of tank.
- ALWAYS stay away from tanks engulfed in fire.

SPILL OR LEAK
- ELIMINATE all ignition sources (no smoking, flares, sparks or flames in immediate area).
- Do not touch or walk through spilled material.
- Stop leak if you can do it without risk.
- Use water spray to reduce vapors or divert vapor cloud drift. Avoid allowing water runoff to contact spilled material.
- **DO NOT GET WATER on spilled substance or inside containers.**

Small Spills • Cover with DRY earth, DRY sand, or other non-combustible material followed with plastic sheet to minimize spreading or contact with rain.
- Dike for later disposal; do not apply water unless directed to do so.

Powder Spills • Cover powder spill with plastic sheet or tarp to minimize spreading and keep powder dry.
- **DO NOT CLEAN-UP OR DISPOSE OF, EXCEPT UNDER SUPERVISION OF A SPECIALIST.**

FIRST AID
- Move victim to fresh air. • Call 911 or emergency medical service.
- Apply artificial respiration if victim is not breathing.
- Administer oxygen if breathing is difficult.
- Remove and isolate contaminated clothing and shoes.
- In case of contact with substance, wipe from skin immediately; flush skin or eyes with running water for at least 20 minutes.
- Keep victim warm and quiet.
- Ensure that medical personnel are aware of the material(s) involved, and take precautions to protect themselves.

POTENTIAL HAZARDS

FIRE OR EXPLOSION
- Produce flammable and toxic gases on contact with water.
- May ignite on contact with water or moist air.
- Some react vigorously or explosively on contact with water.
- May be ignited by heat, sparks or flames.
- May re-ignite after fire is extinguished.
- Some are transported in highly flammable liquids.
- Runoff may create fire or explosion hazard.

HEALTH
- Highly toxic: contact with water produces toxic gas, may be fatal if inhaled.
- Inhalation or contact with vapors, substance, or decomposition products may cause severe injury or death.
- May produce corrosive solutions on contact with water.
- Fire will produce irritating, corrosive and/or toxic gases.
- Runoff from fire control may cause pollution.

PUBLIC SAFETY

- **CALL Emergency Response Telephone Number on Shipping Paper first. If Shipping Paper not available or no answer, refer to appropriate telephone number listed on the inside back cover.**
- Isolate spill or leak area immediately for at least 100 to 150 meters (330 to 490 feet) in all directions.
- Keep unauthorized personnel away.
- Stay upwind.
- Keep out of low areas.
- Ventilate the area before entry.

PROTECTIVE CLOTHING
- Wear positive pressure self-contained breathing apparatus (SCBA).
- Wear chemical protective clothing which is specifically recommended by the manufacturer. It may provide little or no thermal protection.
- Structural firefighters' protective clothing provides limited protection in fire situations ONLY; it is not effective in spill situations.

EVACUATION
Large Spill
- See the Table of Initial Isolation and Protective Action Distances for highlighted substances. For non-highlighted substances, increase, in the downwind direction, as necessary, the isolation distance shown under "PUBLIC SAFETY".

Fire
- If tank, rail car or tank truck is involved in a fire, ISOLATE for 800 meters (1/2 mile) in all directions; also, consider initial evacuation for 800 meters (1/2 mile) in all directions.

EMERGENCY RESPONSE

FIRE
- **DO NOT USE WATER OR FOAM. (FOAM MAY BE USED FOR CHLOROSILANES, SEE BELOW)**

Small Fires
- Dry chemical, soda ash, lime or sand.

Large Fires
- DRY sand, dry chemical, soda ash or lime or withdraw from area and let fire burn.
- **FOR CHLOROSILANES, DO NOT USE WATER; use AFFF alcohol-resistant medium expansion foam; DO NOT USE dry chemicals, soda ash or lime on chlorosilane fires (large or small) as they may release large quantities of hydrogen gas which may explode.**
- Move containers from fire area if you can do it without risk.

Fire involving Tanks or Car/Trailer Loads
- Fight fire from maximum distance or use unmanned hose holders or monitor nozzles.
- Cool containers with flooding quantities of water until well after fire is out.
- Do not get water inside containers.
- Withdraw immediately in case of rising sound from venting safety devices or discoloration of tank.
- ALWAYS stay away from tanks engulfed in fire.

SPILL OR LEAK
- Fully encapsulating, vapor protective clothing should be worn for spills and leaks with no fire.
- ELIMINATE all ignition sources (no smoking, flares, sparks or flames in immediate area).
- Do not touch or walk through spilled material.
- Stop leak if you can do it without risk.
- **DO NOT GET WATER on spilled substance or inside containers.**
- Use water spray to reduce vapors or divert vapor cloud drift. Avoid allowing water runoff to contact spilled material.
- **FOR CHLOROSILANES, use AFFF alcohol-resistant medium expansion foam to reduce vapors.**

Small Spills • Cover with DRY earth, DRY sand, or other non-combustible material followed with plastic sheet to minimize spreading or contact with rain.
- Dike for later disposal; do not apply water unless directed to do so.

Powder Spills • Cover powder spill with plastic sheet or tarp to minimize spreading and keep powder dry.
- **DO NOT CLEAN-UP OR DISPOSE OF, EXCEPT UNDER SUPERVISION OF A SPECIALIST.**

FIRST AID
- Move victim to fresh air. • Call 911 or emergency medical service.
- Apply artificial respiration if victim is not breathing.
- **Do not use mouth-to-mouth method if victim ingested or inhaled the substance; induce artificial respiration with the aid of a pocket mask equipped with a one-way valve or other proper respiratory medical device.**
- Administer oxygen if breathing is difficult. • Remove and isolate contaminated clothing and shoes. • In case of contact with substance, wipe from skin immediately; flush skin or eyes with running water for at least 20 minutes.
- Keep victim warm and quiet. • Ensure that medical personnel are aware of the material(s) involved, and take precautions to protect themselves.

POTENTIAL HAZARDS

FIRE OR EXPLOSION

- These substances will accelerate burning when involved in a fire.
- Some may decompose explosively when heated or involved in a fire.
- May explode from heat or contamination.
- Some will react explosively with hydrocarbons (fuels).
- May ignite combustibles (wood, paper, oil, clothing, etc.).
- Containers may explode when heated.
- Runoff may create fire or explosion hazard.

HEALTH

- Inhalation, ingestion or contact (skin, eyes) with vapors or substance may cause severe injury, burns, or death.
- Fire may produce irritating, corrosive and/or toxic gases.
- Runoff from fire control or dilution water may cause pollution.

PUBLIC SAFETY

- **CALL Emergency Response Telephone Number on Shipping Paper first. If Shipping Paper not available or no answer, refer to appropriate telephone number listed on the inside back cover.**
- Isolate spill or leak area immediately for at least 10 to 25 meters (30 to 80 feet) in all directions.
- Keep unauthorized personnel away.
- Stay upwind.
- Keep out of low areas.
- Ventilate closed spaces before entering.

PROTECTIVE CLOTHING

- Wear positive pressure self-contained breathing apparatus (SCBA).
- Structural firefighters' protective clothing will only provide limited protection.

EVACUATION

Large Spill

- Consider initial downwind evacuation for at least 100 meters (330 feet).

Fire

- If tank, rail car or tank truck is involved in a fire, ISOLATE for 800 meters (1/2 mile) in all directions; also, consider initial evacuation for 800 meters (1/2 mile) in all directions.

EMERGENCY RESPONSE

FIRE

Small Fires
- Use water. Do not use dry chemicals or foams. CO_2 or Halon® may provide limited control.

Large Fires
- Flood fire area with water from a distance.
- Move containers from fire area if you can do it without risk.
- Do not move cargo or vehicle if cargo has been exposed to heat.
- Fight fire from maximum distance or use unmanned hose holders or monitor nozzles.
- Cool containers with flooding quantities of water until well after fire is out.
- ALWAYS stay away from tanks engulfed in fire.
- For massive fire, use unmanned hose holders or monitor nozzles; if this is impossible, withdraw from area and let fire burn.

SPILL OR LEAK
- Keep combustibles (wood, paper, oil, etc.) away from spilled material.
- Do not touch damaged containers or spilled material unless wearing appropriate protective clothing.
- Stop leak if you can do it without risk.
- Do not get water inside containers.

Small Dry Spills
- With clean shovel place material into clean, dry container and cover loosely; move containers from spill area.

Small Liquid Spills
- Use a non-combustible material like vermiculite, sand or earth to soak up the product and place into a container for later disposal.

Large Spills
- Dike far ahead of liquid spill for later disposal.
- **Following product recovery, flush area with water.**

FIRST AID
- Move victim to fresh air. • Call 911 or emergency medical service.
- Apply artificial respiration if victim is not breathing.
- Administer oxygen if breathing is difficult.
- Remove and isolate contaminated clothing and shoes.
- In case of contact with substance, immediately flush skin or eyes with running water for at least 20 minutes.
- Keep victim warm and quiet.
- Ensure that medical personnel are aware of the material(s) involved, and take precautions to protect themselves.

POTENTIAL HAZARDS

FIRE OR EXPLOSION
- These substances will accelerate burning when involved in a fire.
- May explode from heat or contamination.
- Some may burn rapidly.
- Some will react explosively with hydrocarbons (fuels).
- May ignite combustibles (wood, paper, oil, clothing, etc.).
- Containers may explode when heated.
- Runoff may create fire or explosion hazard.

HEALTH
- Toxic by ingestion.
- Inhalation of dust is toxic.
- Fire may produce irritating, corrosive and/or toxic gases.
- Contact with substance may cause severe burns to skin and eyes.
- Runoff from fire control or dilution water may cause pollution.

PUBLIC SAFETY
- **CALL Emergency Response Telephone Number on Shipping Paper first. If Shipping Paper not available or no answer, refer to appropriate telephone number listed on the inside back cover.**
- Isolate spill or leak area immediately for at least 10 to 25 meters (30 to 80 feet) in all directions.
- Keep unauthorized personnel away.
- Stay upwind.
- Keep out of low areas.
- Ventilate closed spaces before entering.

PROTECTIVE CLOTHING
- Wear positive pressure self-contained breathing apparatus (SCBA).
- Wear chemical protective clothing which is specifically recommended by the manufacturer. It may provide little or no thermal protection.
- Structural firefighters' protective clothing will only provide limited protection.

EVACUATION
Large Spill
- Consider initial downwind evacuation for at least 100 meters (330 feet).

Fire
- If tank, rail car or tank truck is involved in a fire, ISOLATE for 800 meters (1/2 mile) in all directions; also, consider initial evacuation for 800 meters (1/2 mile) in all directions.

EMERGENCY RESPONSE

FIRE

Small Fires
- Use water. Do not use dry chemicals or foams. CO_2 or Halon® may provide limited control.

Large Fires
- Flood fire area with water from a distance.
- Move containers from fire area if you can do it without risk.
- Do not move cargo or vehicle if cargo has been exposed to heat.
- Fight fire from maximum distance or use unmanned hose holders or monitor nozzles.
- Cool containers with flooding quantities of water until well after fire is out.
- ALWAYS stay away from tanks engulfed in fire.
- For massive fire, use unmanned hose holders or monitor nozzles; if this is impossible, withdraw from area and let fire burn.

SPILL OR LEAK
- Keep combustibles (wood, paper, oil, etc.) away from spilled material.
- Do not touch damaged containers or spilled material unless wearing appropriate protective clothing.
- Stop leak if you can do it without risk.

Small Dry Spills
- With clean shovel place material into clean, dry container and cover loosely; move containers from spill area.

Large Spills
- Dike far ahead of spill for later disposal.

FIRST AID
- Move victim to fresh air.   • Call 911 or emergency medical service.
- Apply artificial respiration if victim is not breathing.
- Administer oxygen if breathing is difficult.
- Remove and isolate contaminated clothing and shoes.
- In case of contact with substance, immediately flush skin or eyes with running water for at least 20 minutes.
- Keep victim warm and quiet.
- Ensure that medical personnel are aware of the material(s) involved, and take precautions to protect themselves.

POTENTIAL HAZARDS

FIRE OR EXPLOSION

- These substances will accelerate burning when involved in a fire.
- May explode from heat or contamination.
- Some will react explosively with hydrocarbons (fuels).
- May ignite combustibles (wood, paper, oil, clothing, etc.).
- Containers may explode when heated.
- Runoff may create fire or explosion hazard.

HEALTH

- TOXIC; inhalation, ingestion or contact (skin, eyes) with vapors or substance may cause severe injury, burns or death.
- Fire may produce irritating, corrosive and/or toxic gases.
- Toxic/flammable fumes may accumulate in confined areas (basement, tanks, hopper/tank cars, etc.).
- Runoff from fire control or dilution water may cause pollution.

PUBLIC SAFETY

- **CALL Emergency Response Telephone Number on Shipping Paper first. If Shipping Paper not available or no answer, refer to appropriate telephone number listed on the inside back cover.**
- Isolate spill or leak area immediately for at least 50 to 100 meters (160 to 330 feet) in all directions.
- Keep unauthorized personnel away.
- Stay upwind.
- Keep out of low areas.
- Ventilate closed spaces before entering.

PROTECTIVE CLOTHING

- Wear positive pressure self-contained breathing apparatus (SCBA).
- Wear chemical protective clothing which is specifically recommended by the manufacturer. It may provide little or no thermal protection.
- Structural firefighters' protective clothing provides limited protection in fire situations ONLY; it is not effective in spill situations.

EVACUATION

Spill

- See the Table of Initial Isolation and Protective Action Distances for highlighted substances. For non-highlighted substances, increase, in the downwind direction, as necessary, the isolation distance shown under "PUBLIC SAFETY".

Fire

- If tank, rail car or tank truck is involved in a fire, ISOLATE for 800 meters (1/2 mile) in all directions; also, consider initial evacuation for 800 meters (1/2 mile) in all directions.

EMERGENCY RESPONSE

FIRE
Small Fires
- Use water. Do not use dry chemicals or foams. CO_2 or Halon® may provide limited control.

Large Fires
- Flood fire area with water from a distance.
- Move containers from fire area if you can do it without risk.
- Do not move cargo or vehicle if cargo has been exposed to heat.
- Fight fire from maximum distance or use unmanned hose holders or monitor nozzles.
- Cool containers with flooding quantities of water until well after fire is out.
- ALWAYS stay away from tanks engulfed in fire.
- For massive fire, use unmanned hose holders or monitor nozzles; if this is impossible, withdraw from area and let fire burn.

SPILL OR LEAK
- Keep combustibles (wood, paper, oil, etc.) away from spilled material.
- Fully encapsulating, vapor protective clothing should be worn for spills and leaks with no fire.
- Do not touch damaged containers or spilled material unless wearing appropriate protective clothing.
- Stop leak if you can do it without risk.
- Use water spray to reduce vapors or divert vapor cloud drift.
- Do not get water inside containers.

Small Liquid Spills
- Use a non-combustible material like vermiculite, sand or earth to soak up the product and place into a container for later disposal.

Large Spills
- Dike far ahead of liquid spill for later disposal.

FIRST AID
- Move victim to fresh air.   • Call 911 or emergency medical service.
- Apply artificial respiration if victim is not breathing.
- **Do not use mouth-to-mouth method if victim ingested or inhaled the substance; induce artificial respiration with the aid of a pocket mask equipped with a one-way valve or other proper respiratory medical device.**
- Administer oxygen if breathing is difficult.
- Remove and isolate contaminated clothing and shoes.
- In case of contact with substance, immediately flush skin or eyes with running water for at least 20 minutes.
- Keep victim warm and quiet.
- Ensure that medical personnel are aware of the material(s) involved, and take precautions to protect themselves.

POTENTIAL HAZARDS

FIRE OR EXPLOSION

- May explode from friction, heat or contamination.
- These substances will accelerate burning when involved in a fire.
- May ignite combustibles (wood, paper, oil, clothing, etc.).
- Some will react explosively with hydrocarbons (fuels).
- Containers may explode when heated.
- Runoff may create fire or explosion hazard.

HEALTH

- TOXIC; inhalation, ingestion or contact (skin, eyes) with vapors, dusts or substance may cause severe injury, burns, or death.
- Fire may produce irritating and/or toxic gases.
- Toxic fumes or dust may accumulate in confined areas (basement, tanks, hopper/tank cars, etc.).
- Runoff from fire control or dilution water may cause pollution.

PUBLIC SAFETY

- **CALL Emergency Response Telephone Number on Shipping Paper first. If Shipping Paper not available or no answer, refer to appropriate telephone number listed on the inside back cover.**
- Isolate spill or leak area immediately for at least 50 to 100 meters (160 to 330 feet) in all directions.
- Keep unauthorized personnel away.
- Stay upwind.
- Keep out of low areas.
- Ventilate closed spaces before entering.

PROTECTIVE CLOTHING

- Wear positive pressure self-contained breathing apparatus (SCBA).
- Wear chemical protective clothing which is specifically recommended by the manufacturer. It may provide little or no thermal protection.
- Structural firefighters' protective clothing provides limited protection in fire situations ONLY; it is not effective in spill situations.

EVACUATION

Spill

- See the Table of Initial Isolation and Protective Action Distances for highlighted substances. For non-highlighted substances, increase, in the downwind direction, as necessary, the isolation distance shown under "PUBLIC SAFETY".

Fire

- If tank, rail car or tank truck is involved in a fire, ISOLATE for 800 meters (1/2 mile) in all directions; also, consider initial evacuation for 800 meters (1/2 mile) in all directions.

EMERGENCY RESPONSE

FIRE
Small Fires
- Use water. Do not use dry chemicals or foams. CO_2 or Halon® may provide limited control.

Large Fires
- Flood fire area with water from a distance.
- Do not move cargo or vehicle if cargo has been exposed to heat.
- Move containers from fire area if you can do it without risk.
- Do not get water inside containers: a violent reaction may occur.
- Cool containers with flooding quantities of water until well after fire is out.
- Dike fire-control water for later disposal.
- ALWAYS stay away from tanks engulfed in fire.
- For massive fire, use unmanned hose holders or monitor nozzles; if this is impossible, withdraw from area and let fire burn.

SPILL OR LEAK
- Keep combustibles (wood, paper, oil, etc.) away from spilled material.
- Do not touch damaged containers or spilled material unless wearing appropriate protective clothing.
- Use water spray to reduce vapors or divert vapor cloud drift.
- Prevent entry into waterways, sewers, basements or confined areas.

Small Spills
- Flush area with flooding quantities of water.

Large Spills
- **DO NOT CLEAN-UP OR DISPOSE OF, EXCEPT UNDER SUPERVISION OF A SPECIALIST.**

FIRST AID
- Move victim to fresh air.   • Call 911 or emergency medical service.
- Apply artificial respiration if victim is not breathing.
- Administer oxygen if breathing is difficult.
- Remove and isolate contaminated clothing and shoes.
- In case of contact with substance, immediately flush skin or eyes with running water for at least 20 minutes.
- Keep victim warm and quiet.
- Ensure that medical personnel are aware of the material(s) involved, and take precautions to protect themselves.

POTENTIAL HAZARDS

FIRE OR EXPLOSION
- May ignite combustibles (wood, paper, oil, clothing, etc.).
- React vigorously and/or explosively with water.
- Produce toxic and/or corrosive substances on contact with water.
- Flammable/toxic gases may accumulate in tanks and hopper cars.
- Containers may explode when heated.
- Runoff may create fire or explosion hazard.

HEALTH
- TOXIC; inhalation or contact with vapor, substance, or decomposition products may cause severe injury or death.
- Fire will produce irritating, corrosive and/or toxic gases.
- Runoff from fire control or dilution water may cause pollution.

PUBLIC SAFETY
- CALL Emergency Response Telephone Number on Shipping Paper first. If Shipping Paper not available or no answer, refer to appropriate telephone number listed on the inside back cover.
- Isolate spill or leak area immediately for at least 50 to 100 meters (160 to 330 feet) in all directions.
- Keep unauthorized personnel away.
- Stay upwind.
- Keep out of low areas.
- Ventilate closed spaces before entering.

PROTECTIVE CLOTHING
- Wear positive pressure self-contained breathing apparatus (SCBA).
- Wear chemical protective clothing which is specifically recommended by the manufacturer. It may provide little or no thermal protection.
- Structural firefighters' protective clothing provides limited protection in fire situations ONLY; it is not effective in spill situations.

EVACUATION

Spill
- See the Table of Initial Isolation and Protective Action Distances for highlighted substances. For non-highlighted substances, increase, in the downwind direction, as necessary, the isolation distance shown under "PUBLIC SAFETY".

Fire
- If tank, rail car or tank truck is involved in a fire, ISOLATE for 800 meters (1/2 mile) in all directions; also, consider initial evacuation for 800 meters (1/2 mile) in all directions.

EMERGENCY RESPONSE

FIRE
- **DO NOT USE WATER OR FOAM.**

Small Fires
- Dry chemical, soda ash or lime.

Large Fires
- DRY sand, dry chemical, soda ash or lime or withdraw from area and let fire burn.
- Move containers from fire area if you can do it without risk.

Fire involving Tanks or Car/Trailer Loads
- Fight fire from maximum distance or use unmanned hose holders or monitor nozzles.
- Cool containers with flooding quantities of water until well after fire is out.
- Withdraw immediately in case of rising sound from venting safety devices or discoloration of tank.
- ALWAYS stay away from tanks engulfed in fire.

SPILL OR LEAK
- ELIMINATE all ignition sources (no smoking, flares, sparks or flames in immediate area).
- Do not touch damaged containers or spilled material unless wearing appropriate protective clothing.
- Stop leak if you can do it without risk.
- Use water spray to reduce vapors or divert vapor cloud drift. Avoid allowing water runoff to contact spilled material.
- **DO NOT GET WATER on spilled substance or inside containers.**

Small Spills
- Cover with DRY earth, DRY sand, or other non-combustible material followed with plastic sheet to minimize spreading or contact with rain.

Large Spills
- **DO NOT CLEAN-UP OR DISPOSE OF, EXCEPT UNDER SUPERVISION OF A SPECIALIST.**

FIRST AID
- Move victim to fresh air.   • Call 911 or emergency medical service.
- Apply artificial respiration if victim is not breathing.
- **Do not use mouth-to-mouth method if victim ingested or inhaled the substance; induce artificial respiration with the aid of a pocket mask equipped with a one-way valve or other proper respiratory medical device.**
- Administer oxygen if breathing is difficult.
- Remove and isolate contaminated clothing and shoes.
- In case of contact with substance, immediately flush skin or eyes with running water for at least 20 minutes.
- Keep victim warm and quiet.   • Keep victim under observation.
- Effects of contact or inhalation may be delayed.
- Ensure that medical personnel are aware of the material(s) involved, and take precautions to protect themselves.

POTENTIAL HAZARDS

FIRE OR EXPLOSION

- May explode from heat or contamination.
- May ignite combustibles (wood, paper, oil, clothing, etc.).
- May be ignited by heat, sparks or flames.
- May burn rapidly with flare-burning effect.
- Containers may explode when heated.
- Runoff may create fire or explosion hazard.

HEALTH

- Fire may produce irritating, corrosive and/or toxic gases.
- Ingestion or contact (skin, eyes) with substance may cause severe injury or burns.
- Runoff from fire control or dilution water may cause pollution.

PUBLIC SAFETY

- **CALL Emergency Response Telephone Number on Shipping Paper first. If Shipping Paper not available or no answer, refer to appropriate telephone number listed on the inside back cover.**
- Isolate spill or leak area immediately for at least 25 to 50 meters (80 to 160 feet) in all directions.
- Keep unauthorized personnel away.
- Stay upwind.
- Keep out of low areas.

PROTECTIVE CLOTHING

- Wear positive pressure self-contained breathing apparatus (SCBA).
- Wear chemical protective clothing which is specifically recommended by the manufacturer. It may provide little or no thermal protection.
- Structural firefighters' protective clothing will only provide limited protection.

EVACUATION

Large Spill

- Consider initial evacuation for at least 250 meters (800 feet).

Fire

- If tank, rail car or tank truck is involved in a fire, ISOLATE for 800 meters (1/2 mile) in all directions; also, consider initial evacuation for 800 meters (1/2 mile) in all directions.

EMERGENCY RESPONSE

FIRE

Small Fires
- Water spray or fog is preferred; if water not available use dry chemical, CO_2 or regular foam.

Large Fires
- Flood fire area with water from a distance.
- Use water spray or fog; do not use straight streams.
- Move containers from fire area if you can do it without risk.
- Do not move cargo or vehicle if cargo has been exposed to heat.
- Fight fire from maximum distance or use unmanned hose holders or monitor nozzles.
- Cool containers with flooding quantities of water until well after fire is out.
- ALWAYS stay away from tanks engulfed in fire.
- For massive fire, use unmanned hose holders or monitor nozzles; if this is impossible, withdraw from area and let fire burn.

SPILL OR LEAK
- ELIMINATE all ignition sources (no smoking, flares, sparks or flames in immediate area).
- Keep combustibles (wood, paper, oil, etc.) away from spilled material.
- Do not touch damaged containers or spilled material unless wearing appropriate protective clothing.
- Keep substance wet using water spray.
- Stop leak if you can do it without risk.

Small Spills
- Take up with inert, damp, noncombustible material using clean non-sparking tools and place into loosely covered plastic containers for later disposal.

Large Spills
- Wet down with water and dike for later disposal.
- Prevent entry into waterways, sewers, basements or confined areas.
- **DO NOT CLEAN-UP OR DISPOSE OF, EXCEPT UNDER SUPERVISION OF A SPECIALIST.**

FIRST AID
- Move victim to fresh air.   • Call 911 or emergency medical service.
- Apply artificial respiration if victim is not breathing.
- Administer oxygen if breathing is difficult.
- Remove and isolate contaminated clothing and shoes.
- Remove material from skin immediately.
- In case of contact with substance, immediately flush skin or eyes with running water for at least 20 minutes.
- Keep victim warm and quiet.
- Ensure that medical personnel are aware of the material(s) involved, and take precautions to protect themselves.

POTENTIAL HAZARDS

FIRE OR EXPLOSION

- May explode from heat, shock, friction or contamination.
- May ignite combustibles (wood, paper, oil, clothing, etc.).
- May be ignited by heat, sparks or flames.
- May burn rapidly with flare-burning effect.
- Containers may explode when heated.
- Runoff may create fire or explosion hazard.

HEALTH

- Fire may produce irritating, corrosive and/or toxic gases.
- Ingestion or contact (skin, eyes) with substance may cause severe injury or burns.
- Runoff from fire control or dilution water may cause pollution.

PUBLIC SAFETY

- **CALL Emergency Response Telephone Number on Shipping Paper first. If Shipping Paper not available or no answer, refer to appropriate telephone number listed on the inside back cover.**
- Isolate spill or leak area immediately for at least 25 to 50 meters (80 to 160 feet) in all directions.
- Keep unauthorized personnel away.
- Stay upwind.
- Keep out of low areas.

PROTECTIVE CLOTHING

- Wear positive pressure self-contained breathing apparatus (SCBA).
- Wear chemical protective clothing which is specifically recommended by the manufacturer. It may provide little or no thermal protection.
- Structural firefighters' protective clothing will only provide limited protection.

EVACUATION

Large Spill

- Consider initial evacuation for at least 250 meters (800 feet).

Fire

- If tank, rail car or tank truck is involved in a fire, ISOLATE for 800 meters (1/2 mile) in all directions; also, consider initial evacuation for 800 meters (1/2 mile) in all directions.

EMERGENCY RESPONSE

FIRE

Small Fires

- Water spray or fog is preferred; if water not available use dry chemical, CO_2 or regular foam.

Large Fires

- Flood fire area with water from a distance.
- Use water spray or fog; do not use straight streams.
- Move containers from fire area if you can do it without risk.
- Do not move cargo or vehicle if cargo has been exposed to heat.
- Fight fire from maximum distance or use unmanned hose holders or monitor nozzles.
- Cool containers with flooding quantities of water until well after fire is out.
- ALWAYS stay away from tanks engulfed in fire.
- For massive fire, use unmanned hose holders or monitor nozzles; if this is impossible, withdraw from area and let fire burn.

SPILL OR LEAK

- ELIMINATE all ignition sources (no smoking, flares, sparks or flames in immediate area).
- Keep combustibles (wood, paper, oil, etc.) away from spilled material.
- Do not touch damaged containers or spilled material unless wearing appropriate protective clothing.
- Keep substance wet using water spray.
- Stop leak if you can do it without risk.

Small Spills

- Take up with inert, damp, noncombustible material using clean non-sparking tools and place into loosely covered plastic containers for later disposal.

Large Spills

- Wet down with water and dike for later disposal.
- Prevent entry into waterways, sewers, basements or confined areas.
- **DO NOT CLEAN-UP OR DISPOSE OF, EXCEPT UNDER SUPERVISION OF A SPECIALIST.**

FIRST AID

- Move victim to fresh air.   • Call 911 or emergency medical service.
- Apply artificial respiration if victim is not breathing.
- Administer oxygen if breathing is difficult.
- Remove and isolate contaminated clothing and shoes.
- Remove material from skin immediately.
- In case of contact with substance, immediately flush skin or eyes with running water for at least 20 minutes.
- Keep victim warm and quiet.
- Ensure that medical personnel are aware of the material(s) involved, and take precautions to protect themselves.

POTENTIAL HAZARDS

FIRE OR EXPLOSION

- May explode from heat or contamination.
- May ignite combustibles (wood, paper, oil, clothing, etc.).
- May be ignited by heat, sparks or flames.
- May burn rapidly with flare-burning effect.
- Containers may explode when heated.
- Runoff may create fire or explosion hazard.

HEALTH

- TOXIC; inhalation, ingestion or contact (skin, eyes) with vapors, dusts or substance may cause severe injury, burns, or death.
- Contact of vapor or substance with eyes may cause blindness within minutes.
- Fire may produce irritating, corrosive and/or toxic gases.
- Toxic fumes or dust may accumulate in confined areas (basement, tanks, hopper/tank cars, etc.).
- Runoff from fire control or dilution water may cause pollution.

PUBLIC SAFETY

- **CALL Emergency Response Telephone Number on Shipping Paper first. If Shipping Paper not available or no answer, refer to appropriate telephone number listed on the inside back cover.**
- Isolate spill or leak area immediately for at least 25 to 50 meters (80 to 160 feet) in all directions.
- Keep unauthorized personnel away.
- Stay upwind.
- Keep out of low areas.

PROTECTIVE CLOTHING

- Wear positive pressure self-contained breathing apparatus (SCBA).
- Wear chemical protective clothing which is specifically recommended by the manufacturer. It may provide little or no thermal protection.
- Structural firefighters' protective clothing provides limited protection in fire situations ONLY; it is not effective in spill situations.

EVACUATION

Large Spill

- Consider initial evacuation for at least 250 meters (800 feet).

Fire

- If tank, rail car or tank truck is involved in a fire, ISOLATE for 800 meters (1/2 mile) in all directions; also, consider initial evacuation for 800 meters (1/2 mile) in all directions.

EMERGENCY RESPONSE

FIRE

Small Fires
- Water spray or fog is preferred; if water not available use dry chemical, CO_2 or regular foam.

Large Fires
- Flood fire area with water from a distance.
- Use water spray or fog; do not use straight streams.
- Move containers from fire area if you can do it without risk.
- Do not move cargo or vehicle if cargo has been exposed to heat.
- Fight fire from maximum distance or use unmanned hose holders or monitor nozzles.
- Cool containers with flooding quantities of water until well after fire is out.
- ALWAYS stay away from tanks engulfed in fire.
- For massive fire, use unmanned hose holders or monitor nozzles; if this is impossible, withdraw from area and let fire burn.

SPILL OR LEAK
- ELIMINATE all ignition sources (no smoking, flares, sparks or flames in immediate area).
- Keep combustibles (wood, paper, oil, etc.) away from spilled material.
- Do not touch damaged containers or spilled material unless wearing appropriate protective clothing.
- Keep substance wet using water spray.
- Stop leak if you can do it without risk.

Small Spills
- Take up with inert, damp, noncombustible material using clean non-sparking tools and place into loosely covered plastic containers for later disposal.

Large Spills
- Wet down with water and dike for later disposal.
- Prevent entry into waterways, sewers, basements or confined areas.
- **DO NOT CLEAN-UP OR DISPOSE OF, EXCEPT UNDER SUPERVISION OF A SPECIALIST.**

FIRST AID
- Move victim to fresh air.   • Call 911 or emergency medical service.
- Apply artificial respiration if victim is not breathing.
- Administer oxygen if breathing is difficult.
- Remove and isolate contaminated clothing and shoes.
- Remove material from skin immediately.
- In case of contact with substance, immediately flush skin or eyes with running water for at least 20 minutes.
- Keep victim warm and quiet.
- Ensure that medical personnel are aware of the material(s) involved, and take precautions to protect themselves.

POTENTIAL HAZARDS

FIRE OR EXPLOSION

- May explode from heat, contamination or loss of temperature control.
- These materials are particularly sensitive to temperature rises. Above a given "Control Temperature" they decompose violently and catch fire.
- May ignite combustibles (wood, paper, oil, clothing, etc.).
- May ignite spontaneously if exposed to air.
- May be ignited by heat, sparks or flames.
- May burn rapidly with flare-burning effect.
- Containers may explode when heated.
- Runoff may create fire or explosion hazard.

HEALTH

- Fire may produce irritating, corrosive and/or toxic gases.
- Ingestion or contact (skin, eyes) with substance may cause severe injury or burns.
- Runoff from fire control or dilution water may cause pollution.

PUBLIC SAFETY

- **CALL Emergency Response Telephone Number on Shipping Paper first. If Shipping Paper not available or no answer, refer to appropriate telephone number listed on the inside back cover.**
- Isolate spill or leak area immediately for at least 50 to 100 meters (160 to 330 feet) in all directions.
- Keep unauthorized personnel away.
- Stay upwind.
- Keep out of low areas.
- **DO NOT allow the substance to warm up. Obtain liquid nitrogen, dry ice or ice for cooling. If none can be obtained, evacuate the area immediately.**

PROTECTIVE CLOTHING

- Wear positive pressure self-contained breathing apparatus (SCBA).
- Wear chemical protective clothing which is specifically recommended by the manufacturer. It may provide little or no thermal protection.
- Structural firefighters' protective clothing will only provide limited protection.

EVACUATION

Large Spill

- Consider initial evacuation for at least 250 meters (800 feet).

Fire

- If tank, rail car or tank truck is involved in a fire, ISOLATE for 800 meters (1/2 mile) in all directions; also, consider initial evacuation for 800 meters (1/2 mile) in all directions.

EMERGENCY RESPONSE

FIRE
- **The temperature of the substance must be maintained at or below the "Control Temperature" at all times.**

Small Fires
- Water spray or fog is preferred; if water not available use dry chemical, CO_2 or regular foam.

Large Fires
- Flood fire area with water from a distance.
- Use water spray or fog; do not use straight streams.
- Move containers from fire area if you can do it without risk.
- Do not move cargo or vehicle if cargo has been exposed to heat.
- Fight fire from maximum distance or use unmanned hose holders or monitor nozzles.
- Cool containers with flooding quantities of water until well after fire is out.
- **BEWARE OF POSSIBLE CONTAINER EXPLOSION.**
- ALWAYS stay away from tanks engulfed in fire.
- For massive fire, use unmanned hose holders or monitor nozzles; if this is impossible, withdraw from area and let fire burn.

SPILL OR LEAK
- ELIMINATE all ignition sources (no smoking, flares, sparks or flames in immediate area).
- Keep combustibles (wood, paper, oil, etc.) away from spilled material.
- Do not touch or walk through spilled material.
- Stop leak if you can do it without risk.

Small Spills
- Take up with inert, damp, noncombustible material using clean non-sparking tools and place into loosely covered plastic containers for later disposal.

Large Spills
- Dike far ahead of liquid spill for later disposal.
- Prevent entry into waterways, sewers, basements or confined areas.
- **DO NOT CLEAN-UP OR DISPOSE OF, EXCEPT UNDER SUPERVISION OF A SPECIALIST.**

FIRST AID
- Move victim to fresh air.   • Call 911 or emergency medical service.
- Apply artificial respiration if victim is not breathing.
- Administer oxygen if breathing is difficult.
- Remove and isolate contaminated clothing and shoes.
- Remove material from skin immediately.
- In case of contact with substance, immediately flush skin or eyes with running water for at least 20 minutes.
- Keep victim warm and quiet.
- Ensure that medical personnel are aware of the material(s) involved, and take precautions to protect themselves.

POTENTIAL HAZARDS

FIRE OR EXPLOSION

- **Self-decomposition or self-ignition may be triggered by heat, chemical reaction, friction or impact.**
- May be ignited by heat, sparks or flames.
- Some may decompose explosively when heated or involved in a fire.
- May burn violently. Decomposition may be self-accelerating and produce large amounts of gases.
- Vapors or dust may form explosive mixtures with air.

HEALTH

- Inhalation or contact with vapors, substance, or decomposition products may cause severe injury or death.
- May produce irritating, toxic and/or corrosive gases.
- Runoff from fire control may cause pollution.

PUBLIC SAFETY

- **CALL Emergency Response Telephone Number on Shipping Paper first. If Shipping Paper not available or no answer, refer to appropriate telephone number listed on the inside back cover.**
- Isolate spill or leak area immediately for at least 25 to 50 meters (80 to 160 feet) in all directions.
- Keep unauthorized personnel away.
- Stay upwind.
- Keep out of low areas.

PROTECTIVE CLOTHING

- Wear positive pressure self-contained breathing apparatus (SCBA).
- Wear chemical protective clothing which is specifically recommended by the manufacturer. It may provide little or no thermal protection.
- Structural firefighters' protective clothing will only provide limited protection.

EVACUATION

Large Spill

- Consider initial downwind evacuation for at least 250 meters (800 feet).

Fire

- If tank, rail car or tank truck is involved in a fire, ISOLATE for 800 meters (1/2 mile) in all directions; also, consider initial evacuation for 800 meters (1/2 mile) in all directions.

EMERGENCY RESPONSE

FIRE
Small Fires
- Dry chemical, CO_2, water spray or regular foam.

Large Fires
- Flood fire area with water from a distance.
- Move containers from fire area if you can do it without risk.

Fire involving Tanks or Car/Trailer Loads
- BEWARE OF POSSIBLE CONTAINER EXPLOSION.
- Fight fire from maximum distance or use unmanned hose holders or monitor nozzles.
- Cool containers with flooding quantities of water until well after fire is out.
- Withdraw immediately in case of rising sound from venting safety devices or discoloration of tank.
- ALWAYS stay away from tanks engulfed in fire.

SPILL OR LEAK
- ELIMINATE all ignition sources (no smoking, flares, sparks or flames in immediate area).
- Do not touch or walk through spilled material.
- Stop leak if you can do it without risk.

Small Spills
- Take up with inert, damp, noncombustible material using clean non-sparking tools and place into loosely covered plastic containers for later disposal.
- Prevent entry into waterways, sewers, basements or confined areas.

FIRST AID
- Move victim to fresh air.　　• Call 911 or emergency medical service.
- Apply artificial respiration if victim is not breathing.
- Administer oxygen if breathing is difficult.
- Remove and isolate contaminated clothing and shoes.
- In case of contact with substance, immediately flush skin or eyes with running water for at least 20 minutes.
- Keep victim warm and quiet.
- Ensure that medical personnel are aware of the material(s) involved, and take precautions to protect themselves.

POTENTIAL HAZARDS

FIRE OR EXPLOSION

- **Self-decomposition or self-ignition may be triggered by heat, chemical reaction, friction or impact.**
- Self-accelerating decomposition may occur if the specific control temperature is not maintained.
- These materials are particularly sensitive to temperature rises. Above a given "Control Temperature" they decompose violently and catch fire.
- May be ignited by heat, sparks or flames.
- Some may decompose explosively when heated or involved in a fire.
- May burn violently. Decomposition may be self-accelerating and produce large amounts of gases.
- Vapors or dust may form explosive mixtures with air.

HEALTH

- Inhalation or contact with vapors, substance, or decomposition products may cause severe injury or death.
- May produce irritating, toxic and/or corrosive gases.
- Runoff from fire control may cause pollution.

PUBLIC SAFETY

- **CALL Emergency Response Telephone Number on Shipping Paper first. If Shipping Paper not available or no answer, refer to appropriate telephone number listed on the inside back cover.**
- Isolate spill or leak area immediately for at least 50 to 100 meters (160 to 330 feet) in all directions.
- Keep unauthorized personnel away.
- Stay upwind.
- Keep out of low areas.
- **DO NOT allow the substance to warm up. Obtain liquid nitrogen, dry ice or ice for cooling. If none can be obtained, evacuate the area immediately.**

PROTECTIVE CLOTHING

- Wear positive pressure self-contained breathing apparatus (SCBA).
- Wear chemical protective clothing which is specifically recommended by the manufacturer. It may provide little or no thermal protection.
- Structural firefighters' protective clothing will only provide limited protection.

EVACUATION

Large Spill

- Consider initial downwind evacuation for at least 250 meters (800 feet).

Fire

- If tank, rail car or tank truck is involved in a fire, ISOLATE for 800 meters (1/2 mile) in all directions; also, consider initial evacuation for 800 meters (1/2 mile) in all directions.

EMERGENCY RESPONSE

FIRE
- The temperature of the substance must be maintained at or below the "Control Temperature" at all times.

Small Fires
- Dry chemical, CO_2, water spray or regular foam.

Large Fires
- Flood fire area with water from a distance.
- Move containers from fire area if you can do it without risk.

Fire involving Tanks or Car/Trailer Loads
- **BEWARE OF POSSIBLE CONTAINER EXPLOSION.**
- Fight fire from maximum distance or use unmanned hose holders or monitor nozzles.
- Cool containers with flooding quantities of water until well after fire is out.
- Withdraw immediately in case of rising sound from venting safety devices or discoloration of tank.
- ALWAYS stay away from tanks engulfed in fire.

SPILL OR LEAK
- ELIMINATE all ignition sources (no smoking, flares, sparks or flames in immediate area).
- Do not touch or walk through spilled material.
- Stop leak if you can do it without risk.

Small Spills
- Take up with inert, damp, noncombustible material using clean non-sparking tools and place into loosely covered plastic containers for later disposal.
- Prevent entry into waterways, sewers, basements or confined areas.
- **DO NOT CLEAN-UP OR DISPOSE OF, EXCEPT UNDER SUPERVISION OF A SPECIALIST.**

FIRST AID
- Move victim to fresh air.   • Call 911 or emergency medical service.
- Apply artificial respiration if victim is not breathing.
- Administer oxygen if breathing is difficult.
- Remove and isolate contaminated clothing and shoes.
- In case of contact with substance, immediately flush skin or eyes with running water for at least 20 minutes.
- Keep victim warm and quiet.
- Ensure that medical personnel are aware of the material(s) involved, and take precautions to protect themselves.

POTENTIAL HAZARDS

HEALTH
- **Highly toxic,** may be fatal if inhaled, swallowed or absorbed through skin.
- Avoid any skin contact.
- Effects of contact or inhalation may be delayed.
- Fire may produce irritating, corrosive and/or toxic gases.
- Runoff from fire control or dilution water may be corrosive and/or toxic and cause pollution.

FIRE OR EXPLOSION
- Non-combustible, substance itself does not burn but may decompose upon heating to produce corrosive and/or toxic fumes.
- Containers may explode when heated.
- Runoff may pollute waterways.

PUBLIC SAFETY
- **CALL Emergency Response Telephone Number on Shipping Paper first. If Shipping Paper not available or no answer, refer to appropriate telephone number listed on the inside back cover.**
- Isolate spill or leak area immediately for at least 25 to 50 meters (80 to 160 feet) in all directions.
- Keep unauthorized personnel away.
- Stay upwind.
- Keep out of low areas.

PROTECTIVE CLOTHING
- Wear positive pressure self-contained breathing apparatus (SCBA).
- Wear chemical protective clothing which is specifically recommended by the manufacturer. It may provide little or no thermal protection.
- Structural firefighters' protective clothing provides limited protection in fire situations ONLY; it is not effective in spill situations.

EVACUATION
Spill
- See the Table of Initial Isolation and Protective Action Distances for highlighted substances. For non-highlighted substances, increase, in the downwind direction, as necessary, the isolation distance shown under "PUBLIC SAFETY".

Fire
- If tank, rail car or tank truck is involved in a fire, ISOLATE for 800 meters (1/2 mile) in all directions; also, consider initial evacuation for 800 meters (1/2 mile) in all directions.

EMERGENCY RESPONSE

FIRE

Small Fires

- Dry chemical, CO_2 or water spray.

Large Fires

- Water spray, fog or regular foam.
- Move containers from fire area if you can do it without risk.
- Dike fire control water for later disposal; do not scatter the material.
- Use water spray or fog; do not use straight streams.

Fire involving Tanks or Car/Trailer Loads

- Fight fire from maximum distance or use unmanned hose holders or monitor nozzles.
- Do not get water inside containers.
- Cool containers with flooding quantities of water until well after fire is out.
- Withdraw immediately in case of rising sound from venting safety devices or discoloration of tank.
- ALWAYS stay away from tanks engulfed in fire.
- For massive fire, use unmanned hose holders or monitor nozzles; if this is impossible, withdraw from area and let fire burn.

SPILL OR LEAK

- Do not touch damaged containers or spilled material unless wearing appropriate protective clothing.
- Stop leak if you can do it without risk.
- Prevent entry into waterways, sewers, basements or confined areas.
- Cover with plastic sheet to prevent spreading.
- Absorb or cover with dry earth, sand or other non-combustible material and transfer to containers.
- DO NOT GET WATER INSIDE CONTAINERS.

FIRST AID

- Move victim to fresh air.   • Call 911 or emergency medical service.
- Apply artificial respiration if victim is not breathing.
- **Do not use mouth-to-mouth method if victim ingested or inhaled the substance; induce artificial respiration with the aid of a pocket mask equipped with a one-way valve or other proper respiratory medical device.**
- Administer oxygen if breathing is difficult.
- Remove and isolate contaminated clothing and shoes.
- In case of contact with substance, immediately flush skin or eyes with running water for at least 20 minutes.
- For minor skin contact, avoid spreading material on unaffected skin.
- Keep victim warm and quiet.
- Effects of exposure (inhalation, ingestion or skin contact) to substance may be delayed.
- Ensure that medical personnel are aware of the material(s) involved, and take precautions to protect themselves.

POTENTIAL HAZARDS

HEALTH

- **Highly toxic,** may be fatal if inhaled, swallowed or absorbed through skin.
- Contact with molten substance may cause severe burns to skin and eyes.
- Avoid any skin contact.
- Effects of contact or inhalation may be delayed.
- Fire may produce irritating, corrosive and/or toxic gases.
- Runoff from fire control or dilution water may be corrosive and/or toxic and cause pollution.

FIRE OR EXPLOSION

- Combustible material: may burn but does not ignite readily.
- Containers may explode when heated.
- Runoff may pollute waterways.
- Substance may be transported in a molten form.

PUBLIC SAFETY

- **CALL Emergency Response Telephone Number on Shipping Paper first. If Shipping Paper not available or no answer, refer to appropriate telephone number listed on the inside back cover.**
- Isolate spill or leak area immediately for at least 25 to 50 meters (80 to 160 feet) in all directions.
- Keep unauthorized personnel away.
- Stay upwind.
- Keep out of low areas.

PROTECTIVE CLOTHING

- Wear positive pressure self-contained breathing apparatus (SCBA).
- Wear chemical protective clothing which is specifically recommended by the manufacturer. It may provide little or no thermal protection.
- Structural firefighters' protective clothing provides limited protection in fire situations ONLY; it is not effective in spill situations.

EVACUATION

Spill

- See the Table of Initial Isolation and Protective Action Distances for highlighted substances. For non-highlighted substances, increase, in the downwind direction, as necessary, the isolation distance shown under "PUBLIC SAFETY".

Fire

- If tank, rail car or tank truck is involved in a fire, ISOLATE for 800 meters (1/2 mile) in all directions; also, consider initial evacuation for 800 meters (1/2 mile) in all directions.

EMERGENCY RESPONSE

FIRE

Small Fires
- Dry chemical, CO_2 or water spray.

Large Fires
- Water spray, fog or regular foam.
- Move containers from fire area if you can do it without risk.
- Dike fire control water for later disposal; do not scatter the material.
- Use water spray or fog; do not use straight streams.

Fire involving Tanks or Car/Trailer Loads
- Fight fire from maximum distance or use unmanned hose holders or monitor nozzles.
- Do not get water inside containers.
- Cool containers with flooding quantities of water until well after fire is out.
- Withdraw immediately in case of rising sound from venting safety devices or discoloration of tank.
- ALWAYS stay away from tanks engulfed in fire.
- For massive fire, use unmanned hose holders or monitor nozzles; if this is impossible, withdraw from area and let fire burn.

SPILL OR LEAK

- Do not touch damaged containers or spilled material unless wearing appropriate protective clothing.
- Stop leak if you can do it without risk.
- Prevent entry into waterways, sewers, basements or confined areas.
- Cover with plastic sheet to prevent spreading.
- Absorb or cover with dry earth, sand or other non-combustible material and transfer to containers.
- DO NOT GET WATER INSIDE CONTAINERS.

FIRST AID

- Move victim to fresh air. • Call 911 or emergency medical service.
- Apply artificial respiration if victim is not breathing.
- **Do not use mouth-to-mouth method if victim ingested or inhaled the substance; induce artificial respiration with the aid of a pocket mask equipped with a one-way valve or other proper respiratory medical device.**
- Administer oxygen if breathing is difficult.
- Remove and isolate contaminated clothing and shoes.
- In case of contact with substance, immediately flush skin or eyes with running water for at least 20 minutes.
- For minor skin contact, avoid spreading material on unaffected skin.
- Keep victim warm and quiet.
- Effects of exposure (inhalation, ingestion or skin contact) to substance may be delayed.
- Ensure that medical personnel are aware of the material(s) involved, and take precautions to protect themselves.

POTENTIAL HAZARDS

HEALTH

- **TOXIC**; inhalation, ingestion, or skin contact with material may cause severe injury or death.
- Contact with molten substance may cause severe burns to skin and eyes.
- Avoid any skin contact.
- Effects of contact or inhalation may be delayed.
- Fire may produce irritating, corrosive and/or toxic gases.
- Runoff from fire control or dilution water may be corrosive and/or toxic and cause pollution.

FIRE OR EXPLOSION

- Combustible material: may burn but does not ignite readily.
- When heated, vapors may form explosive mixtures with air: indoors, outdoors, and sewers explosion hazards.
- Those substances designated with a "P" may polymerize explosively when heated or involved in a fire.
- Contact with metals may evolve flammable hydrogen gas.
- Containers may explode when heated.
- Runoff may pollute waterways.
- Substance may be transported in a molten form.

PUBLIC SAFETY

- **CALL Emergency Response Telephone Number on Shipping Paper first. If Shipping Paper not available or no answer, refer to appropriate telephone number listed on the inside back cover.**
- Isolate spill or leak area immediately for at least 25 to 50 meters (80 to 160 feet) in all directions.
- Keep unauthorized personnel away.
- Stay upwind.
- Keep out of low areas.
- Ventilate enclosed areas.

PROTECTIVE CLOTHING

- Wear positive pressure self-contained breathing apparatus (SCBA).
- Wear chemical protective clothing which is specifically recommended by the manufacturer. It may provide little or no thermal protection.
- Structural firefighters' protective clothing provides limited protection in fire situations ONLY; it is not effective in spill situations.

EVACUATION

Spill

- See the Table of Initial Isolation and Protective Action Distances for highlighted substances. For non-highlighted substances, increase, in the downwind direction, as necessary, the isolation distance shown under "PUBLIC SAFETY".

Fire

- If tank, rail car or tank truck is involved in a fire, ISOLATE for 800 meters (1/2 mile) in all directions; also, consider initial evacuation for 800 meters (1/2 mile) in all directions.

EMERGENCY RESPONSE

FIRE
Small Fires
- Dry chemical, CO_2 or water spray.

Large Fires
- Dry chemical, CO_2, alcohol-resistant foam or water spray.
- Move containers from fire area if you can do it without risk.
- Dike fire control water for later disposal; do not scatter the material.

Fire involving Tanks or Car/Trailer Loads
- Fight fire from maximum distance or use unmanned hose holders or monitor nozzles.
- Do not get water inside containers.
- Cool containers with flooding quantities of water until well after fire is out.
- Withdraw immediately in case of rising sound from venting safety devices or discoloration of tank.
- ALWAYS stay away from tanks engulfed in fire.

SPILL OR LEAK
- ELIMINATE all ignition sources (no smoking, flares, sparks or flames in immediate area).
- Do not touch damaged containers or spilled material unless wearing appropriate protective clothing.
- Stop leak if you can do it without risk.
- Prevent entry into waterways, sewers, basements or confined areas.
- Absorb or cover with dry earth, sand or other non-combustible material and transfer to containers.
- DO NOT GET WATER INSIDE CONTAINERS.

FIRST AID
- Move victim to fresh air.   • Call 911 or emergency medical service.
- Apply artificial respiration if victim is not breathing.
- **Do not use mouth-to-mouth method if victim ingested or inhaled the substance; induce artificial respiration with the aid of a pocket mask equipped with a one-way valve or other proper respiratory medical device.**
- Administer oxygen if breathing is difficult.
- Remove and isolate contaminated clothing and shoes.
- In case of contact with substance, immediately flush skin or eyes with running water for at least 20 minutes.
- For minor skin contact, avoid spreading material on unaffected skin.
- Keep victim warm and quiet.
- Effects of exposure (inhalation, ingestion or skin contact) to substance may be delayed.
- Ensure that medical personnel are aware of the material(s) involved, and take precautions to protect themselves.

POTENTIAL HAZARDS

HEALTH

- **TOXIC**; inhalation, ingestion, or skin contact with material may cause severe injury or death.
- Contact with molten substance may cause severe burns to skin and eyes.
- Avoid any skin contact.
- Effects of contact or inhalation may be delayed.
- Fire may produce irritating, corrosive and/or toxic gases.
- Runoff from fire control or dilution water may be corrosive and/or toxic and cause pollution.

FIRE OR EXPLOSION

- Non-combustible, substance itself does not burn but may decompose upon heating to produce corrosive and/or toxic fumes.
- Some are oxidizers and may ignite combustibles (wood, paper, oil, clothing, etc.).
- Contact with metals may evolve flammable hydrogen gas.
- Containers may explode when heated.

PUBLIC SAFETY

- **CALL Emergency Response Telephone Number on Shipping Paper first. If Shipping Paper not available or no answer, refer to appropriate telephone number listed on the inside back cover.**
- Isolate spill or leak area immediately for at least 25 to 50 meters (80 to 160 feet) in all directions.
- Keep unauthorized personnel away.
- Stay upwind.
- Keep out of low areas.
- Ventilate enclosed areas.

PROTECTIVE CLOTHING

- Wear positive pressure self-contained breathing apparatus (SCBA).
- Wear chemical protective clothing which is specifically recommended by the manufacturer. It may provide little or no thermal protection.
- Structural firefighters' protective clothing provides limited protection in fire situations ONLY; it is not effective in spill situations.

EVACUATION

Spill

- See the Table of Initial Isolation and Protective Action Distances for highlighted substances. For non-highlighted substances, increase, in the downwind direction, as necessary, the isolation distance shown under "PUBLIC SAFETY".

Fire

- If tank, rail car or tank truck is involved in a fire, ISOLATE for 800 meters (1/2 mile) in all directions; also, consider initial evacuation for 800 meters (1/2 mile) in all directions.

EMERGENCY RESPONSE

FIRE

Small Fires

· Dry chemical, CO_2 or water spray.

Large Fires

· Dry chemical, CO_2, alcohol-resistant foam or water spray.
· Move containers from fire area if you can do it without risk.
· Dike fire control water for later disposal; do not scatter the material.

Fire involving Tanks or Car/Trailer Loads

· Fight fire from maximum distance or use unmanned hose holders or monitor nozzles.
· Do not get water inside containers.
· Cool containers with flooding quantities of water until well after fire is out.
· Withdraw immediately in case of rising sound from venting safety devices or discoloration of tank.
· ALWAYS stay away from tanks engulfed in fire.

SPILL OR LEAK

· ELIMINATE all ignition sources (no smoking, flares, sparks or flames in immediate area).
· Do not touch damaged containers or spilled material unless wearing appropriate protective clothing.
· Stop leak if you can do it without risk.
· Prevent entry into waterways, sewers, basements or confined areas.
· Absorb or cover with dry earth, sand or other non-combustible material and transfer to containers.
· DO NOT GET WATER INSIDE CONTAINERS.

FIRST AID

· Move victim to fresh air.   · Call 911 or emergency medical service.
· Apply artificial respiration if victim is not breathing.
· **Do not use mouth-to-mouth method if victim ingested or inhaled the substance; induce artificial respiration with the aid of a pocket mask equipped with a one-way valve or other proper respiratory medical device.**
· Administer oxygen if breathing is difficult.
· Remove and isolate contaminated clothing and shoes.
· In case of contact with substance, immediately flush skin or eyes with running water for at least 20 minutes.
· For minor skin contact, avoid spreading material on unaffected skin.
· Keep victim warm and quiet.
· Effects of exposure (inhalation, ingestion or skin contact) to substance may be delayed.
· Ensure that medical personnel are aware of the material(s) involved, and take precautions to protect themselves.

POTENTIAL HAZARDS

FIRE OR EXPLOSION

- **HIGHLY FLAMMABLE: Will be easily ignited by heat, sparks or flames.**
- Vapors form explosive mixtures with air: indoors, outdoors, and sewers explosion hazards.
- Most vapors are heavier than air. They will spread along ground and collect in low or confined areas (sewers, basements, tanks).
- Vapors may travel to source of ignition and flash back.
- Substance will react with water (some violently) releasing flammable, toxic or corrosive gases and runoff.
- Contact with metals may evolve flammable hydrogen gas.
- Containers may explode when heated or if contaminated with water.

HEALTH

- TOXIC; inhalation, ingestion or contact (skin, eyes) with vapors, dusts or substance may cause severe injury, burns, or death.
- **Bromoacetates and chloroacetates are extremely irritating/lachrymators.**
- Reaction with water or moist air will release toxic, corrosive or flammable gases.
- Reaction with water may generate much heat which will increase the concentration of fumes in the air.
- Fire will produce irritating, corrosive and/or toxic gases.
- Runoff from fire control or dilution water may be corrosive and/or toxic and cause pollution.

PUBLIC SAFETY

- **CALL Emergency Response Telephone Number on Shipping Paper first. If Shipping Paper not available or no answer, refer to appropriate telephone number listed on the inside back cover.**
- Isolate spill or leak area immediately for at least 50 to 100 meters (160 to 330 feet) in all directions.
- Keep unauthorized personnel away.
- Stay upwind.
- Keep out of low areas.
- Ventilate enclosed areas.

PROTECTIVE CLOTHING

- Wear positive pressure self-contained breathing apparatus (SCBA).
- Wear chemical protective clothing which is specifically recommended by the manufacturer. It may provide little or no thermal protection.
- Structural firefighters' protective clothing provides limited protection in fire situations ONLY; it is not effective in spill situations.

EVACUATION

Spill

- See the Table of Initial Isolation and Protective Action Distances for highlighted substances. For non-highlighted substances, increase, in the downwind direction, as necessary, the isolation distance shown under "PUBLIC SAFETY".

Fire

- If tank, rail car or tank truck is involved in a fire, ISOLATE for 800 meters (1/2 mile) in all directions; also, consider initial evacuation for 800 meters (1/2 mile) in all directions.

EMERGENCY RESPONSE

FIRE
- Note: Most foams will react with the material and release corrosive/toxic gases.
- **Small Fires** • CO_2, dry chemical, dry sand, alcohol-resistant foam.

Large Fires
- Water spray, fog or alcohol-resistant foam.
- **FOR CHLOROSILANES, DO NOT USE WATER**; use AFFF alcohol-resistant medium expansion foam.
- Move containers from fire area if you can do it without risk.
- Use water spray or fog; do not use straight streams.

Fire involving Tanks or Car/Trailer Loads
- Fight fire from maximum distance or use unmanned hose holders or monitor nozzles.
- Do not get water inside containers.
- Cool containers with flooding quantities of water until well after fire is out.
- Withdraw immediately in case of rising sound from venting safety devices or discoloration of tank.
- ALWAYS stay away from tanks engulfed in fire.

SPILL OR LEAK
- ELIMINATE all ignition sources (no smoking, flares, sparks or flames in immediate area).
- All equipment used when handling the product must be grounded.
- Do not touch damaged containers or spilled material unless wearing appropriate protective clothing.
- Stop leak if you can do it without risk.
- A vapor suppressing foam may be used to reduce vapors.
- **FOR CHLOROSILANES**, use AFFF alcohol-resistant medium expansion foam to reduce vapors.
- **DO NOT GET WATER on spilled substance or inside containers.**
- Use water spray to reduce vapors or divert vapor cloud drift. Avoid allowing water runoff to contact spilled material.
- Prevent entry into waterways, sewers, basements or confined areas.
- **Small Spills** • Cover with DRY earth, DRY sand, or other non-combustible material followed with plastic sheet to minimize spreading or contact with rain.
- Use clean non-sparking tools to collect material and place it into loosely covered plastic containers for later disposal.

FIRST AID
- Move victim to fresh air.   • Call 911 or emergency medical service.
- Apply artificial respiration if victim is not breathing.
- **Do not use mouth-to-mouth method if victim ingested or inhaled the substance; induce artificial respiration with the aid of a pocket mask equipped with a one-way valve or other proper respiratory medical device.**
- Administer oxygen if breathing is difficult.
- Remove and isolate contaminated clothing and shoes.
- In case of contact with substance, immediately flush skin or eyes with running water for at least 20 minutes.
- For minor skin contact, avoid spreading material on unaffected skin.
- Keep victim warm and quiet.
- Effects of exposure (inhalation, ingestion or skin contact) to substance may be delayed.
- Ensure that medical personnel are aware of the material(s) involved, and take precautions to protect themselves.

POTENTIAL HAZARDS

FIRE OR EXPLOSION

- Combustible material: may burn but does not ignite readily.
- Substance will react with water (some violently) releasing flammable, toxic or corrosive gases and runoff.
- When heated, vapors may form explosive mixtures with air: indoors, outdoors, and sewers explosion hazards.
- Most vapors are heavier than air. They will spread along ground and collect in low or confined areas (sewers, basements, tanks).
- Vapors may travel to source of ignition and flash back.
- Contact with metals may evolve flammable hydrogen gas.
- Containers may explode when heated or if contaminated with water.

HEALTH

- TOXIC; inhalation, ingestion or contact (skin, eyes) with vapors, dusts or substance may cause severe injury, burns, or death.
- Reaction with water or moist air will release toxic, corrosive or flammable gases.
- Reaction with water may generate much heat which will increase the concentration of fumes in the air.
- Fire will produce irritating, corrosive and/or toxic gases.
- Runoff from fire control or dilution water may be corrosive and/or toxic and cause pollution.

PUBLIC SAFETY

- **CALL Emergency Response Telephone Number on Shipping Paper first. If Shipping Paper not available or no answer, refer to appropriate telephone number listed on the inside back cover.**
- Isolate spill or leak area immediately for at least 50 to 100 meters (160 to 330 feet) in all directions.
- Keep unauthorized personnel away.
- Stay upwind.
- Keep out of low areas.
- Ventilate enclosed areas.

PROTECTIVE CLOTHING

- Wear positive pressure self-contained breathing apparatus (SCBA).
- Wear chemical protective clothing which is specifically recommended by the manufacturer. It may provide little or no thermal protection.
- Structural firefighters' protective clothing provides limited protection in fire situations ONLY; it is not effective in spill situations.

EVACUATION

Spill

- See the Table of Initial Isolation and Protective Action Distances for highlighted substances. For non-highlighted substances, increase, in the downwind direction, as necessary, the isolation distance shown under "PUBLIC SAFETY".

Fire

- If tank, rail car or tank truck is involved in a fire, ISOLATE for 800 meters (1/2 mile) in all directions; also, consider initial evacuation for 800 meters (1/2 mile) in all directions.

EMERGENCY RESPONSE

FIRE
- Note: Most foams will react with the material and release corrosive/toxic gases.

Small Fires • CO_2, dry chemical, dry sand, alcohol-resistant foam.

Large Fires
- Water spray, fog or alcohol-resistant foam.
- **FOR CHLOROSILANES, DO NOT USE WATER;** use AFFF alcohol-resistant medium expansion foam.
- Move containers from fire area if you can do it without risk.
- Use water spray or fog; do not use straight streams.

Fire involving Tanks or Car/Trailer Loads
- Fight fire from maximum distance or use unmanned hose holders or monitor nozzles.
- Do not get water inside containers.
- Cool containers with flooding quantities of water until well after fire is out.
- Withdraw immediately in case of rising sound from venting safety devices or discoloration of tank.
- ALWAYS stay away from tanks engulfed in fire.

SPILL OR LEAK
- ELIMINATE all ignition sources (no smoking, flares, sparks or flames in immediate area).
- All equipment used when handling the product must be grounded.
- Do not touch damaged containers or spilled material unless wearing appropriate protective clothing.
- Stop leak if you can do it without risk.
- A vapor suppressing foam may be used to reduce vapors.
- **FOR CHLOROSILANES**, use AFFF alcohol-resistant medium expansion foam to reduce vapors.
- **DO NOT GET WATER on spilled substance or inside containers.**
- Use water spray to reduce vapors or divert vapor cloud drift. Avoid allowing water runoff to contact spilled material.
- Prevent entry into waterways, sewers, basements or confined areas.

Small Spills • Cover with DRY earth, DRY sand, or other non-combustible material followed with plastic sheet to minimize spreading or contact with rain.
- Use clean non-sparking tools to collect material and place it into loosely covered plastic containers for later disposal.

FIRST AID
- Move victim to fresh air.   • Call 911 or emergency medical service.
- Apply artificial respiration if victim is not breathing.
- **Do not use mouth-to-mouth method if victim ingested or inhaled the substance; induce artificial respiration with the aid of a pocket mask equipped with a one-way valve or other proper respiratory medical device.**
- Administer oxygen if breathing is difficult.
- Remove and isolate contaminated clothing and shoes.
- In case of contact with substance, immediately flush skin or eyes with running water for at least 20 minutes.
- For minor skin contact, avoid spreading material on unaffected skin.
- Keep victim warm and quiet.
- Effects of exposure (inhalation, ingestion or skin contact) to substance may be delayed.
- Ensure that medical personnel are aware of the material(s) involved, and take precautions to protect themselves.

POTENTIAL HAZARDS

HEALTH

- **TOXIC**; inhalation, ingestion or contact (skin, eyes) with vapors, dusts or substance may cause severe injury, burns, or death.
- Reaction with water or moist air will release toxic, corrosive or flammable gases.
- Reaction with water may generate much heat which will increase the concentration of fumes in the air.
- Fire will produce irritating, corrosive and/or toxic gases.
- Runoff from fire control or dilution water may be corrosive and/or toxic and cause pollution.

FIRE OR EXPLOSION

- Non-combustible, substance itself does not burn but may decompose upon heating to produce corrosive and/or toxic fumes.
- Vapors may accumulate in confined areas (basement, tanks, hopper/tank cars etc.).
- Substance will react with water (some violently), releasing corrosive and/or toxic gases.
- Reaction with water may generate much heat which will increase the concentration of fumes in the air.
- Contact with metals may evolve flammable hydrogen gas.
- Containers may explode when heated or if contaminated with water.

PUBLIC SAFETY

- **CALL Emergency Response Telephone Number on Shipping Paper first. If Shipping Paper not available or no answer, refer to appropriate telephone number listed on the inside back cover.**
- Isolate spill or leak area immediately for at least 50 to 100 meters (160 to 330 feet) in all directions.
- Keep unauthorized personnel away.
- Stay upwind.
- Keep out of low areas.
- Ventilate enclosed areas.

PROTECTIVE CLOTHING

- Wear positive pressure self-contained breathing apparatus (SCBA).
- Wear chemical protective clothing which is specifically recommended by the manufacturer. It may provide little or no thermal protection.
- Structural firefighters' protective clothing provides limited protection in fire situations ONLY; it is not effective in spill situations.

EVACUATION

Spill

- See the Table of Initial Isolation and Protective Action Distances for highlighted substances. For non-highlighted substances, increase, in the downwind direction, as necessary, the isolation distance shown under "PUBLIC SAFETY".

Fire

- If tank, rail car or tank truck is involved in a fire, ISOLATE for 800 meters (1/2 mile) in all directions; also, consider initial evacuation for 800 meters (1/2 mile) in all directions.

EMERGENCY RESPONSE

FIRE

- Note: Most foams will react with the material and release corrosive/toxic gases.

Small Fires • CO_2 (except for Cyanides), dry chemical, dry sand, alcohol-resistant foam.

Large Fires

- Water spray, fog or alcohol-resistant foam.
- Move containers from fire area if you can do it without risk.
- Use water spray or fog; do not use straight streams.
- Dike fire control water for later disposal; do not scatter the material.

Fire involving Tanks or Car/Trailer Loads

- Fight fire from maximum distance or use unmanned hose holders or monitor nozzles.
- Do not get water inside containers.
- Cool containers with flooding quantities of water until well after fire is out.
- Withdraw immediately in case of rising sound from venting safety devices or discoloration of tank.
- ALWAYS stay away from tanks engulfed in fire.

SPILL OR LEAK

- ELIMINATE all ignition sources (no smoking, flares, sparks or flames in immediate area).
- All equipment used when handling the product must be grounded.
- Do not touch damaged containers or spilled material unless wearing appropriate protective clothing.
- Stop leak if you can do it without risk.
- A vapor suppressing foam may be used to reduce vapors.
- DO NOT GET WATER INSIDE CONTAINERS.
- Use water spray to reduce vapors or divert vapor cloud drift. Avoid allowing water runoff to contact spilled material.
- Prevent entry into waterways, sewers, basements or confined areas.

Small Spills • Cover with DRY earth, DRY sand, or other non-combustible material followed with plastic sheet to minimize spreading or contact with rain.

- Use clean non-sparking tools to collect material and place it into loosely covered plastic containers for later disposal.

FIRST AID

- Move victim to fresh air.   • Call 911 or emergency medical service.
- Apply artificial respiration if victim is not breathing.
- **Do not use mouth-to-mouth method if victim ingested or inhaled the substance; induce artificial respiration with the aid of a pocket mask equipped with a one-way valve or other proper respiratory medical device.**
- Administer oxygen if breathing is difficult.
- Remove and isolate contaminated clothing and shoes.
- In case of contact with substance, immediately flush skin or eyes with running water for at least 20 minutes.
- For minor skin contact, avoid spreading material on unaffected skin.
- Keep victim warm and quiet.
- Effects of exposure (inhalation, ingestion or skin contact) to substance may be delayed.
- Ensure that medical personnel are aware of the material(s) involved, and take precautions to protect themselves.

POTENTIAL HAZARDS

HEALTH

- Inhalation or contact with substance may cause infection, disease, or death.
- Runoff from fire control may cause pollution.
- **Note: Damaged packages containing solid CO_2 as a refrigerant may produce water or frost from condensation of air. Do not touch this liquid as it could be contaminated by the contents of the parcel.**

FIRE OR EXPLOSION

- Some of these materials may burn, but none ignite readily.
- Some may be transported in flammable liquids.

PUBLIC SAFETY

- CALL Emergency Response Telephone Number on Shipping Paper first. If Shipping Paper not available or no answer, refer to appropriate telephone number listed on the inside back cover.
- Isolate spill or leak area immediately for at least 10 to 25 meters (30 to 80 feet) in all directions.
- Keep unauthorized personnel away.
- Stay upwind.
- Obtain identity of substance involved.

PROTECTIVE CLOTHING

- Wear positive pressure self-contained breathing apparatus (SCBA).
- Structural firefighters' protective clothing will only provide limited protection.

EMERGENCY RESPONSE

FIRE
Small Fires
- Dry chemical, soda ash, lime or sand.

Large Fires
- Use extinguishing agent suitable for type of surrounding fire.
- Move containers from fire area if you can do it without risk.
- Do not scatter spilled material with high pressure water streams.

SPILL OR LEAK
- Do not touch or walk through spilled material.
- Do not touch damaged containers or spilled material unless wearing appropriate protective clothing.
- Absorb with earth, sand or other non-combustible material.
- Cover damaged package or spilled material with damp towel or rag and keep wet with liquid bleach or other disinfectant.
- **DO NOT CLEAN-UP OR DISPOSE OF, EXCEPT UNDER SUPERVISION OF A SPECIALIST.**

FIRST AID
- Move victim to a safe isolated area.

CAUTION: Victim may be a source of contamination.
- Call 911 or emergency medical service.
- Remove and isolate contaminated clothing and shoes.
- In case of contact with substance, immediately flush skin or eyes with running water for at least 20 minutes.
- Effects of exposure (inhalation, ingestion or skin contact) to substance may be delayed.
- **For further assistance, contact your local Poison Control Center.**
- Ensure that medical personnel are aware of the material(s) involved, and take precautions to protect themselves.

POTENTIAL HAZARDS

HEALTH

- Inhalation of vapors or dust is extremely irritating.
- May cause burning of eyes and flow of tears.
- May cause coughing, difficult breathing and nausea.
- Brief exposure effects last only a few minutes.
- Exposure in an enclosed area may be very harmful.
- Fire will produce irritating, corrosive and/or toxic gases.
- Runoff from fire control or dilution water may cause pollution.

FIRE OR EXPLOSION

- Some of these materials may burn, but none ignite readily.
- Containers may explode when heated.

PUBLIC SAFETY

- CALL Emergency Response Telephone Number on Shipping Paper first. If Shipping Paper not available or no answer, refer to appropriate telephone number listed on the inside back cover.
- Isolate spill or leak area immediately for at least 25 to 50 meters (80 to 160 feet) in all directions.
- Keep unauthorized personnel away.
- Stay upwind.
- Keep out of low areas.
- Ventilate closed spaces before entering.

PROTECTIVE CLOTHING

- Wear positive pressure self-contained breathing apparatus (SCBA).
- Wear chemical protective clothing which is specifically recommended by the manufacturer. It may provide little or no thermal protection.
- Structural firefighters' protective clothing provides limited protection in fire situations ONLY; it is not effective in spill situations.

EVACUATION

Large Spill

- Consider initial downwind evacuation for at least 100 meters (330 feet).

Fire

- If tank, rail car or tank truck is involved in a fire, ISOLATE for 800 meters (1/2 mile) in all directions; also, consider initial evacuation for 800 meters (1/2 mile) in all directions.

EMERGENCY RESPONSE

FIRE

Small Fires
- Dry chemical, CO_2, water spray or regular foam.

Large Fires
- Water spray, fog or regular foam.
- Move containers from fire area if you can do it without risk.
- Dike fire control water for later disposal; do not scatter the material.

Fire involving Tanks or Car/Trailer Loads
- Fight fire from maximum distance or use unmanned hose holders or monitor nozzles.
- Do not get water inside containers.
- Cool containers with flooding quantities of water until well after fire is out.
- Withdraw immediately in case of rising sound from venting safety devices or discoloration of tank.
- ALWAYS stay away from tanks engulfed in fire.
- For massive fire, use unmanned hose holders or monitor nozzles; if this is impossible, withdraw from area and let fire burn.

SPILL OR LEAK
- Do not touch or walk through spilled material.
- Stop leak if you can do it without risk.
- Fully encapsulating, vapor protective clothing should be worn for spills and leaks with no fire.

Small Spills
- Take up with sand or other noncombustible absorbent material and place into containers for later disposal.

Large Spills
- Dike far ahead of liquid spill for later disposal.
- Prevent entry into waterways, sewers, basements or confined areas.

FIRST AID
- Move victim to fresh air.   • Call 911 or emergency medical service.
- Apply artificial respiration if victim is not breathing.
- **Do not use mouth-to-mouth method if victim ingested or inhaled the substance; induce artificial respiration with the aid of a pocket mask equipped with a one-way valve or other proper respiratory medical device.**
- Administer oxygen if breathing is difficult.
- Remove and isolate contaminated clothing and shoes.
- In case of contact with substance, immediately flush skin or eyes with running water for at least 20 minutes.
- For minor skin contact, avoid spreading material on unaffected skin.
- Keep victim warm and quiet.
- Effects should disappear after individual has been exposed to fresh air for approximately 10 minutes.
- Ensure that medical personnel are aware of the material(s) involved, and take precautions to protect themselves.

POTENTIAL HAZARDS

HEALTH
- Vapors may cause dizziness or suffocation.
- Exposure in an enclosed area may be very harmful.
- Contact may irritate or burn skin and eyes.
- Fire may produce irritating and/or toxic gases.
- Runoff from fire control or dilution water may cause pollution.

FIRE OR EXPLOSION
- Some of these materials may burn, but none ignite readily.
- Most vapors are heavier than air.
- Air/vapor mixtures may explode when ignited.
- Container may explode in heat of fire.

PUBLIC SAFETY
- **CALL Emergency Response Telephone Number on Shipping Paper first. If Shipping Paper not available or no answer, refer to appropriate telephone number listed on the inside back cover.**
- Isolate spill or leak area immediately for at least 25 to 50 meters (80 to 160 feet) in all directions.
- Keep unauthorized personnel away.
- Stay upwind.
- Many gases are heavier than air and will spread along ground and collect in low or confined areas (sewers, basements, tanks).
- Keep out of low areas.
- Ventilate closed spaces before entering.

PROTECTIVE CLOTHING
- Wear positive pressure self-contained breathing apparatus (SCBA).
- Structural firefighters' protective clothing will only provide limited protection.

EVACUATION
Large Spill
- Consider initial downwind evacuation for at least 100 meters (330 feet).

Fire
- If tank, rail car or tank truck is involved in a fire, ISOLATE for 800 meters (1/2 mile) in all directions; also, consider initial evacuation for 800 meters (1/2 mile) in all directions.

EMERGENCY RESPONSE

FIRE

Small Fires

- Dry chemical, CO_2 or water spray.

Large Fires

- Dry chemical, CO_2, alcohol-resistant foam or water spray.
- Move containers from fire area if you can do it without risk.
- Dike fire control water for later disposal; do not scatter the material.

Fire involving Tanks or Car/Trailer Loads

- Fight fire from maximum distance or use unmanned hose holders or monitor nozzles.
- Cool containers with flooding quantities of water until well after fire is out.
- Withdraw immediately in case of rising sound from venting safety devices or discoloration of tank.
- ALWAYS stay away from tanks engulfed in fire.

SPILL OR LEAK

- ELIMINATE all ignition sources (no smoking, flares, sparks or flames in immediate area).
- Stop leak if you can do it without risk.

Small Liquid Spills

- Take up with sand, earth or other noncombustible absorbent material.

Large Spills

- Dike far ahead of liquid spill for later disposal.
- Prevent entry into waterways, sewers, basements or confined areas.

FIRST AID

- Move victim to fresh air.   • Call 911 or emergency medical service.
- Apply artificial respiration if victim is not breathing.
- Administer oxygen if breathing is difficult.
- Remove and isolate contaminated clothing and shoes.
- In case of contact with substance, immediately flush skin or eyes with running water for at least 20 minutes.
- For minor skin contact, avoid spreading material on unaffected skin.
- Wash skin with soap and water.
- Keep victim warm and quiet.
- Ensure that medical personnel are aware of the material(s) involved, and take precautions to protect themselves.

POTENTIAL HAZARDS

HEALTH

- Radiation presents minimal risk to transport workers, emergency response personnel, and the public during transportation accidents. Packaging durability increases as potential hazard of radioactive content increases.
- Very low levels of contained radioactive materials and low radiation levels outside packages result in low risks to people. Damaged packages may release measurable amounts of radioactive material, but the resulting risks are expected to be low.
- Some radioactive materials cannot be detected by commonly available instruments.
- Packages do not have RADIOACTIVE I, II, or III labels. Some may have EMPTY labels or may have the word "Radioactive" in the package marking.

FIRE OR EXPLOSION

- Some of these materials may burn, but most do not ignite readily.
- Many have cardboard outer packaging; content (physically large or small) can be of many different physical forms.
- Radioactivity does not change flammability or other properties of materials.

PUBLIC SAFETY

- **CALL Emergency Response Telephone Number on Shipping Paper first. If Shipping Paper not available or no answer, refer to appropriate telephone number listed on the inside back cover.**
- **Priorities for rescue, life-saving, first aid, and control of fire and other hazards are higher than the priority for measuring radiation levels.**
- Radiation Authority must be notified of accident conditions. Radiation Authority is usually responsible for decisions about radiological consequences and closure of emergencies.
- Isolate spill or leak area immediately for at least 25 to 50 meters (80 to 160 feet) in all directions.
- Stay upwind.
- Keep unauthorized personnel away.
- Detain or isolate uninjured persons or equipment suspected to be contaminated; delay decontamination and cleanup until instructions are received from Radiation Authority.

PROTECTIVE CLOTHING

- Positive pressure self-contained breathing apparatus (SCBA) and structural firefighters' protective clothing will provide adequate protection.

EVACUATION

Large Spill

- Consider initial downwind evacuation for at least 100 meters (330 feet).

Fire

- When a large quantity of this material is involved in a major fire, consider an initial evacuation distance of 300 meters (1000 feet) in all directions.

EMERGENCY RESPONSE

FIRE

- Presence of radioactive material will not influence the fire control processes and should not influence selection of techniques.
- Move containers from fire area if you can do it without risk.
- Do not move damaged packages; move undamaged packages out of fire zone.

Small Fires

- Dry chemical, CO_2, water spray or regular foam.

Large Fires

- Water spray, fog (flooding amounts).

SPILL OR LEAK

- Do not touch damaged packages or spilled material.
- Cover liquid spill with sand, earth or other noncombustible absorbent material.
- Cover powder spill with plastic sheet or tarp to minimize spreading.

FIRST AID

- Medical problems take priority over radiological concerns.
- Use first aid treatment according to the nature of the injury.
- Do not delay care and transport of a seriously injured person.
- Apply artificial respiration if victim is not breathing.
- Administer oxygen if breathing is difficult.
- In case of contact with substance, immediately flush skin or eyes with running water for at least 20 minutes.
- Injured persons contaminated by contact with released material are not a serious hazard to health care personnel, equipment or facilities.
- Ensure that medical personnel are aware of the material(s) involved, take precautions to protect themselves and prevent spread of contamination.

POTENTIAL HAZARDS

HEALTH

- Radiation presents minimal risk to transport workers, emergency response personnel, and the public during transportation accidents. Packaging durability increases as potential hazard of radioactive content increases.
- Undamaged packages are safe. Contents of damaged packages may cause higher external radiation exposure, or both external and internal radiation exposure if contents are released.
- Low radiation hazard when material is inside container. If material is released from package or bulk container, hazard will vary from low to moderate. Level of hazard will depend on the type and amount of radioactivity, the kind of material it is in, and/or the surfaces it is on.
- Some material may be released from packages during accidents of moderate severity but risks to people are not great.
- Released radioactive materials or contaminated objects usually will be visible if packaging fails.
- Some exclusive use shipments of bulk and packaged materials will not have "RADIOACTIVE" labels. • Placards, markings, and shipping papers provide identification.
- Some packages may have a "RADIOACTIVE" label and a second hazard label. The second hazard is usually greater than the radiation hazard; so follow this Guide as well as the response Guide for the second hazard class label.
- Some radioactive materials cannot be detected by commonly available instruments.
- Runoff from control of cargo fire may cause low-level pollution.

FIRE OR EXPLOSION

- Some of these materials may burn, but most do not ignite readily.
- Uranium and Thorium metal cuttings may ignite spontaneously if exposed to air (see Guide 136).
- Nitrates are oxidizers and may ignite other combustibles (see Guide 141).

PUBLIC SAFETY

- **CALL Emergency Response Telephone Number on Shipping Paper first. If Shipping Paper not available or no answer, refer to appropriate telephone number listed on the inside back cover.**
- **Priorities for rescue, life-saving, first aid, and control of fire and other hazards are higher than the priority for measuring radiation levels.**
- Radiation Authority must be notified of accident conditions. Radiation Authority is usually responsible for decisions about radiological consequences and closure of emergencies.
- Isolate spill or leak area immediately for at least 25 to 50 meters (80 to 160 feet) in all directions. • Stay upwind. • Keep unauthorized persons away.
- Detain or isolate uninjured persons or equipment suspected to be contaminated; delay decontamination and cleanup until instructions are received from Radiation Authority.

PROTECTIVE CLOTHING

- Positive pressure self-contained breathing apparatus (SCBA) and structural firefighters' protective clothing will provide adequate protection.

EVACUATION

Large Spill
- Consider initial downwind evacuation for at least 100 meters (330 feet).

Fire
- When a large quantity of this material is involved in a major fire, consider an initial evacuation distance of 300 meters (1000 feet) in all directions.

EMERGENCY RESPONSE

FIRE

- Presence of radioactive material will not influence the fire control processes and should not influence selection of techniques.
- Move containers from fire area if you can do it without risk.
- Do not move damaged packages; move undamaged packages out of fire zone.

Small Fires

- Dry chemical, CO_2, water spray or regular foam.

Large Fires

- Water spray, fog (flooding amounts).
- Dike fire-control water for later disposal.

SPILL OR LEAK

- Do not touch damaged packages or spilled material.
- Cover liquid spill with sand, earth or other noncombustible absorbent material.
- Dike to collect large liquid spills.
- Cover powder spill with plastic sheet or tarp to minimize spreading.

FIRST AID

- Medical problems take priority over radiological concerns.
- Use first aid treatment according to the nature of the injury.
- Do not delay care and transport of a seriously injured person.
- Apply artificial respiration if victim is not breathing.
- Administer oxygen if breathing is difficult.
- In case of contact with substance, wipe from skin immediately; flush skin or eyes with running water for at least 20 minutes.
- Injured persons contaminated by contact with released material are not a serious hazard to health care personnel, equipment or facilities.
- Ensure that medical personnel are aware of the material(s) involved, take precautions to protect themselves and prevent spread of contamination.

POTENTIAL HAZARDS

HEALTH

- Radiation presents minimal risk to transport workers, emergency response personnel, and the public during transportation accidents. Packaging durability increases as potential hazard of radioactive content increases.
- Undamaged packages are safe. Contents of damaged packages may cause higher external radiation exposure, or both external and internal radiation exposure if contents are released.
- Type A packages (cartons, boxes, drums, articles, etc.) identified as "Type A" by marking on packages or by shipping papers contain non-life endangering amounts. Partial releases might be expected if "Type A" packages are damaged in moderately severe accidents.
- Type B packages, and the rarely occurring Type C packages, (large and small, usually metal) contain the most hazardous amounts. They can be identified by package markings or by shipping papers. Life threatening conditions may exist only if contents are released or package shielding fails. Because of design, evaluation, and testing of packages, these conditions would be expected only for accidents of utmost severity.
- The rarely occurring "Special Arrangement" shipments may be of Type A, Type B or Type C packages. Package type will be marked on packages, and shipment details will be on shipping papers.
- Radioactive White-I labels indicate radiation levels outside spill, isolated, undamaged packages are very low (less than 0.005 mSv/h (0.5 mrem/h)).
- Radioactive Yellow-II and Yellow-III labeled packages have higher radiation levels. The transport index (TI) on the label identifies the maximum radiation level in mrem/h one meter from a single, isolated, undamaged package.
- Some radioactive materials cannot be detected by commonly available instruments.
- Water from cargo fire control may cause pollution.

FIRE OR EXPLOSION

- Some of these materials may burn, but most do not ignite readily.
- Radioactivity does not change flammability or other properties of materials.
- Type B packages are designed and evaluated to withstand total engulfment in flames at temperatures of 800°C (1475°F) for a period of 30 minutes.

PUBLIC SAFETY

- **CALL Emergency Response Telephone Number on Shipping Paper first. If Shipping Paper not available or no answer, refer to appropriate telephone number listed on the inside back cover.**
- Priorities for rescue, life-saving, first aid, and control of fire and other hazards are higher than the priority for measuring radiation levels.
- Radiation Authority must be notified of accident conditions. Radiation Authority is usually responsible for decisions about radiological consequences and closure of emergencies.
- Isolate spill or leak area immediately for at least 25 to 50 meters (80 to 160 feet) in all directions.
  - Stay upwind.   • Keep unauthorized personnel away.
- Detain or isolate uninjured persons or equipment suspected to be contaminated; delay decontamination and cleanup until instructions are received from Radiation Authority.

PROTECTIVE CLOTHING

- Positive pressure self-contained breathing apparatus (SCBA) and structural firefighters' protective clothing will provide adequate protection against internal radiation exposure, but not external radiation exposure.

EVACUATION

Large Spill
- Consider initial downwind evacuation for at least 100 meters (330 feet).

Fire
- When a large quantity of this material is involved in a major fire, consider an initial evacuation distance of 300 meters (1000 feet) in all directions.

EMERGENCY RESPONSE

FIRE
- Presence of radioactive material will not influence the fire control processes and should not influence selection of techniques.
- Move containers from fire area if you can do it without risk.
- Do not move damaged packages; move undamaged packages out of fire zone.

Small Fires
- Dry chemical, CO_2, water spray or regular foam.

Large Fires
- Water spray, fog (flooding amounts).
- Dike fire-control water for later disposal.

SPILL OR LEAK
- Do not touch damaged packages or spilled material.
- Damp surfaces on undamaged or slightly damaged packages are seldom an indication of packaging failure. Most packaging for liquid content have inner containers and/or inner absorbent materials.
- Cover liquid spill with sand, earth or other noncombustible absorbent material.

FIRST AID
- Medical problems take priority over radiological concerns.
- Use first aid treatment according to the nature of the injury.
- Do not delay care and transport of a seriously injured person.
- Apply artificial respiration if victim is not breathing.
- Administer oxygen if breathing is difficult.
- In case of contact with substance, immediately flush skin or eyes with running water for at least 20 minutes.
- Injured persons contaminated by contact with released material are not a serious hazard to health care personnel, equipment or facilities.
- Ensure that medical personnel are aware of the material(s) involved, take precautions to protect themselves and prevent spread of contamination.

POTENTIAL HAZARDS

HEALTH

- Radiation presents minimal risk to transport workers, emergency response personnel, and the public during transportation accidents. Packaging durability increases as potential hazard of radioactive content increases.
- Undamaged packages are safe; contents of damaged packages may cause external radiation exposure, and much higher external radiation exposure if contents (source capsules) are released.
- Contamination and internal radiation hazards are not expected, but not impossible.
- Type A packages (cartons, boxes, drums, articles, etc.) identified as "Type A" by marking on packages or by shipping papers contain non-life endangering amounts. Radioactive sources may be released if "Type A" packages are damaged in moderately severe accidents.
- Type B packages, and the rarely occurring Type C packages, (large and small, usually metal) contain the most hazardous amounts. They can be identified by package markings or by shipping papers. Life threatening conditions may exist only if contents are released or package shielding fails. Because of design, evaluation, and testing of packages, these conditions would be expected only for accidents of utmost severity.
- Radioactive White-I labels indicate radiation levels outside single, isolated, undamaged packages are very low (less than 0.005 mSv/h (0.5 mrem/h)).
- Radioactive Yellow-II and Yellow-III labeled packages have higher radiation levels. The transport index (TI) on the label identifies the maximum radiation level in mrem/h one meter from a single, isolated, undamaged package.
- Radiation from the package contents, usually in durable metal capsules, can be detected by most radiation instruments.
- Water from cargo fire control is not expected to cause pollution.

FIRE OR EXPLOSION

- Packagings can burn completely without risk of content loss from sealed source capsule.
- Radioactivity does not change flammability or other properties of materials.
- Radioactive source capsules and Type B packages are designed and evaluated to withstand total engulfment in flames at temperatures of 800°C (1475°F).

PUBLIC SAFETY

- **CALL Emergency Response Telephone Number on Shipping Paper first. If Shipping Paper not available or no answer, refer to appropriate telephone number listed on the inside back cover.**
- **Priorities for rescue, life-saving, first aid, and control of fire and other hazards are higher than the priority for measuring radiation levels.**
- Radiation Authority must be notified of accident conditions. Radiation Authority is usually responsible for decisions about radiological consequences and closure of emergencies.
- Isolate spill or leak area immediately for at least 25 to 50 meters (80 to 160 feet) in all directions.
- Stay upwind. • Keep unauthorized personnel away.
- Delay final cleanup until instructions or advice is received from Radiation Authority.

PROTECTIVE CLOTHING

- Positive pressure self-contained breathing apparatus (SCBA) and structural firefighters' protective clothing will provide adequate protection against internal radiation exposure, but not external radiation exposure.

EVACUATION

Large Spill

- Consider initial downwind evacuation for at least 100 meters (330 feet).

Fire

- When a large quantity of this material is involved in a major fire, consider an initial evacuation distance of 300 meters (1000 feet) in all directions.

EMERGENCY RESPONSE

FIRE
- Presence of radioactive material will not influence the fire control processes and should not influence selection of techniques.
- Move containers from fire area if you can do it without risk.
- Do not move damaged packages; move undamaged packages out of fire zone.

Small Fires
- Dry chemical, CO_2, water spray or regular foam.

Large Fires
- Water spray, fog (flooding amounts).

SPILL OR LEAK
- Do not touch damaged packages or spilled material.
- Damp surfaces on undamaged or slightly damaged packages are seldom an indication of packaging failure. Contents are seldom liquid. Content is usually a metal capsule, easily seen if released from package.
- If source capsule is identified as being out of package, **DO NOT TOUCH**. Stay away and await advice from Radiation Authority.

FIRST AID
- Medical problems take priority over radiological concerns.
- Use first aid treatment according to the nature of the injury.
- Do not delay care and transport of a seriously injured person.
- Persons exposed to special form sources are not likely to be contaminated with radioactive material.
- Apply artificial respiration if victim is not breathing.
- Administer oxygen if breathing is difficult.
- Injured persons contaminated by contact with released material are not a serious hazard to health care personnel, equipment or facilities.
- Ensure that medical personnel are aware of the material(s) involved, take precautions to protect themselves and prevent spread of contamination.

POTENTIAL HAZARDS

HEALTH
- Radiation presents minimal risk to transport workers, emergency response personnel, and the public during transportation accidents. Packaging durability increases as potential radiation and criticality hazards of the content increase.
- Undamaged packages are safe. Contents of damaged packages may cause higher external radiation exposure, or both external and internal radiation exposure if contents are released.
- Type AF or IF packages, identified by package markings, do not contain life-threatening amounts of material. External radiation levels are low and packages are designed, evaluated, and tested to control releases and to prevent a fission chain reaction under severe transport conditions.
- Type B(U)F, B(M)F and CF packages (identified by markings on packages or shipping papers) contain potentially life endangering amounts. Because of design, evaluation, and testing of packages, fission chain reactions are prevented and releases are not expected to be life endangering for all accidents except those of utmost severity.
- The rarely occurring "Special Arrangement" shipments may be of Type AF, BF or CF packages. Package type will be marked on packages, and shipment details will be on shipping papers.
- The transport index (TI) shown on labels or a shipping paper might not indicate the radiation level at one meter from a single, isolated, undamaged package; instead, it might relate to controls needed during transport because of the fissile properties of the materials.
- Some radioactive materials cannot be detected by commonly available instruments.
- Water from cargo fire control is not expected to cause pollution.

FIRE OR EXPLOSION
- These materials are seldom flammable. Packages are designed to withstand fires without damage to contents.
- Radioactivity does not change flammability or other properties of materials.
- Type AF, IF, B(U)F, B(M)F and CF packages are designed and evaluated to withstand total engulfment in flames at temperatures of 800°C (1475°F) for a period of 30 minutes.

PUBLIC SAFETY

- **CALL Emergency Response Telephone Number on Shipping Paper first. If Shipping Paper not available or no answer, refer to appropriate telephone number listed on the inside back cover.**
- **Priorities for rescue, life-saving, first aid, and control of fire and other hazards are higher than the priority for measuring radiation levels.**
- Radiation Authority must be notified of accident conditions. Radiation Authority is usually responsible for decisions about radiological consequences and closure of emergencies.
- Isolate spill or leak area immediately for at least 25 to 50 meters (80 to 160 feet) in all directions.
  - Stay upwind.   • Keep unauthorized personnel away.
- Detain or isolate uninjured persons or equipment suspected to be contaminated; delay decontamination and cleanup until instructions are received from Radiation Authority.

PROTECTIVE CLOTHING
- Positive pressure self-contained breathing apparatus (SCBA) and structural firefighters' protective clothing will provide adequate protection against internal radiation exposure, but not external radiation exposure.

EVACUATION
Large Spill
- Consider initial downwind evacuation for at least 100 meters (330 feet).

Fire
- When a large quantity of this material is involved in a major fire, consider an initial evacuation distance of 300 meters (1000 feet) in all directions.

EMERGENCY RESPONSE

FIRE
- Presence of radioactive material will not influence the fire control processes and should not influence selection of techniques.
- Move containers from fire area if you can do it without risk.
- Do not move damaged packages; move undamaged packages out of fire zone.

Small Fires
- Dry chemical, CO_2, water spray or regular foam.

Large Fires
- Water spray, fog (flooding amounts).

SPILL OR LEAK
- Do not touch damaged packages or spilled material.
- Damp surfaces on undamaged or slightly damaged packages are seldom an indication of packaging failure. Most packaging for liquid content have inner containers and/or inner absorbent materials.

Liquid Spills
- Package contents are seldom liquid. If any radioactive contamination resulting from a liquid release is present, it probably will be low-level.

FIRST AID
- Medical problems take priority over radiological concerns.
- Use first aid treatment according to the nature of the injury.
- Do not delay care and transport of a seriously injured person.
- Apply artificial respiration if victim is not breathing.
- Administer oxygen if breathing is difficult.
- In case of contact with substance, immediately flush skin or eyes with running water for at least 20 minutes.
- Injured persons contaminated by contact with released material are not a serious hazard to health care personnel, equipment or facilities.
- Ensure that medical personnel are aware of the material(s) involved, take precautions to protect themselves and prevent spread of contamination.

POTENTIAL HAZARDS

HEALTH

- Radiation presents minimal risk to transport workers, emergency response personnel, and the public during transportation accidents. Packaging durability increases as potential radiation and criticality hazards of the content increase.
- Chemical hazard greatly exceeds radiation hazard.
- Substance reacts with water and water vapor in air to form toxic and corrosive hydrogen fluoride gas and an extremely irritating and corrosive, white-colored, water-soluble residue.
- If inhaled, may be fatal.
- Direct contact causes burns to skin, eyes, and respiratory tract.
- Low-level radioactive material; very low radiation hazard to people.
- Runoff from control of cargo fire may cause low-level pollution.

FIRE OR EXPLOSION

- Substance does not burn.
- Containers in protective overpacks (horizontal cylindrical shape with short legs for tie-downs), are identified with "AF" or "B(U)F" on shipping papers or by markings on the overpacks. They are designed and evaluated to withstand severe conditions including total engulfment in flames at temperatures of 800°C (1475°F).
- Bare filled cylinders, identified with UN2978 as part of the marking, may rupture in heat of engulfing fire; bare empty (except for residue) cylinders will not rupture in fires.
- The material may react violently with fuels.
- Radioactivity does not change flammability or other properties of materials.

PUBLIC SAFETY

- **CALL Emergency Response Telephone Number on Shipping Paper first. If Shipping Paper not available or no answer, refer to appropriate telephone number listed on the inside back cover.**
- **Priorities for rescue, life-saving, first aid, and control of fire and other hazards are higher than the priority for measuring radiation levels.**
- Radiation Authority must be notified of accident conditions. Radiation Authority is usually responsible for decisions about radiological consequences and closure of emergencies.
- Isolate spill or leak area immediately for at least 25 to 50 meters (80 to 160 feet) in all directions. • Stay upwind. • Keep unauthorized personnel away.
- Detain or isolate uninjured persons or equipment suspected to be contaminated; delay decontamination and cleanup until instructions are received from Radiation Authority.

PROTECTIVE CLOTHING

- Wear positive pressure self-contained breathing apparatus (SCBA).
- Wear chemical protective clothing which is specifically recommended by the manufacturer. It may provide little or no thermal protection.
- Structural firefighters' protective clothing provides limited protection in fire situations ONLY; it is not effective in spill situations.

EVACUATION

Large Spill

- Consider initial downwind evacuation for at least 100 meters (330 feet).

Fire

- When a large quantity of this material is involved in a major fire, consider an initial evacuation distance of 300 meters (1000 feet) in all directions.

EMERGENCY RESPONSE

FIRE
- DO NOT USE WATER OR FOAM ON MATERIAL ITSELF.
- Move containers from fire area if you can do it without risk.

Small Fires
- Dry chemical or CO_2.

Large Fires
- Water spray, fog or regular foam.
- Cool containers with flooding quantities of water until well after fire is out.
- If this is impossible, withdraw from area and let fire burn.
- ALWAYS stay away from tanks engulfed in fire.

SPILL OR LEAK
- Do not touch damaged packages or spilled material.
- Without fire or smoke, leak will be evident by visible and irritating vapors and residue forming at the point of release.
- Use fine water spray to reduce vapors; do not put water directly on point of material release from container.
- Residue buildup may self-seal small leaks.
- Dike far ahead of spill to collect runoff water.

FIRST AID
- Medical problems take priority over radiological concerns.
- Use first aid treatment according to the nature of the injury.
- Do not delay care and transport of a seriously injured person.
- Apply artificial respiration if victim is not breathing.
- Administer oxygen if breathing is difficult.
- In case of contact with substance, immediately flush skin or eyes with running water for at least 20 minutes.
- Effects of exposure (inhalation, ingestion or skin contact) to substance may be delayed.
- Injured persons contaminated by contact with released material are not a serious hazard to health care personnel, equipment or facilities.
- Ensure that medical personnel are aware of the material(s) involved, take precautions to protect themselves and prevent spread of contamination.

POTENTIAL HAZARDS

HEALTH
- **TOXIC; may be fatal if inhaled.**
- Vapors are extremely irritating.
- Contact with gas or liquefied gas will cause burns, severe injury and/or frostbite.
- Vapors from liquefied gas are initially heavier than air and spread along ground.
- Runoff from fire control may cause pollution.

FIRE OR EXPLOSION
- Substance does not burn but will support combustion.
- This is a strong oxidizer and will react vigorously or explosively with many materials including fuels.
- May ignite combustibles (wood, paper, oil, clothing, etc.).
- Vapor explosion and poison hazard indoors, outdoors or in sewers.
- Containers may explode when heated.
- Ruptured cylinders may rocket.

PUBLIC SAFETY
- CALL Emergency Response Telephone Number on Shipping Paper first. If Shipping Paper not available or no answer, refer to appropriate telephone number listed on the inside back cover.
- Isolate spill or leak area immediately for at least 100 to 200 meters (330 to 660 feet) in all directions.
- Keep unauthorized personnel away.
- Stay upwind.
- Many gases are heavier than air and will spread along ground and collect in low or confined areas (sewers, basements, tanks).
- Keep out of low areas.
- Ventilate closed spaces before entering.

PROTECTIVE CLOTHING
- Wear positive pressure self-contained breathing apparatus (SCBA).
- Wear chemical protective clothing which is specifically recommended by the manufacturer. It may provide little or no thermal protection.
- Structural firefighters' protective clothing provides limited protection in fire situations ONLY; it is not effective in spill situations.
- Always wear thermal protective clothing when handling refrigerated/cryogenic liquids.

EVACUATION
Spill
- See the Table of Initial Isolation and Protective Action Distances for highlighted substances. For non-highlighted substances, increase, in the downwind direction, as necessary, the isolation distance shown under "PUBLIC SAFETY".

Fire
- If tank, rail car or tank truck is involved in a fire, ISOLATE for 1600 meters (1 mile) in all directions; also, consider initial evacuation for 1600 meters (1 mile) in all directions.

EMERGENCY RESPONSE

FIRE
Small Fires
- Dry chemical, soda ash, lime or sand.

Large Fires
- Water spray, fog (flooding amounts).
- Do not get water inside containers.
- Move containers from fire area if you can do it without risk.

Fire involving Tanks
- Fight fire from maximum distance or use unmanned hose holders or monitor nozzles.
- Cool containers with flooding quantities of water until well after fire is out.
- Do not direct water at source of leak or safety devices; icing may occur.
- Withdraw immediately in case of rising sound from venting safety devices or discoloration of tank.
- ALWAYS stay away from tanks engulfed in fire.
- For massive fire, use unmanned hose holders or monitor nozzles; if this is impossible, withdraw from area and let fire burn.

SPILL OR LEAK
- Do not touch or walk through spilled material.
- If you have not donned special protective clothing approved for this material, do not expose yourself to any risk of this material touching you.
- **Do not direct water at spill or source of leak.**
- A fine water spray remotely directed to the edge of the spill pool can be used to direct and maintain a hot flare fire which will burn the spilled material in a controlled manner.
- Keep combustibles (wood, paper, oil, etc.) away from spilled material.
- Stop leak if you can do it without risk.
- Use water spray to reduce vapors or divert vapor cloud drift. Avoid allowing water runoff to contact spilled material.
- If possible, turn leaking containers so that gas escapes rather than liquid.
- Prevent entry into waterways, sewers, basements or confined areas.
- Isolate area until gas has dispersed.
- Ventilate the area.

FIRST AID
- Move victim to fresh air.   • Call 911 or emergency medical service.
- Apply artificial respiration if victim is not breathing.
- Administer oxygen if breathing is difficult.
- Clothing frozen to the skin should be thawed before being removed.
- Remove and isolate contaminated clothing and shoes.
- In case of contact with substance, immediately flush skin or eyes with running water for at least 20 minutes.
- Keep victim warm and quiet.   • Keep victim under observation.
- Effects of contact or inhalation may be delayed.
- Ensure that medical personnel are aware of the material(s) involved, and take precautions to protect themselves.

POTENTIAL HAZARDS

HEALTH

- **TOXIC; Extremely Hazardous.**
- Inhalation extremely dangerous; may be fatal.
- Contact with gas or liquefied gas may cause burns, severe injury and/or frostbite.
- Odorless, will not be detected by sense of smell.

FIRE OR EXPLOSION

- **EXTREMELY FLAMMABLE.**
- May be ignited by heat, sparks or flames.
- Flame may be invisible.
- Containers may explode when heated.
- Vapor explosion and poison hazard indoors, outdoors or in sewers.
- Vapors from liquefied gas are initially heavier than air and spread along ground.
- Vapors may travel to source of ignition and flash back.
- Runoff may create fire or explosion hazard.

PUBLIC SAFETY

- CALL Emergency Response Telephone Number on Shipping Paper first. If Shipping Paper not available or no answer, refer to appropriate telephone number listed on the inside back cover.
- Isolate spill or leak area immediately for at least 100 to 200 meters (330 to 660 feet) in all directions.
- Keep unauthorized personnel away.
- Stay upwind.
- Many gases are heavier than air and will spread along ground and collect in low or confined areas (sewers, basements, tanks).
- Keep out of low areas.
- Ventilate closed spaces before entering.

PROTECTIVE CLOTHING

- Wear positive pressure self-contained breathing apparatus (SCBA).
- Wear chemical protective clothing which is specifically recommended by the manufacturer. It may provide little or no thermal protection.
- Structural firefighters' protective clothing provides limited protection in fire situations ONLY; it is not effective in spill situations.
- Always wear thermal protective clothing when handling refrigerated/cryogenic liquids.

EVACUATION

Spill

- See the Table of Initial Isolation and Protective Action Distances for highlighted substances. For non-highlighted substances, increase, in the downwind direction, as necessary, the isolation distance shown under "PUBLIC SAFETY".

Fire

- If tank, rail car or tank truck is involved in a fire, ISOLATE for 800 meters (1/2 mile) in all directions; also, consider initial evacuation for 800 meters (1/2 mile) in all directions.

EMERGENCY RESPONSE

FIRE
- **DO NOT EXTINGUISH A LEAKING GAS FIRE UNLESS LEAK CAN BE STOPPED.**

Small Fires
- Dry chemical, CO_2 or water spray.

Large Fires
- Water spray, fog or regular foam.
- Move containers from fire area if you can do it without risk.

Fire involving Tanks
- Fight fire from maximum distance or use unmanned hose holders or monitor nozzles.
- Cool containers with flooding quantities of water until well after fire is out.
- Do not direct water at source of leak or safety devices; icing may occur.
- Withdraw immediately in case of rising sound from venting safety devices or discoloration of tank.
- ALWAYS stay away from tanks engulfed in fire.

SPILL OR LEAK
- ELIMINATE all ignition sources (no smoking, flares, sparks or flames in immediate area).
- All equipment used when handling the product must be grounded.
- Fully encapsulating, vapor protective clothing should be worn for spills and leaks with no fire.
- Do not touch or walk through spilled material.
- Stop leak if you can do it without risk.
- Use water spray to reduce vapors or divert vapor cloud drift. Avoid allowing water runoff to contact spilled material.
- Do not direct water at spill or source of leak.
- If possible, turn leaking containers so that gas escapes rather than liquid.
- Prevent entry into waterways, sewers, basements or confined areas.
- Isolate area until gas has dispersed.

FIRST AID
- Move victim to fresh air.   • Call 911 or emergency medical service.
- Apply artificial respiration if victim is not breathing.
- Administer oxygen if breathing is difficult.
- Remove and isolate contaminated clothing and shoes.
- In case of contact with substance, immediately flush skin or eyes with running water for at least 20 minutes.
- In case of contact with liquefied gas, thaw frosted parts with lukewarm water.
- Keep victim warm and quiet.   • Keep victim under observation.
- Effects of contact or inhalation may be delayed.
- Ensure that medical personnel are aware of the material(s) involved, and take precautions to protect themselves.

POTENTIAL HAZARDS

FIRE OR EXPLOSION

- Substance is transported in molten form at a temperature above 705°C (1300°F).
- Violent reaction with water; contact may cause an explosion or may produce a flammable gas.
- Will ignite combustible materials (wood, paper, oil, debris, etc.).
- Contact with nitrates or other oxidizers may cause an explosion.
- Contact with containers or other materials, including cold, wet or dirty tools, may cause an explosion.
- Contact with concrete will cause spalling and small pops.

HEALTH

- Contact causes severe burns to skin and eyes.
- Fire may produce irritating and/or toxic gases.

PUBLIC SAFETY

- **CALL Emergency Response Telephone Number on Shipping Paper first. If Shipping Paper not available or no answer, refer to appropriate telephone number listed on the inside back cover.**
- Isolate spill or leak area immediately for at least 50 to 100 meters (160 to 330 feet) in all directions.
- Keep unauthorized personnel away.
- Ventilate closed spaces before entering.

PROTECTIVE CLOTHING

- Wear positive pressure self-contained breathing apparatus (SCBA).
- Wear flame retardant structural firefighters' protective clothing, including faceshield, helmet and gloves, this will provide limited thermal protection.

EMERGENCY RESPONSE

FIRE
- **Do Not Use Water, except in life threatening situations and then only in a fine spray.**
- **Do not use halogenated extinguishing agents or foam.**
- Move combustibles out of path of advancing pool if you can do so without risk.
- Extinguish fires started by molten material by using appropriate method for the burning material; keep water, halogenated extinguishing agents and foam away from the molten material.

SPILL OR LEAK
- Do not touch or walk through spilled material.
- Do not attempt to stop leak, due to danger of explosion.
- Keep combustibles (wood, paper, oil, etc.) away from spilled material.
- Substance is very fluid, spreads quickly, and may splash. Do not try to stop it with shovels or other objects.
- Dike far ahead of spill; use dry sand to contain the flow of material.
- Where possible allow molten material to solidify naturally.
- Avoid contact even after material solidifies. Molten, heated and cold aluminum look alike; do not touch unless you know it is cold.
- Clean up under the supervision of an expert after material has solidified.

FIRST AID
- Move victim to fresh air.   • Call 911 or emergency medical service.
- Apply artificial respiration if victim is not breathing.
- Administer oxygen if breathing is difficult.
- For severe burns, immediate medical attention is required.
- Removal of solidified molten material from skin requires medical assistance.
- Remove and isolate contaminated clothing and shoes.
- In case of contact with substance, immediately flush skin or eyes with running water for at least 20 minutes.
- Keep victim warm and quiet.

POTENTIAL HAZARDS

FIRE OR EXPLOSION

- May react violently or explosively on contact with water.
- Some are transported in flammable liquids.
- May be ignited by friction, heat, sparks or flames.
- Some of these materials will burn with intense heat.
- Dusts or fumes may form explosive mixtures in air.
- Containers may explode when heated.
- May re-ignite after fire is extinguished.

HEALTH

- Oxides from metallic fires are a severe health hazard.
- Inhalation or contact with substance or decomposition products may cause severe injury or death.
- Fire may produce irritating, corrosive and/or toxic gases.
- Runoff from fire control or dilution water may cause pollution.

PUBLIC SAFETY

- **CALL Emergency Response Telephone Number on Shipping Paper first. If Shipping Paper not available or no answer, refer to appropriate telephone number listed on the inside back cover.**
- Isolate spill or leak area immediately for at least 25 to 50 meters (80 to 160 feet) in all directions.
- Stay upwind.
- Keep unauthorized personnel away.

PROTECTIVE CLOTHING

- Wear positive pressure self-contained breathing apparatus (SCBA).
- Structural firefighters' protective clothing will only provide limited protection.

EVACUATION

Large Spill

- Consider initial downwind evacuation for at least 50 meters (160 feet).

Fire

- If tank, rail car or tank truck is involved in a fire, ISOLATE for 800 meters (1/2 mile) in all directions; also, consider initial evacuation for 800 meters (1/2 mile) in all directions.

EMERGENCY RESPONSE

FIRE

- **DO NOT USE WATER, FOAM OR CO_2.**
- Dousing metallic fires with water may generate hydrogen gas, an extremely dangerous explosion hazard, particularly if fire is in a confined environment (i.e., building, cargo hold, etc.).
- Use DRY sand, graphite powder, dry sodium chloride based extinguishers, G-1® or Met-L-X® powder.
- Confining and smothering metal fires is preferable rather than applying water.
- Move containers from fire area if you can do it without risk.

Fire involving Tanks or Car/Trailer Loads

- If impossible to extinguish, protect surroundings and allow fire to burn itself out.

SPILL OR LEAK

- ELIMINATE all ignition sources (no smoking, flares, sparks or flames in immediate area).
- Do not touch or walk through spilled material.
- Stop leak if you can do it without risk.
- Prevent entry into waterways, sewers, basements or confined areas.

FIRST AID

- Move victim to fresh air. • Call 911 or emergency medical service.
- Apply artificial respiration if victim is not breathing.
- Administer oxygen if breathing is difficult.
- Remove and isolate contaminated clothing and shoes.
- In case of contact with substance, immediately flush skin or eyes with running water for at least 20 minutes.
- Keep victim warm and quiet.
- Ensure that medical personnel are aware of the material(s) involved, and take precautions to protect themselves.

POTENTIAL HAZARDS

FIRE OR EXPLOSION

- Some may burn but none ignite readily.
- Those substances designated with a "P" may polymerize explosively when heated or involved in a fire.
- Containers may explode when heated.
- Some may be transported hot.

HEALTH

- Inhalation of material may be harmful.
- Contact may cause burns to skin and eyes.
- Inhalation of Asbestos dust may have a damaging effect on the lungs.
- Fire may produce irritating, corrosive and/or toxic gases.
- Runoff from fire control may cause pollution.

PUBLIC SAFETY

- **CALL Emergency Response Telephone Number on Shipping Paper first. If Shipping Paper not available or no answer, refer to appropriate telephone number listed on the inside back cover.**
- Isolate spill or leak area immediately for at least 10 to 25 meters (30 to 80 feet) in all directions.
- Keep unauthorized personnel away.
- Stay upwind.

PROTECTIVE CLOTHING

- Wear positive pressure self-contained breathing apparatus (SCBA).
- Structural firefighters' protective clothing will only provide limited protection.

EVACUATION

Fire

- If tank, rail car or tank truck is involved in a fire, ISOLATE for 800 meters (1/2 mile) in all directions; also, consider initial evacuation for 800 meters (1/2 mile) in all directions.

EMERGENCY RESPONSE

FIRE

Small Fires

- Dry chemical, CO_2, water spray or regular foam.

Large Fires

- Water spray, fog or regular foam.
- Move containers from fire area if you can do it without risk.
- Do not scatter spilled material with high pressure water streams.
- Dike fire-control water for later disposal.

Fire involving Tanks

- Cool containers with flooding quantities of water until well after fire is out.
- Withdraw immediately in case of rising sound from venting safety devices or discoloration of tank.
- ALWAYS stay away from tanks engulfed in fire.

SPILL OR LEAK

- Do not touch or walk through spilled material.
- Stop leak if you can do it without risk.
- Prevent dust cloud.
- Avoid inhalation of asbestos dust.

Small Dry Spills

- With clean shovel place material into clean, dry container and cover loosely; move containers from spill area.

Small Spills

- Take up with sand or other noncombustible absorbent material and place into containers for later disposal.

Large Spills

- Dike far ahead of liquid spill for later disposal.
- Cover powder spill with plastic sheet or tarp to minimize spreading.
- Prevent entry into waterways, sewers, basements or confined areas.

FIRST AID

- Move victim to fresh air.   • Call 911 or emergency medical service.
- Apply artificial respiration if victim is not breathing.
- Administer oxygen if breathing is difficult.
- Remove and isolate contaminated clothing and shoes.
- In case of contact with substance, immediately flush skin or eyes with running water for at least 20 minutes.
- Ensure that medical personnel are aware of the material(s) involved, and take precautions to protect themselves.

POTENTIAL HAZARDS

HEALTH

- Inhalation of vapors or contact with substance will result in contamination and potential harmful effects.
- Fire will produce irritating, corrosive and/or toxic gases.

FIRE OR EXPLOSION

- Non-combustible, substance itself does not burn but may react upon heating to produce corrosive and/or toxic fumes.
- Runoff may pollute waterways.

PUBLIC SAFETY

- **CALL Emergency Response Telephone Number on Shipping Paper first. If Shipping Paper not available or no answer, refer to appropriate telephone number listed on the inside back cover.**
- Isolate spill or leak area immediately for at least 10 to 25 meters (30 to 80 feet) in all directions.
- Stay upwind.
- Keep unauthorized personnel away.

PROTECTIVE CLOTHING

- Wear positive pressure self-contained breathing apparatus (SCBA).
- Structural firefighters' protective clothing will only provide limited protection.

EVACUATION

Large Spill

- Consider initial downwind evacuation for at least 100 meters (330 feet).

Fire

- When any large container is involved in a fire, consider initial evacuation for 500 meters (1/3 mile) in all directions.

EMERGENCY RESPONSE

FIRE
- Use extinguishing agent suitable for type of surrounding fire.
- **Do not direct water at the heated metal.**

SPILL OR LEAK
- Do not touch or walk through spilled material.
- Do not touch damaged containers or spilled material unless wearing appropriate protective clothing.
- Stop leak if you can do it without risk.
- Prevent entry into waterways, sewers, basements or confined areas.
- Do not use steel or aluminum tools or equipment.
- Cover with earth, sand, or other non-combustible material followed with plastic sheet to minimize spreading or contact with rain.
- For mercury, use a mercury spill kit.
- Mercury spill areas may be subsequently treated with calcium sulphide/calcium sulfide or with sodium thiosulphate/sodium thiosulfate wash to neutralize any residual mercury.

FIRST AID
- Move victim to fresh air.   • Call 911 or emergency medical service.
- Apply artificial respiration if victim is not breathing.
- Administer oxygen if breathing is difficult.
- Remove and isolate contaminated clothing and shoes.
- In case of contact with substance, immediately flush skin or eyes with running water for at least 20 minutes.
- Keep victim warm and quiet.
- Ensure that medical personnel are aware of the material(s) involved, and take precautions to protect themselves.

INTRODUCTION TO THE TABLE OF INITIAL ISOLATION AND PROTECTIVE ACTION DISTANCES

The Table of Initial Isolation and Protective Action Distances suggests distances useful to protect people from vapors resulting from spills involving dangerous goods which are considered toxic by inhalation (TIH), including certain chemical warfare agents, or which produce toxic gases upon contact with water. The Table provides first responders with initial guidance until technically qualified emergency response personnel are available. **Distances show areas likely to be affected during the first 30 minutes after materials are spilled and could increase with time.**

The **Initial Isolation Zone** defines an area SURROUNDING the incident in which persons may be exposed to dangerous (upwind) and life threatening (downwind) concentrations of material. The **Protective Action Zone** defines an area DOWNWIND from the incident in which persons may become incapacitated and unable to take protective action and/or incur serious or irreversible health effects. The Table provides specific guidance for small and large spills occurring day or night.

Adjusting distances for a specific incident involves many interdependent variables and should be made only by personnel technically qualified to make such adjustments. For this reason, no precise guidance can be provided in this document to aid in adjusting the table distances; however, general guidance follows.

Factors That May Change the Protective Action Distances

The guide for a material clearly indicates the evacuation distance required to protect against fragmentation hazard. If the material becomes involved in a **FIRE**, the toxic hazard may become less important than the fire or explosion hazard.

If more than one tank car, cargo tank, portable tank, or large cylinder involved in the incident is leaking, LARGE SPILL distances may need to be increased.

For material with a protective action distance of 11.0+ km (7.0+ miles), the actual distance can be larger in certain atmospheric conditions. If the dangerous goods vapor plume is channeled in a valley or between many tall buildings, distances may be larger than shown in the Table due to less mixing of the plume with the atmosphere. Daytime spills in regions with known strong inversions or snow cover, or occurring near sunset, accompanied by a steady wind, may require an increase in protective action distance. When these conditions are present, airborne contaminants mix and disperse more slowly and may travel much farther downwind. In addition, protective action distances may be larger for liquid spills when either the material or outdoor temperature exceeds 30°C (86°F).

Materials which react with water to produce significant toxic gases are included in the Table of Initial Isolation and Protective Action Distances. Note that some materials which are TIH (e.g., bromine trifluoride, thionyl chloride, etc.) produce additional TIH materials when spilled in water. For these materials, two entries are provided in the Table of Initial Isolation and Protective Action Distances. If it is not clear whether the spill is on land or in water, or in cases where the spill occurs both on land and in water, choose the larger Protective Action Distance. Following the Table of Initial Isolation and Protective Action Distances is a table that lists the materials which, when spilled in water, produce toxic gases and the toxic gases that these water reactive materials produce.

When a water reactive TIH producing material is spilled into a river or stream, the source of the toxic gas may move with the current or stretch from the spill point downstream for a substantial distance.

Certain chemical warfare agents have been added to the Table of Initial Isolation and Protective Action Distances. The distances shown were calculated using worst case scenarios for these agents **when used as a weapon**.

PROTECTIVE ACTION DECISION FACTORS TO CONSIDER

The choice of protective options for a given situation depends on a number of factors. For some cases, evacuation may be the best option; in others, sheltering in-place may be the best course. Sometimes, these two actions may be used in combination. In any emergency, officials need to quickly give the public instructions. The public will need continuing information and instructions while being evacuated or sheltered in-place.

Proper evaluation of the factors listed below will determine the effectiveness of evacuation or in-place protection. The importance of these factors can vary with emergency conditions. In specific emergencies, other factors may need to be identified and considered as well. This list indicates what kind of information may be needed to make the initial decision.

The Dangerous Goods

- Degree of health hazard
- Amount involved
- Containment/control of release
- Rate of vapor movement

The Population Threatened

- Location
- Number of people
- Time available to evacuate or shelter in-place
- Ability to control evacuation or shelter in-place
- Building types and availability
- Special institutions or populations, e.g., nursing homes, hospitals, prisons

Weather Conditions

- Effect on vapor and cloud movement
- Potential for change
- Effect on evacuation or protection in-place

PROTECTIVE ACTIONS

Protective Actions are those steps taken to preserve the health and safety of emergency responders and the public during an incident involving releases of dangerous goods. The Table of Initial Isolation and Protective Action Distances (green-bordered pages) predicts the size of downwind areas which could be affected by a cloud of toxic gas. People in this area should be evacuated and/or sheltered in-place inside buildings.

Isolate Hazard Area and Deny Entry means keep everybody away from the area if they are not directly involved in emergency response operations. Unprotected emergency responders should not be allowed to enter the isolation zone. This "isolation" task is done first to establish control over the area of operations. This is the first step for any protective actions that may follow. See the Table of Isolation and Protective Action Distances (green-bordered pages) for more detailed information on specific materials.

Evacuate means move all people from a threatened area to a safer place. To perform an evacuation, there must be enough time for people to be warned, to get ready, and to leave an area. If there is enough time, evacuation is the best protective action. Begin evacuating people nearby and those outdoors in direct view of the scene. When additional help arrives, expand the area to be evacuated downwind and crosswind to at least the extent recommended in this guidebook. Even after people move to the distances recommended, they may not be completely safe from harm. They should not be permitted to congregate at such distances. Send evacuees to a definite place, by a specific route, far enough away so they will not have to be moved again if the wind shifts.

Shelter In-Place means people should seek shelter inside a building and remain inside until the danger passes. **Sheltering in-place is used when evacuating the public would cause greater risk than staying where they are, or when an evacuation cannot be performed.** Direct the people inside to **close all doors and windows** and to **shut off all ventilating, heating and cooling systems.** In-place protection may not be the best option if (a) the vapors are flammable; (b) if it will take a long time for the gas to clear the area; or (c) if buildings cannot be closed tightly. Vehicles can offer some protection for a short period if the windows are closed and the ventilating systems are shut off. Vehicles are not as effective as buildings for in-place protection.

It is vital to maintain communications with competent persons inside the building so that they are advised about changing conditions. **Persons protected-in-place should be warned to stay far from windows** because of the danger from glass and projected metal fragments in a fire and/or explosion.

Every dangerous goods incident is different. Each will have special problems and concerns. Action to protect the public must be selected carefully. These pages can help with **initial** decisions on how to protect the public. Officials must continue to gather information and monitor the situation until the threat is removed.

BACKGROUND ON THE INITIAL ISOLATION
AND PROTECTIVE ACTION DISTANCE TABLE

Initial Isolation and Protective Action Distances in this guidebook were determined for small and large spills occurring during day or night. The overall analysis was statistical in nature and utilized state-of-the-art emission rate and dispersion models; statistical release data from the U.S. DOT HMIS (Hazardous Materials Incident Reporting System) database; 5 years of meteorological observations from over 120 locations in United States, Canada and Mexico; and the most current toxicological exposure guidelines.

For each chemical, thousands of hypothetical releases were modeled to account for the statistical variation in both release amount and atmospheric conditions. Based on this statistical sample, the 90% percentile Protective Action Distance for each chemical and category was selected to appear in the Table. A brief description of the analysis is provided below. A detailed report outlining the methodology and data used in the generation of the Initial Isolation and Protective Action Distances may be obtained from the U.S. Department of Transportation, Research and Special Programs Administration.

Release amounts and emission rates into the atmosphere were statistically modeled based on (1) data from the U.S. DOT HMIS database; (2) container types and sizes authorized for transport as specified in 49 CFR §172.101 and Part 173; (3) physical properties of the materials involved, and (4) atmospheric data from a historical database. The emission model calculated the release of vapor due to evaporation of pools on the ground, direct release of vapors from the container, or a combination of both, as would occur for liquefied gases which can flash to form both a vapor/ aerosol mixture and an evaporating pool. In addition, the emission model also calculated the emission of toxic vapor by-products generated from spilling water-reactive chemicals in water. Spills that involve releases of approximately 200 liters or less are considered Small Spills, while spills that involve quantities greater than 200 liters are considered Large Spills.

Downwind dispersion of the vapor was estimated for each case modeled. Atmospheric parameters affecting the dispersion, and the emission rate, were selected in a statistical fashion from a database containing hourly meteorological data from 120 cities in United States, Canada and Mexico. The dispersion calculation accounted for the time dependent emission rate from the source as well as the density of the vapor plume (i.e., heavy gas effects). Since atmospheric mixing is less effective at dispersing vapor plumes during nighttime, day and night were separated in the analysis. In the Table, "Day" refers to time periods after sunrise and before sunset, while "Night" includes all hours between sunset and sunrise.

Toxicological short-term exposure guidelines for the chemicals were applied to determine the downwind distance to which persons may become incapacitated and unable to take protective action or may incur serious health effects. Toxicological exposure guidelines were chosen from (1) emergency response guidelines, (2) occupational health guidelines, or (3) lethal concentrations determined from animal studies, as recommended by an independent panel of toxicological experts from industry and academia.

HOW TO USE THE TABLE OF INITIAL ISOLATION AND PROTECTIVE ACTION DISTANCES

(1) The responder should already have:

- Identified the material by its ID Number and Name; (if an ID Number cannot be found, use the name of material index in the blue-bordered pages to locate that number.)
- Found the three-digit guide for that material in order to consult the emergency actions recommended jointly with this table;
- **Noted the wind direction.**

(2) Look in this Table (the green-bordered pages) for the ID Number and Name of the Material involved in the incident. Some ID Numbers have more than one shipping name listed—look for the specific name of the material. (If the shipping name is not known and the Table lists more than one name for the same ID Number, use the entry with the largest protective action distances.)

(3) Determine if the incident involves a SMALL or LARGE spill and if DAY or NIGHT. Generally, a SMALL SPILL is one which involves a single, small package (e.g., a drum containing up to approximately 200 liters), a small cylinder, or a small leak from a large package. A LARGE SPILL is one which involves a spill from a large package, or multiple spills from many small packages. DAY is any time after sunrise and before sunset. NIGHT is any time between sunset and sunrise.

(4) Look up the initial ISOLATION distance. Direct all persons to move, in a crosswind direction, away from the spill to the distance specified—in meters and feet.

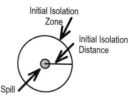

(5) Look up the initial PROTECTIVE ACTION DISTANCE shown in the Table. For a given dangerous goods, spill size, and whether day or night, the Table gives the downwind distance—in kilometers and miles— for which protective actions should be considered. For practical purposes, the Protective Action Zone (i.e., the area in which people are at risk of harmful exposure) is a square, whose length and width are the same as the downwind distance shown in the Table.

(6) Initiate Protective Actions to the extent possible, beginning with those closest to the spill site and working away from the site in the downwind direction. When a water-reactive TIH producing material is spilled into a river or stream, the source of the toxic gas may move with the current or stretch from the spill point downstream for a substantial distance.

The shape of the area in which protective actions should be taken (the Protective Action Zone) is shown in this figure. The spill is located at the center of the small circle. The larger circle represents the INITIAL ISOLATION zone around the spill.

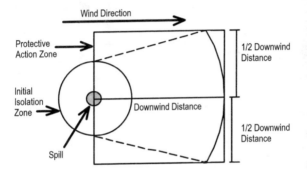

NOTE: See "Introduction To The Table Of Initial Isolation And Protective Action Distances" for factors which may increase or decrease Protective Action Distances.

Call the emergency response telephone number listed on the shipping paper, or the appropriate response agency as soon as possible for additional information on the material, safety precautions, and mitigation procedures.

TABLE OF INITIAL ISOLATION AND PROTECTIVE ACTION DISTANCES

		SMALL SPILLS				LARGE SPILLS			
		(From a small package or small leak from a large package)				(From a large package or from many small packages)			
		First ISOLATE in all Directions		Then PROTECT persons Downwind during-		First ISOLATE in all Directions		Then PROTECT persons Downwind during-	
				DAY	NIGHT			DAY	NIGHT
ID No.	NAME OF MATERIAL	Meters	(Feet)	Kilometers (Miles)	Kilometers (Miles)	Meters	(Feet)	Kilometers (Miles)	Kilometers (Miles)
1005	Ammonia, anhydrous	30 m	(100 ft)	0.2 km (0.1 mi)	0.2 km (0.1 mi)	60 m	(200 ft)	0.5 km (0.3 mi)	1.1 km (0.7 mi)
1005	Ammonia, anhydrous, liquefied								
1005	Ammonia, solution, with more than 50% Ammonia								
1005	Anhydrous ammonia								
1005	Anhydrous ammonia, liquefied								
1008	Boron trifluoride	30 m	(100 ft)	0.2 km (0.1 mi)	0.6 km (0.4 mi)	215 m	(700 ft)	1.6 km (1.0 mi)	5.1 km (3.2 mi)
1008	Boron trifluoride, compressed								
1016	Carbon monoxide	30 m	(100 ft)	0.2 km (0.1 mi)	0.2 km (0.1 mi)	125 m	(400 ft)	0.6 km (0.4 mi)	1.8 km (1.1 mi)
1016	Carbon monoxide, compressed								
1017	Chlorine	30 m	(100 ft)	0.3 km (0.2 mi)	1.1 km (0.7 mi)	275 m	(900 ft)	2.7 km (1.7 mi)	6.8 km (4.2 mi)
1023	Coal gas	30 m	(100 ft)	0.2 km (0.1 mi)	0.2 km (0.1 mi)	60 m	(200 ft)	0.3 km (0.2 mi)	0.5 km (0.3 mi)
1023	Coal gas, compressed								
1026	Cyanogen	30 m	(100 ft)	0.3 km (0.2 mi)	1.1 km (0.7 mi)	305 m	(1000 ft)	3.1 km (1.9 mi)	7.7 km (4.8 mi)
1026	Cyanogen, liquefied								
1026	Cyanogen gas								
1040	Ethylene oxide	30 m	(100 ft)	0.2 km (0.1 mi)	0.2 km (0.1 mi)	60 m	(200 ft)	0.5 km (0.3 mi)	1.8 km (1.1 mi)
1040	Ethylene oxide with Nitrogen								
1045	Fluorine	30 m	(100 ft)	0.2 km (0.1 mi)	0.5 km (0.3 mi)	185 m	(600 ft)	1.4 km (0.9 mi)	4.0 km (2.5 mi)
1045	Fluorine, compressed								
1048	Hydrogen bromide, anhydrous	30 m	(100 ft)	0.2 km (0.1 mi)	0.5 km (0.3 mi)	125 m	(400 ft)	1.1 km (0.7 mi)	3.4 km (2.1 mi)
1050	Hydrogen chloride, anhydrous	30 m	(100 ft)	0.2 km (0.1 mi)	0.6 km (0.4 mi)	185 m	(600 ft)	1.6 km (1.0 mi)	4.3 km (2.7 mi)
1051	AC (when used as a weapon)	60 m	(200 ft)	0.2 km (0.1 mi)	0.5 km (0.3 mi)	460 m	(1500 ft)	1.5 km (1.0 mi)	3.9 km (2.4 mi)

ID No.	Name of Material	SMALL SPILLS First ISOLATE in all Directions	Then PROTECT persons Downwind during DAY	Then PROTECT persons Downwind during NIGHT	LARGE SPILLS First ISOLATE in all Directions	Then PROTECT persons Downwind during DAY	Then PROTECT persons Downwind during NIGHT
1051 1051 1051 1051	Hydrocyanic acid, aqueous solutions, with more than 20% Hydrogen cyanide; Hydrocyanic acid, liquefied; Hydrogen cyanide, anhydrous, stabilized; Hydrogen cyanide, stabilized	60 m (200 ft)	0.2 km (0.1 mi)	0.5 km (0.3 mi)	400 m (1300 ft)	1.3 km (0.8 mi)	3.4 km (2.1 mi)
1052	Hydrogen fluoride, anhydrous	30 m (100 ft)	0.2 km (0.1 mi)	0.6 km (0.4 mi)	125 m (400 ft)	1.1 km (0.7 mi)	2.9 km (1.8 mi)
1053 1053 1053 1053	Hydrogen sulfide; Hydrogen sulfide, liquefied; Hydrogen sulphide; Hydrogen sulphide, liquefied	30 m (100 ft)	0.2 km (0.1 mi)	0.3 km (0.2 mi)	215 m (700 ft)	1.4 km (0.9 mi)	4.3 km (2.7 mi)
1062	Methyl bromide	30 m (100 ft)	0.2 km (0.1 mi)	0.3 km (0.2 mi)	95 m (300 ft)	0.5 km (0.3 mi)	1.4 km (0.9 mi)
1064	Methyl mercaptan	30 m (100 ft)	0.2 km (0.1 mi)	0.3 km (0.2 mi)	95 m (300 ft)	0.8 km (0.5 mi)	2.7 km (1.7 mi)
1067 1067 1067 1067 1067 1067	Dinitrogen tetroxide; Dinitrogen tetroxide, liquefied; Nitrogen dioxide; Nitrogen dioxide, liquefied; Nitrogen peroxide, liquid; Nitrogen tetroxide, liquid	30 m (100 ft)	0.2 km (0.1 mi)	0.5 km (0.3 mi)	305 m (1000 ft)	1.3 km (0.8 mi)	3.9 km (2.4 mi)
1069	Nitrosyl chloride	30 m (100 ft)	0.3 km (0.2 mi)	1.4 km (0.9 mi)	365 m (1200 ft)	3.5 km (2.2 mi)	9.8 km (6.1 mi)
1071 1071	Oil gas; Oil gas, compressed	30 m (100 ft)	0.2 km (0.1 mi)	0.2 km (0.1 mi)	30 m (100 ft)	0.3 km (0.2 mi)	0.5 km (0.3 mi)
1076	CG (when used as a weapon)	155 m (500 ft)	1.3 km (0.8 mi)	3.2 km (2.0 mi)	765 m (2500 ft)	7.2 km (4.5 mi)	11.0+ km (7.0+ mi)
1076	Diphosgene	60 m (200 ft)	0.2 km (0.1 mi)	0.5 km (0.3 mi)	95 m (300 ft)	1.0 km (0.6 mi)	1.9 km (1.2 mi)
1076	DP (when used as a weapon)	60 m (200 ft)	0.3 km (0.2 mi)	1.0 km (0.6 mi)	185 m (600 ft)	1.6 km (1.0 mi)	4.5 km (2.8 mi)
1076	Phosgene	95 m (300 ft)	0.8 km (0.5 mi)	2.7 km (1.7 mi)	765 m (2500 ft)	6.6 km (4.1 mi)	11.0 km (6.9 mi)
1079 1079 1079 1079	Sulfur dioxide; Sulfur dioxide, liquefied; Sulphur dioxide; Sulphur dioxide, liquefied	30 m (100 ft)	0.3 km (0.2 mi)	1.1 km (0.7 mi)	185 m (600 ft)	3.1 km (1.9 mi)	7.2 km (4.5 mi)

"+" means distance can be larger in certain atmospheric conditions

TABLE OF INITIAL ISOLATION AND PROTECTIVE ACTION DISTANCES

ID No.	NAME OF MATERIAL	SMALL SPILLS (From a small package or small leak from a large package)				LARGE SPILLS (From a large package or from many small packages)			
		First ISOLATE in all Directions		Then PROTECT persons Downwind during-		First ISOLATE in all Directions		Then PROTECT persons Downwind during-	
				DAY	NIGHT			DAY	NIGHT
		Meters	(Feet)	Kilometers (Miles)	Kilometers (Miles)	Meters	(Feet)	Kilometers (Miles)	Kilometers (Miles)
1082 1082	Trifluorochloroethylene Trifluorochloroethylene, inhibited	30 m	(100 ft)	0.2 km (0.1 mi)	0.2 km (0.1 mi)	30 m	(100 ft)	0.3 km (0.2 mi)	0.8 km (0.5 mi)
1092	Acrolein, inhibited	60 m	(200 ft)	0.5 km (0.3 mi)	1.6 km (1.0 mi)	400 m	(1300 ft)	3.9 km (2.4 mi)	7.9 km (4.9 mi)
1098	Allyl alcohol	30 m	(100 ft)	0.2 km (0.1 mi)	0.2 km (0.1 mi)	30 m	(100 ft)	0.3 km (0.2 mi)	0.6 km (0.4 mi)
1135	Ethylene chlorohydrin	30 m	(100 ft)	0.2 km (0.1 mi)	0.3 km (0.2 mi)	60 m	(200 ft)	0.6 km (0.4 mi)	1.3 km (0.8 mi)
1143 1143	Crotonaldehyde, inhibited Crotonaldehyde, stabilized	30 m	(100 ft)	0.2 km (0.1 mi)	0.2 km (0.1 mi)	30 m	(100 ft)	0.3 km (0.2 mi)	0.8 km (0.5 mi)
1162	Dimethyldichlorosilane (when spilled in water)	30 m	(100 ft)	0.2 km (0.1 mi)	0.3 km (0.2 mi)	125 m	(400 ft)	1.1 km (0.7 mi)	2.9 km (1.8 mi)
1163 1163	1,1-Dimethylhydrazine Dimethylhydrazine, unsymmetrical	30 m	(100 ft)	0.2 km (0.1 mi)	0.2 km (0.1 mi)	60 m	(200 ft)	0.5 km (0.3 mi)	1.1 km (0.7 mi)
1182	Ethyl chloroformate	30 m	(100 ft)	0.2 km (0.1 mi)	0.3 km (0.2 mi)	60 m	(200 ft)	0.6 km (0.4 mi)	1.4 km (0.9 mi)
1185	Ethyleneimine, inhibited	30 m	(100 ft)	0.3 km (0.2 mi)	0.8 km (0.5 mi)	155 m	(500 ft)	1.4 km (0.9 mi)	3.5 km (2.2 mi)
1238	Methyl chloroformate	30 m	(100 ft)	0.3 km (0.2 mi)	1.1 km (0.7 mi)	155 m	(500 ft)	1.6 km (1.0 mi)	3.4 km (2.1 mi)
1239	Methyl chloromethyl ether	30 m	(100 ft)	0.2 km (0.1 mi)	0.6 km (0.4 mi)	125 m	(400 ft)	1.1 km (0.7 mi)	2.7 km (1.7 mi)
1242	Methyldichlorosilane (when spilled in water)	30 m	(100 ft)	0.2 km (0.1 mi)	0.2 km (0.1 mi)	60 m	(200 ft)	0.5 km (0.3 mi)	1.6 km (1.0 mi)
1244	Methylhydrazine	30 m	(100 ft)	0.3 km (0.2 mi)	0.8 km (0.5 mi)	125 m	(400 ft)	1.1 km (0.7 mi)	2.7 km (1.7 mi)
1250	Methyltrichlorosilane (when spilled in water)	30 m	(100 ft)	0.2 km (0.1 mi)	0.3 km (0.2 mi)	125 m	(400 ft)	1.1 km (0.7 mi)	2.9 km (1.8 mi)
1251 1251	Methyl vinyl ketone Methyl vinyl ketone, stabilized	155 m	(500 ft)	1.3 km (0.8 mi)	3.4 km (2.1 mi)	915 m	(3000 ft)	8.7 km (5.4 mi)	11.0+ km (7.0+ mi)

ID No.	Name of Material	SMALL SPILLS First ISOLATE in all Directions	SMALL SPILLS Then PROTECT persons Downwind DAY	SMALL SPILLS Then PROTECT persons Downwind NIGHT	LARGE SPILLS First ISOLATE in all Directions	LARGE SPILLS Then PROTECT persons Downwind DAY	LARGE SPILLS Then PROTECT persons Downwind NIGHT
1259	Nickel carbonyl	60 m (200 ft)	0.6 km (0.4 mi)	2.1 km (1.3 mi)	215 m (700 ft)	2.1 km (1.3 mi)	4.3 km (2.7 mi)
1295	Trichlorosilane (when spilled in water)	30 m (100 ft)	0.2 km (0.1 mi)	0.3 km (0.2 mi)	125 m (400 ft)	1.3 km (0.8 mi)	3.2 km (2.0 mi)
1298	Trimethylchlorosilane (when spilled in water)	30 m (100 ft)	0.2 km (0.1 mi)	0.2 km (0.1 mi)	95 m (300 ft)	0.8 km (0.5 mi)	2.3 km (1.4 mi)
1340	Phosphorus pentasulfide, free from yellow or white Phosphorus (when spilled in water)	30 m (100 ft)	0.2 km (0.1 mi)	0.5 km (0.3 mi)	155 m (500 ft)	1.3 km (0.8 mi)	3.2 km (2.0 mi)
1340	Phosphorus pentasulphide, free from yellow or white Phosphorus (when spilled in water)						
1360	Calcium phosphide (when spilled in water)	30 m (100 ft)	0.2 km (0.1 mi)	0.8 km (0.5 mi)	215 m (700 ft)	2.1 km (1.3 mi)	5.3 km (3.3 mi)
1380	Pentaborane	155 m (500 ft)	1.3 km (0.8 mi)	3.7 km (2.3 mi)	765 m (2500 ft)	6.6 km (4.1 mi)	10.6 km (6.6 mi)
1384	Sodium dithionite (when spilled in water)	30 m (100 ft)	0.2 km (0.1 mi)	0.2 km (0.1 mi)	30 m (100 ft)	0.3 km (0.2 mi)	1.1 km (0.7 mi)
1384	Sodium hydrosulfite (when spilled in water)						
1384	Sodium hydrosulphite (when spilled in water)						
1397	Aluminum phosphide (when spilled in water)	30 m (100 ft)	0.2 km (0.1 mi)	0.8 km (0.5 mi)	245 m (800 ft)	2.4 km (1.5 mi)	6.4 km (4.0 mi)
1412	Lithium amide (when spilled in water)	30 m (100 ft)	0.2 km (0.1 mi)	0.2 km (0.1 mi)	95 m (300 ft)	0.8 km (0.5 mi)	1.9 km (1.2 mi)
1419	Magnesium aluminum phosphide (when spilled in water)	30 m (100 ft)	0.2 km (0.1 mi)	0.8 km (0.5 mi)	215 m (700 ft)	2.1 km (1.3 mi)	5.5 km (3.4 mi)
1432	Sodium phosphide (when spilled in water)	30 m (100 ft)	0.2 km (0.1 mi)	0.5 km (0.3 mi)	155 m (500 ft)	1.4 km (0.9 mi)	4.0 km (2.5 mi)
1433	Stannic phosphides (when spilled in water)	30 m (100 ft)	0.2 km (0.1 mi)	0.8 km (0.5 mi)	185 m (600 ft)	1.6 km (1.0 mi)	4.7 km (2.9 mi)
1510	Tetranitromethane	30 m (100 ft)	0.3 km (0.2 mi)	0.5 km (0.3 mi)	60 m (200 ft)	0.6 km (0.4 mi)	1.3 km (0.8 mi)

"+" means distance can be larger in certain atmospheric conditions

TABLE OF INITIAL ISOLATION AND PROTECTIVE ACTION DISTANCES

ID No.	NAME OF MATERIAL	SMALL SPILLS (From a small package or small leak from a large package)			LARGE SPILLS (From a large package or from many small packages)		
		First ISOLATE in all Directions Meters (Feet)	Then PROTECT persons Downwind during— DAY Kilometers (Miles)	NIGHT Kilometers (Miles)	First ISOLATE in all Directions Meters (Feet)	Then PROTECT persons Downwind during— DAY Kilometers (Miles)	NIGHT Kilometers (Miles)
1541	Acetone cyanohydrin, stabilized (when spilled in water)	30 m (100 ft)	0.2 km (0.1 mi)	0.2 km (0.1 mi)	95 m (300 ft)	0.8 km (0.5 mi)	2.1 km (1.3 mi)
1556	MD (when used as a weapon)	30 m (100 ft)	0.3 km (0.2 mi)	0.8 km (0.5 mi)	125 m (400 ft)	1.3 km (0.8 mi)	3.5 km (2.2 mi)
1556	Methyldichloroarsine	30 m (100 ft)	0.2 km (0.1 mi)	0.3 km (0.2 mi)	60 m (200 ft)	0.5 km (0.3 mi)	1.0 km (0.6 mi)
1556	PD (when used as a weapon)	30 m (100 ft)	0.2 km (0.1 mi)	0.2 km (0.1 mi)	30 m (100 ft)	0.2 km (0.1 mi)	0.3 km (0.2 mi)
1560 1560	Arsenic chloride Arsenic trichloride	30 m (100 ft)	0.2 km (0.1 mi)	0.3 km (0.2 mi)	60 m (200 ft)	0.6 km (0.4 mi)	1.4 km (0.9 mi)
1569	Bromoacetone	30 m (100 ft)	0.2 km (0.1 mi)	0.3 km (0.2 mi)	95 m (300 ft)	0.8 km (0.5 mi)	1.9 km (1.2 mi)
1580	Chloropicrin	60 m (200 ft)	0.5 km (0.3 mi)	1.3 km (0.8 mi)	185 m (600 ft)	1.8 km (1.1 mi)	4.0 km (2.5 mi)
1581	Chloropicrin and Methyl bromide mixture	30 m (100 ft)	0.2 km (0.1 mi)	0.5 km (0.3 mi)	125 m (400 ft)	1.3 km (0.8 mi)	3.1 km (1.9 mi)
1581	Methyl bromide and Chloropicrin mixtures						
1581	Methyl bromide and more than 2% Chloropicrin mixture, liquid	30 m (100 ft)	0.3 km (0.2 mi)	1.1 km (0.7 mi)	215 m (700 ft)	2.1 km (1.3 mi)	5.6 km (3.5 mi)
1582	Chloropicrin and Methyl chloride mixture	30 m (100 ft)	0.2 km (0.1 mi)	0.8 km (0.5 mi)	95 m (300 ft)	1.0 km (0.6 mi)	3.2 km (2.0 mi)
1582	Methyl chloride and Chloropicrin mixtures						
1583	Chloropicrin, absorbed	60 m (200 ft)	0.5 km (0.3 mi)	1.3 km (0.8 mi)	185 m (600 ft)	1.8 km (1.1 mi)	4.0 km (2.5 mi)
1583	Chloropicrin mixture, n.o.s.	30 m (100 ft)	0.3 km (0.2 mi)	1.1 km (0.7 mi)	215 m (700 ft)	2.1 km (1.3 mi)	5.6 km (3.5 mi)
1589	CK (when used as a weapon)	60 m (200 ft)	0.6 km (0.4 mi)	2.4 km (1.5 mi)	400 m (1300 ft)	4.0 km (2.5 mi)	8.0 km (5.0 mi)

ID No.	Name of Material	SMALL SPILLS First ISOLATE in all Directions	Then PROTECT persons Downwind during DAY	Then PROTECT persons Downwind during NIGHT	LARGE SPILLS First ISOLATE in all Directions	Then PROTECT persons Downwind during DAY	Then PROTECT persons Downwind during NIGHT
1589	Cyanogen chloride, inhibited	60 m (200 ft)	0.5 km (0.3 mi)	1.8 km (1.1 mi)	275 m (900 ft)	2.7 km (1.7 mi)	6.8 km (4.2 mi)
1595 1595	Dimethyl sulfate Dimethyl sulphate	30 m (100 ft)	0.2 km (0.1 mi)	0.2 km (0.1 mi)	30 m (100 ft)	0.3 km (0.2 mi)	0.6 km (0.4 mi)
1605	Ethylene dibromide	30 m (100 ft)	0.2 km (0.1 mi)	0.2 km (0.1 mi)	30 m (100 ft)	0.3 km (0.2 mi)	0.5 km (0.3 mi)
1612	Hexaethyl tetraphosphate and compressed gas mixture	30 m (100 ft)	0.2 km (0.1 mi)	0.2 km (0.1 mi)	30 m (100 ft)	0.3 km (0.2 mi)	1.4 km (0.9 mi)
1613 1613	Hydrocyanic acid, aqueous solution, with not more than 20% Hydrogen cyanide (when "Inhalation Hazard" is on a package or shipping paper) Hydrogen cyanide, aqueous solution, with not more than 20% Hydrogen cyanide (when "Inhalation Hazard" is on a package or shipping paper)	30 m (100 ft)	0.2 km (0.1 mi)	0.2 km (0.1 mi)	125 m (400 ft)	0.5 km (0.3 mi)	1.3 km (0.8 mi)
1614 1614	Hydrogen cyanide, anhydrous, stabilized (absorbed) Hydrogen cyanide, stabilized (absorbed)	60 m (200 ft)	0.2 km (0.1 mi)	0.5 km (0.3 mi)	400 m (1300 ft)	1.3 km (0.8 mi)	3.4 km (2.1 mi)
1647 1647	Ethylene dibromide and Methyl bromide mixture, liquid Methyl bromide and Ethylene dibromide mixture, liquid	30 m (100 ft)	0.2 km (0.1 mi)	0.2 km (0.1 mi)	30 m (100 ft)	0.3 km (0.2 mi)	0.5 km (0.3 mi)
1660 1660	Nitric oxide Nitric oxide, compressed	30 m (100 ft)	0.3 km (0.2 mi)	1.3 km (0.8 mi)	155 m (500 ft)	1.3 km (0.8 mi)	3.5 km (2.2 mi)
1670	Perchloromethylmercaptan	30 m (100 ft)	0.2 km (0.1 mi)	0.3 km (0.2 mi)	60 m (200 ft)	0.5 km (0.3 mi)	1.1 km (0.7 mi)
1680	Potassium cyanide (when spilled in water)	30 m (100 ft)	0.2 km (0.1 mi)	0.3 km (0.2 mi)	95 m (300 ft)	0.8 km (0.5 mi)	2.6 km (1.6 mi)
1689	Sodium cyanide (when spilled in water)	30 m (100 ft)	0.2 km (0.1 mi)	0.3 km (0.2 mi)	95 m (300 ft)	1.0 km (0.6 mi)	2.6 km (1.6 mi)
1694	CA (when used as a weapon)	30 m (100 ft)	0.2 km (0.1 mi)	0.5 km (0.3 mi)	155 m (500 ft)	1.6 km (1.0 mi)	4.2 km (2.6 mi)

"+" means distance can be larger in certain atmospheric conditions

TABLE OF INITIAL ISOLATION AND PROTECTIVE ACTION DISTANCES

		SMALL SPILLS				LARGE SPILLS			
		(From a small package or small leak from a large package)				(From a large package or from many small packages)			
		First ISOLATE in all Directions	Then PROTECT persons Downwind during-			First ISOLATE in all Directions	Then PROTECT persons Downwind during-		
				DAY	NIGHT			DAY	NIGHT
ID No.	NAME OF MATERIAL	Meters (Feet)		Kilometers (Miles)	Kilometers (Miles)	Meters (Feet)		Kilometers (Miles)	Kilometers (Miles)
1695	Chloroacetone, stabilized	30 m	(100 ft)	0.2 km (0.1 mi)	0.3 km (0.2 mi)	60 m	(200 ft)	0.6 km (0.4 mi)	1.3 km (0.8 mi)
1697	CN (when used as a weapon)	30 m	(100 ft)	0.2 km (0.1 mi)	0.5 km (0.3 mi)	125 m	(400 ft)	1.1 km (0.7 mi)	3.2 km (2.0 mi)
1698 1698	Adamsite (when used as a weapon) DM (when used as a weapon)	60 m	(200 ft)	0.3 km (0.2 mi)	1.1 km (0.7 mi)	185 m	(600 ft)	2.3 km (1.4 mi)	5.1 km (3.2 mi)
1699	DA (when used as a weapon)	60 m	(200 ft)	0.3 km (0.2 mi)	1.1 km (0.7 mi)	185 m	(600 ft)	2.3 km (1.4 mi)	5.1 km (3.2 mi)
1703 1703	Tetraethyl dithiopyrophosphate and gases, in solution Tetraethyl dithiopyrophosphate and gases, mixtures	30 m	(100 ft)	0.3 km (0.2 mi)	1.1 km (0.7 mi)	365 m	(1200 ft)	3.7 km (2.3 mi)	6.9 km (4.3 mi)
1703	Tetraethyl dithiopyrophosphate and gases, mixtures, or in solution (LC50 more than 200 ppm but not more than 5000 ppm)	30 m	(100 ft)	0.2 km (0.1 mi)	0.5 km (0.3 mi)	125 m	(400 ft)	0.8 km (0.5 mi)	2.9 km (1.8 mi)
1703	Tetraethyl dithiopyrophosphate and gases, mixtures, or in solution (LC50 not more than 200 ppm)	30 m	(100 ft)	0.3 km (0.2 mi)	1.1 km (0.7 mi)	365 m	(1200 ft)	3.7 km (2.3 mi)	6.9 km (4.3 mi)
1705	Tetraethyl pyrophosphate and compressed gas mixtures	30 m	(100 ft)	0.3 km (0.2 mi)	1.3 km (0.8 mi)	400 m	(1300 ft)	4.0 km (2.5 mi)	7.2 km (4.5 mi)
1705	Tetraethyl pyrophosphate and compressed gas mixtures (LC50 more than 200 ppm but not more than 5000 ppm)	30 m	(100 ft)	0.2 km (0.1 mi)	0.5 km (0.3 mi)	125 m	(400 ft)	0.8 km (0.5 mi)	2.9 km (1.8 mi)
1705	Tetraethyl pyrophosphate and compressed gas mixtures (LC50 not more than 200 ppm)	30 m	(100 ft)	0.3 km (0.2 mi)	1.3 km (0.8 mi)	400 m	(1300 ft)	4.0 km (2.5 mi)	7.2 km (4.5 mi)

ID No.	Name of Material	SMALL SPILLS First ISOLATE in all Directions		Then PROTECT persons Downwind during DAY		Then PROTECT persons Downwind during NIGHT		LARGE SPILLS First ISOLATE in all Directions		Then PROTECT persons Downwind during DAY		Then PROTECT persons Downwind during NIGHT	
1714	Zinc phosphide (when spilled in water)	30 m	(100 ft)	0.2 km	(0.1 mi)	0.8 km	(0.5 mi)	185 m	(600 ft)	1.8 km	(1.1 mi)	5.1 km	(3.2 mi)
1716	Acetyl bromide (when spilled in water)	30 m	(100 ft)	0.2 km	(0.1 mi)	0.3 km	(0.2 mi)	95 m	(300 ft)	0.8 km	(0.5 mi)	2.3 km	(1.4 mi)
1717	Acetyl chloride (when spilled in water)	30 m	(100 ft)	0.2 km	(0.1 mi)	0.3 km	(0.2 mi)	95 m	(300 ft)	1.0 km	(0.6 mi)	2.7 km	(1.7 mi)
1722 1722	Allyl chlorocarbonate Allyl chloroformate	155 m	(500 ft)	1.3 km	(0.8 mi)	2.7 km	(1.7 mi)	610 m	(2000 ft)	6.1 km	(3.8 mi)	10.8 km	(6.7 mi)
1724	Allyltrichlorosilane, stabilized (when spilled in water)	30 m	(100 ft)	0.2 km	(0.1 mi)	0.3 km	(0.2 mi)	125 m	(400 ft)	1.0 km	(0.6 mi)	2.9 km	(1.8 mi)
1725	Aluminum bromide, anhydrous (when spilled in water)	30 m	(100 ft)	0.2 km	(0.1 mi)	0.3 km	(0.2 mi)	95 m	(300 ft)	1.0 km	(0.6 mi)	2.7 km	(1.7 mi)
1726	Aluminum chloride, anhydrous (when spilled in water)	30 m	(100 ft)	0.2 km	(0.1 mi)	0.2 km	(0.1 mi)	60 m	(200 ft)	0.5 km	(0.3 mi)	1.6 km	(1.0 mi)
1728	Amyltrichlorosilane (when spilled in water)	30 m	(100 ft)	0.2 km	(0.1 mi)	0.2 km	(0.1 mi)	60 m	(200 ft)	0.5 km	(0.3 mi)	1.6 km	(1.0 mi)
1732	Antimony pentafluoride (when spilled in water)	30 m	(100 ft)	0.2 km	(0.1 mi)	0.6 km	(0.4 mi)	155 m	(500 ft)	1.6 km	(1.0 mi)	3.7 km	(2.3 mi)
1736	Benzoyl chloride (when spilled in water)	30 m	(100 ft)	0.2 km	(0.1 mi)	0.2 km	(0.1 mi)	30 m	(100 ft)	0.3 km	(0.2 mi)	1.1 km	(0.7 mi)
1741	Boron trichloride	30 m	(100 ft)	0.2 km	(0.1 mi)	0.3 km	(0.2 mi)	60 m	(200 ft)	0.6 km	(0.4 mi)	1.6 km	(1.0 mi)
1744 1744	Bromine Bromine, solution	60 m	(200 ft)	0.3 km	(0.2 mi)	1.1 km	(0.7 mi)	185 m	(600 ft)	1.6 km	(1.0 mi)	4.0 km	(2.5 mi)
1745	Bromine pentafluoride (when spilled on land)	60 m	(200 ft)	0.5 km	(0.3 mi)	1.3 km	(0.8 mi)	245 m	(800 ft)	2.3 km	(1.4 mi)	5.0 km	(3.1 mi)
1745	Bromine pentafluoride (when spilled in water)	30 m	(100 ft)	0.2 km	(0.1 mi)	0.8 km	(0.5 mi)	215 m	(700 ft)	1.9 km	(1.2 mi)	4.2 km	(2.6 mi)
1746	Bromine trifluoride (when spilled on land)	30 m	(100 ft)	0.2 km	(0.1 mi)	0.3 km	(0.2 mi)	60 m	(200 ft)	0.3 km	(0.2 mi)	0.8 km	(0.5 mi)

"+" means distance can be larger in certain atmospheric conditions

TABLE OF INITIAL ISOLATION AND PROTECTIVE ACTION DISTANCES

ID No.	NAME OF MATERIAL	SMALL SPILLS (From a small package or small leak from a large package)					LARGE SPILLS (From a large package or from many small packages)				
		First ISOLATE in all Directions		Then PROTECT persons Downwind during:				First ISOLATE in all Directions		Then PROTECT persons Downwind during:			
				DAY		NIGHT				DAY		NIGHT	
		Meters	(Feet)	Kilometers	(Miles)	Kilometers	(Miles)	Meters	(Feet)	Kilometers	(Miles)	Kilometers	(Miles)
1746	Bromine trifluoride (when spilled in water)	30 m	(100 ft)	0.2 km	(0.1 mi)	0.6 km	(0.4 mi)	185 m	(600 ft)	2.1 km	(1.3 mi)	5.5 km	(3.4 mi)
1747	Butyltrichlorosilane (when spilled in water)	30 m	(100 ft)	0.2 km	(0.1 mi)	0.2 km	(0.1 mi)	60 m	(200 ft)	0.5 km	(0.3 mi)	1.8 km	(1.1 mi)
1749	Chlorine trifluoride	60 m	(200 ft)	0.5 km	(0.3 mi)	1.6 km	(1.0 mi)	335 m	(1100 ft)	3.4 km	(2.1 mi)	7.7 km	(4.8 mi)
1752	Chloroacetyl chloride (when spilled on land)	30 m	(100 ft)	0.2 km	(0.1 mi)	0.5 km	(0.3 mi)	95 m	(300 ft)	0.8 km	(0.5 mi)	1.6 km	(1.0 mi)
1752	Chloroacetyl chloride (when spilled in water)	30 m	(100 ft)	0.2 km	(0.1 mi)	0.2 km	(0.1 mi)	60 m	(200 ft)	0.3 km	(0.2 mi)	1.3 km	(0.8 mi)
1754	Chlorosulfonic acid (when spilled on land)	30 m	(100 ft)	0.2 km	(0.1 mi)	0.2 km	(0.1 mi)	30 m	(100 ft)	0.2 km	(0.1 mi)	0.5 km	(0.3 mi)
1754	Chlorosulfonic acid (when spilled in water)	30 m	(100 ft)	0.2 km	(0.1 mi)	0.2 km	(0.1 mi)	60 m	(200 ft)	0.5 km	(0.3 mi)	1.4 km	(0.9 mi)
1754	Chlorosulfonic acid and Sulfur trioxide mixture (when spilled on land)	60 m	(200 ft)	0.3 km	(0.2 mi)	1.1 km	(0.7 mi)	305 m	(1000 ft)	2.1 km	(1.3 mi)	5.6 km	(3.5 mi)
1754	Chlorosulfonic acid and Sulfur trioxide mixture (when spilled in water)												
1754	Chlorosulphonic acid (when spilled on land)	30 m	(100 ft)	0.2 km	(0.1 mi)	0.2 km	(0.1 mi)	30 m	(100 ft)	0.2 km	(0.1 mi)	0.5 km	(0.3 mi)
1754	Chlorosulphonic acid (when spilled in water)	30 m	(100 ft)	0.2 km	(0.1 mi)	0.2 km	(0.1 mi)	60 m	(200 ft)	0.5 km	(0.3 mi)	1.4 km	(0.9 mi)

ID No.	Name of Material	Meters	(Feet)	km	(mi)	km	(mi)	Meters	(Feet)	km	(mi)	km	(mi)
1754	Chlorosulphonic acid and Sulphur trioxide mixture (when spilled on land)	60 m	(200 ft)	0.3 km	(0.2 mi)	1.1 km	(0.7 mi)	305 m	(1000 ft)	2.1 km	(1.3 mi)	5.6 km	(3.5 mi)
1754	Chlorosulphonic acid and Sulphur trioxide mixture (when spilled in water)												
1754	Sulfur trioxide and Chlorosulfonic acid mixture (when spilled on land)												
1754	Sulfur trioxide and Chlorosulfonic acid mixture (when spilled in water)												
1754	Sulphur trioxide and Chlorosulphonic acid mixture (when spilled on land)												
1754	Sulphur trioxide and Chlorosulphonic acid mixture (when spilled in water)												
1758	Chromium oxychloride (when spilled in water)	30 m	(100 ft)	0.2 km	(0.1 mi)	0.2 km	(0.1 mi)	60 m	(200 ft)	0.3 km	(0.2 mi)	1.3 km	(0.8 mi)
1777	Fluorosulfonic acid (when spilled in water)	30 m	(100 ft)	0.2 km	(0.1 mi)	0.2 km	(0.1 mi)	60 m	(200 ft)	0.5 km	(0.3 mi)	1.4 km	(0.9 mi)
1777	Fluorosulphonic acid (when spilled in water)												
1801	Octyltrichlorosilane (when spilled in water)	30 m	(100 ft)	0.2 km	(0.1 mi)	0.3 km	(0.2 mi)	95 m	(300 ft)	0.8 km	(0.5 mi)	2.4 km	(1.5 mi)
1806	Phosphorus pentachloride (when spilled in water)	30 m	(100 ft)	0.2 km	(0.1 mi)	0.3 km	(0.2 mi)	125 m	(400 ft)	1.0 km	(0.6 mi)	2.9 km	(1.8 mi)
1809	Phosphorus trichloride (when spilled on land)	30 m	(100 ft)	0.2 km	(0.1 mi)	0.6 km	(0.4 mi)	125 m	(400 ft)	1.1 km	(0.7 mi)	2.7 km	(1.7 mi)
1809	Phosphorus trichloride (when spilled in water)	30 m	(100 ft)	0.2 km	(0.1 mi)	0.3 km	(0.2 mi)	125 m	(400 ft)	1.1 km	(0.7 mi)	2.6 km	(1.6 mi)
1810	Phosphorus oxychloride (when spilled on land)	30 m	(100 ft)	0.2 km	(0.1 mi)	0.5 km	(0.3 mi)	95 m	(300 ft)	0.8 km	(0.5 mi)	1.8 km	(1.1 mi)
1810	Phosphorus oxychloride (when spilled in water)	30 m	(100 ft)	0.2 km	(0.1 mi)	0.3 km	(0.2 mi)	95 m	(300 ft)	1.0 km	(0.6 mi)	2.6 km	(1.6 mi)

"+" means distance can be larger in certain atmospheric conditions

TABLE OF INITIAL ISOLATION AND PROTECTIVE ACTION DISTANCES

ID No.	NAME OF MATERIAL	SMALL SPILLS (From a small package or small leak from a large package)					LARGE SPILLS (From a large package or from many small packages)					
		First ISOLATE in all Directions		Then PROTECT persons Downwind during-				First ISOLATE in all Directions		Then PROTECT persons Downwind during-		
				DAY		NIGHT				DAY		NIGHT	
		Meters	(Feet)	Kilometers	(Miles)	Kilometers	(Miles)	Meters	(Feet)	Kilometers	(Miles)	Kilometers	(Miles)
1818	Silicon tetrachloride (when spilled in water)	30 m	(100 ft)	0.2 km	(0.1 mi)	0.3 km	(0.2 mi)	125 m	(400 ft)	1.3 km	(0.8 mi)	3.4 km	(2.1 mi)
1828	Sulfur chlorides (when spilled on land)	30 m	(100 ft)	0.2 km	(0.1 mi)	0.3 km	(0.2 mi)	60 m	(200 ft)	0.5 km	(0.3 mi)	1.0 km	(0.6 mi)
1828	Sulfur chlorides (when spilled in water)	30 m	(100 ft)	0.2 km	(0.1 mi)	0.2 km	(0.1 mi)	60 m	(200 ft)	0.6 km	(0.4 mi)	2.3 km	(1.4 mi)
1828	Sulphur chlorides (when spilled on land)	30 m	(100 ft)	0.2 km	(0.1 mi)	0.3 km	(0.2 mi)	60 m	(200 ft)	0.5 km	(0.3 mi)	1.0 km	(0.6 mi)
1828	Sulphur chlorides (when spilled in water)	30 m	(100 ft)	0.2 km	(0.1 mi)	0.2 km	(0.1 mi)	60 m	(200 ft)	0.6 km	(0.4 mi)	2.3 km	(1.4 mi)
1829 1829 1829 1829 1829 1829 1829	Sulfur trioxide Sulfur trioxide, inhibited Sulfur trioxide, stabilized Sulfur trioxide, uninhibited Sulphur trioxide Sulphur trioxide, inhibited Sulphur trioxide, stabilized Sulphur trioxide, uninhibited	60 m	(200 ft)	0.3 km	(0.2 mi)	1.1 km	(0.7 mi)	305 m	(1000 ft)	2.1 km	(1.3 mi)	5.6 km	(3.5 mi)
1831 1831 1831 1831 1831 1831 1831	Oleum, with not less than 30% free Sulfur trioxide Oleum, with not less than 30% free Sulphur trioxide Sulfuric acid, fuming Sulfuric acid, fuming, with not less than 30% free Sulfur trioxide Sulphuric acid, fuming Sulphuric acid, fuming, with not less than 30% free Sulphur trioxide	60 m	(200 ft)	0.3 km	(0.2 mi)	1.1 km	(0.7 mi)	305 m	(1000 ft)	2.1 km	(1.3 mi)	5.6 km	(3.5 mi)

ID	Name						
1834	Sulfuryl chloride (when spilled on land)	30 m (100 ft)	0.2 km (0.1 mi)	0.2 km (0.1 mi)	30 m (100 ft)	0.3 km (0.2 mi)	0.6 km (0.4 mi)
1834	Sulfuryl chloride (when spilled in water)	30 m (100 ft)	0.2 km (0.1 mi)	0.2 km (0.1 mi)	125 m (400 ft)	1.1 km (0.7 mi)	2.4 km (1.5 mi)
1834	Sulphuryl chloride (when spilled on land)	30 m (100 ft)	0.2 km (0.1 mi)	0.2 km (0.1 mi)	30 m (100 ft)	0.3 km (0.2 mi)	0.6 km (0.4 mi)
1834	Sulphuryl chloride (when spilled in water)	30 m (100 ft)	0.2 km (0.1 mi)	0.2 km (0.1 mi)	125 m (400 ft)	1.1 km (0.7 mi)	2.4 km (1.5 mi)
1836	Thionyl chloride (when spilled on land)	30 m (100 ft)	0.2 km (0.1 mi)	0.5 km (0.3 mi)	60 m (200 ft)	0.5 km (0.3 mi)	1.1 km (0.7 mi)
1836	Thionyl chloride (when spilled in water)	30 m (100 ft)	0.2 km (0.1 mi)	1.0 km (0.6 mi)	335 m (1100 ft)	3.2 km (2.0 mi)	7.1 km (4.4 mi)
1838	Titanium tetrachloride (when spilled on land)	30 m (100 ft)	0.2 km (0.1 mi)	0.2 km (0.1 mi)	30 m (100 ft)	0.3 km (0.2 mi)	0.8 km (0.5 mi)
1838	Titanium tetrachloride (when spilled in water)	30 m (100 ft)	0.2 km (0.1 mi)	0.3 km (0.2 mi)	125 m (400 ft)	1.1 km (0.7 mi)	2.9 km (1.8 mi)
1859	Silicon tetrafluoride	30 m (100 ft)	0.2 km (0.1 mi)	0.5 km (0.3 mi)	60 m (200 ft)	0.5 km (0.3 mi)	1.6 km (1.0 mi)
1859	Silicon tetrafluoride, compressed						
1892	ED (when used as a weapon)	30 m (100 ft)	0.3 km (0.2 mi)	0.8 km (0.5 mi)	125 m (400 ft)	1.3 km (0.8 mi)	2.6 km (1.6 mi)
1892	Ethyldichloroarsine	30 m (100 ft)	0.2 km (0.1 mi)	0.3 km (0.2 mi)	60 m (200 ft)	0.5 km (0.3 mi)	1.0 km (0.6 mi)
1898	Acetyl iodide (when spilled in water)	30 m (100 ft)	0.2 km (0.1 mi)	0.2 km (0.1 mi)	60 m (200 ft)	0.6 km (0.4 mi)	1.6 km (1.0 mi)
1911	Diborane	30 m (100 ft)	0.2 km (0.1 mi)	0.3 km (0.2 mi)	95 m (300 ft)	1.0 km (0.6 mi)	2.7 km (1.7 mi)
1911	Diborane, compressed						
1923	Calcium dithionite	30 m (100 ft)	0.2 km (0.1 mi)	0.2 km (0.1 mi)	30 m (100 ft)	0.3 km (0.2 mi)	1.1 km (0.7 mi)
1923	Calcium hydrosulfite (when spilled in water)						
1923	Calcium hydrosulphite (when spilled in water)						

"+" means distance can be larger in certain atmospheric conditions

TABLE OF INITIAL ISOLATION AND PROTECTIVE ACTION DISTANCES

ID No.	NAME OF MATERIAL	SMALL SPILLS (From a small package or small leak from a large package)				LARGE SPILLS (From a large package or from many small packages)			
		First ISOLATE in all Directions	Then PROTECT persons Downwind during—			First ISOLATE in all Directions	Then PROTECT persons Downwind during—		
				DAY	NIGHT			DAY	NIGHT
		Meters (Feet)		Kilometers (Miles)	Kilometers (Miles)	Meters (Feet)		Kilometers (Miles)	Kilometers (Miles)
1939	Phosphorus oxybromide (when spilled in water)	30 m (100 ft)		0.2 km (0.1 mi)	0.3 km (0.2 mi)	95 m (300 ft)		0.6 km (0.4 mi)	1.9 km (1.2 mi)
1939	Phosphorus oxybromide, solid (when spilled in water)								
1953	Compressed gas, flammable, poisonous, n.o.s. (Inhalation Hazard Zone A)	185 m (600 ft)		1.8 km (1.1 mi)	5.6 km (3.5 mi)	915 m (3000 ft)		10.8 km (6.7 mi)	11.0+ km (7.0+ mi)
1953	Compressed gas, flammable, poisonous, n.o.s (Inhalation Hazard Zone B)	30 m (100 ft)		0.3 km (0.2 mi)	1.1 km (0.7 mi)	305 m (1000 ft)		3.1 km (1.9 mi)	7.7 km (4.8 mi)
1953	Compressed gas, flammable, poisonous, n.o.s. (Inhalation Hazard Zone C)	30 m (100 ft)		0.2 km (0.1 mi)	1.0 km (0.6 mi)	215 m (700 ft)		2.1 km (1.3 mi)	5.6 km (3.5 mi)
1953	Compressed gas, flammable, poisonous, n.o.s. (Inhalation Hazard Zone D)	30 m (100 ft)		0.2 km (0.1 mi)	0.6 km (0.4 mi)	185 m (600 ft)		1.6 km (1.0 mi)	4.3 km (2.7 mi)
1953	Compressed gas, flammable, toxic, n.o.s. (Inhalation Hazard Zone A)	185 m (600 ft)		1.8 km (1.1 mi)	5.6 km (3.5 mi)	915 m (3000 ft)		10.8 km (6.7 mi)	11.0+ km (7.0+ mi)
1953	Compressed gas, flammable, toxic, n.o.s. (Inhalation Hazard Zone B)	30 m (100 ft)		0.3 km (0.2 mi)	1.1 km (0.7 mi)	305 m (1000 ft)		3.1 km (1.9 mi)	7.7 km (4.8 mi)
1953	Compressed gas, flammable, toxic, n.o.s. (Inhalation Hazard Zone C)	30 m (100 ft)		0.2 km (0.1 mi)	1.0 km (0.6 mi)	215 m (700 ft)		2.1 km (1.3 mi)	5.6 km (3.5 mi)
1953	Compressed gas, flammable, toxic, n.o.s. (Inhalation Hazard Zone D)	30 m (100 ft)		0.2 km (0.1 mi)	0.6 km (0.4 mi)	185 m (600 ft)		1.6 km (1.0 mi)	4.3 km (2.7 mi)

ID No.	Name of Material	Small Spills — First ISOLATE	Small Spills — Then PROTECT (Day)	Small Spills — Then PROTECT (Night)	Large Spills — First ISOLATE	Large Spills — Then PROTECT (Day)	Large Spills — Then PROTECT (Night)
1953	Compressed gas, poisonous, flammable, n.o.s.	185 m (600 ft)	1.8 km (1.1 mi)	5.6 km (3.5 mi)	915 m (3000 ft)	10.8 km (6.7 mi)	11.0+ km (7.0+ mi)
1953	Compressed gas, poisonous, flammable, n.o.s. (Inhalation Hazard Zone A)	185 m (600 ft)	1.8 km (1.1 mi)	5.6 km (3.5 mi)	915 m (3000 ft)	10.8 km (6.7 mi)	11.0+ km (7.0+ mi)
1953	Compressed gas, poisonous, flammable, n.o.s. (Inhalation Hazard Zone B)	30 m (100 ft)	0.3 km (0.2 mi)	1.1 km (0.7 mi)	305 m (1000 ft)	3.1 km (1.9 mi)	7.7 km (4.8 mi)
1953	Compressed gas, poisonous, flammable, n.o.s. (Inhalation Hazard Zone C)	30 m (100 ft)	0.2 km (0.1 mi)	1.0 km (0.6 mi)	215 m (700 ft)	2.1 km (1.3 mi)	5.6 km (3.5 mi)
1953	Compressed gas, poisonous, flammable, n.o.s. (Inhalation Hazard Zone D)	30 m (100 ft)	0.2 km (0.1 mi)	0.6 km (0.4 mi)	185 m (600 ft)	1.6 km (1.0 mi)	4.3 km (2.7 mi)
1953	Compressed gas, toxic, flammable, n.o.s.	185 m (600 ft)	1.8 km (1.1 mi)	5.6 km (3.5 mi)	915 m (3000 ft)	10.8 km (6.7 mi)	11.0+ km (7.0+ mi)
1953	Compressed gas, toxic, flammable, n.o.s. (Inhalation Hazard Zone A)	185 m (600 ft)	1.8 km (1.1 mi)	5.6 km (3.5 mi)	915 m (3000 ft)	10.8 km (6.7 mi)	11.0+ km (7.0+ mi)
1953	Compressed gas, toxic, flammable, n.o.s. (Inhalation Hazard Zone B)	30 m (100 ft)	0.3 km (0.2 mi)	1.1 km (0.7 mi)	305 m (1000 ft)	3.1 km (1.9 mi)	7.7 km (4.8 mi)
1953	Compressed gas, toxic, flammable, n.o.s. (Inhalation Hazard Zone C)	30 m (100 ft)	0.2 km (0.1 mi)	1.0 km (0.6 mi)	215 m (700 ft)	2.1 km (1.3 mi)	5.6 km (3.5 mi)
1953	Compressed gas, toxic, flammable, n.o.s. (Inhalation Hazard Zone D)	30 m (100 ft)	0.2 km (0.1 mi)	0.6 km (0.4 mi)	185 m (600 ft)	1.6 km (1.0 mi)	4.3 km (2.7 mi)
1953	Liquefied gas, flammable, poisonous, n.o.s.	185 m (600 ft)	1.8 km (1.1 mi)	5.6 km (3.5 mi)	915 m (3000 ft)	10.8 km (6.7 mi)	11.0+ km (7.0+ mi)
1953	Liquefied gas, flammable, poisonous, n.o.s. (Inhalation Hazard Zone A)	185 m (600 ft)	1.8 km (1.1 mi)	5.6 km (3.5 mi)	915 m (3000 ft)	10.8 km (6.7 mi)	11.0+ km (7.0+ mi)

"+" means distance can be larger in certain atmospheric conditions

TABLE OF INITIAL ISOLATION AND PROTECTIVE ACTION DISTANCES

ID No.	NAME OF MATERIAL	SMALL SPILLS (From a small package or small leak from a large package)			LARGE SPILLS (From a large package or from many small packages)		
		First ISOLATE in all Directions Meters (Feet)	Then PROTECT persons Downwind during— DAY Kilometers (Miles)	NIGHT Kilometers (Miles)	First ISOLATE in all Directions Meters (Feet)	Then PROTECT persons Downwind during— DAY Kilometers (Miles)	NIGHT Kilometers (Miles)
1953	Liquefied gas, flammable, poisonous, n.o.s. (Inhalation Hazard Zone B)	30 m (100 ft)	0.3 km (0.2 mi)	1.1 km (0.7 mi)	305 m (1000 ft)	3.1 km (1.9 mi)	7.7 km (4.8 mi)
1953	Liquefied gas, flammable, poisonous, n.o.s. (Inhalation Hazard Zone C)	30 m (100 ft)	0.2 km (0.1 mi)	1.0 km (0.6 mi)	215 m (700 ft)	2.1 km (1.3 mi)	5.6 km (3.5 mi)
1953	Liquefied gas, flammable, poisonous, n.o.s. (Inhalation Hazard Zone D)	30 m (100 ft)	0.2 km (0.1 mi)	0.6 km (0.4 mi)	185 m (600 ft)	1.6 km (1.0 mi)	4.3 km (2.7 mi)
1953 1953	Liquefied gas, flammable, toxic, n.o.s. Liquefied gas, flammable, toxic, n.o.s. (Inhalation Hazard Zone A)	185 m (600 ft)	1.8 km (1.1 mi)	5.6 km (3.5 mi)	915 m (3000 ft)	10.8 km (6.7 mi)	11.0+ km (7.0+ mi)
1953	Liquefied gas, flammable, toxic, n.o.s. (Inhalation Hazard Zone B)	30 m (100 ft)	0.3 km (0.2 mi)	1.1 km (0.7 mi)	305 m (1000 ft)	3.1 km (1.9 mi)	7.7 km (4.8 mi)
1953	Liquefied gas, flammable, toxic, n.o.s. (Inhalation Hazard Zone C)	30 m (100 ft)	0.2 km (0.1 mi)	1.0 km (0.6 mi)	215 m (700 ft)	2.1 km (1.3 mi)	5.6 km (3.5 mi)
1953	Liquefied gas, flammable, toxic, n.o.s. (Inhalation Hazard Zone D)	30 m (100 ft)	0.2 km (0.1 mi)	0.6 km (0.4 mi)	185 m (600 ft)	1.6 km (1.0 mi)	4.3 km (2.7 mi)
1953	Poisonous gas, flammable, n.o.s.	185 m (600 ft)	1.8 km (1.1 mi)	5.6 km (3.5 mi)	915 m (3000 ft)	10.8 km (6.7 mi)	11.0+ km (7.0+ mi)
1953	Poisonous liquid, flammable, n.o.s.	155 m (500 ft)	1.3 km (0.8 mi)	3.4 km (2.1 mi)	915 m (3000 ft)	8.7 km (5.4 mi)	11.0+ km (7.0+ mi)
1955 1955	Compressed gas, poisonous, n.o.s. Compressed gas, poisonous, n.o.s. (Inhalation Hazard Zone A)	430 m (1400 ft)	4.2 km (2.6 mi)	8.4 km (5.2 mi)	915 m (3000 ft)	11.0+ km (7.0+ mi)	11.0+ km (7.0+ mi)
1955	Compressed gas, poisonous, n.o.s. (Inhalation Hazard Zone B)	60 m (200 ft)	0.5 km (0.3 mi)	1.6 km (1.0 mi)	430 m (1400 ft)	4.0 km (2.5 mi)	9.8 km (6.1 mi)

ID No.	Name of Material	SMALL SPILLS First ISOLATE in all Directions	SMALL SPILLS Then PROTECT persons Downwind during DAY	SMALL SPILLS Then PROTECT persons Downwind during NIGHT	LARGE SPILLS First ISOLATE in all Directions	LARGE SPILLS Then PROTECT persons Downwind during DAY	LARGE SPILLS Then PROTECT persons Downwind during NIGHT
1955	Compressed gas, poisonous, n.o.s. (Inhalation Hazard Zone C)	30 m (100 ft)	0.3 km (0.2 mi)	1.3 km (0.8 mi)	215 m (700 ft)	3.1 km (1.9 mi)	7.2 km (4.5 mi)
1955	Compressed gas, poisonous, n.o.s. (Inhalation Hazard Zone D)	30 m (100 ft)	0.2 km (0.1 mi)	0.6 km (0.4 mi)	185 m (600 ft)	1.6 km (1.0 mi)	4.3 km (2.7 mi)
1955 1955	Compressed gas, toxic, n.o.s. Compressed gas, toxic, n.o.s. (Inhalation Hazard Zone A)	430 m (1400 ft)	4.2 km (2.6 mi)	8.4 km (5.2 mi)	915 m (3000 ft)	11.0+ km (7.0+ mi)	11.0+ km (7.0+ mi)
1955	Compressed gas, toxic, n.o.s. (Inhalation Hazard Zone B)	60 m (200 ft)	0.5 km (0.3 mi)	1.6 km (1.0 mi)	430 m (1400 ft)	4.0 km (2.5 mi)	9.8 km (6.1 mi)
1955	Compressed gas, toxic, n.o.s. (Inhalation Hazard Zone C)	30 m (100 ft)	0.3 km (0.2 mi)	1.3 km (0.8 mi)	215 m (700 ft)	3.1 km (1.9 mi)	7.2 km (4.5 mi)
1955	Compressed gas, toxic, n.o.s. (Inhalation Hazard Zone D)	30 m (100 ft)	0.2 km (0.1 mi)	0.6 km (0.4 mi)	185 m (600 ft)	1.6 km (1.0 mi)	4.3 km (2.7 mi)
1955 1955	Liquefied gas, poisonous, n.o.s. Liquefied gas, poisonous, n.o.s. (Inhalation Hazard Zone A)	430 m (1400 ft)	4.2 km (2.6 mi)	8.4 km (5.2 mi)	915 m (3000 ft)	11.0+ km (7.0+ mi)	11.0+ km (7.0+ mi)
1955	Liquefied gas, poisonous, n.o.s. (Inhalation Hazard Zone B)	60 m (200 ft)	0.5 km (0.3 mi)	1.6 km (1.0 mi)	430 m (1400 ft)	4.0 km (2.5 mi)	9.8 km (6.1 mi)
1955	Liquefied gas, poisonous, n.o.s. (Inhalation Hazard Zone C)	30 m (100 ft)	0.3 km (0.2 mi)	1.3 km (0.8 mi)	215 m (700 ft)	3.1 km (1.9 mi)	7.2 km (4.5 mi)
1955	Liquefied gas, poisonous, n.o.s. (Inhalation Hazard Zone D)	30 m (100 ft)	0.2 km (0.1 mi)	0.6 km (0.4 mi)	185 m (600 ft)	1.6 km (1.0 mi)	4.3 km (2.7 mi)
1955 1955	Liquefied gas, toxic, n.o.s. Liquefied gas, toxic, n.o.s. (Inhalation Hazard Zone A)	430 m (1400 ft)	4.2 km (2.6 mi)	8.4 km (5.2 mi)	915 m (3000 ft)	11.0+ km (7.0+ mi)	11.0+ km (7.0+ mi)
1955	Liquefied gas, toxic, n.o.s. (Inhalation Hazard Zone B)	60 m (200 ft)	0.5 km (0.3 mi)	1.6 km (1.0 mi)	430 m (1400 ft)	4.0 km (2.5 mi)	9.8 km (6.1 mi)
1955	Liquefied gas, toxic, n.o.s. (Inhalation Hazard Zone C)	30 m (100 ft)	0.3 km (0.2 mi)	1.3 km (0.8 mi)	215 m (700 ft)	3.1 km (1.9 mi)	7.2 km (4.5 mi)
1955	Liquefied gas, toxic, n.o.s. (Inhalation Hazard Zone D)	30 m (100 ft)	0.2 km (0.1 mi)	0.6 km (0.4 mi)	185 m (600 ft)	1.6 km (1.0 mi)	4.3 km (2.7 mi)

"+" means distance can be larger in certain atmospheric conditions

TABLE OF INITIAL ISOLATION AND PROTECTIVE ACTION DISTANCES

ID No.	NAME OF MATERIAL	SMALL SPILLS (From a small package or small leak from a large package)					LARGE SPILLS (From a large package or from many small packages)					
		First ISOLATE in all Directions		Then PROTECT persons Downwind during—				First ISOLATE in all Directions		Then PROTECT persons Downwind during—		
				DAY		NIGHT				DAY		NIGHT	
		Meters	(Feet)	Kilometers (Miles)		Kilometers (Miles)		Meters	(Feet)	Kilometers (Miles)		Kilometers (Miles)	
1955	Methyl bromide and nonflammable, nonliquefied compressed gas mixture	30 m	(100 ft)	0.2 km	(0.1 mi)	0.3 km	(0.2 mi)	95 m	(300 ft)	0.5 km	(0.3 mi)	1.4 km	(0.9 mi)
1955	Organic phosphate compound mixed with compressed gas	30 m	(100 ft)	0.3 km	(0.2 mi)	1.3 km	(0.8 mi)	400 m	(1300 ft)	4.0 km	(2.5 mi)	7.2 km	(4.5 mi)
1955	Organic phosphate mixed with compressed gas												
1955	Organic phosphorus compound mixed with compressed gas												
1967	Insecticide gas, poisonous, n.o.s.	30 m	(100 ft)	0.3 km	(0.2 mi)	1.3 km	(0.8 mi)	400 m	(1300 ft)	4.0 km	(2.5 mi)	7.2 km	(4.5 mi)
1967	Insecticide gas, toxic, n.o.s.												
1967	Parathion and compressed gas mixture	30 m	(100 ft)	0.2 km	(0.1 mi)	0.3 km	(0.2 mi)	95 m	(300 ft)	1.0 km	(0.6 mi)	3.2 km	(2.0 mi)
1975	Dinitrogen tetroxide and Nitric oxide mixture	30 m	(100 ft)	0.3 km	(0.2 mi)	1.3 km	(0.8 mi)	155 m	(500 ft)	1.3 km	(0.8 mi)	3.5 km	(2.2 mi)
1975	Nitric oxide and Dinitrogen tetroxide mixture												
1975	Nitric oxide and Nitrogen dioxide mixture												
1975	Nitric oxide and Nitrogen tetroxide mixture												
1975	Nitrogen dioxide and Nitric oxide mixture												
1975	Nitrogen tetroxide and Nitric oxide mixture												
1994	Iron pentacarbonyl	30 m	(100 ft)	0.3 km	(0.2 mi)	0.6 km	(0.4 mi)	125 m	(400 ft)	1.1 km	(0.7 mi)	2.4 km	(1.5 mi)
2004	Magnesium diamide (when spilled in water)	30 m	(100 ft)	0.2 km	(0.1 mi)	0.2 km	(0.1 mi)	60 m	(200 ft)	0.5 km	(0.3 mi)	1.3 km	(0.8 mi)

ID No.	Name of Material	SMALL SPILLS First ISOLATE in all Directions	SMALL SPILLS Then PROTECT persons Downwind DAY	SMALL SPILLS Then PROTECT persons Downwind NIGHT	LARGE SPILLS First ISOLATE in all Directions	LARGE SPILLS Then PROTECT persons Downwind DAY	LARGE SPILLS Then PROTECT persons Downwind NIGHT
2011	Magnesium phosphide (when spilled in water)	30 m (100 ft)	0.2 km (0.1 mi)	0.8 km (0.5 mi)	245 m (800 ft)	2.3 km (1.4 mi)	6.0 km (3.7 mi)
2012	Potassium phosphide (when spilled in water)	30 m (100 ft)	0.2 km (0.1 mi)	0.5 km (0.3 mi)	155 m (500 ft)	1.3 km (0.8 mi)	4.0 km (2.5 mi)
2013	Strontium phosphide (when spilled in water)	30 m (100 ft)	0.2 km (0.1 mi)	0.5 km (0.3 mi)	155 m (500 ft)	1.3 km (0.8 mi)	3.7 km (2.3 mi)
2032 2032	Nitric acid, fuming Nitric acid, red fuming	95 m (300 ft)	0.3 km (0.2 mi)	0.5 km (0.3 mi)	400 m (1300 ft)	1.3 km (0.8 mi)	3.5 km (2.2 mi)
2186	Hydrogen chloride, refrigerated liquid	30 m (100 ft)	0.2 km (0.1 mi)	0.6 km (0.4 mi)	185 m (600 ft)	1.6 km (1.0 mi)	4.3 km (2.7 mi)
2188	Arsine	60 m (200 ft)	0.5 km (0.3 mi)	2.1 km (1.3 mi)	335 m (1100 ft)	3.2 km (2.0 mi)	6.6 km (4.1 mi)
2188	SA (when used as a weapon)	60 m (200 ft)	0.8 km (0.5 mi)	2.4 km (1.5 mi)	400 m (1300 ft)	4.0 km (2.5 mi)	8.0 km (5.0 mi)
2189	Dichlorosilane	30 m (100 ft)	0.3 km (0.2 mi)	1.0 km (0.6 mi)	245 m (800 ft)	2.4 km (1.5 mi)	6.3 km (3.9 mi)
2190 2190	Oxygen difluoride Oxygen difluoride, compressed	430 m (1400 ft)	4.2 km (2.6 mi)	8.4 km (5.2 mi)	915 m (3000 ft)	11.0+ km (7.0+ mi)	11.0+ km (7.0+ mi)
2191 2191	Sulfuryl fluoride Sulphuryl fluoride	30 m (100 ft)	0.2 km (0.1 mi)	0.3 km (0.2 mi)	95 m (300 ft)	0.8 km (0.5 mi)	2.3 km (1.4 mi)
2192	Germane	30 m (100 ft)	0.2 km (0.1 mi)	0.8 km (0.5 mi)	275 m (900 ft)	2.7 km (1.7 mi)	6.6 km (4.1 mi)
2194	Selenium hexafluoride	30 m (100 ft)	0.3 km (0.2 mi)	1.3 km (0.8 mi)	245 m (800 ft)	2.3 km (1.4 mi)	6.0 km (3.7 mi)
2195	Tellurium hexafluoride	60 m (200 ft)	0.6 km (0.4 mi)	2.3 km (1.4 mi)	365 m (1200 ft)	3.5 km (2.2 mi)	7.6 km (4.7 mi)
2196	Tungsten hexafluoride	30 m (100 ft)	0.3 km (0.2 mi)	1.3 km (0.8 mi)	155 m (500 ft)	1.3 km (0.8 mi)	3.7 km (2.3 mi)
2197	Hydrogen iodide, anhydrous	30 m (100 ft)	0.2 km (0.1 mi)	0.5 km (0.3 mi)	95 m (300 ft)	0.8 km (0.5 mi)	2.6 km (1.6 mi)
2198 2198	Phosphorus pentafluoride Phosphorus pentafluoride, compressed	30 m (100 ft)	0.3 km (0.2 mi)	1.1 km (0.7 mi)	125 m (400 ft)	1.1 km (0.7 mi)	3.5 km (2.2 mi)
2199	Phosphine	95 m (300 ft)	0.3 km (0.2 mi)	1.3 km (0.8 mi)	490 m (1600 ft)	1.8 km (1.1 mi)	5.5 km (3.4 mi)
2202	Hydrogen selenide, anhydrous	185 m (600 ft)	1.8 km (1.1 mi)	5.6 km (3.5 mi)	915 m (3000 ft)	10.8 km (6.7 mi)	11.0+ km (7.0+ mi)
2204 2204	Carbonyl sulfide Carbonyl sulphide	30 m (100 ft)	0.2 km (0.1 mi)	0.6 km (0.4 mi)	215 m (700 ft)	1.9 km (1.2 mi)	5.6 km (3.5 mi)

"+" means distance can be larger in certain atmospheric conditions

TABLE OF INITIAL ISOLATION AND PROTECTIVE ACTION DISTANCES

		SMALL SPILLS					LARGE SPILLS				
		(From a small package or small leak from a large package)					(From a large package or from many small packages)				
		First ISOLATE in all Directions		Then PROTECT persons Downwind during—				First ISOLATE in all Directions		Then PROTECT persons Downwind during—		
				DAY		NIGHT				DAY		NIGHT
ID No.	NAME OF MATERIAL	Meters	(Feet)	Kilometers	(Miles)	Kilometers	(Miles)	Meters	(Feet)	Kilometers	(Miles)	Kilometers	(Miles)
2232 2232	Chloroacetaldehyde 2-Chloroethanal	30 m	(100 ft)	0.2 km	(0.1 mi)	0.5 km	(0.3 mi)	60 m	(200 ft)	0.6 km	(0.4 mi)	1.6 km	(1.0 mi)
2334	Allylamine	30 m	(100 ft)	0.2 km	(0.1 mi)	0.5 km	(0.3 mi)	95 m	(300 ft)	1.0 km	(0.6 mi)	2.4 km	(1.5 mi)
2337	Phenylmercaptan	30 m	(100 ft)	0.2 km	(0.1 mi)	0.2 km	(0.1 mi)	30 m	(100 ft)	0.3 km	(0.2 mi)	0.6 km	(0.4 mi)
2382 2382	1,2-Dimethylhydrazine Dimethylhydrazine, symmetrical	30 m	(100 ft)	0.2 km	(0.1 mi)	0.3 km	(0.2 mi)	60 m	(200 ft)	0.5 km	(0.3 mi)	1.1 km	(0.7 mi)
2407	Isopropyl chloroformate	30 m	(100 ft)	0.2 km	(0.1 mi)	0.3 km	(0.2 mi)	95 m	(300 ft)	0.8 km	(0.5 mi)	1.9 km	(1.2 mi)
2417 2417	Carbonyl fluoride Carbonyl fluoride, compressed	30 m	(100 ft)	0.2 km	(0.1 mi)	1.1 km	(0.7 mi)	125 m	(400 ft)	1.0 km	(0.6 mi)	3.1 km	(1.9 mi)
2418 2418	Sulfur tetrafluoride Sulphur tetrafluoride	60 m	(200 ft)	0.5 km	(0.3 mi)	1.9 km	(1.2 mi)	305 m	(1000 ft)	2.9 km	(1.8 mi)	6.9 km	(4.3 mi)
2420	Hexafluoroacetone	30 m	(100 ft)	0.3 km	(0.2 mi)	1.4 km	(0.9 mi)	365 m	(1200 ft)	3.7 km	(2.3 mi)	8.5 km	(5.3 mi)
2421	Nitrogen trioxide	30 m	(100 ft)	0.2 km	(0.1 mi)	0.2 km	(0.1 mi)	155 m	(500 ft)	0.6 km	(0.4 mi)	2.1 km	(1.3 mi)
2438	Trimethylacetyl chloride	30 m	(100 ft)	0.2 km	(0.1 mi)	0.2 km	(0.1 mi)	30 m	(100 ft)	0.3 km	(0.2 mi)	0.8 km	(0.5 mi)
2442	Trichloroacetyl chloride (when spilled on land)	30 m	(100 ft)	0.2 km	(0.1 mi)	0.3 km	(0.2 mi)	60 m	(200 ft)	0.6 km	(0.4 mi)	1.4 km	(0.9 mi)
2442	Trichloroacetyl chloride (when spilled in water)	30 m	(100 ft)	0.2 km	(0.1 mi)	0.2 km	(0.1 mi)	30 m	(100 ft)	0.3 km	(0.2 mi)	1.3 km	(0.8 mi)
2474	Thiophosgene	60 m	(200 ft)	0.6 km	(0.4 mi)	1.8 km	(1.1 mi)	275 m	(900 ft)	2.6 km	(1.6 mi)	5.0 km	(3.1 mi)
2477	Methylisothiocyanate	30 m	(100 ft)	0.2 km	(0.1 mi)	0.3 km	(0.2 mi)	60 m	(200 ft)	0.5 km	(0.3 mi)	1.1 km	(0.7 mi)
2480	Methyl isocyanate	95 m	(300 ft)	0.8 km	(0.5 mi)	2.7 km	(1.7 mi)	490 m	(1600 ft)	4.8 km	(3.0 mi)	9.8 km	(6.1 mi)
2481	Ethyl isocyanate	215 m	(700 ft)	1.9 km	(1.2 mi)	4.3 km	(2.7 mi)	915 m	(3000 ft)	11.0+ km	(7.0+ mi)	11.0+ km	(7.0+ mi)

ID No.	Name of Material	SMALL SPILLS First ISOLATE in all Directions	Then PROTECT persons Downwind during DAY	Then PROTECT persons Downwind during NIGHT	LARGE SPILLS First ISOLATE in all Directions	Then PROTECT persons Downwind during DAY	Then PROTECT persons Downwind during NIGHT
2482	n-Propyl isocyanate	125 m (400 ft)	1.1 km (0.7 mi)	2.4 km (1.5 mi)	765 m (2500 ft)	6.3 km (3.9 mi)	10.6 km (6.6 mi)
2483	Isopropyl isocyanate	185 m (600 ft)	1.8 km (1.1 mi)	3.9 km (2.4 mi)	430 m (1400 ft)	4.2 km (2.6 mi)	7.4 km (4.6 mi)
2484	tert-Butyl isocyanate	125 m (400 ft)	1.0 km (0.6 mi)	2.4 km (1.5 mi)	550 m (1800 ft)	5.3 km (3.3 mi)	10.3 km (6.4 mi)
2485	n-Butyl isocyanate	95 m (300 ft)	0.8 km (0.5 mi)	1.6 km (1.0 mi)	335 m (1100 ft)	3.1 km (1.9 mi)	6.3 km (3.9 mi)
2486	Isobutyl isocyanate	60 m (200 ft)	0.6 km (0.4 mi)	1.4 km (0.9 mi)	155 m (500 ft)	1.6 km (1.0 mi)	3.2 km (2.0 mi)
2487	Phenyl isocyanate	30 m (100 ft)	0.3 km (0.2 mi)	0.8 km (0.5 mi)	155 m (500 ft)	1.3 km (0.8 mi)	2.6 km (1.6 mi)
2488	Cyclohexyl isocyanate	30 m (100 ft)	0.2 km (0.1 mi)	0.3 km (0.2 mi)	95 m (300 ft)	0.8 km (0.5 mi)	1.4 km (0.9 mi)
2495	Iodine pentafluoride (when spilled in water)	30 m (100 ft)	0.2 km (0.1 mi)	0.5 km (0.3 mi)	125 m (400 ft)	1.1 km (0.7 mi)	3.1 km (1.9 mi)
2521	Diketene, inhibited	30 m (100 ft)	0.2 km (0.1 mi)	0.2 km (0.1 mi)	30 m (100 ft)	0.3 km (0.2 mi)	0.5 km (0.3 mi)
2534	Methylchlorosilane	30 m (100 ft)	0.2 km (0.1 mi)	1.0 km (0.6 mi)	215 m (700 ft)	2.1 km (1.3 mi)	5.6 km (3.5 mi)
2548	Chlorine pentafluoride	30 m (100 ft)	0.3 km (0.2 mi)	1.0 km (0.6 mi)	365 m (1200 ft)	3.7 km (2.3 mi)	8.7 km (5.4 mi)
2576	Phosphorus oxybromide, molten (when spilled in water)	30 m (100 ft)	0.2 km (0.1 mi)	0.3 km (0.2 mi)	95 m (300 ft)	0.6 km (0.4 mi)	1.9 km (1.2 mi)
2600	Carbon monoxide and Hydrogen mixture	30 m (100 ft)	0.2 km (0.1 mi)	0.2 km (0.1 mi)	125 m (400 ft)	0.6 km (0.4 mi)	1.8 km (1.1 mi)
2600	Carbon monoxide and Hydrogen mixture, compressed						
2600	Hydrogen and Carbon monoxide mixture						
2600	Hydrogen and Carbon monoxide mixture, compressed						
2605	Methoxymethyl isocyanate	60 m (200 ft)	0.3 km (0.2 mi)	0.8 km (0.5 mi)	125 m (400 ft)	1.3 km (0.8 mi)	2.6 km (1.6 mi)
2606	Methyl orthosilicate	30 m (100 ft)	0.2 km (0.1 mi)	0.2 km (0.1 mi)	30 m (100 ft)	0.3 km (0.2 mi)	0.6 km (0.4 mi)
2644	Methyl iodide	30 m (100 ft)	0.2 km (0.1 mi)	0.3 km (0.2 mi)	60 m (200 ft)	0.3 km (0.2 mi)	1.0 km (0.6 mi)
2646	Hexachlorocyclopentadiene	30 m (100 ft)	0.2 km (0.1 mi)	0.2 km (0.1 mi)	30 m (100 ft)	0.2 km (0.1 mi)	0.3 km (0.2 mi)
2668	Chloroacetonitrile	30 m (100 ft)	0.2 km (0.1 mi)	0.2 km (0.1 mi)	30 m (100 ft)	0.3 km (0.2 mi)	0.5 km (0.3 mi)
2676	Stibine	30 m (100 ft)	0.3 km (0.2 mi)	1.6 km (1.0 mi)	245 m (800 ft)	2.3 km (1.4 mi)	6.0 km (3.7 mi)

"+" means distance can be larger in certain atmospheric conditions

TABLE OF INITIAL ISOLATION AND PROTECTIVE ACTION DISTANCES

ID No.	NAME OF MATERIAL	SMALL SPILLS (From a small package or small leak from a large package)				LARGE SPILLS (From a large package or from many small packages)			
		First ISOLATE in all Directions		Then PROTECT persons Downwind during—		First ISOLATE in all Directions		Then PROTECT persons Downwind during—	
				DAY	NIGHT			DAY	NIGHT
		Meters	(Feet)	Kilometers (Miles)	Kilometers (Miles)	Meters	(Feet)	Kilometers (Miles)	Kilometers (Miles)
2691	Phosphorus pentabromide (when spilled in water)	30 m	(100 ft)	0.2 km (0.1 mi)	0.3 km (0.2 mi)	95 m	(300 ft)	0.8 km (0.5 mi)	2.4 km (1.5 mi)
2692	Boron tribromide (when spilled on land)	30 m	(100 ft)	0.2 km (0.1 mi)	0.3 km (0.2 mi)	60 m	(200 ft)	0.6 km (0.4 mi)	1.4 km (0.9 mi)
2692	Boron tribromide (when spilled in water)	30 m	(100 ft)	0.2 km (0.1 mi)	0.2 km (0.1 mi)	60 m	(200 ft)	0.5 km (0.3 mi)	1.6 km (1.0 mi)
2740	n-Propyl chloroformate	30 m	(100 ft)	0.2 km (0.1 mi)	0.3 km (0.2 mi)	60 m	(200 ft)	0.5 km (0.3 mi)	1.4 km (0.9 mi)
2742	sec-Butyl chloroformate	30 m	(100 ft)	0.2 km (0.1 mi)	0.2 km (0.1 mi)	30 m	(100 ft)	0.3 km (0.2 mi)	0.6 km (0.4 mi)
2742	Isobutyl chloroformate	30 m	(100 ft)	0.2 km (0.1 mi)	0.2 km (0.1 mi)	60 m	(200 ft)	0.3 km (0.2 mi)	0.8 km (0.5 mi)
2743	n-Butyl chloroformate	30 m	(100 ft)	0.2 km (0.1 mi)	0.2 km (0.1 mi)	30 m	(100 ft)	0.3 km (0.2 mi)	0.5 km (0.3 mi)
2806	Lithium nitride (when spilled in water)	30 m	(100 ft)	0.2 km (0.1 mi)	0.2 km (0.1 mi)	95 m	(300 ft)	0.8 km (0.5 mi)	2.1 km (1.3 mi)
2810 2810 2810 2810	Bis-2-chloroethyl ethylamine Bis-2-chloroethyl methylamine Bis-2-chloroethyl sulfide Bis-2-chloroethyl sulphide	30 m	(100 ft)	0.2 km (0.1 mi)	0.2 km (0.1 mi)	30 m	(100 ft)	0.2 km (0.1 mi)	0.3 km (0.2 mi)
2810 2810	Buzz (when used as a weapon) BZ (when used as a weapon)	30 m	(100 ft)	0.2 km (0.1 mi)	0.5 km (0.3 mi)	60 m	(200 ft)	0.5 km (0.3 mi)	1.9 km (1.2 mi)
2810	CS (when used as a weapon)	60 m	(200 ft)	0.3 km (0.2 mi)	1.1 km (0.7 mi)	245 m	(800 ft)	2.6 km (1.6 mi)	5.6 km (3.5 mi)
2810	DC (when used as a weapon)	30 m	(100 ft)	0.2 km (0.1 mi)	0.8 km (0.5 mi)	245 m	(800 ft)	2.3 km (1.4 mi)	5.3 km (3.3 mi)
2810	O-Ethyl S-(2-diisopropylaminoethyl) methylphosphonothioate	30 m	(100 ft)	0.2 km (0.1 mi)	0.2 km (0.1 mi)	30 m	(100 ft)	0.2 km (0.1 mi)	0.2 km (0.1 mi)

ID No.	Name of Material	SMALL SPILLS First ISOLATE in all Directions		SMALL SPILLS Then PROTECT Day	SMALL SPILLS Then PROTECT Night	LARGE SPILLS First ISOLATE in all Directions		LARGE SPILLS Then PROTECT Day	LARGE SPILLS Then PROTECT Night
2810	Ethyl N,N-dimethylphosphoramidocyanidate	30 m	(100 ft)	0.2 km (0.1 mi)	0.2 km (0.1 mi)	60 m	(200 ft)	0.5 km (0.3 mi)	1.0 km (0.6 mi)
2810	GA (when used as a weapon)	30 m	(100 ft)	0.3 km (0.2 mi)	0.6 km (0.4 mi)	155 m	(500 ft)	1.6 km (1.0 mi)	3.1 km (1.9 mi)
2810	GB (when used as a weapon)	155 m	(500 ft)	1.6 km (1.0 mi)	3.4 km (2.1 mi)	915 m	(3000 ft)	11.0+ km (7.0+ mi)	11.0+ km (7.0+ mi)
2810	GD (when used as a weapon)	95 m	(300 ft)	0.8 km (0.5 mi)	1.8 km (1.1 mi)	765 m	(2500 ft)	6.8 km (4.2 mi)	10.5 km (6.5 mi)
2810	GF (when used as a weapon)	30 m	(100 ft)	0.3 km (0.2 mi)	0.6 km (0.4 mi)	245 m	(800 ft)	2.3 km (1.4 mi)	5.1 km (3.2 mi)
2810 2810	H (when used as a weapon) HD (when used as a weapon)	30 m	(100 ft)	0.2 km (0.1 mi)	0.2 km (0.1 mi)	60 m	(200 ft)	0.6 km (0.4 mi)	1.1 km (0.7 mi)
2810	HL (when used as a weapon)	30 m	(100 ft)	0.2 km (0.1 mi)	0.3 km (0.2 mi)	95 m	(300 ft)	1.0 km (0.6 mi)	1.8 km (1.1 mi)
2810	HN-1 (when used as a weapon)	30 m	(100 ft)	0.2 km (0.1 mi)	0.2 km (0.1 mi)	60 m	(200 ft)	0.6 km (0.4 mi)	1.3 km (0.8 mi)
2810	HN-2 (when used as a weapon)	30 m	(100 ft)	0.2 km (0.1 mi)	0.2 km (0.1 mi)	60 m	(200 ft)	0.5 km (0.3 mi)	1.1 km (0.7 mi)
2810	HN-3 (when used as a weapon)	30 m	(100 ft)	0.2 km (0.1 mi)	0.2 km (0.1 mi)	30 m	(100 ft)	0.2 km (0.1 mi)	0.3 km (0.2 mi)
2810	Isopropyl methylphosphonofluoridate	125 m	(400 ft)	1.3 km (0.8 mi)	2.3 km (1.4 mi)	550 m	(1800 ft)	5.3 km (3.3 mi)	8.7 km (5.4 mi)
2810	L (Lewisite) (when used as a weapon) Lewisite when used as a weapon	30 m	(100 ft)	0.2 km (0.1 mi)	0.3 km (0.2 mi)	95 m	(300 ft)	1.0 km (0.6 mi)	1.8 km (1.1 mi)
2810	Mustard (when used as a weapon)	30 m	(100 ft)	0.2 km (0.1 mi)	0.2 km (0.1 mi)	30 m	(100 ft)	0.2 km (0.1 mi)	0.3 km (0.2 mi)
2810	Mustard Lewisite (when used as a weapon)	30 m	(100 ft)	0.2 km (0.1 mi)	0.3 km (0.2 mi)	95 m	(300 ft)	1.0 km (0.6 mi)	1.8 km (1.1 mi)
2810	Pinacolyl methylphosphonofluoridate	60 m	(200 ft)	0.5 km (0.3 mi)	0.8 km (0.5 mi)	215 m	(700 ft)	2.1 km (1.3 mi)	3.1 km (1.9 mi)
2810	Poisonous liquid, n.o.s. (when Inhalation Hazard is on a package or shipping paper)	215 m	(700 ft)	1.9 km (1.2 mi)	4.3 km (2.7 mi)	915 m	(3000 ft)	11.0+ km (7.0+ mi)	11.0+ km (7.0+ mi)
2810	Poisonous liquid, n.o.s. (Inhalation Hazard Zone A)								

"+" means distance can be larger in certain atmospheric conditions

TABLE OF INITIAL ISOLATION AND PROTECTIVE ACTION DISTANCES

ID No.	NAME OF MATERIAL	SMALL SPILLS (From a small package or small leak from a large package)			LARGE SPILLS (From a large package or from many small packages)			
		First ISOLATE in all Directions	Then PROTECT persons Downwind during-		First ISOLATE in all Directions	Then PROTECT persons Downwind during-		
		Meters (Feet)	DAY Kilometers (Miles)	NIGHT Kilometers (Miles)	Meters (Feet)	DAY Kilometers (Miles)	NIGHT Kilometers (Miles)	
2810	Poisonous liquid, n.o.s. (Inhalation Hazard Zone B)	60 m (200 ft)	0.5 km (0.3 mi)	1.3 km (0.8 mi)	245 m (800 ft)	2.3 km (1.4 mi)	5.0 km (3.1 mi)	
2810	Poisonous liquid, organic, n.o.s. (when "Inhalation Hazard" is on a package or shipping paper)	215 m (700 ft)	1.9 km (1.2 mi)	4.3 km (2.7 mi)	915 m (3000 ft)	11.0+ km (7.0+ mi)	11.0+ km (7.0+ mi)	
2810	Poisonous liquid, organic, n.o.s. (Inhalation Hazard Zone A)							
2810	Poisonous liquid, organic, n.o.s. (Inhalation Hazard Zone B)	60 m (200 ft)	0.3 km (0.2 mi)	1.1 km (0.7 mi)	185 m (600 ft)	1.6 km (1.0 mi)	4.0 km (2.5 mi)	
2810	Sarin (when used as a weapon)	155 m (500 ft)	1.6 km (1.0 mi)	3.4 km (2.1 mi)	915 m (3000 ft)	11.0+ km (7.0+ mi)	11.0+ km (7.0+ mi)	
2810	Soman (when used as a weapon)	95 m (300 ft)	0.8 km (0.5 mi)	1.8 km (1.1 mi)	765 m (2500 ft)	6.8 km (4.2 mi)	10.5 km (6.5 mi)	
2810	Tabun (when used as a weapon)	30 m (100 ft)	0.3 km (0.2 mi)	0.6 km (0.4 mi)	155 m (500 ft)	1.6 km (1.0 mi)	3.1 km (1.9 mi)	
2810	Thickened GD (when used as a weapon)	95 m (300 ft)	0.8 km (0.5 mi)	1.8 km (1.1 mi)	765 m (2500 ft)	6.8 km (4.2 mi)	10.5 km (6.5 mi)	
2810	Toxic liquid, n.o.s. (when "Inhalation Hazard" is on a package or shipping paper)	215 m (700 ft)	1.9 km (1.2 mi)	4.3 km (2.7 mi)	915 m (3000 ft)	11.0+ km (7.0+ mi)	11.0+ km (7.0+ mi)	
2810	Toxic liquid, n.o.s. (Inhalation Hazard Zone A)							
2810	Toxic liquid, n.o.s. (Inhalation Hazard Zone B)	60 m (200 ft)	0.5 km (0.3 mi)	1.3 km (0.8 mi)	245 m (800 ft)	2.3 km (1.4 mi)	5.0 km (3.1 mi)	
2810	Toxic liquid, organic, n.o.s. (when "Inhalation Hazard" is on a package or shipping paper)	215 m (700 ft)	1.9 km (1.2 mi)	4.3 km (2.7 mi)	915 m (3000 ft)	11.0+ km (7.0+ mi)	11.0+ km (7.0+ mi)	
2810	Toxic liquid, organic, n.o.s. (Inhalation Hazard Zone A)							

ID No.	Name of Material						
2810	Toxic liquid, organic, n.o.s. (Inhalation Hazard Zone B)	60 m (200 ft)	0.3 km (0.2 mi)	1.1 km (0.7 mi)	185 m (600 ft)	1.6 km (1.0 mi)	4.0 km (2.5 mi)
2810	Tris-(2-chloroethyl) amine	30 m (100 ft)	0.2 km (0.1 mi)	0.2 km (0.1 mi)	30 m (100 ft)	0.2 km (0.1 mi)	0.2 km (0.1 mi)
2811	VX (when used as a weapon)	30 m (100 ft)	0.2 km (0.1 mi)	0.2 km (0.1 mi)	60 m (200 ft)	0.6 km (0.4 mi)	1.0 km (0.6 mi)
2811	CX (when used as a weapon)	30 m (100 ft)	0.2 km (0.1 mi)	0.5 km (0.3 mi)	95 m (300 ft)	1.0 km (0.6 mi)	3.1 km (1.9 mi)
2826	Ethyl chlorothioformate	30 m (100 ft)	0.2 km (0.1 mi)	0.2 km (0.1 mi)	60 m (200 ft)	0.5 km (0.3 mi)	0.8 km (0.5 mi)
2845	Ethyl phosphonous dichloride, anhydrous	60 m (200 ft)	0.5 km (0.3 mi)	1.3 km (0.8 mi)	155 m (500 ft)	1.6 km (1.0 mi)	3.4 km (2.1 mi)
2845	Methylphosphonous dichloride	60 m (200 ft)	0.5 km (0.3 mi)	1.3 km (0.8 mi)	245 m (800 ft)	2.3 km (1.4 mi)	5.0 km (3.1 mi)
2901	Bromine chloride	30 m (100 ft)	0.3 km (0.2 mi)	1.0 km (0.6 mi)	155 m (500 ft)	1.6 km (1.0 mi)	4.0 km (2.5 mi)
2927	Ethyl phosphonothioic dichloride, anhydrous	30 m (100 ft)	0.2 km (0.1 mi)	0.2 km (0.1 mi)	30 m (100 ft)	0.2 km (0.1 mi)	0.2 km (0.1 mi)
2927	Ethyl phosphorodichloridate	30 m (100 ft)	0.2 km (0.1 mi)	0.2 km (0.1 mi)	30 m (100 ft)	0.2 km (0.1 mi)	0.3 km (0.2 mi)
2927	Poisonous liquid, corrosive, n.o.s. (when "Inhalation Hazard" is on a package or shipping paper)	215 m (700 ft)	1.9 km (1.2 mi)	4.3 km (2.7 mi)	915 m (3000 ft)	11.0+ km (7.0+ mi)	11.0+ km (7.0+ mi)
2927	Poisonous liquid, corrosive, n.o.s. (Inhalation Hazard Zone A)						
2927	Poisonous liquid, corrosive, n.o.s. (Inhalation Hazard Zone B)	60 m (200 ft)	0.3 km (0.2 mi)	1.1 km (0.7 mi)	245 m (800 ft)	1.6 km (1.0 mi)	5.0 km (2.5 mi)
2927	Poisonous liquid, corrosive, organic, n.o.s. (when "Inhalation Hazard" is on a package or shipping paper)	215 m (700 ft)	1.9 km (1.2 mi)	4.3 km (2.7 mi)	915 m (3000 ft)	11.0+ km (7.0+ mi)	11.0+ km (7.0+ mi)
2927	Poisonous liquid, corrosive, organic, n.o.s. (Inhalation Hazard Zone A)						
2927	Toxic liquid, corrosive, n.o.s. (Inhalation Hazard Zone B)	60 m (200 ft)	0.3 km (0.2 mi)	1.1 km (0.7 mi)	245 m (800 ft)	1.6 km (1.0 mi)	5.0 km (2.5 mi)
2929	Poisonous liquid, flammable, n.o.s. (when "Inhalation	155 m (500 ft)	1.3 km (0.8 mi)	3.4 km (2.1 mi)	915 m (3000 ft)	8.7 km (5.4 mi)	11.0+ km (7.0+ mi)

"+" means distance can be larger in certain atmospheric conditions

TABLE OF INITIAL ISOLATION AND PROTECTIVE ACTION DISTANCES

ID No.	NAME OF MATERIAL	SMALL SPILLS (From a small package or small leak from a large package)			LARGE SPILLS (From a large package or from many small packages)		
		First ISOLATE in all Directions	Then PROTECT persons Downwind during—		First ISOLATE in all Directions	Then PROTECT persons Downwind during—	
		Meters (Feet)	DAY Kilometers (Miles)	NIGHT Kilometers (Miles)	Meters (Feet)	DAY Kilometers (Miles)	NIGHT Kilometers (Miles)
2929	Hazard" is on a package or shipping paper) Poisonous liquid, flammable, n.o.s. (Inhalation Hazard Zone A)						
2929	Poisonous liquid, flammable, n.o.s. (Inhalation Hazard Zone B)	30 m (100 ft)	0.2 km (0.1 mi)	0.6 km (0.4 mi)	125 m (400 ft)	1.1 km (0.7 mi)	2.7 km (1.7 mi)
2929	Poisonous liquid, flammable, organic, n.o.s. (when "Inhalation Hazard" is on a package or shipping paper)	155 m (500 ft)	1.3 km (0.8 mi)	3.4 km (2.1 mi)	915 m (3000 ft)	8.7 km (5.4 mi)	11.0+ km (7.0+ mi)
2929	Poisonous liquid, flammable, organic, n.o.s. (Inhalation Hazard Zone A)						
2929	Poisonous liquid, flammable, organic, n.o.s. (Inhalation Hazard Zone B)	30 m (100 ft)	0.2 km (0.1 mi)	0.6 km (0.4 mi)	125 m (400 ft)	1.1 km (0.7 mi)	2.7 km (1.7 mi)
2929	Toxic liquid, flammable, n.o.s. (when "Inhalation Hazard" is on a package or shipping paper) Toxic liquid, flammable, n.o.s. (Inhalation Hazard Zone A)	155 m (500 ft)	1.3 km (0.8 mi)	3.4 km (2.1 mi)	915 m (3000 ft)	8.7 km (5.4 mi)	11.0+ km (7.0+ mi)
2929	Toxic liquid, flammable, n.o.s. (Inhalation Hazard Zone B)	30 m (100 ft)	0.2 km (0.1 mi)	0.6 km (0.4 mi)	125 m (400 ft)	1.1 km (0.7 mi)	2.7 km (1.7 mi)
2929	Toxic liquid, flammable, organic, n.o.s. (when "Inhalation Hazard" is on a package or shipping paper) Toxic liquid, flammable, organic, n.o.s. (Inhalation Hazard Zone A)	155 m (500 ft)	1.3 km (0.8 mi)	3.4 km (2.1 mi)	915 m (3000 ft)	8.7 km (5.4 mi)	11.0+ km (7.0+ mi)

ID No.	NAME OF MATERIAL	SMALL SPILLS First ISOLATE in all Directions	Then PROTECT persons Downwind during DAY	Then PROTECT persons Downwind during NIGHT	LARGE SPILLS First ISOLATE in all Directions	Then PROTECT persons Downwind during DAY	Then PROTECT persons Downwind during NIGHT
2929	Toxic liquid, flammable, organic, n.o.s. (Inhalation Hazard Zone B)	30 m (100 ft)	0.2 km (0.1 mi)	0.6 km (0.4 mi)	125 m (400 ft)	1.1 km (0.7 mi)	2.7 km (1.7 mi)
2977	Radioactive material, Uranium hexafluoride, fissile **(when spilled in water)**	30 m (100 ft)	0.2 km (0.1 mi)	0.5 km (0.3 mi)	95 m (300 ft)	1.0 km (0.6 mi)	3.1 km (1.9 mi)
2977	Uranium hexafluoride, fissile containing more than 1% Uranium-235 **(when spilled in water)**						
2978	Radioactive material, Uranium hexafluoride, non fissile or fissile-excepted **(when spilled in water)**	30 m (100 ft)	0.2 km (0.1 mi)	0.5 km (0.3 mi)	95 m (300 ft)	1.0 km (0.6 mi)	3.1 km (1.9 mi)
2978	Uranium hexafluoride, fissile-excepted **(when spilled in water)**						
2978	Uranium hexafluoride, low specific activity **(when spilled in water)**						
2978	Uranium hexafluoride, non-fissile **(when spilled in water)**						
2985	Chlorosilanes, flammable, corrosive, n.o.s. **(when spilled in water)**	30 m (100 ft)	0.2 km (0.1 mi)	0.3 km (0.2 mi)	125 m (400 ft)	1.1 km (0.7 mi)	2.9 km (1.8 mi)
2985	Chlorosilanes, n.o.s. **(when spilled in water)**						
2986	Chlorosilanes, corrosive, flammable, n.o.s. **(when spilled in water)**	30 m (100 ft)	0.2 km (0.1 mi)	0.3 km (0.2 mi)	125 m (400 ft)	1.1 km (0.7 mi)	2.9 km (1.8 mi)
2986	Chlorosilanes, n.o.s. **(when spilled in water)**						
2987	Chlorosilanes, corrosive, n.o.s. **(when spilled in water)**	30 m (100 ft)	0.2 km (0.1 mi)	0.3 km (0.2 mi)	125 m (400 ft)	1.1 km (0.7 mi)	2.9 km (1.8 mi)
2987	Chlorosilanes, n.o.s. **(when spilled in water)**						

"+" means distance can be larger in certain atmospheric conditions

TABLE OF INITIAL ISOLATION AND PROTECTIVE ACTION DISTANCES

ID No.	NAME OF MATERIAL	SMALL SPILLS (From a small package or small leak from a large package)					LARGE SPILLS (From a large package or from many small packages)				
		First ISOLATE in all Directions		Then PROTECT persons Downwind during-			First ISOLATE in all Directions		Then PROTECT persons Downwind during-		
				DAY		NIGHT			DAY		NIGHT
		Meters	(Feet)	Kilometers (Miles)		Kilometers (Miles)	Meters	(Feet)	Kilometers (Miles)		Kilometers (Miles)
2988	Chlorosilanes, n.o.s. (When spilled in water) Chlorosilanes, water-reactive, flammable, corrosive, n.o.s. (When spilled in water)	30 m	(100 ft)	0.2 km	(0.1 mi)	0.3 km (0.2 mi)	125 m	(400 ft)	1.1 km	(0.7 mi)	2.9 km (1.8 mi)
3023 3023	2-Methyl-2-heptanethiol tert-Octyl mercaptan	30 m	(100 ft)	0.2 km	(0.1 mi)	0.2 km (0.1 mi)	60 m	(200 ft)	0.5 km	(0.3 mi)	1.1 km (0.7 mi)
3048	Aluminum phosphide pesticide (when spilled in water)	30 m	(100 ft)	0.2 km	(0.1 mi)	0.8 km (0.5 mi)	215 m	(700 ft)	1.9 km	(1.2 mi)	5.3 km (3.3 mi)
3049 3049 3049 3049	Metal alkyl halides, n.o.s. (when spilled in water) Metal alkyl halides, water-reactive, n.o.s. (when spilled in water) Metal aryl halides, n.o.s. (when spilled in water) Metal aryl halides, water-reactive, n.o.s. (when spilled in water)	30 m	(100 ft)	0.2 km	(0.1 mi)	0.2 km (0.1 mi)	30 m	(100 ft)	0.3 km	(0.2 mi)	1.3 km (0.8 mi)
3052	Aluminum alkyl halides (when spilled in water)	30 m	(100 ft)	0.2 km	(0.1 mi)	0.2 km (0.1 mi)	30 m	(100 ft)	0.3 km	(0.2 mi)	1.3 km (0.8 mi)
3057	Trifluoroacetyl chloride	30 m	(100 ft)	0.3 km	(0.2 mi)	1.4 km (0.9 mi)	430 m	(1400 ft)	4.0 km	(2.5 mi)	8.5 km (5.3 mi)
3079	Methacrylonitrile, inhibited	30 m	(100 ft)	0.2 km	(0.1 mi)	0.5 km (0.3 mi)	60 m	(200 ft)	0.6 km	(0.4 mi)	1.6 km (1.0 mi)
3083	Perchloryl fluoride	30 m	(100 ft)	0.2 km	(0.1 mi)	1.0 km (0.6 mi)	215 m	(700 ft)	2.3 km	(1.4 mi)	5.6 km (3.5 mi)

ID No.	Name of Material	SMALL SPILLS First ISOLATE in all Directions	SMALL SPILLS Then PROTECT persons Downwind during DAY	SMALL SPILLS Then PROTECT persons Downwind during NIGHT	LARGE SPILLS First ISOLATE in all Directions	LARGE SPILLS Then PROTECT persons Downwind during DAY	LARGE SPILLS Then PROTECT persons Downwind during NIGHT
3122	Poisonous liquid, oxidizing, n.o.s. (when "Inhalation Hazard" is on a package or shipping paper) (Inhalation Hazard Zone A)	155 m (500 ft)	1.3 km (0.8 mi)	3.4 km (2.1 mi)	915 m (3000 ft)	8.7 km (5.4 mi)	11.0+ km (7.0+ mi)
3122	Poisonous liquid, oxidizing, n.o.s. (Inhalation Hazard Zone B)	30 m (100 ft)	0.2 km (0.1 mi)	0.6 km (0.4 mi)	125 m (400 ft)	1.1 km (0.7 mi)	2.7 km (1.7 mi)
3122	Toxic liquid, oxidizing, n.o.s. (when "Inhalation Hazard" is on a package or shipping paper) Toxic liquid, oxidizing, n.o.s. (Inhalation Hazard Zone A)	155 m (500 ft)	1.3 km (0.8 mi)	3.4 km (2.1 mi)	915 m (3000 ft)	8.7 km (5.4 mi)	11.0+ km (7.0+ mi)
3122	Toxic liquid, oxidizing, n.o.s. (Inhalation Hazard Zone B)	30 m (100 ft)	0.2 km (0.1 mi)	0.6 km (0.4 mi)	125 m (400 ft)	1.1 km (0.7 mi)	2.7 km (1.7 mi)
3123	Poisonous liquid, water-reactive, n.o.s. (when "Inhalation Hazard" is on a package or shipping paper) Poisonous liquid, water-reactive, n.o.s. (Inhalation Hazard Zone A)	215 m (700 ft)	1.9 km (1.2 mi)	4.3 km (2.7 mi)	915 m (3000 ft)	11.0+ km (7.0+ mi)	11.0+ km (7.0+ mi)
3123	Poisonous liquid, water-reactive, n.o.s. (Inhalation Hazard Zone B)	60 m (200 ft)	0.5 km (0.3 mi)	1.3 km (0.8 mi)	245 m (800 ft)	2.3 km (1.4 mi)	5.0 km (3.1 mi)
3123	Poisonous liquid, which in contact with water emits flammable gases, n.o.s. (when "Inhalation Hazard" is on a package or shipping paper) Poisonous liquid, which in contact with water emits flammable gases, n.o.s. (Inhalation Hazard Zone A)	215 m (700 ft)	1.9 km (1.2 mi)	4.3 km (2.7 mi)	915 m (3000 ft)	11.0+ km (7.0+ mi)	11.0+ km (7.0+ mi)
3123	Poisonous liquid, which in contact with water emits flammable gases, n.o.s. (Inhalation Hazard Zone B)	60 m (200 ft)	0.5 km (0.3 mi)	1.3 km (0.8 mi)	245 m (800 ft)	2.3 km (1.4 mi)	5.0 km (3.1 mi)

"+" means distance can be larger in certain atmospheric conditions

TABLE OF INITIAL ISOLATION AND PROTECTIVE ACTION DISTANCES

		SMALL SPILLS				LARGE SPILLS			
		(From a small package or small leak from a large package)				(From a large package or from many small packages)			
		First ISOLATE in all Directions		Then PROTECT persons Downwind during-		First ISOLATE in all Directions		Then PROTECT persons Downwind during-	
				DAY	NIGHT			DAY	NIGHT
ID No.	NAME OF MATERIAL	Meters	(Feet)	Kilometers (Miles)	Kilometers (Miles)	Meters	(Feet)	Kilometers (Miles)	Kilometers (Miles)
3123	Toxic liquid, water-reactive, n.o.s. when "Inhalation Hazard" is on a package or shipping paper)	215 m	(700 ft)	1.9 km (1.2 mi)	4.3 km (2.7 mi)	915 m	(3000 ft)	11.0+ km (7.0+ mi)	11.0+ km (7.0+ mi)
3123	Toxic liquid, water-reactive, n.o.s. (Inhalation Hazard Zone A)	60 m	(200 ft)	0.5 km (0.3 mi)	1.3 km (0.8 mi)	245 m	(800 ft)	2.3 km (1.4 mi)	5.0 km (3.1 mi)
3123	Toxic liquid, water-reactive, n.o.s. (Inhalation Hazard Zone B)	215 m	(700 ft)	1.9 km (1.2 mi)	4.3 km (2.7 mi)	915 m	(3000 ft)	11.0+ km (7.0+ mi)	11.0+ km (7.0+ mi)
3123	Toxic liquid, which in contact with water emits flammable gases, n.o.s. (when "Inhalation Hazard" is on a package or shipping paper)								
3123	Toxic liquid, which in contact with water emits flammable gases, n.o.s. (Inhalation Hazard Zone A)	60 m	(200 ft)	0.5 km (0.3 mi)	1.3 km (0.8 mi)	245 m	(800 ft)	2.3 km (1.4 mi)	5.0 km (3.1 mi)
3123	Toxic liquid, which in contact with water emits flammable gases, n.o.s. (Inhalation Hazard Zone B)	185 m	(600 ft)	1.8 km (1.1 mi)	5.6 km (3.5 mi)	915 m	(3000 ft)	10.8 km (6.7 mi)	11.0+ km (7.0+ mi)
3160	Liquefied gas, poisonous, flammable, n.o.s.								
3160	Liquefied gas, poisonous, flammable, n.o.s. (Inhalation Hazard Zone A)								
3160	Liquefied gas, poisonous, flammable, n.o.s. (Inhalation Hazard Zone B)	30 m	(100 ft)	0.3 km (0.2 mi)	1.1 km (0.7 mi)	305 m	(1000 ft)	3.1 km (1.9 mi)	7.7 km (4.8 mi)

ID No.	Name of Material	SMALL SPILLS — First ISOLATE in all Directions	SMALL SPILLS — Then PROTECT persons Downwind during DAY	SMALL SPILLS — during NIGHT	LARGE SPILLS — First ISOLATE in all Directions	LARGE SPILLS — Then PROTECT persons Downwind during DAY	LARGE SPILLS — during NIGHT
3160	Liquefied gas, poisonous, flammable, n.o.s. (Inhalation Hazard Zone C)	30 m (100 ft)	0.2 km (0.1 mi)	1.0 km (0.6 mi)	215 m (700 ft)	2.1 km (1.3 mi)	5.6 km (3.5 mi)
3160	Liquefied gas, poisonous, flammable, n.o.s. (Inhalation Hazard Zone D)	30 m (100 ft)	0.2 km (0.1 mi)	0.6 km (0.4 mi)	185 m (600 ft)	1.6 km (1.0 mi)	4.3 km (2.7 mi)
3160 3160	Liquefied gas, toxic, flammable, n.o.s. Liquefied gas, toxic, flammable, n.o.s. (Inhalation Hazard Zone A)	185 m (600 ft)	1.8 km (1.1 mi)	5.6 km (3.5 mi)	915 m (3000 ft)	10.8 km (6.7 mi)	11.0+ km (7.0+ mi)
3160	Liquefied gas, toxic, flammable, n.o.s. (Inhalation Hazard Zone B)	30 m (100 ft)	0.3 km (0.2 mi)	1.1 km (0.7 mi)	305 m (1000 ft)	3.1 km (1.9 mi)	7.7 km (4.8 mi)
3160	Liquefied gas, toxic, flammable, n.o.s. (Inhalation Hazard Zone C)	30 m (100 ft)	0.2 km (0.1 mi)	1.0 km (0.6 mi)	215 m (700 ft)	2.1 km (1.3 mi)	5.6 km (3.5 mi)
3160	Liquefied gas, toxic, flammable, n.o.s. (Inhalation Hazard Zone D)	30 m (100 ft)	0.2 km (0.1 mi)	0.6 km (0.4 mi)	185 m (600 ft)	1.6 km (1.0 mi)	4.3 km (2.7 mi)
3162 3162	Liquefied gas, poisonous, n.o.s. Liquefied gas, poisonous, n.o.s. (Inhalation Hazard Zone A)	430 m (1400 ft)	4.2 km (2.6 mi)	8.4 km (5.2 mi)	915 m (3000 ft)	11.0+ km (7.0+ mi)	11.0+ km (7.0+ mi)
3162	Liquefied gas, poisonous, n.o.s. (Inhalation Hazard Zone B)	60 m (200 ft)	0.5 km (0.3 mi)	1.6 km (1.0 mi)	430 m (1400 ft)	4.0 km (2.5 mi)	9.8 km (6.1 mi)
3162	Liquefied gas, poisonous, n.o.s. (Inhalation Hazard Zone C)	30 m (100 ft)	0.3 km (0.2 mi)	1.3 km (0.8 mi)	215 m (700 ft)	3.1 km (1.9 mi)	7.2 km (4.5 mi)
3162	Liquefied gas, poisonous, n.o.s. (Inhalation Hazard Zone D)	30 m (100 ft)	0.2 km (0.1 mi)	0.6 km (0.4 mi)	185 m (600 ft)	1.6 km (1.0 mi)	4.3 km (2.7 mi)
3162 3162	Liquefied gas, toxic, n.o.s. Liquefied gas, toxic, n.o.s. (Inhalation Hazard Zone A)	430 m (1400 ft)	4.2 km (2.6 mi)	8.4 km (5.2 mi)	915 m (3000 ft)	11.0+ km (7.0+ mi)	11.0+ km (7.0+ mi)
3162	Liquefied gas, toxic, n.o.s. (Inhalation Hazard Zone B)	60 m (200 ft)	0.5 km (0.3 mi)	1.6 km (1.0 mi)	430 m (1400 ft)	4.0 km (2.5 mi)	9.8 km (6.1 mi)
3162	Liquefied gas, toxic, n.o.s. (Inhalation Hazard Zone C)	30 m (100 ft)	0.3 km (0.2 mi)	1.3 km (0.8 mi)	215 m (700 ft)	3.1 km (1.9 mi)	7.2 km (4.5 mi)

"+" means distance can be larger in certain atmospheric conditions

TABLE OF INITIAL ISOLATION AND PROTECTIVE ACTION DISTANCES

ID No.	NAME OF MATERIAL	SMALL SPILLS (From a small package or small leak from a large package)					LARGE SPILLS (From a large package or from many small packages)					
		First ISOLATE in all Directions		Then PROTECT persons Downwind during—				First ISOLATE in all Directions		Then PROTECT persons Downwind during—		
				DAY		NIGHT				DAY		NIGHT	
		Meters	(Feet)	Kilometers (Miles)		Kilometers (Miles)		Meters	(Feet)	Kilometers (Miles)		Kilometers (Miles)	
3162	Liquefied gas, toxic, n.o.s. (Inhalation Hazard Zone D)	30 m	(100 ft)	0.2 km	(0.1 mi)	0.6 km	(0.4 mi)	185 m	(600 ft)	1.6 km	(1.0 mi)	4.3 km	(2.7 mi)
3246 3246	Methanesulfonyl chloride Methanesulphonyl chloride	95 m	(300 ft)	0.6 km	(0.4 mi)	2.4 km	(1.5 mi)	245 m	(800 ft)	2.3 km	(1.4 mi)	5.1 km	(3.2 mi)
3275	Nitriles, poisonous, flammable, n.o.s. (when "Inhalation Hazard" is on a package or shipping paper)	30 m	(100 ft)	0.2 km	(0.1 mi)	0.5 km	(0.3 mi)	60 m	(200 ft)	0.6 km	(0.4 mi)	1.6 km	(1.0 mi)
3275	Nitriles, toxic, flammable, n.o.s. (when "Inhalation Hazard" is on a package or shipping paper)												
3276 3276	Nitriles, poisonous, n.o.s. Nitriles, toxic, n.o.s.	30 m	(100 ft)	0.2 km	(0.1 mi)	0.5 km	(0.3 mi)	60 m	(200 ft)	0.6 km	(0.4 mi)	1.6 km	(1.0 mi)
3278	Organophosphorus compound, poisonous, n.o.s. (when "Inhalation Hazard" is on a package or shipping paper)	60 m	(200 ft)	0.5 km	(0.3 mi)	1.3 km	(0.8 mi)	245 m	(800 ft)	2.3 km	(1.4 mi)	5.0 km	(3.1 mi)
3278	Organophosphorus compound, toxic, n.o.s. (when "Inhalation Hazard" is on a package or shipping paper)												
3279	Organophosphorus compound, poisonous, flammable, n.o.s. (when "Inhalation Hazard" is on a package or shipping paper)	60 m	(200 ft)	0.5 km	(0.3 mi)	1.3 km	(0.8 mi)	245 m	(800 ft)	2.3 km	(1.4 mi)	5.0 km	(3.1 mi)
3279	Organophosphorus compound, toxic, flammable, n.o.s. (when "Inhalation Hazard" is on a package or shipping paper)												

ID No.	Name of Material	SMALL SPILLS First ISOLATE in all Directions	SMALL SPILLS Then PROTECT persons Downwind during DAY	SMALL SPILLS Then PROTECT persons Downwind during NIGHT	LARGE SPILLS First ISOLATE in all Directions	LARGE SPILLS Then PROTECT persons Downwind during DAY	LARGE SPILLS Then PROTECT persons Downwind during NIGHT
3280	Organoarsenic compound, n.o.s. (when "Inhalation Hazard" is on a package or shipping paper)	30 m (100 ft)	0.2 km (0.1 mi)	0.8 km (0.5 mi)	185 m (600 ft)	1.8 km (1.1 mi)	4.3 km (2.7 mi)
3281	Metal carbonyls, n.o.s.	60 m (200 ft)	0.6 km (0.4 mi)	2.1 km (1.3 mi)	215 m (700 ft)	2.1 km (1.3 mi)	4.3 km (2.7 mi)
3287	Poisonous liquid, inorganic, n.o.s. (when "Inhalation Hazard" is on a package or shipping paper)	155 m (500 ft)	1.3 km (0.8 mi)	3.7 km (2.3 mi)	765 m (2500 ft)	6.6 km (4.1 mi)	10.6 km (6.6 mi)
3287	Poisonous liquid, inorganic, n.o.s. (Inhalation Hazard Zone A)						
3287	Poisonous liquid, inorganic, n.o.s. (Inhalation Hazard Zone B)	60 m (200 ft)	0.5 km (0.3 mi)	1.3 km (0.8 mi)	245 m (800 ft)	2.3 km (1.4 mi)	5.0 km (3.1 mi)
3287	Toxic liquid, inorganic, n.o.s. (when "Inhalation Hazard" is on a package or shipping paper)	155 m (500 ft)	1.3 km (0.8 mi)	3.7 km (2.3 mi)	765 m (2500 ft)	6.6 km (4.1 mi)	10.6 km (6.6 mi)
3287	Toxic liquid, inorganic, n.o.s. (Inhalation Hazard Zone A)						
3287	Toxic liquid, inorganic, n.o.s. (Inhalation Hazard Zone B)	60 m (200 ft)	0.5 km (0.3 mi)	1.3 km (0.8 mi)	245 m (800 ft)	2.3 km (1.4 mi)	5.0 km (3.1 mi)
3289	Poisonous liquid, corrosive, inorganic, n.o.s. (when "Inhalation Hazard" is on a package or shipping paper)	95 m (300 ft)	0.6 km (0.4 mi)	1.8 km (1.1 mi)	400 m (1300 ft)	2.6 km (1.6 mi)	5.0 km (3.1 mi)
3289	Poisonous liquid, corrosive, inorganic, n.o.s. (Inhalation Hazard Zone A)						
3289	Poisonous liquid, corrosive, inorganic, n.o.s. (Inhalation Hazard Zone B)	60 m (200 ft)	0.3 km (0.2 mi)	1.1 km (0.7 mi)	185 m (600 ft)	1.6 km (1.0 mi)	4.0 km (2.5 mi)
3289	Toxic liquid, corrosive, inorganic, n.o.s. (when "Inhalation Hazard" is on a package or shipping paper)	95 m (300 ft)	0.6 km (0.4 mi)	1.8 km (1.1 mi)	400 m (1300 ft)	2.6 km (1.6 mi)	5.0 km (3.1 mi)
3289	Toxic liquid, corrosive, inorganic, n.o.s. (Inhalation Hazard Zone A)						

"+" means distance can be larger in certain atmospheric conditions

TABLE OF INITIAL ISOLATION AND PROTECTIVE ACTION DISTANCES

ID No.	NAME OF MATERIAL	SMALL SPILLS (From a small package or small leak from a large package)				LARGE SPILLS (From a large package or from many small packages)			
		First ISOLATE in all Directions		Then PROTECT persons Downwind during—		First ISOLATE in all Directions		Then PROTECT persons Downwind during—	
				DAY	NIGHT			DAY	NIGHT
		Meters	(Feet)	Kilometers (Miles)	Kilometers (Miles)	Meters	(Feet)	Kilometers (Miles)	Kilometers (Miles)
3289	Toxic liquid, corrosive, inorganic, n.o.s. (Inhalation Hazard Zone B)	60 m	(200 ft)	0.3 km (0.2 mi)	1.1 km (0.7 mi)	185 m	(600 ft)	1.6 km (1.0 mi)	4.0 km (2.5 mi)
3294	Hydrogen cyanide, solution in alcohol, with not more than 45% Hydrogen cyanide (when "Inhalation Hazard" is on a package or shipping paper)	30 m	(100 ft)	0.2 km (0.1 mi)	0.3 km (0.2 mi)	215 m	(700 ft)	0.6 km (0.4 mi)	1.9 km (1.2 mi)
3300	Carbon dioxide and Ethylene oxide mixture, with more than 87% Ethylene oxide	30 m	(100 ft)	0.2 km (0.1 mi)	0.2 km (0.1 mi)	60 m	(200 ft)	0.5 km (0.3 mi)	1.8 km (1.1 mi)
3300	Ethylene oxide and Carbon dioxide mixture, with more than 87% Ethylene oxide								
3303	Compressed gas, poisonous, oxidizing, n.o.s.	430 m	(1400 ft)	4.2 km (2.6 mi)	8.4 km (5.2 mi)	915 m	(3000 ft)	11.0+ km (7.0+ mi)	11.0+ km (7.0+ mi)
3303	Compressed gas, poisonous, oxidizing, n.o.s. (Inhalation Hazard Zone A)								
3303	Compressed gas, poisonous, oxidizing, n.o.s. (Inhalation Hazard Zone B)	60 m	(200 ft)	0.5 km (0.3 mi)	1.6 km (1.0 mi)	335 m	(1100 ft)	3.4 km (2.1 mi)	7.7 km (4.8 mi)
3303	Compressed gas, poisonous, oxidizing, n.o.s. (Inhalation Hazard Zone C)	30 m	(100 ft)	0.3 km (0.2 mi)	1.3 km (0.8 mi)	215 m	(700 ft)	3.1 km (1.9 mi)	7.2 km (4.5 mi)
3303	Compressed gas, poisonous, oxidizing, n.o.s. (Inhalation Hazard Zone D)	30 m	(100 ft)	0.2 km (0.1 mi)	0.6 km (0.4 mi)	185 m	(600 ft)	1.6 km (1.0 mi)	4.3 km (2.7 mi)

ID No.	Name of Material	First ISOLATE in all Directions	Then PROTECT persons Downwind during- DAY	Then PROTECT persons Downwind during- NIGHT	First ISOLATE in all Directions	Then PROTECT persons Downwind during- DAY	Then PROTECT persons Downwind during- NIGHT
3303	Compressed gas, toxic, oxidizing, n.o.s. Compressed gas, toxic, oxidizing, n.o.s. (Inhalation Hazard Zone A)	430 m (1400 ft)	4.2 km (2.6 mi)	8.4 km (5.2 mi)	915 m (3000 ft)	11.0+ km (7.0+ mi)	11.0+ km (7.0+ mi)
3303	Compressed gas, toxic, oxidizing, n.o.s. (Inhalation Hazard Zone B)	60 m (200 ft)	0.5 km (0.3 mi)	1.6 km (1.0 mi)	335 m (1100 ft)	3.4 km (2.1 mi)	7.7 km (4.8 mi)
3303	Compressed gas, toxic, oxidizing, n.o.s. (Inhalation Hazard Zone C)	30 m (100 ft)	0.3 km (0.2 mi)	1.3 km (0.8 mi)	215 m (700 ft)	3.1 km (1.9 mi)	7.2 km (4.5 mi)
3303	Compressed gas, toxic, oxidizing, n.o.s. (Inhalation Hazard Zone D)	30 m (100 ft)	0.2 km (0.1 mi)	0.6 km (0.4 mi)	185 m (600 ft)	1.6 km (1.0 mi)	4.3 km (2.7 mi)
3304	Compressed gas, poisonous, corrosive, n.o.s. Compressed gas, poisonous, corrosive, n.o.s. (Inhalation Hazard Zone A)	430 m (1400 ft)	4.2 km (2.6 mi)	8.4 km (5.2 mi)	915 m (3000 ft)	11.0+ km (7.0+ mi)	11.0+ km (7.0+ mi)
3304	Compressed gas, poisonous, corrosive, n.o.s. (Inhalation Hazard Zone B)	60 m (200 ft)	0.5 km (0.3 mi)	1.6 km (1.0 mi)	430 m (1400 ft)	4.0 km (2.5 mi)	9.8 km (6.1 mi)
3304	Compressed gas, poisonous, corrosive, n.o.s. (Inhalation Hazard Zone C)	30 m (100 ft)	0.3 km (0.2 mi)	1.3 km (0.8 mi)	185 m (600 ft)	3.1 km (1.9 mi)	7.2 km (4.5 mi)
3304	Compressed gas, poisonous, corrosive, n.o.s. (Inhalation Hazard Zone D)	30 m (100 ft)	0.2 km (0.1 mi)	0.6 km (0.4 mi)	185 m (600 ft)	1.6 km (1.0 mi)	4.3 km (2.7 mi)
3304	Compressed gas, toxic, corrosive, n.o.s. Compressed gas, toxic, corrosive, n.o.s. (Inhalation Hazard Zone A)	430 m (1400 ft)	4.2 km (2.6 mi)	8.4 km (5.2 mi)	915 m (3000 ft)	11.0+ km (7.0+ mi)	11.0+ km (7.0+ mi)

"+" means distance can be larger in certain atmospheric conditions

TABLE OF INITIAL ISOLATION AND PROTECTIVE ACTION DISTANCES

		SMALL SPILLS					LARGE SPILLS					
		(From a small package or small leak from a large package)					(From a large package or from many small packages)					
		First ISOLATE in all Directions		Then PROTECT persons Downwind during-				First ISOLATE in all Directions		Then PROTECT persons Downwind during-		
					DAY		NIGHT				DAY		NIGHT
ID No.	NAME OF MATERIAL	Meters	(Feet)	Kilometers (Miles)		Kilometers (Miles)		Meters	(Feet)	Kilometers (Miles)		Kilometers (Miles)
3304	Compressed gas, toxic, corrosive, n.o.s. (Inhalation Hazard Zone B)	60 m	(200 ft)	0.5 km	(0.3 mi)	1.6 km	(1.0 mi)	430 m	(1400 ft)	4.0 km	(2.5 mi)	9.8 km (6.1 mi)
3304	Compressed gas, toxic, corrosive, n.o.s. (Inhalation Hazard Zone C)	30 m	(100 ft)	0.3 km	(0.2 mi)	1.3 km	(0.8 mi)	185 m	(600 ft)	3.1 km	(1.9 mi)	7.2 km (4.5 mi)
3304	Compressed gas, toxic, corrosive, n.o.s. (Inhalation Hazard Zone D)	30 m	(100 ft)	0.2 km	(0.1 mi)	0.6 km	(0.4 mi)	185 m	(600 ft)	1.6 km	(1.0 mi)	4.3 km (2.7 mi)
3305	Compressed gas, poisonous, flammable, corrosive, n.o.s.	430 m	(1400 ft)	4.2 km	(2.6 mi)	8.4 km	(5.2 mi)	915 m	(3000 ft)	11.0+ km	(7.0+ mi)	11.0+ km (7.0+ mi)
3305	Compressed gas, poisonous, flammable, corrosive, n.o.s. (Inhalation Hazard Zone A)											
3305	Compressed gas, poisonous, flammable, corrosive, n.o.s. (Inhalation Hazard Zone B)	60 m	(200 ft)	0.5 km	(0.3 mi)	1.6 km	(1.0 mi)	430 m	(1400 ft)	4.0 km	(2.5 mi)	9.8 km (6.1 mi)
3305	Compressed gas, poisonous, flammable, corrosive, n.o.s. (Inhalation Hazard Zone C)	30 m	(100 ft)	0.3 km	(0.2 mi)	1.3 km	(0.8 mi)	185 m	(600 ft)	3.1 km	(1.9 mi)	7.2 km (4.5 mi)
3305	Compressed gas, poisonous, flammable, corrosive, n.o.s. (Inhalation Hazard Zone D)	30 m	(100 ft)	0.2 km	(0.1 mi)	0.6 km	(0.4 mi)	185 m	(600 ft)	1.6 km	(1.0 mi)	4.3 km (2.7 mi)
3305	Compressed gas, toxic, flammable, corrosive, n.o.s. (Inhalation Hazard Zone A)	430 m	(1400 ft)	4.2 km	(2.6 mi)	8.4 km	(5.2 mi)	915 m	(3000 ft)	11.0+ km	(7.0+ mi)	11.0+ km (7.0+ mi)

ID No.	Name of Material	SMALL SPILLS First ISOLATE in all Directions	SMALL SPILLS Then PROTECT Day	SMALL SPILLS Then PROTECT Night	LARGE SPILLS First ISOLATE in all Directions	LARGE SPILLS Then PROTECT Day	LARGE SPILLS Then PROTECT Night
3305	Compressed gas, toxic, flammable, corrosive, n.o.s. (Inhalation Hazard Zone B)	60 m (200 ft)	0.5 km (0.3 mi)	1.6 km (1.0 mi)	430 m (1400 ft)	4.0 km (2.5 mi)	9.8 km (6.1 mi)
3305	Compressed gas, toxic, flammable, corrosive, n.o.s. (Inhalation Hazard Zone C)	30 m (100 ft)	0.3 km (0.2 mi)	1.3 km (0.8 mi)	185 m (600 ft)	3.1 km (1.9 mi)	7.2 km (4.5 mi)
3305	Compressed gas, toxic, flammable, corrosive, n.o.s. (Inhalation Hazard Zone D)	30 m (100 ft)	0.2 km (0.1 mi)	0.6 km (0.4 mi)	185 m (600 ft)	1.6 km (1.0 mi)	4.3 km (2.7 mi)
3306	Compressed gas, poisonous, oxidizing, corrosive, n.o.s. / Compressed gas, poisonous, oxidizing, corrosive, n.o.s. (Inhalation Hazard Zone A)	430 m (1400 ft)	4.2 km (2.6 mi)	8.4 km (5.2 mi)	915 m (3000 ft)	11.0+ km (7.0+ mi)	11.0+ km (7.0+ mi)
3306	Compressed gas, poisonous, oxidizing, corrosive, n.o.s. (Inhalation Hazard Zone B)	60 m (200 ft)	0.5 km (0.3 mi)	1.6 km (1.0 mi)	335 m (1100 ft)	3.4 km (2.1 mi)	7.7 km (4.8 mi)
3306	Compressed gas, poisonous, oxidizing, corrosive, n.o.s. (Inhalation Hazard Zone C)	30 m (100 ft)	0.3 km (0.2 mi)	1.3 km (0.8 mi)	185 m (600 ft)	3.1 km (1.9 mi)	7.2 km (4.5 mi)
3306	Compressed gas, poisonous, oxidizing, corrosive, n.o.s. (Inhalation Hazard Zone D)	30 m (100 ft)	0.2 km (0.1 mi)	0.6 km (0.4 mi)	185 m (600 ft)	1.6 km (1.0 mi)	4.3 km (2.7 mi)
3306	Compressed gas, toxic, oxidizing, corrosive, n.o.s. / Compressed gas, toxic, oxidizing, corrosive, n.o.s. (Inhalation Hazard Zone A)	430 m (1400 ft)	4.2 km (2.6 mi)	8.4 km (5.2 mi)	915 m (3000 ft)	11.0+ km (7.0+ mi)	11.0+ km (7.0+ mi)
3306	Compressed gas, toxic, oxidizing, corrosive, n.o.s. (Inhalation Hazard Zone B)	60 m (200 ft)	0.5 km (0.3 mi)	1.6 km (1.0 mi)	335 m (1100 ft)	3.4 km (2.1 mi)	7.7 km (4.8 mi)
3306	Compressed gas, toxic, oxidizing, corrosive, n.o.s. (Inhalation Hazard Zone C)	30 m (100 ft)	0.3 km (0.2 mi)	1.3 km (0.8 mi)	185 m (600 ft)	3.1 km (1.9 mi)	7.2 km (4.5 mi)

"+" means distance can be larger in certain atmospheric conditions

TABLE OF INITIAL ISOLATION AND PROTECTIVE ACTION DISTANCES

ID No.	NAME OF MATERIAL	SMALL SPILLS (From a small package or small leak from a large package)				LARGE SPILLS (From a large package or from many small packages)			
		First ISOLATE in all Directions		Then PROTECT persons Downwind during-		First ISOLATE in all Directions		Then PROTECT persons Downwind during-	
				DAY	NIGHT			DAY	NIGHT
		Meters	(Feet)	Kilometers (Miles)	Kilometers (Miles)	Meters	(Feet)	Kilometers (Miles)	Kilometers (Miles)
3306	Compressed gas, toxic, oxidizing, corrosive, n.o.s. (Inhalation Hazard Zone D)	30 m	(100 ft)	0.2 km (0.1 mi)	0.6 km (0.4 mi)	185 m	(600 ft)	1.6 km (1.0 mi)	4.3 km (2.7 mi)
3307	Liquefied gas, poisonous, oxidizing, n.o.s.	430 m	(1400 ft)	4.2 km (2.6 mi)	8.4 km (5.2 mi)	915 m	(3000 ft)	11.0+ km (7.0+ mi)	11.0+ km (7.0+ mi)
3307	Liquefied gas, poisonous, oxidizing, n.o.s. (Inhalation Hazard Zone A)								
3307	Liquefied gas, poisonous, oxidizing, n.o.s. (Inhalation Hazard Zone B)	60 m	(200 ft)	0.5 km (0.3 mi)	1.6 km (1.0 mi)	335 m	(1100 ft)	3.4 km (2.1 mi)	7.7 km (4.8 mi)
3307	Liquefied gas, poisonous, oxidizing, n.o.s. (Inhalation Hazard Zone C)	30 m	(100 ft)	0.3 km (0.2 mi)	1.3 km (0.8 mi)	215 m	(700 ft)	3.1 km (1.9 mi)	7.2 km (4.5 mi)
3307	Liquefied gas, poisonous, oxidizing, n.o.s. (Inhalation Hazard Zone D)	30 m	(100 ft)	0.2 km (0.1 mi)	0.6 km (0.4 mi)	185 m	(600 ft)	1.6 km (1.0 mi)	4.3 km (2.7 mi)
3307	Liquefied gas, toxic, oxidizing, n.o.s.	430 m	(1400 ft)	4.2 km (2.6 mi)	8.4 km (5.2 mi)	915 m	(3000 ft)	11.0+ km (7.0+ mi)	11.0+ km (7.0+ mi)
3307	Liquefied gas, toxic, oxidizing, n.o.s. (Inhalation Hazard Zone A)								
3307	Liquefied gas, toxic, oxidizing, n.o.s. (Inhalation Hazard Zone B)	60 m	(200 ft)	0.5 km (0.3 mi)	1.6 km (1.0 mi)	335 m	(1100 ft)	3.4 km (2.1 mi)	7.7 km (4.8 mi)
3307	Liquefied gas, toxic, oxidizing, n.o.s. (Inhalation Hazard Zone C)	30 m	(100 ft)	0.3 km (0.2 mi)	1.3 km (0.8 mi)	215 m	(700 ft)	3.1 km (1.9 mi)	7.2 km (4.5 mi)
3307	Liquefied gas, toxic, oxidizing, n.o.s. (Inhalation Hazard Zone D)	30 m	(100 ft)	0.2 km (0.1 mi)	0.6 km (0.4 mi)	185 m	(600 ft)	1.6 km (1.0 mi)	4.3 km (2.7 mi)

ID No.	Name of Material	First ISOLATE in all Directions (m)	(ft)	Then PROTECT persons Downwind — Day (km)	(mi)	Then PROTECT persons Downwind — Night (km)	(mi)	First ISOLATE in all Directions (m)	(ft)	Then PROTECT persons Downwind — Day (km)	(mi)	Then PROTECT persons Downwind — Night (km)	(mi)
3308	Liquefied gas, poisonous, corrosive, n.o.s.	430 m	(1400 ft)	4.2 km	(2.6 mi)	8.4 km	(5.2 mi)	915 m	(3000 ft)	11.0+ km	(7.0+ mi)	11.0+ km	(7.0+ mi)
3308	Liquefied gas, poisonous, corrosive, n.o.s. (Inhalation Hazard Zone A)												
3308	Liquefied gas, poisonous, corrosive, n.o.s. (Inhalation Hazard Zone B)	60 m	(200 ft)	0.5 km	(0.3 mi)	1.6 km	(1.0 mi)	430 m	(1400 ft)	4.0 km	(2.5 mi)	9.8 km	(6.1 mi)
3308	Liquefied gas, poisonous, corrosive, n.o.s. (Inhalation Hazard Zone C)	30 m	(100 ft)	0.3 km	(0.2 mi)	1.3 km	(0.8 mi)	185 m	(600 ft)	3.1 km	(1.9 mi)	7.2 km	(4.5 mi)
3308	Liquefied gas, poisonous, corrosive, n.o.s. (Inhalation Hazard Zone D)	30 m	(100 ft)	0.2 km	(0.1 mi)	0.6 km	(0.4 mi)	185 m	(600 ft)	1.6 km	(1.0 mi)	4.3 km	(2.7 mi)
3308 3308	Liquefied gas, toxic, corrosive, n.o.s. Liquefied gas, toxic, corrosive, n.o.s. (Inhalation Hazard Zone A)	430 m	(1400 ft)	4.2 km	(2.6 mi)	8.4 km	(5.2 mi)	915 m	(3000 ft)	11.0+ km	(7.0+ mi)	11.0+ km	(7.0+ mi)
3308	Liquefied gas, toxic, corrosive, n.o.s. (Inhalation Hazard Zone B)	60 m	(200 ft)	0.5 km	(0.3 mi)	1.6 km	(1.0 mi)	430 m	(1400 ft)	4.0 km	(2.5 mi)	9.8 km	(6.1 mi)
3308	Liquefied gas, toxic, corrosive, n.o.s. (Inhalation Hazard Zone C)	30 m	(100 ft)	0.3 km	(0.2 mi)	1.3 km	(0.8 mi)	185 m	(600 ft)	3.1 km	(1.9 mi)	7.2 km	(4.5 mi)
3308	Liquefied gas, toxic, corrosive, n.o.s. (Inhalation Hazard Zone D)	30 m	(100 ft)	0.2 km	(0.1 mi)	0.6 km	(0.4 mi)	185 m	(600 ft)	1.6 km	(1.0 mi)	4.3 km	(2.7 mi)
3309 3009	Liquefied gas, poisonous, flammable, corrosive, n.o.s. Liquefied gas, poisonous, flammable, corrosive, n.o.s. (Inhalation Hazard Zone A)	430 m	(1400 ft)	4.2 km	(2.6 mi)	8.4 km	(5.2 mi)	915 m	(3000 ft)	11.0+ km	(7.0+ mi)	11.0+ km	(7.0+ mi)
3309	Liquefied gas, poisonous, flammable, corrosive, n.o.s. (Inhalation Hazard Zone B)	60 m	(200 ft)	0.5 km	(0.3 mi)	1.6 km	(1.0 mi)	430 m	(1400 ft)	4.0 km	(2.5 mi)	9.8 km	(6.1 mi)
3309	Liquefied gas, poisonous, flammable, corrosive, n.o.s. (Inhalation Hazard Zone C)	30 m	(100 ft)	0.3 km	(0.2 mi)	1.3 km	(0.8 mi)	185 m	(600 ft)	3.1 km	(1.9 mi)	7.2 km	(4.5 mi)

"+" means distance can be larger in certain atmospheric conditions

TABLE OF INITIAL ISOLATION AND PROTECTIVE ACTION DISTANCES

ID No.	NAME OF MATERIAL	SMALL SPILLS (From a small package or small leak from a large package)			LARGE SPILLS (From a large package or from many small packages)		
		First ISOLATE in all Directions	Then PROTECT persons Downwind during—		First ISOLATE in all Directions	Then PROTECT persons Downwind during—	
		Meters (Feet)	DAY Kilometers (Miles)	NIGHT Kilometers (Miles)	Meters (Feet)	DAY Kilometers (Miles)	NIGHT Kilometers (Miles)
3309	Liquefied gas, poisonous, flammable, corrosive, n.o.s. (Inhalation Hazard Zone D)	30 m (100 ft)	0.2 km (0.1 mi)	0.6 km (0.4 mi)	185 m (600 ft)	1.6 km (1.0 mi)	4.3 km (2.7 mi)
3309	Liquefied gas, toxic, flammable, corrosive, n.o.s.	430 m (1400 ft)	4.2 km (2.6 mi)	8.4 km (5.2 mi)	915 m (3000 ft)	11.0+ km (7.0+ mi)	11.0+ km (7.0+ mi)
3309	Liquefied gas, toxic, flammable, corrosive, n.o.s. (Inhalation Hazard Zone A)						
3309	Liquefied gas, toxic, flammable, corrosive, n.o.s. (Inhalation Hazard Zone B)	60 m (200 ft)	0.5 km (0.3 mi)	1.6 km (1.0 mi)	430 m (1400 ft)	4.0 km (2.5 mi)	9.8 km (6.1 mi)
3309	Liquefied gas, toxic, flammable, corrosive, n.o.s. (Inhalation Hazard Zone C)	30 m (100 ft)	0.3 km (0.2 mi)	1.3 km (0.8 mi)	185 m (600 ft)	3.1 km (1.9 mi)	7.2 km (4.5 mi)
3309	Liquefied gas, toxic, flammable, corrosive, n.o.s. (Inhalation Hazard Zone D)	30 m (100 ft)	0.2 km (0.1 mi)	0.6 km (0.4 mi)	185 m (600 ft)	1.6 km (1.0 mi)	4.3 km (2.7 mi)
3310	Liquefied gas, poisonous, oxidizing, corrosive, n.o.s.	430 m (1400 ft)	4.2 km (2.6 mi)	8.4 km (5.2 mi)	915 m (3000 ft)	11.0+ km (7.0+ mi)	11.0+ km (7.0+ mi)
3310	Liquefied gas, poisonous, oxidizing, corrosive, n.o.s. (Inhalation Hazard Zone A)						
3310	Liquefied gas, poisonous, oxidizing, corrosive, n.o.s. (Inhalation Hazard Zone B)	60 m (200 ft)	0.5 km (0.3 mi)	1.6 km (1.0 mi)	335 m (1100 ft)	3.4 km (2.1 mi)	7.7 km (4.8 mi)
3310	Liquefied gas, poisonous, oxidizing, corrosive, n.o.s. (Inhalation Hazard Zone C)	30 m (100 ft)	0.3 km (0.2 mi)	1.3 km (0.8 mi)	185 m (600 ft)	3.1 km (1.9 mi)	7.2 km (4.5 mi)

ID No.	Name of Material						
3310	Liquefied gas, poisonous, oxidizing, corrosive, n.o.s. (Inhalation Hazard Zone D)	30 m (100 ft)	0.2 km (0.1 mi)	0.6 km (0.4 mi)	185 m (600 ft)	1.6 km (1.0 mi)	4.3 km (2.7 mi)
3310	Liquefied gas, toxic, oxidizing, corrosive, n.o.s.	430 m (1400 ft)	4.2 km (2.6 mi)	8.4 km (5.2 mi)	915 m (3000 ft)	11.0+ km (7.0+ mi)	11.0+ km (7.0+ mi)
3310	Liquefied gas, toxic, oxidizing, corrosive, n.o.s. (Inhalation Hazard Zone A)						
3310	Liquefied gas, toxic, oxidizing, corrosive, n.o.s. (Inhalation Hazard Zone B)	60 m (200 ft)	0.5 km (0.3 mi)	1.6 km (1.0 mi)	335 m (1100 ft)	3.4 km (2.1 mi)	7.7 km (4.8 mi)
3310	Liquefied gas, toxic, oxidizing, corrosive, n.o.s. (Inhalation Hazard Zone C)	30 m (100 ft)	0.3 km (0.2 mi)	1.3 km (0.8 mi)	185 m (600 ft)	3.1 km (1.9 mi)	7.2 km (4.5 mi)
3310	Liquefied gas, toxic, oxidizing, corrosive, n.o.s. (Inhalation Hazard Zone D)	30 m (100 ft)	0.2 km (0.1 mi)	0.6 km (0.4 mi)	185 m (600 ft)	1.6 km (1.0 mi)	4.3 km (2.7 mi)
3318	Ammonia solution, with more than 50% Ammonia	30 m (100 ft)	0.2 km (0.1 mi)	0.2 km (0.1 mi)	60 m (200 ft)	0.5 km (0.3 mi)	1.1 km (0.7 mi)
3355	Insecticide gas, poisonous, flammable, n.o.s	430 m (1400 ft)	4.2 km (2.6 mi)	8.4 km (5.2 mi)	915 m (3000 ft)	11.0+ km (7.0+ mi)	11.0+ km (7.0+ mi)
3355	Insecticide gas, poisonous, flammable, n.o.s. (Inhalation Hazard Zone A)						
3355	Insecticide gas, poisonous, flammable, n.o.s. (Inhalation Hazard Zone B)	60 m (200 ft)	0.5 km (0.3 mi)	1.6 km (1.0 mi)	430 m (1400 ft)	4.0 km (2.5 mi)	9.8 km (6.1 mi)
3355	Insecticide gas, poisonous, flammable, n.o.s. (Inhalation Hazard Zone C)	30 m (100 ft)	0.3 km (0.2 mi)	1.3 km (0.8 mi)	215 m (700 ft)	3.1 km (1.9 mi)	7.2 km (4.5 mi)
3355	Insecticide gas, poisonous, flammable, n.o.s. (Inhalation Hazard Zone D)	30 m (100 ft)	0.2 km (0.1 mi)	0.6 km (0.4 mi)	185 m (600 ft)	1.6 km (1.0 mi)	4.3 km (2.7 mi)

"+" means distance can be larger in certain atmospheric conditions

TABLE OF INITIAL ISOLATION AND PROTECTIVE ACTION DISTANCES

ID No.	NAME OF MATERIAL	SMALL SPILLS (From a small package or small leak from a large package)			LARGE SPILLS (From a large package or from many small packages)		
		First ISOLATE in all Directions	Then PROTECT persons Downwind during-		First ISOLATE in all Directions	Then PROTECT persons Downwind during-	
		Meters (Feet)	DAY Kilometers (Miles)	NIGHT Kilometers (Miles)	Meters (Feet)	DAY Kilometers (Miles)	NIGHT Kilometers (Miles)
3355	Insecticide gas, toxic, flammable, n.o.s	430 m (1400 ft)	4.2 km (2.6 mi)	8.4 km (5.2 mi)	915 m (3000 ft)	11.0+ km (7.0+ mi)	11.0+ km (7.0+ mi)
3355	Insecticide gas, toxic, flammable, n.o.s. (Inhalation Hazard Zone A)						
3355	Insecticide gas, toxic, flammable, n.o.s. (Inhalation Hazard Zone B)	60 m (200 ft)	0.5 km (0.3 mi)	1.6 km (1.0 mi)	430 m (1400 ft)	4.0 km (2.5 mi)	9.8 km (6.1 mi)
3355	Insecticide gas, toxic, flammable, n.o.s. (Inhalation Hazard Zone C)	30 m (100 ft)	0.3 km (0.2 mi)	1.3 km (0.8 mi)	215 m (700 ft)	3.1 km (1.9 mi)	7.2 km (4.5 mi)
3355	Insecticide gas, toxic, flammable, n.o.s. (Inhalation Hazard Zone D)	30 m (100 ft)	0.2 km (0.1 mi)	0.6 km (0.4 mi)	185 m (600 ft)	1.6 km (1.0 mi)	4.3 km (2.7 mi)
9191	Chlorine dioxide, hydrate, frozen (when spilled in water)	30 m (100 ft)	0.2 km (0.1 mi)	0.2 km (0.1 mi)	30 m (100 ft)	0.2 km (0.1 mi)	0.6 km (0.4 mi)
9192	Fluorine, refrigerated liquid (cryogenic liquid)	30 m (100 ft)	0.2 km (0.1 mi)	0.5 km (0.3 mi)	185 m (600 ft)	1.4 km (0.9 mi)	4.0 km (2.5 mi)
9202	Carbon monoxide, refrigerated liquid (cryogenic liquid)	30 m (100 ft)	0.2 km (0.1 mi)	0.2 km (0.1 mi)	125 m (400 ft)	0.6 km (0.4 mi)	1.8 km (1.1 mi)
9206	Methyl phosphonic-dichloride	30 m (100 ft)	0.2 km (0.1 mi)	0.2 km (0.1 mi)	30 m (100 ft)	0.2 km (0.1 mi)	0.3 km (0.2 mi)
9263	Chloropivaloylchloride	30 m (100 ft)	0.2 km (0.1 mi)	0.2 km (0.1 mi)	30 m (100 ft)	0.3 km (0.2 mi)	0.5 km (0.3 mi)
9264	3,5-Dichloro-2,4,6-trifluoropyridine	30 m (100 ft)	0.2 km (0.1 mi)	0.2 km (0.1 mi)	30 m (100 ft)	0.3 km (0.2 mi)	0.5 km (0.3 mi)
9269	Trimethoxysilane	30 m (100 ft)	0.3 km (0.2 mi)	1.0 km (0.6 mi)	215 m (700 ft)	2.1 km (1.3 mi)	4.2 km (2.6 mi)

See Next Page for Table of Water-Reactive Materials Which Produce Toxic Gases

"+" means distance can be larger in certain atmospheric conditions

TABLE OF WATER-REACTIVE MATERIALS WHICH PRODUCE TOXIC GASE[S]

Materials Which Produce Large Amounts of Toxic-by-Inhalation (TIH) Gas(es) When Spilled in Water

ID No.	Guide No.	Name of Material	TIH Gas(es) Produced
1162	155	Dimethyldichlorosilane	HCl
1242	139	Methyldichlorosilane	HCl
1250	155	Methyltrichlorosilane	HCl
1295	139	Trichlorosilane	HCl
1298	155	Trimethylchlorosilane	HCl
1340	139	Phosphorus pentasulfide, free from yellow and white Phosphorus	H_2S
1340	139	Phosphorus pentasulphide, free from yellow and white Phosphorus	H_2S
1360	139	Calcium phosphide	PH_3
1384	135	Sodium dithionite	H_2S SO_2
1384	135	Sodium hydrosulfite	H_2S SO_2
1384	135	Sodium hydrosulphite	H_2S SO_2
1397	139	Aluminum phosphide	PH_3
1412	139	Lithium amide	NH_3
1419	139	Magnesium aluminum phosphide	PH_3
1432	139	Sodium phosphide	PH_3
1433	139	Stannic phosphides	PH_3
1541	155	Acetone cyanohydrin, stabilized	HCN
1680	157	Potassium cyanide	HCN
1689	157	Sodium cyanide	HCN
1714	139	Zinc phosphide	PH_3
1716	156	Acetyl bromide	HBr
1717	132	Acetyl chloride	HCl
1724	155	Allyl trichlorosilane, stabilized	HCl
1725	137	Aluminum bromide, anhydrous	HBr

Chemical Symbols for TIH Gases:

Br_2	Bromine	HF	Hydrogen fluoride	PH_3	Phosphine
Cl_2	Chlorine	HI	Hydrogen iodide	SO_2	Sulfur dioxide
HBr	Hydrogen bromide	H_2S	Hydrogen sulfide	SO_2	Sulphur dioxide
HCl	Hydrogen chloride	H_2S	Hydrogen sulphide	SO_3	Sulfur trioxide
HCN	Hydrogen cyanide	NH_3	Ammonia	SO_3	Sulphur trioxide

Use this list only when material is spilled in water.

Materials Which Produce Large Amounts of Toxic-by-Inhalation (TIH) Gas(es) When Spilled in Water

ID No.	Guide No.	Name of Material	TIH Gas(es) Produced		
1726	137	Aluminum chloride, anhydrous	HCl		
1728	155	Amyltrichlorosilane	HCl		
1732	157	Antimony pentafluoride	HF		
1736	137	Benzoyl chloride	HCl		
1745	144	Bromine pentafluoride	HF	HBr	Br$_2$
1746	144	Bromine trifluoride	HF	HBr	Br$_2$
1747	155	Butyltrichlorosilane	HCl		
1752	156	Chloroacetyl chloride	HCl		
1754	137	Chlorosulfonic acid	HCl		
1754	137	Chlorosulfonic acid and Sulfur trioxide mixture	HCl		
1754	137	Chlorosulphonic acid	HCl		
1754	137	Chlorosulphonic acid and Sulphur trioxide mixture	HCl		
1754	137	Sulfur trioxide and Chlorosulfonic acid	HCl		
1754	137	Sulphur trioxide and Chlorosulphonic acid	HCl		
1758	137	Chromium oxychloride	HCl		
1777	137	Fluorosulfonic acid	HF		
1777	137	Fluorosulphonic acid	HF		
1801	156	Octyltrichlorosilane	HCl		
1806	137	Phosphorus pentachloride	HCl		
1809	137	Phosphorus trichloride	HCl		
1810	137	Phosphorus oxychloride	HCl		
1818	157	Silicon tetrachloride	HCl		
1828	137	Sulfur chlorides	HCl	SO$_2$	H$_2$S
1828	137	Sulphur chlorides	HCl	SO$_2$	H$_2$S

Chemical Symbols for TIH Gases:

Br$_2$	Bromine	HF	Hydrogen fluoride	PH$_3$	Phosphine
Cl$_2$	Chlorine	HI	Hydrogen iodide	SO$_2$	Sulfur dioxide
HBr	Hydrogen bromide	H$_2$S	Hydrogen sulfide	SO$_2$	Sulphur dioxide
HCl	Hydrogen chloride	H$_2$S	Hydrogen sulphide	SO$_3$	Sulfur trioxide
HCN	Hydrogen cyanide	NH$_3$	Ammonia	SO$_3$	Sulphur trioxide

Use this list only when material is spilled in water.

TABLE OF WATER-REACTIVE MATERIALS WHICH PRODUCE TOXIC GASE

Materials Which Produce Large Amounts of Toxic-by-Inhalation (TIH) Gas(es) When Spilled in Water

ID No.	Guide No.	Name of Material	TIH Gas(es) Produced	
1834	137	Sulfuryl chloride	HCl	SO₃
1834	137	Sulphuryl chloride	HCl	SO₃
1836	137	Thionyl chloride	HCl	SO₂
1838	137	Titanium tetrachloride	HCl	
1898	156	Acetyl iodide	HI	
1923	135	Calcium dithionite	H₂S	SO₂
1923	135	Calcium hydrosulfite	H₂S	SO₂
1923	135	Calcium hydrosulphite	H₂S	SO₂
1939	137	Phosphorus oxybromide	HBr	
1939	137	Phosphorus oxybromide, solid	HBr	
2004	135	Magnesium diamide	NH₃	
2011	139	Magnesium phosphide	PH₃	
2012	139	Potassium phosphide	PH₃	
2013	139	Strontium phosphide	PH₃	
2442	156	Trichloroacetyl chloride	HCl	
2495	144	Iodine pentafluoride	HF	
2576	137	Phosphorus oxybromide, molten	HBr	
2691	137	Phosphorus pentabromide	HBr	
2692	157	Boron tribromide	HBr	
2806	138	Lithium nitride	NH₃	
2977	166	Radioactive material, Uranium hexafluoride, fissile	HF	
2977	166	Uranium hexafluoride, fissile containing more than 1% Uranium-235	HF	
2978	166	Radioactive material, Uranium hexafluoride, non-fissile or fissile excepted	HF	

Chemical Symbols for TIH Gases:

Br₂	Bromine	HF	Hydrogen fluoride	PH₃	Phosphine
Cl₂	Chlorine	HI	Hydrogen iodide	SO₂	Sulfur dioxide
HBr	Hydrogen bromide	H₂S	Hydrogen sulfide	SO₂	Sulphur dioxide
HCl	Hydrogen chloride	H₂S	Hydrogen sulphide	SO₃	Sulfur trioxide
HCN	Hydrogen cyanide	NH₃	Ammonia	SO₃	Sulphur trioxide

Use this list only when material is spilled in water.

TABLE OF WATER-REACTIVE MATERIALS WHICH PRODUCE TOXIC GASES

Materials Which Produce Large Amounts of Toxic-by-Inhalation (TIH) Gas(es) When Spilled in Water

ID No.	Guide No.	Name of Material	TIH Gas(es) Produced
2978	166	Uranium hexafluoride, fissile excepted	HF
2978	166	Uranium hexafluoride, low specific activity	HF
2978	166	Uranium hexafluoride, non-fissile	HF
2985	155	Chlorosilanes, flammable, corrosive, n.o.s.	HCl
2985	155	Chlorosilanes, n.o.s.	HCl
2986	155	Chlorosilanes, corrosive, flammable, n.o.s.	HCl
2986	155	Chlorosilanes, n.o.s.	HCl
2987	156	Chlorosilanes, corrosive, n.o.s.	HCl
2987	156	Chlorosilanes, n.o.s.	HCl
2988	139	Chlorosilanes, n.o.s.	HCl
2988	139	Chlorosilanes, water-reactive, flammable, corrosive, n.o.s.	HCl
3048	157	Aluminum phosphide pesticide	PH_3
3049	138	Metal alkyl halides, n.o.s.	HCl
3049	138	Metal alkyl halides, water-reactive, n.o.s.	HCl
3049	138	Metal aryl halides, n.o.s.	HCl
3049	138	Metal aryl halides, water-reactive, n.o.s.	HCl
3052	135	Aluminum alkyl halides	HCl
9191	143	Chlorine dioxide, hydrate, frozen	Cl_2

Chemical Symbols for TIH Gases:

Br_2	Bromine	HF	Hydrogen fluoride	PH_3	Phosphine
Cl_2	Chlorine	HI	Hydrogen iodide	SO_2	Sulfur dioxide
HBr	Hydrogen bromide	H_2S	Hydrogen sulfide	SO_2	Sulphur dioxide
HCl	Hydrogen chloride	H_2S	Hydrogen sulphide	SO_3	Sulfur trioxide
HCN	Hydrogen cyanide	NH_3	Ammonia	SO_3	Sulphur trioxide

Use this list only when material is spilled in water.

PROTECTIVE CLOTHING

Street Clothing and Work Uniforms. These garments, such as uniforms worn by police and emergency medical services personnel, provide almost no protection from the harmful effects of dangerous goods.

Structural Fire Fighters' Protective Clothing (SFPC). This category of clothing, often called turnout or bunker gear, means the protective clothing normally worn by fire fighters during structural fire fighting operations. It includes a helmet, coat, pants, boots, gloves and a hood to cover parts of the head not protected by the helmet and facepiece. This clothing must be used with full-facepiece positive pressure self-contained breathing apparatus (SCBA). This protective clothing should, at a minimum, meet the OSHA Fire Brigades Standard (29 CFR 1910.156). Structural fire fighters' protective clothing provides limited protection from heat and cold, but may not provide adequate protection from the harmful vapors or liquids that are encountered during dangerous goods incidents. Each guide includes a statement about the use of SFPC in incidents involving those materials referenced by that guide. Some guides state that SFPC provides limited protection. In those cases, the responder wearing SFPC and SCBA may be able to perform an expedient, that is quick "in-and-out", operation. However, this type of operation can place the responder at risk of exposure, injury or death. The incident commander makes the decision to perform this operation only if an overriding benefit can be gained (i.e., perform an immediate rescue, turn off a valve to control a leak, etc.). The coverall-type protective clothing customarily worn to fight fires in forests or wildlands is **not** SFPC and is not recommended nor referred to elsewhere in this guidebook.

Positive Pressure Self-Contained Breathing Apparatus (SCBA). This apparatus provides a constant, positive pressure flow of air within the facepiece, even if one inhales deeply while doing heavy work. Use apparatus certified by NIOSH and the Department of Labor/Mine Safety and Health Administration in accordance with 42 CFR Part 84. Use it in accordance with the requirements for respiratory protection specified in OSHA 29 CFR 1910.134 (Respiratory Protection) and/or 29 CFR 1910.156 (f) (Fire Brigades Standard.) Chemical-cartridge respirators or other filtering masks are not acceptable substitutes for positive pressure self-contained breathing apparatus. Demand-type SCBA does not meet the OSHA 29 CFR 1910.156 (f)(1)(i) Fire Brigade Standard.

Chemical Protective Clothing and Equipment. Safe use of this type of protective clothing and equipment requires specific skills developed through training and experience. It is generally not available to, or used by, first responders. This type of special clothing may protect against one chemical, yet be readily permeated by chemicals for which it was not designed. Therefore, protective clothing should not be used unless it is compatible with the released material. This type of special clothing offers little or no protection against heat and/or cold. Examples of this type of equipment have been described as (1) Vapor Protective Suits (NFPA 1991), also known as Totally-Encapsulating Chemical Protective (TECP) Suits or Level A* protection (OSHA 29 CFR 1910.120, Appendix A & B), and (2) Liquid-Splash Protective Suits (NFPA 1992 & 1993), also known as Level B* or C* protection (OSHA 29

CFR 1910.120, Appendix A & B). No single protective clothing material will protect you from all dangerous goods. Do not assume any protective clothing is resistant to cold and/or heat or flame exposure unless it is so certified by the manufacturer. (NFPA 1991 5-3 Flammability Resistance Test and 5-6 Cold Temperature Performance Test.)

* Consult glossary for additional protection levels under the heading "Protective Clothing".

FIRE AND SPILL CONTROL

FIRE CONTROL

Water is the most common and generally most available fire extinguishing agent. Exercise caution in selecting a fire extinguishing method since there are many factors to be considered in an incident. Water may be ineffective in fighting fires involving some materials; its effectiveness depends greatly on the method of application.

Spill fires involving flammable liquids are generally controlled by applying a fire fighting foam to the surface of the burning material. Fighting flammable liquid fires requires foam concentrate which is <u>chemically compatible</u> with the burning material, <u>correct mixing</u> of the foam concentrate with water and air, and <u>careful application and maintenance</u> of the foam blanket. There are two general types of fire fighting foam: regular and alcohol-resistant. Examples of regular foam are protein-base, fluoroprotein, and aqueous film forming foam (AFFF). Some flammable liquids, including many petroleum products, can be controlled by applying regular foam. Other flammable liquids, including polar solvents (flammable liquids which are water soluble) such as alcohols and ketones, have different chemical properties. A fire involving these materials cannot be easily controlled with regular foam and requires application of alcohol-resistant foam. Polar-solvent fires may be difficult to control and require a higher foam application rate than other flammable liquid fires (see NFPA/ANSI Standards 11 and 11A for further information). Refer to the appropriate guide to determine which type of foam is recommended. Although it is impossible to make specific recommendations for flammable liquids which have subsidiary corrosive or toxic hazards, alcohol-resistant foam may be effective for many of these materials. The emergency response telephone number on the shipping document, or the appropriate emergency response agency, should be contacted as soon as possible for guidance on the proper fire extinguishing agent to use. The final selection of the agent and method depends on many factors such as incident location, exposure hazards, size of the fire, environmental concerns, as well as the availability of extinguishing agents and equipment at the scene.

WATER REACTIVE MATERIALS

Water is sometimes used to flush spills and to reduce or direct vapors in spill situations. Some of the materials covered by the guidebook can react violently or even explosively with water. In these cases, consider letting the fire burn or leaving the spill alone (except to prevent its spreading by diking) until additional technical advice can be obtained. The applicable guides clearly warn you of these potentially dangerous reactions. These materials require technical advice since

(1) water getting inside a ruptured or leaking container may cause an explosion;

(2) water may be needed to cool adjoining containers to prevent their rupturing (exploding) or further spread of the fires;

(3) water may be effective in mitigating an incident involving a water-reactive material only if it can be applied at a sufficient flooding rate for an extended period; and

(4) the products from the reaction with water may be more toxic, corrosive, or otherwise more undesirable than the product of the fire without water applied.

When responding to an incident involving water-reactive chemicals, take into account the existing conditions such as wind, precipitation, location and accessibility to the incident, as well as the availability of the agents to control the fire or spill. Because there are variables to consider, the decision to use water on fires or spills involving water-reactive materials should be based on information from an authoritative source; for example, a producer of the material, who can be contacted through the emergency response telephone number or the appropriate emergency response agency.

VAPOR CONTROL

Limiting the amount of vapor released from a pool of flammable or corrosive liquids is an operational concern. It requires the use of proper protective clothing, specialized equipment, appropriate chemical agents, and skilled personnel. Before engaging in vapor control, get advice from an authoritative source as to the proper tactics.

There are several ways to minimize the amount of vapors escaping from pools of spilled liquids, such as special foams, adsorbing agents, absorbing agents, and neutralizing agents. To be effective, these vapor control methods must be selected for the specific material involved and performed in a manner that will mitigate, not worsen, the incident.

Where specific materials are known, such as at manufacturing or storage facilities, it is desirable for the dangerous goods response team to prearrange with the facility operators to select and stockpile these control agents in advance of a spill. In the field, first responders may not have the most effective vapor control agent for the material available. They are likely to have only water and only one type of fire fighting foam on their vehicles. If the available foam is inappropriate for use, they are likely to use water spray. Because the water is being used to form a vapor seal, care must be taken not to churn or further spread the spill during application. Vapors that do not react with water may be directed away from the site using the air currents surrounding the water spray. Before using water spray or other methods to safely control vapor emission or to suppress ignition, obtain technical advice, based on specific chemical name identification.

CRIMINAL/TERRORIST USE OF CHEMICAL/BIOLOGICAL AGENTS

The following is intended to supply information to first responders for use in making a preliminary assessment of a situation that they suspect involves criminal/terrorist use of chemical and/or biological (CB) agents. To aid in the assessment, a list of observable indicators of the use and/or presence of a CB agent is provided in the following paragraphs.

DIFFERENCES BETWEEN A CHEMICAL AND A BIOLOGICAL AGENT

Chemical and biological agents can be dispersed in the air we breathe, the water we drink, or on surfaces we physically contact. Dispersion methods may be as simple as opening a container, using conventional (garden) spray devices, or as elaborate as detonating an improvised explosive device.

Chemical Incidents are characterized by the rapid onset of medical symptoms (minutes to hours) and easily observed signatures (colored residue, dead foliage, pungent odor, dead insects and animals).

Biological Incidents are characterized by the onset of symptoms in hours to days. Typically, there will be no characteristic signatures because biological agents are usually odorless and colorless. Because of the delayed onset of symptoms in a biological incident, the area affected may be greater due to the movement of infected individuals.

INDICATORS OF A POSSIBLE CHEMICAL INCIDENT

Dead animals/birds/fish	Not just an occasional road kill, but numerous animals (wild and domestic, small and large), birds, and fish in the same area.
Lack of insect life	If normal insect activity (ground, air, and/or water) is missing, check the ground/water surface/shore line for dead insects. If near water, check for dead fish/aquatic birds.
Unexplained odors	Smells may range from fruity to flowery to sharp/pungent to garlic/ horseradish-like to bitter almonds/peach kernels to new mown hay. It is important to note that the particular odor is completely out of character with its surroundings.
Unusual numbers of dying or sick people (mass casualties)	Health problems including nausea, disorientation, difficulty in breathing, convulsions, localized sweating, conjunctivitis (reddening of eyes/nerve agent symptoms), erythema (reddening of skin/vesicant symptoms) and death.
Pattern of casualties	Casualties will likely be distributed downwind, or if indoors, by the air ventilation system.

INDICATORS OF A POSSIBLE CHEMICAL INCIDENT (Continued)

Blisters/rashes Numerous individuals experiencing unexplained water-like blisters, weals (like bee stings), and/or rashes.

Illness in confined area Different casualty rates for people working indoors versus outdoors dependent on where the agent was released.

Unusual liquid droplets Numerous surfaces exhibit oily droplets/film; numerous water surfaces have an oily film. (No recent rain.)

Different looking areas Not just a patch of dead weeds, but trees, shrubs, bushes, food crops, and/or lawns that are dead, discolored, or withered. (No current drought.)

Low-lying clouds Low-lying cloud/fog-like condition that is not consistent with its surroundings.

Unusual metal debris Unexplained bomb/munitions-like material, especially if it contains a liquid.

INDICATORS OF A POSSIBLE BIOLOGICAL INCIDENT

Unusual numbers of sick or dying people or animals Any number of symptoms may occur. Casualties may occur hours to days after an incident has occurred. The time required before symptoms are observed is dependent on the agent used.

Unscheduled and unusual spray being disseminated Especially if outdoors during periods of darkness.

Abandoned spray devices Devices may not have distinct odors.

PERSONAL SAFETY CONSIDERATIONS

When approaching a scene that may involve CB agents, the most critical consideration is the safety of oneself and other responders. Protective clothing and respiratory protection of appropriate level of safety must be used. Be aware that the presence and identification of CB agents may not be verifiable, especially in the case of biological agents. The following actions/measures to be considered are applicable to either a chemical or biological incident. The guidance is general in nature, not all encompassing, and its applicability should be evaluated on a case-by-case basis.

Approach and response strategies. Protect yourself and use a safe approach (minimize any exposure time, maximize the distance between you and the item that is likely to harm you, use cover as protection and wear appropriate personal protective equipment and respiratory protection). Identify and estimate the hazard by using indicators as provided above. Isolate the area and secure the scene; potentially contaminated people should be isolated and decontaminated as soon as possible. In the event of a chemical incident, the fading of chemical odors is not necessarily an indication of reduced vapor concentrations. Some chemicals deaden the senses giving the false perception that the chemical is no longer present.

Decontamination measures. Emergency responders should follow standard decontamination procedures (flush-strip-flush). Mass casualty decontamination should begin as soon as possible by stripping (all clothing) and flushing (soap and water). If biological agents are involved or suspected, careful washing and use of a brush are more effective. If chemical agents are suspected, the most important and effective decontamination will be that done within the first one or two minutes. If possible, further decontamination should be performed using a 0.5% hypochlorite solution (1 part household bleach mixed with 9 parts water). If biological agents are suspected, a contact time of 10 to 15 minutes should be allowed before rinsing. The solution can be used on soft tissue wounds, but must not be used in eyes or open wounds of the abdomen, chest, brain, or spine. For further information contact the agencies listed in this guidebook.

NOTE: The above information was developed by the Department of National Defence (Canada) and the U.S. Department of the Army, Edgewood Arsenal.

Glossary

Alcohol resistant foam	A foam that is resistant to "polar" chemicals such as ketones and esters which may break down other types of foam.
Biological agents	Living organisms that cause disease, sickness and mortality in humans. Anthrax and Ebola are examples of biological agents. **Refer to Guide 158.**
Blister agents (vesicants)	Substances that cause blistering of the skin. Exposure is through liquid or vapor contact with any exposed tissue (eyes, skin, lungs). Mustard (H), Distilled Mustard (HD), Nitrogen Mustard (HN) and Lewisite (L) are blister agents. **Symptoms:** Red eyes, skin irritation, burning of skin, blisters, upper respiratory damage, cough, hoarseness.
Blood agents	Substances that injure a person by interfering with cell respiration (the exchange of oxygen and carbon dioxide between blood and tissues). Hydrogen cyanide (AC) and Cyanogen chloride (CK) are blood agents. **Symptoms:** Respiratory distress, headache, unresponsiveness, seizures, coma.
Burn	Refers to either a chemical or thermal burn, the former may be caused by corrosive substances and the latter by liquefied cryogenic gases, hot molten substances, or flames.
Choking agents	Substances that cause physical injury to the lungs. Exposure is through inhalation. In extreme cases, membranes swell and lungs become filled with liquid (pulmonary edema). Death results from lack of oxygen; hence, the victim is "choked". Phosgene (CG) is a choking agent. **Symptoms:** irritation to eyes/nose/throat, respiratory distress, nausea and vomiting, burning of exposed skin.
CO_2	Carbon dioxide gas.
Cold zone	Area where the command post and support functions that are necessary to control the incident are located. This is also referred to as the clean zone, green zone or support zone in other documents. (EPA Standard Operating Safety Guidelines, OSHA 29 CFR 1910.120, NFPA 472)

Glossary

Combustible liquid

Liquids which have a flash point greater than 60.5°C (141°F) and below 93°C (200°F). U.S. regulations permit a flammable liquid with a flash point between 38°C (100°F) and 60.5°C (141°F) to be reclassed as a combustible liquid.

Compatibility Group

Letters identify explosives that are deemed to be compatible. Class 1 materials are considered to be "compatible" if they can be transported together without significantly increasing either the probability of an incident or, for a given quantity, the magnitude of the effects of such an incident.

A   Substances which are expected to mass detonate very soon after fire reaches them.

B   Articles which are expected to mass detonate very soon after fire reaches them.

C   Substances or articles which may be readily ignited and burn violently without necessarily exploding.

D   Substances or articles which may mass detonate (with blast and/or fragment hazard) when exposed to fire.

E&F Articles which may mass detonate in a fire.

G   Substances and articles which may mass explode and give off smoke or toxic gases.

H   Articles which in a fire may eject hazardous projectiles and dense white smoke.

J   Articles which may mass explode.

K   Articles which in a fire may eject hazardous projectiles and toxic gases.

L   Substances and articles which present a special risk and could be activated by exposure to air or water.

N   Articles which contain only extremely insensitive detonating substances and demonstrate a negligible probability of accidental ignition or propagation.

S   Packaged substances or articles which, if accidentally initiated, produce effects that are usually confined to the immediate vicinity.

Glossary

Control zones	Designated areas at dangerous goods incidents, based on safety and the degree of hazard. Many terms are used to describe control zones; however, in this guidebook, these zones are defined as the hot/exclusion/restricted zone, warm/contamination reduction/limited access zone, and cold/support/clean zone. (EPA Standard Operating Safety Guidelines, OSHA 29 CFR 1910.120, NFPA 472)
Cryogenic liquid	A refrigerated, liquefied gas that has a boiling point colder than -90°C (-130°F) at atmospheric pressure.
Dangerous Water Reactive Material	Produces significant toxic gas when it comes in contact with water.
Decomposition products	Products of a chemical or thermal break-down of a substance.
Decontamination	The removal of dangerous goods from personnel and equipment to the extent necessary to prevent potential adverse health effects. Always avoid direct or indirect contact with dangerous goods; however, if contact occurs, personnel should be decontaminated as soon as possible. Since the methods used to decontaminate personnel and equipment differ from one chemical to another, contact the chemical manufacturer, through the agencies listed on the inside back cover, to determine the appropriate procedure. Contaminated clothing and equipment should be removed after use and stored in a controlled area (warm/contamination reduction/limited access zone) until cleanup procedures can be initiated. In some cases, protective clothing and equipment cannot be decontaminated and must be disposed of in a proper manner.
Dry chemical	A preparation designed for fighting fires involving flammable liquids, pyrophoric substances and electrical equipment. Common types contain sodium bicarbonate or potassium bicarbonate.
Edema	The accumulation of an excessive amount of watery fluid in cells and tissues. Pulmonary edema is an excessive buildup of water in the lungs, for instance, after inhalation of a gas that is corrosive to lung tissue.
Flammable liquid	A liquid that has a flash point of 60.5°C (141°F) or lower.
Flash point	Lowest temperature at which a liquid or solid gives off vapor in such a concentration that, when the vapor combines with air near the surface of the liquid or solid, a flammable mixture is formed. Hence, the lower the flash point, the more flammable the material.

Glossary

Hazard zones (Inhalation Hazard Zones)	**HAZARD ZONE A:** LC50 of less than or equal to 200 ppm, **HAZARD ZONE B:** LC50 greater than 200 ppm and less than or equal to 1000 ppm, **HAZARD ZONE C:** LC50 greater than 1000 ppm and less than or equal to 3000 ppm, **HAZARD ZONE D:** LC50 greater than 3000 ppm and less than or equal to 5000 ppm.
Hot zone	Area immediately surrounding a dangerous goods incident which extends far enough to prevent adverse effects from released dangerous goods to personnel outside the zone. This zone is also referred to as exclusion zone, red zone or restricted zone in other documents. (EPA Standard Operating Safety Guidelines, OSHA 29 CFR 1910.120, NFPA 472)
Immiscible	In this guidebook, means that a material does not mix readily with water.
Mass explosion	Explosion which affects almost the entire load virtually instantaneously.
Miscible	In this guidebook, means that a material mixes readily with water.
Nerve agents	Substances that interfere with the central nervous system. Exposure is primarily through contact with the liquid (via skin and eyes) and secondarily through inhalation of the vapor. Tabun (GA), Sarin (GB), Soman (GD) and VX are nerve agents. **Symptoms:** Pinpoint pupils, extreme headache, severe tightness in the chest, dyspnea, runny nose, coughing, salivation, unresponsiveness, seizures.
Non-polar	See "Immiscible".
n.o.s.	These letters refer to not otherwise specified. The entries which use this description are generic names such as "Corrosive liquid, n.o.s." This means that the actual chemical name for that corrosive liquid is not listed in the regulations; therefore, a generic name must be used to describe it on shipping papers.
Noxious	In this guidebook, means that a material may be harmful or injurious to health or physical well-being.
Oxidizer	A chemical which supplies its own oxygen and which helps other combustible material burn more readily.

Glossary

P	The letter "P" following a guide number in the yellow-bordered and blue-bordered pages identifies a material which may polymerize violently under high temperature conditions or contamination with other products. This polymerization will produce heat and high pressure buildup in containers which may explode or rupture. (See polymerization below.)
pH	pH is a value that represents the acidity or alkalinity of a water solution. Pure water has a pH of 7. A pH value below 7 indicates an acid solution (a pH of 1 is extremely acidic). A pH above 7 indicates an alkaline solution (a pH of 14 is extremely alkaline). Acids and alkalies (bases) are commonly referred to as corrosive materials.
PIH	Poison Inhalation Hazard. Term used to describe gases and volatile liquids that are toxic when inhaled. (Same as TIH)
Polar	See "Miscible".
Polymerization	This term describes a chemical reaction which is generally associated with the production of plastic substances. Basically, the individual molecules of the chemical (liquid or gas) react with each other to produce what can be described as a long chain. These chains can be formed in many useful applications. A well known example is the styrofoam (polystyrene) coffee cup which is formed when liquid molecules of styrene react with each other or polymerize forming a solid, therefore changing the name from styrene to polystyrene (poly means many).
Protective clothing	Includes both respiratory and physical protection. One cannot assign a level of protection to clothing or respiratory devices separately. These levels were accepted and defined by response organizations such as U.S. Coast Guard, NIOSH, and U.S. EPA.
	Level A: SCBA plus totally encapsulating chemical resistant clothing (permeation resistant).
	Level B: SCBA plus hooded chemical resistant clothing (splash suit).
	Level C: Full or half-face respirator plus hooded chemical resistant clothing (splash suit).
	Level D: Coverall with no respiratory protection.
Pyrophoric	A material which ignites spontaneously upon exposure to air (or oxygen).
Radioactivity	The property of some substances to emit invisible and potentially harmful radiation.

Glossary

Radiation Authority

As referred to in Guides 161 through 166 for radioactive materials, the Radiation Authority is either a Federal, state/provincial agency or state/province designated official. The responsibilities of this authority include evaluating radiological hazard conditions during normal operations and during emergencies. If the identity and telephone number of the authority are not known by emergency responders, or included in the local response plan, the information can be obtained from the agencies listed on the inside back cover. They maintain a periodically updated list of radiation authorities.

Refrigerated liquid

See "Cryogenic liquid".

Straight (solid) stream

Method used to apply or distribute water from the end of a hose. The water is delivered under pressure for penetration. In an efficient straight (solid) stream, approximately 90% of the water passes through an imaginary circle 38 cm (15 inches) in diameter at the breaking point. Hose (solid or straight) streams are frequently used to cool tanks and other equipment exposed to flammable liquid fires, or for washing burning spills away from danger points. However, straight streams will cause a spill fire to spread if improperly used or when directed into open containers of flammable and combustible liquids.

TIH

Toxic Inhalation Hazard. Term used to describe gases and volatile liquids that are toxic when inhaled. (Same as PIH)

Vapor density

Weight of a volume of pure vapor or gas (with no air present) compared to the weight of an equal volume of dry air at the same temperature and pressure. A vapor density less than 1 (one) indicates that the vapor is lighter than air and will tend to rise. A vapor density greater than 1 (one) indicates that the vapor is heavier than air and may travel along the ground.

Vapor pressure

Pressure at which a liquid and its vapor are in equilibrium at a given temperature. Liquids with high vapor pressures evaporate rapidly.

Viscosity

Measure of a liquid's internal resistance to flow. This property is important because it indicates how fast a material will leak out through holes in containers or tanks.

Glossary

Warm zone

Area between Hot and Cold zones where personnel and equipment decontamination and hot zone support take place. It includes control points for the access corridor and thus assists in reducing the spread of contamination. Also referred to as the contamination reduction corridor (CRC), contamination reduction zone (CRZ), yellow zone or limited access zone in other documents. (EPA Standard Operating Safety Guidelines, OSHA 29 CFR 1910.120, NFPA 472)

Water-sensitive

Substances which may produce flammable and/or toxic decomposition products upon contact with water.

Water spray (fog)

Method or way to apply or distribute water. The water is finely divided to provide for high heat absorption. Water spray patterns can range from about 10 to 90 degrees. Water spray streams can be used to extinguish or control the burning of a fire or to provide exposure protection for personnel, equipment, buildings, etc. **(This method can be used to absorb vapors, knock-down vapors or disperse vapors. Direct a water spray (fog), rather than a straight (solid) stream, into the vapor cloud to accomplish any of the above).**

Water spray is particularly effective on fires of flammable liquids and volatile solids having flash points above 37.8°C (100°F).

Regardless of the above, water spray can be used successfully on flammable liquids with low flash points. The effectiveness depends particularly on the method of application. With proper nozzles, even gasoline spill fires of some types have been extinguished when coordinated hose lines were used to sweep the flames off the surface of the liquid. Furthermore, water spray carefully applied has frequently been used with success in extinguishing fires involving flammable liquids with high flash points (or any viscous liquids) by causing frothing to occur only on the surface, and this foaming action blankets and extinguishes the fire.

PUBLICATION DATA

The 2000 Emergency Response Guidebook (ERG2000) was prepared by the staff of Transport Canada, the U.S. Department of Transportation, and the Secretariat of Communications and Transport of Mexico with the assistance of many interested parties from government and industry.

ERG2000 is based on earlier Transport Canada, U.S. DOT, and Secretariat of Communications and Transport emergency response guidebooks. The Emergency Response Guidebook has been translated and printed in many languages, including French, Spanish, Chinese, German, Hebrew, Japanese, Portuguese, and Thai.

We encourage countries that wish to participate in future editions of the Guidebook to provide their emergency response center information for inclusion. Please contact any of the websites or telephone numbers in the paragraph below.

DISTRIBUTION OF THIS GUIDEBOOK

The primary objective is to place one copy of the ERG2000 in each emergency service vehicle through distribution to Federal, state, provincial and local public safety authorities. The distribution of this guidebook is being accomplished through the voluntary cooperation of a network of key agencies. Emergency service organizations that have not yet received copies of ERG2000 should contact the respective distribution center in their country, state or province. In the U.S., information about the distribution center for your location may be obtained from the Hazardous Material Safety web site at http://hazmat.dot.gov or call 202-366-4900. In Canada, contact CANUTEC at 613-992-4624 or via the web site at http://www.canutec.gc.ca for information. In Mexico, call SCT at 52-5-684-1275 or 684-0188.

REPRODUCTION and RESALE

Copies of this document which are provided free of charge to fire, police and other emergency services may not be resold. ERG2000 (RSPA P 5800.8) may be reproduced without further permission subject to the following:

> The names and the seals of the participating governments may not be reproduced on a copy of this document unless that copy accurately reproduces the entire content (text, format, and coloration) of this document without modification. In addition, the publisher's full name and address must be displayed on the outside back cover of each copy, replacing the wording placed on the center of the back cover.

Constructive comments concerning ERG2000 are solicited; in particular, comments concerning its use in handling incidents involving dangerous goods. Comments should be addressed to:

In Canada:

Chief, CANUTEC
Transport Dangerous Goods
Transport Canada
Ottawa, Ontario
Canada K1A 0N5

Phone: 613-992-4624 (information)
FAX: 613-954-5101
Internet: canutec@tc.gc.ca

In the U.S.:

U. S. Department of Transportation
Research and Special Programs Administration
Office of Hazardous Materials Initiatives and Training (DHM-50)
Washington, DC 20590-0001

Phone: 202-366-4900
FAX: 202-366-7342
Internet: welisten@rspa.dot.gov

In Mexico:

Secretariat for Communications and Transport
Land Transport Directorate
Hazardous Materials and Wastes Directorate
Calz. de las Bombas No. 411-9 piso
Col. San Bartolo Coapa
Coyoacan 04800, D.F.
Mexico

Phone and FAX: 52-5-684-1275 and 684-0188

NOTES

EMERGENCY RESPONSE TELEPHONE NUMBERS

CANADA

1. CANUTEC

613-996-6666

(Collect calls are accepted)
*666 cellular (in Canada only)

UNITED STATES

1. CHEMTREC®

1-800-424-9300

(Toll-free in the U.S., Canada, and the U.S. Virgin Islands)
703-527-3887 For calls originating elsewhere
(Collect calls are accepted)

2. CHEM-TEL, INC.

1-800-255-3924

(Toll-free in the U.S., Canada, and the U.S. Virgin Islands)
813-248-0585 For calls originating elsewhere
(Collect calls are accepted)

3. INFOTRAC

1-800-535-5053

(Toll-free in the U.S., Canada, and the U.S. Virgin Islands)
352-323-3500 For calls originating elsewhere
(Collect calls are accepted)

4. 3E COMPANY

1-800-451-8346

(Toll-free in the U.S., Canada, and the U.S. Virgin Islands)
760-602-8703 For calls originating elsewhere
(Collect calls are accepted)

5. MILITARY SHIPMENTS

703-697-0218 - Explosives/ammunition incidents
(Collect calls are accepted)
1-800-851-8061 - All other dangerous goods incidents